Reading Aids for Every Class

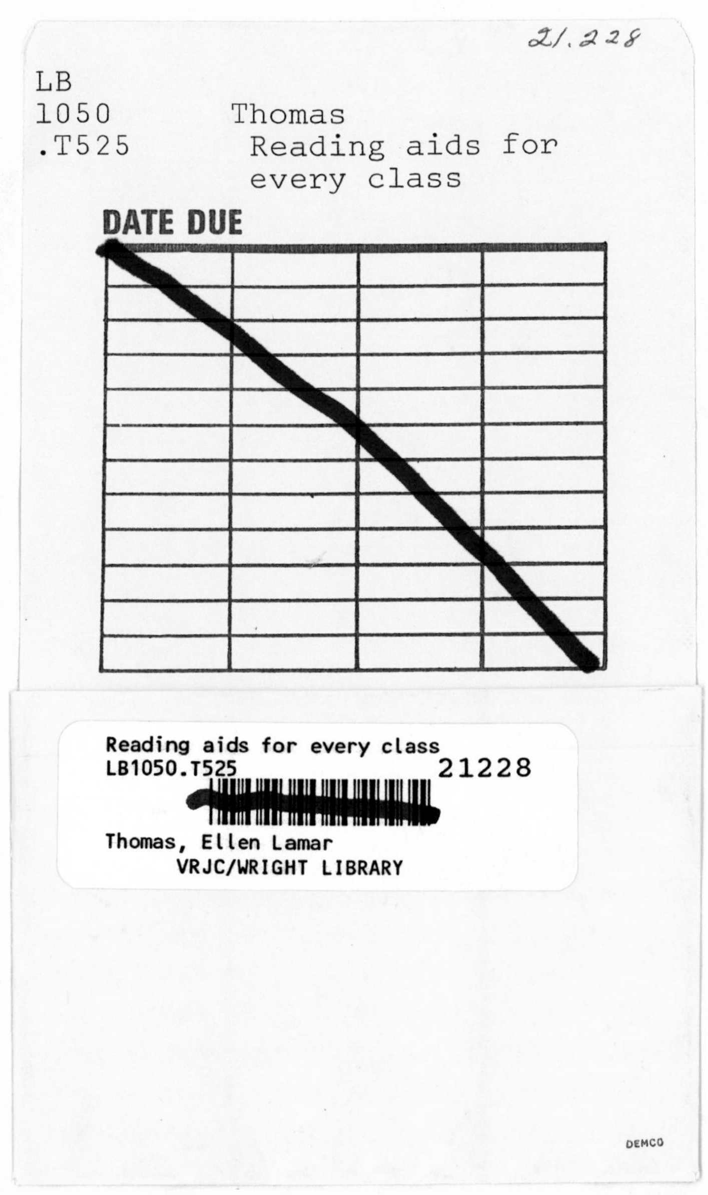

Reading Aids for Every Class

400 Activities for Instruction and Enrichment

Ellen Lamar Thomas

Allyn and Bacon, Inc.

Boston London Sydney Toronto

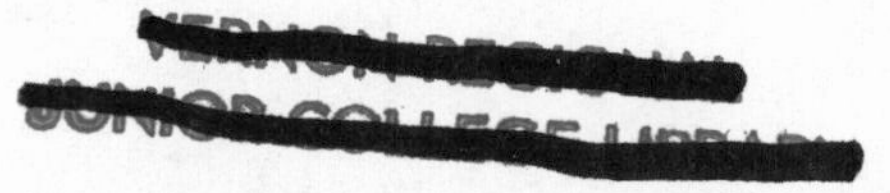

Library of Congress Cataloging in Publication Data

Thomas, Ellen Lamar.
Reading aids for every class.

Includes indexes.
1. Reading. 2. Reading games. 3. Study, Method of. I. Title.
LB1050.T525 428.4'07'1 79-26836
ISBN 0-205-06955-X

Production Editor/Designer: Paula Carroll
Preparation Buyer: Sharlene Queenan
Managing Editor: Robert Roen

Printed in the United States of America

For Margaret Ellen Hillman, ''Peggy''—
master teacher, person, and friend.

Contents

Preface xi

1 HOW TO USE THIS BOOK 1

What Will You Find Here? 1
How Should This Book Prove Useful? 2
How Will You Read This Book? 2
You Will Want to Select Carefully from Among the Reading Aids 3
Teachers Will Want to Make Adjustments 3
Teachers Will Want Students to Acquire a Full Complement of Reading Skills 4
Real Reading Improvement Is Not Easy but Worth Our Dedicated Effort 4
"To Each His Own" 5

2 HELPING STUDENTS TO ATTACK WORDS 7

Exploring What Students Need in Word Attack 10
Helping Students Attack Words through Context Clues 14
Helping Students Attack Words through Structural Analysis 17
Helping Students Attack Words through Syllable Division 19
Helping Students Use Accent in Attacking Words 25
Helping Students Attack Words through Phonic Aids 27
Helping Students Use the Dictionary in Identifying Words 46
Helping Students Develop Their Sight Vocabularies 48

3 HELPING STUDENTS LEARN THE MEANINGS OF WORDS 53

Learning About Vocabulary Strengths and Weaknesses 55
Helping Students Want to Grow in Vocabulary 58
Using, Providing, or Enriching Background Experience 61
Wide Reading Builds Word Power 62
Pre-Teaching "Stopper" Words 63
Helping Students Use Context Clues as an Aid in Reasoning Out Meanings 67

Learning Word Meanings through Structural Analysis 74
Learning New Words through Word Origins 80
Developing Dictionary Competence—A Must 80
Students Need On-Their-Own Techniques for Learning and Retaining Words 86
How to Crack Down on a Word 91
Lively, Lighthearted Activities with Words 92

IMPROVING COMPREHENSION 99

SOME WAYS TO HELP YOUR STUDENTS COMPREHEND 99

Finding Out about Their Reading 100
Remove Roadblocks before Students Read 103
Help Students Step into Their Reading with a Mini-Preview 104
Building Bridges to Students' Concerns 107
Use That Wonder-Worker—Interest 109
Tie Reading in with Exciting Doing 113
Help Students Read with Purpose through Questions 115
Study Guides Can Turn on Reading Power 117
Utilize or Provide Background Experience 118
Walk Students through the Opening 119
Open Book Lessons Can Develop Skills 120
Read Aloud—and Build Reading Power 120
Students Can Become "Special Investigators" 121
Have a "Silent Reading Teacher" in Your Classroom 122
School Librarians Can Be Right-Hand Angels 123
Arrange Readings in an Easier-to-Harder Sequence 124
Teachers Can Turn Author 125

HELPING STUDENTS PULL OUT THE MAIN IDEAS FROM PARAGRAPHS 127

Paragraph Pattern 1-Main Idea Sentence Placed First 130
Paragraph Pattern 2-Main Idea Sentence Placed Last 131
Paragraph Pattern 3-Main Idea Sentence in Between 132
Paragraph Pattern 4-A "Split" Main Idea 133
Paragraph Pattern 5-Main Idea Not Stated 133
Paragraph Pattern 6-Is the Main Idea Always the Broadest Idea? 134
Paragraph Pattern 7-A Seeming Contradiction 134
Paragraph Pattern 8-Main Idea Clarified by an Anecdote 135
Paragraph Pattern 9-Main Idea Supported by an Example 135
Paragraph Pattern 10-Main Idea in Part of a Sentence 135

HELPING STUDENTS IDENTIFY IMPORTANT DETAILS IN PARAGRAPHS 138

Spotting Details with "Full Signals" 138
What Details Can Be Disregarded? 139
Spotting Details with "Half Signals" 141
Moving on to No Signals 143

HELPING STUDENTS PULL OUT THE MAIN CONTENT OF A LONGER SELECTION 145

5 HELPING STUDENTS STREAMLINE THEIR STUDY 153

Activities for Teaching and Practicing the Ten Strategies 155
Strategy 1: Overview—To Save Time 155
Strategy 2: Go in with a Question 158
Strategy 3: Do "Stop-and-Go" Reading 160
Strategy 4: Remove the Roadblocks of "Official" Terms 161
Strategy 5: Use a "Back-and-Forth" Strategy 161
Strategy 6: Make Important Points Flag You 162
Strategy 7: Adjust Your Speed to the Task at Hand 162
Strategy 8: Use "The Most Powerful Study Technique" 162
Strategy 9: Zero in on the Self-Checks 163
Strategy 10: Review to Firm Up Learning 163
A Conclusion to the Ten Strategies 164
A Postscript—The OK5R Approach to College Reading 164

6 HELPING STUDENTS ADJUST THEIR READING RATE TO THE TASK AT HAND 169

Learning Students' Attainments and Needs in Rate Adjustment 169
Introducing the Concept of Rate Adjustment 171
Helping Students Acquire a Full Range of Reading Rates 172
Helping Students Read More Rapidly When This Is Appropriate 177

7 TURN YOUR STUDENTS INTO READERS—FOR LIFE 185

Finding Out about Their Personal Reading 188
Matching Book and Student 189
"Turning On" Readers 192
Sharing Reading Enthusiasms 205
How Are We Succeeding? 211

HELPING STUDENTS READ WITH CRITICAL EVALUATION 215 

Critical Reading Belongs in Our Students'—and in Planet Earth's—Survival Kit! 215
Students Should Become Aware of Strong Forces within Themselves That May Affect Their Reading 219

"PLEASE HELP ME LEARN TO STUDY!" 235 

Helping Students Want *to Improve Their Study Habits* 238
Helping Students Learn to Control Their Time 240
"Time-Stretchers" for Students with Part-Time Jobs 250
Spacing Out Long-Term Projects 250
Is the Place Where Students Study "On Their Side"? 251
When Notebooks Are a "Disaster Area" 253
Keeping a Record of Work Assigned 254
"How Can I Learn to Concentrate?" 254
Students Need to Be Kept Going 256
Enlisting Parents in Encouraging Effective Study 257

APPENDIX

Some Productive Greek and Latin Prefixes and Roots 261
Some Frequently Recurring Suffixes 266
Tips for Dividing Words into Syllables 267

Index 359

Preface

You will find in this book almost 400 reading aids, aids for instruction and enrichment which, in my experience and that of others, have helped students become more successful readers. You will also find, as a convenient and time-saving feature, around seventy-five master copy pages of lesson materials and guidelines for students, ready for instant reproduction in the form of dittoed or xeroxed copies. You have the publisher's permission to reproduce these items in any quantities.

At this moment, you hold in your hands my "dream book." A favorite dream has been to share the contents of shelves and file cases bursting with the resources of many years—years when I first met troubled readers in English classes, years when I worked with such readers in a public school reading center, years when I served as reading consultant and teacher in the University of Chicago Laboratory School. Through those years, I worked closely with students and observed their response to materials and methods. I have lived the problems and the joys of classroom teachers—the disappointment and discouragement when progress comes slowly, the satisfaction when students take hold, attitudes change, and real progress follows.

You will find in this book a great many reading aids borrowed from others. I express special thanks to Bernice Bragstad, reading consultant of LaFollette High School in Madison, Wisconsin, for generously sharing reading aids that have worked in her school. Mary Lee Hoganson, a counselor close to students at the University of Chicago Laboratory School, helped me bring some of the activities closer to young people. Three master teachers contributed ideas and inspiration—Murray Hozinsky, Mr. Enthusiasm in his biology classes at the University of Chicago Laboratory School; Earl Bell, who is just as enthusiastic in social studies; and Elizabeth K. Lynch, earnest and dedicated social studies teacher at Neshaminy Langhorne High School in Langhorne, Pennsylvania.

Did a bookstore owner ever before contribute to a professional book on teaching reading? Here is a special thank you to Elizabeth Haslam, co-owner of Haslam's Book Store in St. Petersburg, Florida, who shared with the writer her ideas on winning young people to books. Mrs. Haslam invites young people who have no books in their homes to browse and to read in the attractive young people's section of her book store. The only credential is clean hands!

I express appreciation to my friend, Dr. H. Alan Robinson, for first focusing my interest on reading aids for every classroom and for years of encouragement and faith; to Dr. Sam Weintraub, for never wearying of answering my questions; and to Dr. Michael F. Graves, for making this a *far* better book through his insightful suggestions. I should like to thank Virginia Jacques and Evelyn Pope, model secretaries as well as right-hand angels. I want to thank Paula Carroll, Design Editor, at Allyn and Bacon for her very special contribution to the quality of this book. Last, I express most earnest thanks to Robert Roen, Managing Editor for Allyn and Bacon, a ready helper, an *instant* problem solver, and, to authors in his charge, Mr. CARE in person.

The Reading-Achievement-Level Index

The reading activities and other aids in this book span a wide range in reading achievement—from under-par readers in the middle school to more academically oriented, very capable upperclassmen in high school. The reading-achievement-level index that follows offers teachers *rough* guidance in selecting activities for under-par, average, and advanced readers. Of course, a diagnosis of students' needs in word attack, vocabulary, comprehension, and so on, is essential if one is to determine the specific needs of individuals. Teachers will also wish to consider the age and the personality of the student. The abbreviation R. A. below stands for Reading Aid. An asterisk placed after the R. A. indicates that the *principle* on which the student is instructed in the Reading Aid is appropriate for under-par readers, but that the *material would need to be adjusted* for them so that it is *on an easier level*. In Reading Aids 101* and 102*, for example, teaching the derivations of words is appropriate for under-par readers but the "example" words, *mnemonic* and *excruciating*, are, of course, too difficult for most under-par readers. References below to the companion volume are to Ellen Lamar Thomas and H. Alan Robinson, *Improving Reading in Every Class*, unabridged 2nd edition (Boston: Allyn and Bacon, 1977).

READING AIDS FOR UNDER-PAR AND YOUNGER READERS

Helping students to attack words, R. A. 1–39, R. A. 41–54

Helping students learn the meanings of words, R. A. 55–63, 64*, 65–70, 71*, 72–76, 77*, 78*, 79*, 80–85, 86*, 88, 89*, 90, 91, 92*, 93*, 94, 95*, 96, 97, 101*, 102*, 103, 104, 105*, 106–109, 110*, 112–120, 121*, 122*, 123*, 126*

Some ways to help your students comprehend, R. A. 128–132, 133*, 134, 135*, 136*, 137*, 138*, 139*, 140–166

Helping students pull out the main ideas of paragraphs, R. A. 167–186.

Note: The basic work on finding the main idea offered in the companion volume, pages 184–189, is likely to be appropriate for under-par readers in middle school and junior high who need to work with main ideas. High school teachers who wish to use the master copies offered in the present book will want to select carefully those that are within the reading reach of their students and meet their specific needs.

Helping students identify the important details of paragraphs, R. A. 187–192.

Note: In working with under-par readers in middle school and junior high and with seriously handicapped readers in high school, teachers will want to adjust the explanations and the practice materials so that they are on an easier level.

Helping students pull out the main content of a longer selection, R. A. 193.

Note: The note just above also applies here.

Helping students streamline their study, R. A. 194–235*.

Note: The master copies in this section were developed for use with capable high school sophomores and upperclassmen, but the pointers offered are appropriate on a wide range of levels. Teachers may want to use the *principles* on the master copies but simplify the *presentation* for younger or less capable readers.

Helping students adjust their reading rate to the task at hand, R. A. 236–240, 241*, 242–243, 245–252.

Note: Students are *not* candidates for training in rapid reading if they are blocked by deficiencies in the basic skills of word attack, vocabulary, or comprehension. Instruction in these basic skills may be essential before speed can be developed. When interfering factors are no longer present, direct attention to rapid reading is appropriate when students need it on or above the high school level; in that case, R. A. 253–260 are appropriate.

Turning students into readers—for life, R. A. 261–334.

Note: Of course, teachers will want to select from the great variety of activities offered here those suitable to the age, the level of maturity, and the personality of their students.

Helping students read with critical evaluation, R. A. 335–365*.

Note: While the principles in the Reading Aids just cited are of value to all students, teachers may wish to simplify the explanations and the practice work for younger or less capable readers.

Improving general study habits, R. A. 366–397*.

Note: Students enrolled for remedial reading instruction usually need help with their study habits along with work on their actual reading. Teachers will want to adapt the Reading Aids just cited so that they are suitable for younger students.

READING AIDS FOR AVERAGE READERS

Helping students to attack words

Average Middle School Readers, R. A. 1–54.

Note: Middle-school teachers can select from Reading Aids 1–54 those that meet the needs of their students, developing and reinforcing, as needed, skills of context analysis, structural analysis, syllable division, accent, phonic analysis, and the dictionary, and also working with sight vocabulary as needed.

Average High School Readers, R. A. 5–14, 15–16, 25–32, 50.

Note: High school students who are average in reading achievement will not ordinarily need to devote much time to word attack. In this writer's experience, however, a number of these students, especially underclassmen, can profitably acquire or reinforce the learnings involved in the Reading Aids cited above.

Helping students learn the meanings of words, R. A. 55, 57–77, 78 (the words should be appropriate in difficulty for the students), 79–97, 98–99 (both intended for upperclassmen), 100–104, 106–123, 124 and 125 (intended for upperclassmen), 126, 127 (intended for upperclassmen).

Some ways to help your students comprehend, R. A. 128–139, 141–144, 146–160, 162–166.

Helping students pull out the main ideas of paragraphs, R. A. 167–186.

Note: The basic work on finding the main idea offered in the companion volume, pages 184–189, may be appropriate for middle school and junior high readers who need to work with main ideas. High school teachers who wish to use the master copies offered in the present book will want to select carefully those that are within the reading reach and meet the specific needs of their students.

Helping students identify the important details in paragraphs, R. A. 187–192.

Note: Middle school and junior high teachers who use these Reading Aids will want to adjust the explanations and the practice materials so that they are on an easier level.

Helping students pull out the main content of a longer selection, R. A. 193.

Note: Middle school and junior high teachers will want to adjust the explanations and the practice materials so that they are on an easier level.

Helping students streamline their study, R. A. 194–235*.

Note: The master copies in this section were developed for use with capable high school sophomores and upperclassmen but the pointers offered are appropriate on a wide range of levels. Teachers may want to use the *principles* on the master copies but simplify the *presentation* for younger or less capable readers.

Helping students adjust their reading rate to the task at hand, R. A. 236–260.

Turning students into readers—for life, R. A. 261–273, 275–334.

Note: Of course, teachers will want to select from the great variety of activities offered here those suitable for the age, the level of maturity, and the personality of their students.

Helping students read with critical evaluation, R. A. 335–365.

Note: While the principles in the Reading Aids just cited are of value to all students, teachers may wish to simplify the explanations and the practice work for younger or less capable readers.

Improving general study habits, R. A. 366–397.

Note: Teachers will wish to adapt for younger students the Reading Aids just cited.

READING AIDS FOR SUPERIOR READERS

Helping students learn the meanings of words, R. A. 55, 57–102, 108–127.

Some ways to help your students comprehend, R. A. 128–139, 141–144, 146–155, 157–160, 162–165.

Helping students pull out the main ideas of paragraphs, R. A. 167–186.

Note: The basic work on finding the main idea offered in the companion volume, pages 184–189, is likely to be appropriate for middle school or junior high school readers who need to work with main ideas.

Helping students identify important details in paragraphs, R. A. 187–192.

Note: Middle school and junior high teachers who use these Reading Aids will probably want to adjust the explanations and the practice materials so that they are on an easier level.

Helping students pull out the main content of a longer selection, R. A. 193.

Note: Middle school and junior high teachers who work with longer selections will probably want to adjust the explanations and the practice materials so that they are on an easier level.

Helping students streamline their study, R. A. 194–235.

Note: The master copies in this section were developed for use with capable high school sophomores and upperclassmen. Those who work with superior readers in grades below these levels may want to use the *principles* on the master copies but simplify the *presentation.*

Helping students adjust their reading rate to the task at hand, R. A. 236–251, 253–260.

Turning students into readers—for life, R. A. 261–265, 267–272, 276–334.

Helping students read with critical evaluation, R. A. 335–365.

Note: While the principles in the Reading Aids just cited are valuable for all students, teachers may wish to simplify the explanations and the practice work for younger readers.

Improving general study habits, R. A. 366–397.

Note: Teachers will want to adapt for younger students the Reading Aids just cited.

The Subject-Area Index

The index at the back of this book is like other indexes in directing you to a great variety of topics. The subject-area index on the pages that follow is different. The headings, as you will note, are various subject areas; reading, English, social studies, and others. It is placed in this introduction to guide content area teachers and reading specialists to all the parts of the book that offer help in improving reading in one particular subject. The numerals below refer you to pages, not to Reading Aids.

Certain sections of the companion volume offer additional help—very specific help—in improving reading in the various subject areas. In the index below you will find cross references to that volume, Ellen Lamar Thomas and H. Alan Robinson, *Improving Reading in Every Class,* unabridged 2nd ed. (Boston: Allyn and Bacon, 1977).

READING

Reading teachers and reading consultants, whose interest in the reading of students is broad, are likely to be interested in the pages of this book to which they are referred below. In general, the contents of the companion volume will also be of interest to these specialists.

Helping students to attack words, 7–51
Helping students learn the meanings of words, 53–97
Some ways to help your students comprehend, 99–127
Helping students pull out the main ideas from paragraphs, 127–138
Helping students identify important details in paragraphs, 138–145
Helping students pull out the main content of a longer selection, 145–151
Helping students streamline their study, 153–166
Helping students adjust their reading rate to the task at hand, 169–183
Turning students into readers—for life, 185–213
Helping students read with critical evaluation, 215–233
Improving general study habits, 235–258

ENGLISH

English teachers, whose interest in reading is broad and who may be in day-to-day contact with both troubled and gifted readers, are likely to be interested in much of the present volume.

They will find additional helps—very specific for English—in the companion volume, pages 325–373.

Helping students to attack words, 7–27, 46–47
Helping students learn the meanings of words, 53–97
Some ways to help your students comprehend, 99–127
Helping students pull out the main ideas from paragraphs, 127–138
Helping students identify important details in paragraphs, 138–145

Helping students pull out the main content of a longer selection, 145–151
Helping students streamline their study, 153–166
Helping students adjust their reading rate to the task at hand, 169–183
Turning students into readers—for life, 185–213
Helping students read with critical evaluation, 215–228, 231–232
Improving general study habits, 235–258

GUIDANCE

Guidance counsellors who have a special interest in improving the quality of study are referred to the pages below. They are also offered background understandings about how to improve reading throughout the book.

Helping students learn to study, pages 235–258

SCIENCE

The pages listed below will guide you to specific opportunities to improve reading in science and also to broad background understandings about how to improve reading.

You will find additional helps—very specific to science—in the companion volume, pages 377–399.

Helping students to attack words, 7–9, 14–19, 21 (R. A. 16), 24 (R. A. 25), 46–47 (including R. A. 49)
Helping students learn the meanings of words, 53–59, 61–73, 74–77, 80–92
Some ways to help your students comprehend, 99–105, 109–111, 112–126
Helping students pull out the main ideas in paragraphs, 127–138
Helping students identify important details in paragraphs, 138–145
Helping students pull out the main content of a longer selection, 145–151
Helping students streamline their study, 153–166
Helping students adjust their reading rate to the task at hand, 169–178
Turning students into readers—for life, 185–194, 195–200, 200–206, 208 (R. A. 310)
Helping students read with critical evaluation, 215–225, 225 (R. A. 347 and 348), 227 (R. A. 352)–228 (R. A. 353), 231 (R. A. 365)

SOCIAL STUDIES

The pages listed below will guide you to specific opportunities for improving reading in social studies and also to broad background understandings about how to improve reading.

You will find additional helps—very specific to social studies—in the companion volume, pages 277–321.

Helping students to attack words, 7–9, 14–19, 21, (R. A. 16), 24 (R. A. 25), 46–47
Helping students learn the meanings of words, 53–59, 61–73, 74–77, 80–92
Some ways to help your students comprehend, 99–105, 107, 109–111, 112–126
Helping students pull out the main ideas in paragraphs, 127–138
Helping students identify important details in paragraphs, 138–145
Helping students pull out the main content of a longer selection, 145–151
Helping students streamline their study, 153–166
Helping students adjust their reading rate to the task at hand, 169–178
Turning students into readers—for life, 185–200, 200–211
Helping students read with critical evaluation, 215–228, 231–232
Improving general study habits, 235–258

MATHEMATICS

The pages below will guide you to specific opportunities to improve reading in mathematics and also to broad background understandings about how to improve reading.

You will find additional helps—very specific to mathematics—in the companion volume, pages 401–447.

Helping students to attack words 7–9, 14–19, 21 (R. A. 16), 24 (R. A. 25), 46–47 (including R. A. 49)
Helping students learn the meanings of words 53–59, 61–72, 74–77, 80–88, 92 (R. A. 120)
Some ways to help your students comprehend, 99–105, 109, 115–116, 118–120, 122–125 114 (R. A. 151)–120, 122–124, 125 (R. A. 166)
Helping students streamline their study, 153–166
Helping students adjust their reading rate to the task at hand, 169–173, 173–177
Turning students into readers—for life, 185–194, 195–200, 200 (R. A. 288)–204, 208 (R. A. 310)
Improving general study habits, 235–258

INDUSTRIAL ARTS AND VOCATIONAL EDUCATION

The pages below will guide you to specific opportunities to improve reading in industrial arts and vocational education and also to broad background understandings about how to improve reading.

You will find additional helps—very specific to industrial arts—in the companion volume, pages 449–469.

Helping students to attack words, 7–9, 14–19, 21 (R. A. 16), 24 (R. A. 25), 46–47
Helping students learn the meanings of words, 53–59, 61–72, 74–77, 80–88, 92 (R. A. 120)
Some ways to help your students comprehend, 99–105, 109, 111 (R. A. 144), 112 (R. A. 146), 114 (R. A. 151)–120, 122–124, 125 (R. A. 166)
Helping students streamline their study, 153–166
Helping students adjust their reading rate to the task at hand, 169–178
Turning students into readers—for life, 185–194, 195 (R. A. 276)–199, 200 (R.A. 288)–204, 208 (R. A. 310)
Helping students read with critical evaluation, 215–221, 223, 414 (R. A. 357)–229, 231 (R. A. 265)
Improving general study habits, 235–258

BUSINESS EDUCATION

The pages cited below will guide you to specific opportunities to improve reading in business education and also to broad background understandings about how to improve reading.

You will find additional helps—specific to typewriting—in the companion volume, pages 471–495.

Helping students to attack words, 7–9, 14–19, 21 (R. A. 16), 24 (R. A. 25), 46–47
Helping students learn the meanings of words, 53–59, 61–62, 62–67, 67–72, 74–78, 80–88, 92 (R. A. 120)
Some ways to help your students comprehend, 99–105, 109, 111 (R. A. 144), 117–120, 122–125
Helping students streamline their study, 153–166
Helping students adjust their reading rate to the task at hand, 169–178
Turning students into readers—for life, 185–194, 195 (R. A. 276)–197, 200 (R. A. 288)–202, 203 (R. A. 295)–204, 208 (R. A. 310)
Helping students read with critical evaluation, 215–221, 229 (R. A. 359), 230 (R. A. 362), 231 (R. A. 365)
Improving general study habits, 235–258

FOREIGN LANGUAGES

The techniques for learning to read English that are discussed on the pages cited below should also help students in reading a foreign language. The procedures suggested for expanding English vocabulary will promote vocabulary accretion in the foreign language, and the procedures for improving comprehension of a passage in English will help students center their attention on *meaning* in foreign language reading. Foreign language teachers are referred to other miscellaneous helps below—helps just as effective in a foreign language as they are in reading English.

You will find additional helps—specific to foreign languages—in the companion volume, pages 497–523.

Helping students learn the meanings of words, 53–55, 62 (R. A. 72), 63 (R. A. 73), 67–72, 74–78, 84–85, 86–88, 92 (R. A. 120)
Some ways to help your students comprehend, 99–100, 102 (R. A. 130), 103 (R. A. 132)–109, 113, 115–116, 118–119, 122–123
Helping students streamline their study. Strategies 1, 2, 4, 8, and 10 in Chapter 5 will help students focus on the meaning *of informational writing in a foreign language.*
Helping students adjust their reading rate to the task at hand, 169, 171 (R. A. 240)–178
Turning students into readers—for life, 185–188, 195 (R. A. 276)–197, 200 (R. A. 288)–202, 205–209
Improving general study habits, 235–258

LIBRARY

School librarians, whose interest in the reading of students is both broad and deep, are likely to be interested in the broad background understandings that are shared on the pages cited here.

They will find further background information in the companion volume. Specific suggestions for librarians are offered on pages 555–561.

Helping students to attack words, 7–51
Helping students learn the meanings of words, 53–97
Some ways to help your students comprehend, 99–127
Helping students pull out the main ideas from paragraphs, 127–138
Helping students identify important details in paragraphs, 138–145
Helping students pull out the main content of a longer selection, 145–151
Helping students streamline their study, 153–166
Helping students adjust their reading rate to the task at hand, 169–183
Turning students into readers—for life, 185–213
Helping students read with critical evaluation, 215–233
Improving general study habits, 235–258

HOMEMAKING

The pages below will guide you to specific opportunities to improve reading in homemaking and also to broad background understandings about how to improve reading.

You will find additional helps—specific to homemaking—in the companion volume, pages 525–543.

Helping students to attack words, 7–9, 14–19, 21 (R. A. 16), 24 (R. A. 25), 46–47
Helping students learn the meanings of words, 53–55, 58–59, 61–62, 62 (R. A. 72)–72, 74–77, 80–81, 84–85, 86–88, 92 (R. A. 120)
Some ways to help your students comprehend, 99–105, 109, 115–116, 118–120, 122–126
Helping students streamline their study. Strategies 1, 2, 3, 4, 5, 6, 7, 8, 9, 10 in Chapter 5.
Helping students adjust their reading rate to the task at hand, 169–178
Turning students into readers—for life, 185–192, 195 (R. A. 276)–199, 200 (R. A. 288)–202, 204 (R. A. 296), 208 (R. A. 310)

Helping students read with critical evaluation, 215–221, 223 (R. A. 340), 229 (R. A. 359)–230, 231 (R. A. 365)
Improving general study habits, 235–258

MUSIC

Teachers of music history, music theory, and music appreciation will, of course, be concerned that their students have the reading competency they need for the reading essential in their course work. The pages cited below will guide you to specific opportunities to improve reading in music courses and will also share broad background understandings.

You will find additional helps—specific to music—in the companion volume, pages 545–554.

Helping students to attack words, 7–9, 14–19, 21 (R. A. 16), 24 (R. A. 25), 46–47
Helping students learn the meanings of words, 53–59, 61–62, 62 (R. A. 72),–67, 67–72, 74–78, 80–81, 84–86, 86–88, 92 (R. A. 120)
Some ways to help your students comprehend, 99–105, 108 (R. A. 140)–109, 115–116, 117–120, 122–125
Helping students adjust their reading rate to the task at hand, 169–178
Turning students into readers—for life, 185–192, 193 (R. A. 271), 195 (R. A. 276)–197, 198 (R. A. 284), 200 (R. A. 288)–202, 204 (R. A. 296), 208 (R. A. 310)
Helping students read with critical evaluation, 215–221, 231–232
Improving general study habits, 235–258

ART

Teachers of art history, art appreciation, design, photography, and related courses, will, of course, be concerned that their students have the competency they need for successful reading. The pages cited below will guide you to specific opportunities to improve reading in the field of art and also to broad background understandings that you may relate to art courses as you see opportunities.

You will find additional helps—specific to the field of art—in the companion volume, pages 563–571.

Helping students to attack words, 7–9, 14–19, 21 (R. A. 16), 24 (R. A. 25), 46–47
Helping students know the meanings of words, 53–55, 56–58, 61–62, 62 (R. A. 72)–72, 74–78, 80–81, 84–85, 86–88, 92 (R. A. 120)
Some ways to help your students comprehend, 99–105, 109, 114 (R. A. 151)–116, 118–120, 122–126
Helping students streamline their study, 153–166
Helping students adjust their reading rate to the task at hand, 169–178
Turning students into readers—for life, 185–192, 193 (R. A. 271), 195 (R. A. 276)–197, 198, 200 (R. A. 288)–202, 204 (R. A. 296), 208 (R. A. 310)
Helping students read with critical evaluation, 215–221, 229 (R. A. 358), 231 (R. A. 365)
Improving general study habits, 235–258

PHYSICAL EDUCATION

Physical education teachers and athletic coaches have a remarkable opportunity to reach the unreached reader—to get students, particularly reluctant readers, to turn to books about sports—action-packed fiction, "how-to-do-it" non-fiction, biographies and autobiographies of sports heroes, reference materials about sports. Members of athletic departments whose interest in young people is broad, are also likely to welcome suggestions for improving their students' general study habits. The pages cited below offer suggestions both for "turning on" readers and improving the quality of study. Physical education teachers will find additional helps—specific to physical education—in the companion volume, pages 573–579.

Turning students into readers—for life, 185–192, 195–196, 198–199, 200 (R. A. 288)–202, 204 (R. A. 296), 208 (R. A. 310)
Improving general study habits, 235–258

Reading Aids for Every Class

1

How to Use This Book

If you are reading this book, you are concerned—in some way—with improving the reading of young people. You may be a reading or language arts specialist, a classroom teacher, a college or university instructor of a reading methods course, a curriculum consultant, a school administrator, or a college student planning to enter one of these fields. I hope this book will be of some help to people in all these occupations.

What Will You Find Here?

You will find in this book about four hundred reading aids—some for instruction, some for enrichment—aids which, in the experience of the writer and others, have worked with students. You will find among them diagnostic questionnaires to explore the attainments and needs of students, suggestions for formal and teacher-made diagnostic tests, word-by-word accounts of possible lessons, lively motivators, fresh, new ways to strengthen basic skills.

You will find, as a convenient and time-saving feature, around seventy-five master copy pages, ready for instant reproduction in the form of dittoed or xeroxed copies. You will find on these pages a variety of items: letters to go home to parents to encourage effective study and also personal reading; actual lesson materials for vocabulary, comprehension, and speed; paragraph patterns to project on a screen; how-to-do-it guidelines for students for streamlining their textbook study; eye-catching record forms to invite students to take pride in a record of their personal reading. You have the publisher's permission to reproduce these master copy pages in any quantities.

You will find, for the most part, activities that are self-contained—with *solid help for the teacher* built right into the explanations. With most of the activities, no prerequisites are intended in the way of special training in the field of reading. When further background would be a decided advantage, the reader will find references to readily available sources.

How Should This Book Prove Useful?

If you are a reading or language arts specialist working with classroom teachers, you hope to involve teachers throughout your school in helping students become more effective readers. Most teachers are eager to upgrade their students' reading but sometimes feel either inadequately trained or lacking in specific teaching techniques for the particular situation in which they find themselves. They ask, "How can I actually do this?" You may find this book a useful tool in in-service training—the *what to do* and the *how to do it* are built right into most of these materials. You may find the master copies of student materials, ready for reproduction, especially useful in advertising to teachers practical ways they can improve or extend reading skills within the classroom. A master copy shared with a teacher can be a persuasive "ad," suggesting just how that teacher can go into action. The teacher should be aware that you have the materials available in quantities and can quickly supply them for all of his or her students.

If you are a teacher in a subject classroom, you will find in this book practical procedures for building reading improvement right into the regular day to day work of your course. Many of these procedures were actually contributed by classroom teachers, who have used them with good results in their own classrooms.

If you are a college or university instructor of a reading methods course, this book should be suggestive, to pre-service or in-service teachers, of procedures for teaching certain important reading strategies and skills. You may find the duplicated materials useful as ready-made handouts for these teachers. In that case you will save time that would otherwise be used in preparing similar handouts.

If you are a reading teacher working with small remedial groups or with reading improvement classes, you doubtless have accumulated your own ready classroom resources. You may wish to add to your collection some of the resources offered here as aids to troubled readers.

If you are a curriculum specialist, you are interested in the reading competencies students must develop for successful learning. You may wish to share with others the view that these competencies can be developed and extended in the subject classroom. You may also want to examine materials and methods that have been used with good results in actual classrooms.

If you are a school administrator, you are concerned that the retarded readers of your school make progress and that the average and the highly gifted approach their full potential. You may wish to examine procedures and materials than can be shared with teachers to help achieve this purpose.

If you are a college student planning to enter one of the fields above, you may wish to broaden your general background concerning the teaching of reading and to become more familiar with practical ways to help the young people you will work with read more effectively.

How Will You Read This Book?

How will this book be read most effectively? You may wish to peruse the book from cover to cover. More likely, you will prefer to go through it once to gain a general familiarity with its contents so that you can return when you feel a specific need and locate related material quickly.

For your convenience I have repeated in certain sections content that is found in another section. Instead of reading the book page by page all the way through, you may dip into the final chapter first! For this reason, I have tried to make each section, so far as possible, a self-contained unit. You will not often need to leaf through the pages to locate related material.

You Will Want to Select Carefully from among the Reading Aids

For what student groups are the reading aids in this book intended? They should prove useful in content area classes, in developmental and remedial reading classes, and in reading and learning centers, depending on the teacher's judgment about what is appropriate for the particular situation.

As you will see, *everything in this book is definitely not for every teacher. Teachers will want to choose from among the reading aids most carefully.* The reading skills developed range from lower level, basic skills to higher level skills. The activities included span a wide range in reading achievement—from under-par readers to the highly gifted. The age range, too, is broad—with some activities intended for "middle-schoolers" and some for sophisticated upperclassmen. Chapter 2, "Helping Students to Attack Words," for example, was written to meet a special need of under-par readers for basic skills of word identification. While informative to all who want general background on the reading process, this chapter will probably prove most useful to remedial teachers and special education teachers. At the other end of the spectrum, the systematic approach to textbook study, OK5R (discussed in Chapter 5), and some of the study helps offered in Chapter 9 will probably make their greatest appeal to teachers of more academically oriented, already capable readers.

Since matching activities to students will be of major interest, two specialized indexes have been provided at the close of this chapter—a subject area index and a reading achievement level index. The *subject area index* on pages 16–20 will direct content area teachers and reading specialists to those parts of the book that offer help in improving reading in the particular subject in which they are interested. The *reading achievement level index* on pages 13–15 offers teachers guidance in selecting activities for under-par, average, and advanced readers. Of course, the regular index at the back of the book guides readers to information on a great variety of topics.

For what grade levels are the reading aids intended? As you will see, they are not labeled with specific grade levels. The individual items range in appropriateness from middle school through junior college; with adaptations, many of them should be appropriate anywhere within that range. Activities that appear juvenile will not, of course, appeal to older students. Teachers will wish to select the aids most appropriate for the immediate situation, considering the reading level, the age, the personality, and the special needs of the student.

Teachers Will Want to Make Adjustments

Teachers will want to make adjustments, adapting the strategies, procedures, and materials for older or younger students, for more capable or less capable readers, for particular situations, for a diversity of purposes. As they now appear, the guidelines, "How To Streamline Your Study," for example, were developed for use with capable high school sophomores and upperclassmen, but the pointers offered students are appropriate on a wide range of levels. You may wish to use the content in this section but simplify the *presentation* for younger or less capable readers. You may wish to use only parts of items, to add parts of your own, or to revise items for your immediate needs. You have the publisher's permission to do this. You may wish to use certain ideas as a stimulus for your own creativity and to prepare materials that closely match your students. Perhaps that will be one of the book's most rewarding uses.

Teachers Will Want Students to Acquire a Full Complement of Reading Skills

A caution seems appropriate in a book of activities which, it is hoped, will look inviting to teachers. Each activity selected for use with students should serve a purpose and should have its place in a well-balanced program. In actual practice, activities are sometimes drawn from an activity book and used simply because they are "there" and look inviting. Thus, activities on word attack sometimes run away with time for *practicing* word attack through wide reading. Activities to encourage reading for enjoyment sometimes run away with time for developing skills. The hours that teachers have available to spend with young people on reading improvement are limited—and infinitely precious. Teachers will want to "budget" those hours most carefully.

The contents of this book are not intended to constitute a complete and balanced reading program. The book is, in part, a fill-the-shortage volume! As I pondered over what its contents should be, one criterion was to supply resources in areas where a sufficiency did not appear to exist for upper level teachers. The section for middle/secondary school teachers who exclaim, "I don't know how to teach phonics!" seemed to fill a need. The paragraph patterns to project on a screen looked like a welcome addition to the resources of teachers. Possible procedures for improving general study habits are not usually included in books on teaching reading. For a picture of a complete and balanced reading program, as one authority perceives it, the reader may wish to examine the scope and sequence of various phases of the reading program covered in Robert Karlin, *Teaching Reading in High School,* Third Edition (Indianapolis: Bobbs-Merrill, 1977).

This book was prepared as a companion volume to *Improving Reading in Every Class* by Dr. H. Alan Robinson and the writer (Boston: Allyn and Bacon, 1977). You will find in the present book numerous cross references to useful additional material that is offered in that volume. The activities and guidelines in this book, however, are self-contained and can be used independently. If you are familiar with *Improving Reading in Every Class,* you will notice that parts of this book repeat ideas from that book, ideas the writer considered "musts" in any book on middle/secondary school reading.

Real Reading Improvement Is Not Easy but Worth Our Dedicated Effort

Let no one, including this writer (who is often caught up with enthusiasm for activities that have worked with students), give the impression that bringing solid improvement to handicapped readers is easy! With slightly below-grade, average, and gifted readers, much can be accomplished to extend and upgrade their reading skills—and without great difficulty. With disabled readers, however, even under the most favorable circumstances—in the nation's top reading clinics staffed with highly trained specialists—progress comes slowly. Reading teachers and content area teachers should not yearn for the impossible but try to accomplish the possible with the time, resources, and energies available in the classroom situation.

A precious gift that classroom teachers can give their under-par readers from day to day is experiences of success and approval in and through reading. Such experiences can cause disheartened students to take hold and renew their effort—then the success experiences, together with the renewed effort, may bring progress. Each reading activity carefully selected for students and matched to their needs can mean a success experience for a group or individual. While miracles of reading progress occur more often in ads for commercial reading courses than in the nation's finest classrooms, the sum total of all the success experiences provided by a single teacher in the course of a school year can have a tremendous effect on the attitudes of students and an important effect on reading progress.

"To Each His Own"

This sharing of three hundred pages of reading aids—with materials for reproduction, even with word-by-word accounts of what teachers might do and say in certain lessons—is not intended to suggest that the book is prescribing *the* procedures for others. And it is not intended to suggest that there are not other, different and highly effective ways. I would like to sit down and talk with you, my reader, and ask you to share your own effective methods. Many of the ideas in this book I owe to just such talks!

A closing word might be "to each his own." Nothing succeeds like the teacher's enthusiasm! Perhaps many of the activities in this book succeeded because of the personal enthusiasm of the users. You are invited to take from the coming pages reading aids to your liking, adjust them even more to your liking, and, perhaps with parts of this book as stimulus, devise your own creative reading aids exactly to your liking.

As my years with this book draw to a close, I hope that you will find my efforts useful, that they will ease your way a little as you work with teachers or students, and that you will devise other still more effective ways to help young people grow to their fullest potential in reading.

2

Helping Students to Attack Words

How can teachers help older students who have lost out on the basic skills of word attack? This chapter offers possible ways to help students build or rebuild this ''first story'' of the reading structure.

Classroom teachers sometimes ask with concern, ''How can we help our students read better if they can't recognize the words on the page?'' And remedial teachers sometimes ask, ''How can we make work on basic skills of word attack palatable to older students?'' To suggest some possible answers to these questions, the writer has prepared this comprehensive chapter.

Deficiency in word attack, even with students on the college level, is often found to be at the root of the problem of disabled readers. With some, the need for these skills is so great that unless we help them, they will always be blocked in reading. And even competent readers will, in many cases, read more efficiently if they upgrade some of their word attack skills.

Who should work with *what* in word attack? With which areas can the classroom teacher—realistically—help? And which areas must—realistically—be the province of the remedial teacher? Before we turn to these questions, let us first consider two others: ''What is word attack?'' and ''What tools of word attack should our students master?''

Word Attack

We sometimes see students stop helplessly before a word that appears to be unfamiliar. With no method for attacking the word, they give up and, looking very lost, turn to their teacher to supply it. Sometimes the word is well known to these students when they hear it spoken, but they fail to recognize it in its printed form. If they are guided in attacking the word, they exclaim, ''Oh, I know that word!''

Just what is word attack? Where does it fit into the reading structure? Obviously, in order to get meaning from the page, the student must be able to *recognize* the words. While students recognize on sight some of the words they meet in reading, others they must *attack* in various ways for clues to their identity. What, then, is *word attack?* As the term is used in this book, it means working on a word in order to recognize it, in one or more of the following ways: through clues in the context, through structural analysis including syllable division, through phonic analysis, through use of the dictionary, or through a combination of these methods.

What is the difference between *learning to recognize a word* and *learning a new vocabulary word?* Why not just teach students word meanings? In the act of *recognizing a word,* students come to identify on the page before them a word whose meaning they already know—a word already familiar in its spoken form, already in their speaking-listening vocabularies. They identify in printed form a word they can already say or understand when they hear it spoken by another. In learning a new vocabulary word, they learn a word whose meaning is unknown to them.

A boy may have met the words *chassis, ignition,* and *carburetor* many times through his ears, may have spoken them many times, and may know their meanings better than his teacher—yet he may never have seen them in their printed form. Helping him to read these words will involve word recognition learning. In contrast, the word *philatelist* may be completely unknown to this student. It will call for vocabulary learning, which includes work on both meaning and word attack.

What Tools of Word Attack Should the Student Master?

Our students need the following tools in order to attack and identify words on the pages before them:

1. *Context analysis*—the use of clues to be found in the language surrounding the word to identify the word
2. *Structural analysis*—the method of analyzing meaningful parts of words—their roots, prefixes, suffixes, and inflectional endings—to help identify a word. Dividing words into syllables and accenting them correctly are other components of structural analysis.
3. *Phonic analysis*—the method of figuring out the sounds the letters stand for and blending these sounds together to form and identify the word
4. *Use of the dictionary*—the method of using the dictionary to determine the pronunciation of a word or to check on a pronunciation or meaning tentatively arrived at through methods 1–3.

Incidentally, there is another important way for teachers to develop their students' proficiency in word attack—a way which, though indirect, is basic. We have defined word attack as working on a word in order to recognize it, a word *already known to the student in its spoken form*. Durkin (1976, p. 57, 66) stresses that the productivity of all we teach in word identification is directly related to the size of the reader's speaking-listening vocabulary and that *we should therefore do all we can to help students grow in their oral language abilities*. This growth, Durkin stresses, will have positive effects on their efforts to become successful readers.

Who *Should Work with* What *in Word Attack?*

Who should work with *what areas* of word attack—context analysis, structural analysis (including syllabication and accent), phonic analysis, use of the dictionary? Will classroom teachers of secondary students ordinarily work with skills of phonics? Most secondary teachers will certainly answer, "No." Should remedial teachers, then, go it alone in word attack? Here again, if students are to acquire a full complement of word attack skills, the answer is surely "No."

Which tools of word attack can teachers help students acquire within the regular classroom? Older students, including capable readers, have much to gain from work with context analysis. They can be given practice with context clues "in action" within their classrooms and, at the same time, gain in subject-matter learning. Content area textbooks and other course materials *abound* in words made up of prefixes, suffixes, and roots. Accordingly, structural analysis is another area where classroom teachers can make a productive contribution. Middle-school teachers of self-contained classrooms will, appropriately, develop and reinforce certain skills of phonics, skills of syllable division, and an awareness of accent. And through instruction and practice in natural situations, *all* classroom teachers can strengthen their students' skills in the use of the dictionary.

What will be the province of the remedial teacher? Surely it will be basic skills of phonics, syllable division, and accent for secondary students as well as work with the other word attack tools. Students seriously deficient in word attack will, of course, need concentrated help from this teacher.

You will find this chapter on word attack, then, to be a "pick and choose" chapter—with certain helps appropriate for some and not for others. Readers will wish to use their own judgment about what is appropriate in a given situation.

How Can We Make Work on Word Attack Palatable to Older Students?

A teacher confronted with the prospect of teaching word attack to older students might exclaim, "You've mentioned strengthening the basis of the reading structure, including phonics. Can a teacher make these 'lower level' skills palatable to older students? The reaction to work in phonics may be 'That's baby stuff!' The reaction to work on syllable division may be 'What good is that?' The reaction to work on the dictionary may be 'I can use the dictionary already!'"

Can a teacher of older students make work on word attack palatable? In her own work with high school students, the writer has found these insights helpful:

1. Work on word attack need not be "the same old stuff"—we can sometimes serve it up in a fresh, new format.
2. We will need to help students understand the *why* of work on word attack, to show them what the tools they are acquiring are good for. Nothing succeeds like the teacher's excitement about an activity and confidence that it will help.
3. The work can be related to the *need of the moment* to identify a word. Students will be more strongly motivated if the word is one that has just blocked them in reading or one that they will need to use immediately.
4. The reading matter on which students practice word attack should, ideally, be high in student appeal. When the students are strongly motivated to read the material, naturally they will try harder to attack the words!
5. With older students, work on word attack should be fast moving—perhaps five or ten minutes at a time. Skills they have been taught in the past can sometimes receive a "booster shot" in a few moments.
6. Some skills of word attack lend themselves to fun-to-do activities. Here teachers have an opportunity to collect—and create—original ideas for a "fun kit."

7. With every skill taught, students will need to *observe* their progress. Lessons should be planned for guaranteed success. This is extremely important in word attack.
8. For what it is worth to others, the writer has used popular books on how to read in college to give "lowly" word attack skills status with older students. From these books, some of which include word attack skills on sophisticated levels, she has drawn explanations and practice work, adapting them for high school students. The students see the college books nearby on a desk or table, are made aware of the source of their lesson material, and realize that even college students need and use word attack skills.*

Word Attack Will Be Just Part of a Broader Program

Disabled readers who lack strategies for word attack may, as we have noted, be permanently blocked in reading. If the student cannot recognize the words on the page, he or she cannot comprehend the meaning of the passage and, most assuredly, cannot read faster. *Important as it is, though, work on word attack should, of course, be just part of a broad, well-structured reading program*. It should not run away with time and attention but should proceed simultaneously with work on vocabulary, comprehension, and other components of the students' total reading progress. *With developmental students, students making normal progress, on the secondary level, word attack is the area that will demand the least attention.*

The rest of this chapter offers guidelines and practical how-to-do-its for strengthening students' basic skills of word attack. For further background and a detailed discussion of a broad, well-structured program, teachers have available some excellent additional resources. Much background information is offered in Dolores Durkin, *Strategies for Identifying Words* (Boston: Allyn and Bacon, 1976). Lou Burmeister offers lively, informative reading and a bookful of how-to do-its in *Words—from Print to Meaning* (Reading, Mass.: Addison-Wesley Publishing Co., 1975). Practice exercises to use with students or to serve as patterns for teacher-made materials are available in Nila Banton Smith, *Be a Better Reader* Series, Basic Skills Edition, Third Edition, books A–G (Englewood Cliffs, N.J.: Prentice-Hall, 1977, 1978) and in Olive Stafford Niles, Mildred Dougherty, and David Memory, *Reading Tactics,* A–F (Glenview, Ill.: Scott, Foresman and Co., 1977). From these workbooks for students, teachers will wish to make a careful selection of practices that match their students' reading levels and that will strengthen the specific skills those students need.

Exploring What Students Need in Word Attack

If a problem in word attack is suspected, teachers may wish to ask these questions: How do the students attack unfamiliar words in order to identify them? What methods do they already know and use? What methods do they lack and need? Since students within a group will be on different levels in various phases of word attack, it will be helpful early in the year to learn the answers to these questions. The diagnostic procedures that follow are likely to be most useful for remedial reading teachers and for teachers in self-contained classrooms.

*Among the college books that include useful material on word attack are Julia Florence Sherbourne, *Toward Reading Comprehension,* 2nd ed. (Lexington, Mass.: D.C. Heath and Co., 1977), pp. 482–499.

A Standardized Diagnostic Test Can Be Revealing

READING AID 1

Which students have a serious word attack problem? What specific areas of word attack need strengthening? The following standardized test should be of some help in answering these questions:

> *McCullough Word Analysis Tests* (Lexington, Mass.: Personnel Press, 1963). Seven tests, designed to be used for individual or group analysis, will suggest particular areas of need in phonetic and structural analysis. The tests may be used at all levels from the fourth or fifth grade through college. Individual record sheets enable the teacher to appraise the strengths and needs of each student. Class record sheets serve this purpose for a group. The seven tests cover the following areas: Test I, Initial Blends and Digraphs; Test II, Phonetic Discrimination; Test III, Matching Letters to Vowel Sounds; Test IV, Sounding Whole Words; Test V, Interpreting Phonetic Symbols; Test VI, Dividing Words into Syllables; and Test VII, Root Words in Affixed Forms.

Of course, a teacher may select and administer from among the seven tests only those that probe for insights the teacher is concerned with at the moment.

We Can Observe from Day to Day

READING AID 2

While we cannot assume that students perform the same when they read orally as when they read silently, students reveal something about their needs in word attack through oral reading. As a student does incidental oral reading, the teacher can pick up clues to possible needs, quietly reach for an index card, and quickly make notes on that card.* An index card for a student appears in Figure 2–1. The teacher fills in the first two columns at the moment, then later analyzes the information and completes the third column.

Obviously, teachers will not want to jump to a conclusion about a student's needs on the basis of a single misreading. A *pattern* of misreadings collected over a period of time will be more accurate and helpful. After the student has revealed a possible need, the teacher will wish to check further.

The jottings on the cards in Figures 2–1 and 2–2 suggest how often students need to be guided to attend to *meaning*—to take care that the words they are reading *make sense in the passage*.

Students Can Read Aloud for Diagnostic Purposes

READING AID 3

We have just mentioned incidental oral reading as a source of insights about a student's needs in word attack. A teacher who wants more comprehensive information can ask a student to read a passage aloud *for diagnostic purposes*. Having in hand a typed or xeroxed copy of the passage, the teacher can record on that copy the student's misreadings. Or the teacher may prefer to tape record the student's reading and do the analyzing later. Since reading aloud before an audience can be a devastating exposure for a troubled reader, reading for diagnostic purposes should be done in private with the teacher. The teacher can make the reading a more positive experience by matching the selection to the student's strong interests and by *inviting* rather than requiring the reading: "Would you

*The author is grateful to Nila Banton Smith and H. Alan Robinson for this practical suggestion. Dr. Robinson gleaned it from notes he took during one of Dr. Smith's lectures at New York University in 1951.

Brian S—

THE WORD WAS	HE SAID	MAY NEED HELP WITH
soldier	solder	examining letter patterns in context
advisability	advi — (He gave up)	scrutinizing middles and endings of words
knob	k-nob	silent k; using context
fugitive	fugitive (hard g)	hard and soft g

FIGURE 2–1

A quick way to record clues to students' needs in word attack.

The card for another student appears in Figure 2–2.

Ginny J—

THE WORD WAS	SHE SAID	MAY NEED HELP WITH
internationalization	int—	attacking each syllable
misled	MIZ'eled	using context the prefix mis-; accent
lounge	long	using context; sound of ou

FIGURE 2–2

Another student's possible needs in word attack.

like to read this aloud? This will help us analyze your needs. Any misreadings will be our opportunity—they will tell us how to help you! This isn't a test. There isn't any grade on this." As a check on comprehension, the teacher asks the student at the close of the reading to retell or sum up the story. Care should be taken to select a passage suitable in difficulty. The reading consultant of a school or system may be available to assist a less experienced teacher.

As teachers analyze their students' oral reading, they will want to evaluate the miscues thoughtfully. Insights to be gained from students' miscues will be discussed in Reading Aid 4.

Miscues Are "Windows" on the Student's Reading

READING AID 4

We can learn much about a student's competencies in word attack by *thoughtfully analyzing* that student's miscues in oral reading. Thought-provoking insights about this diagnostic process are offered in *Miscue Analysis: Applications to Reading Instruction,* edited by Kenneth S. Goodman (Urbana, Ill.: National Council of Teachers of English, 1973). While we cannot in our limited space give this subject the explanation it deserves, Dr. Goodman leads us to view a reader's miscues as "windows on the reading process." The fact that he calls deviations from what is printed *miscues* instead of errors is full of import. Dr. Goodman sees certain miscues as quite acceptable.

He leads us to these understandings:

- that all readers, including good readers, make miscues
- that the miscues students make have much to tell us about their *strengths* as well as weaknesses
- that getting meaning from the passage should always be central
- that some miscues, while they differ from the expected response, show us that the reader is keeping his focus successfully on meaning and that these miscues are acceptable
- that, as we analyze our students' oral reading, we should be primarily concerned with the *quality* of their miscues.

Dr. Goodman suggests that instead of merely counting up a student's deviations and designating all of them as "bad," we will wish to *evaluate* his or her miscues through asking these and other questions:

1. Does the reader rely on the sound-letter similarity to the exclusion of concern with getting meaning; that is, does the miscue *sound like* or *look like* the word on the page but make no sense in the context?
2. Does the student have correction strategies to use when that student realizes that what he or she read at first needs correction?
3. How much use of phonic [and structural] strategies does the reader make?
4. Does the reader tend to correct his or her own miscues that result in a loss of meaning? (Miscues that are successfully corrected tell us the reader really comprehends the material.)
5. How many of the miscues are just "editings" or correct interpretations and result in acceptable meaning? These miscues, too, are telling us that the reader is keeping the focus successfully on meaning.
6. Are the miscues shifts to the reader's own dialect? If they are, Goodman observes, they are not really errors. They are what we should expect that particular reader to say.
7. How many of the reader's miscues resulted in an unacceptable meaning but were successfully corrected?

8. Is the reader constantly asking himself if what he is reading makes sense and sounds like language?
9. Does the student's retelling of the content of the passage following the oral reading indicate that he or she has gained a deeper comprehension of the passage than the miscues at first led us to believe?
10. What specific reading strategies would you consider for this student's next lesson?

This all too brief introduction to miscues as "windows" on the student's reading is an invitation to further study. Much practical help is available in Yetta Goodman and Carolyn L. Burke, *Reading Miscue Inventory Manual: Procedure for Diagnosis and Evaluation* (New York: Macmillan Publishing Co., 1972). There the reader will find a discussion of choosing the selection, taping the student's reading, recording, analyzing, and interpreting the miscues, checking on the student's comprehension, and finally, using the information as a basis for specific follow-up instruction. The Reading Miscue Inventory requires training on the part of the teacher and time for administration and interpretation. It is recommended to teachers who want detailed information and can invest considerable time with the individual student.

Helping Students Attack Words through Context Clues

Examining the context for clues will be the most important single aid for readers if they do not recognize a word at sight. As the student attacks a word, *context clues to the word's identity should always be tried first.* Many older students, including good readers will profit from guided practice with the use of context clues.

Students Should Focus on Meaning

The suggestion, "Read to the end of the sentence or paragraph to see what word makes sense here," will encourage the attitude and habit of seeking meaning. As Stauffer (1969) observes, you will be focusing attention sharply on these questions: "What is the writer trying to say? What words would you, the student, use to say the same thing?" You will be inviting the student to reconstruct the author's ideas and to think.

Students, he notes, have had many experiences doing the same thing when communicating orally: "Often when two people are having a conversation, a speaker hesitates on a word and, before he can supply it and finish his idea, the listener has supplied it for him. How does the listener know what word to supply? He does so because he is listening intently and has grasped the speaker's ideas. So, with his attention focused on meaning, he is ready to . . . supply the word. It is the same intentness on meaning that should characterize the circumstance in which a pupil reads on and uses printed language-context clues to word recognition. . . ." Referring to the printed page as a "reading detective's paradise of clues," he points out, "Every word, every word order; each idea, each idea order; every line, sentence, paragraph, and page; all punctuation; all mechanics—all aid the knowing reader in his search for understanding" (Stauffer, 1969, p. 304).

Words Are Like Chameleons

READING AID 5

Many students, including competent readers, need to understand that many words shift and change their meanings frequently—that they take on their meaning from the context. The teacher might share with students—or elicit from students—insights like these:

A chameleon is a remarkable little lizard that changes the color of its skin to match its surroundings. Words are like chameleons!

What does this word mean?*

RUN

. . . to jog fast?
. . . a ravel in a stocking?
. . . a score in baseball?
. . . to campaign for office?
. . . to manage something, like a business?
. . . to slip past something, like a blockade?
. . . to be affected by something, like a high fever?

As you see, the word *run* has no exact meaning apart from surrounding words or context. But what meaning does *run* clearly take on in the sentence below?

Urged by his classmates, Dave decided that he would *run* for class president.

Like the changeable chameleon, the word *run* "takes its color" from its surroundings. The context that surrounds a word, then, helps you determine which meaning from among a number of familiar meanings is intended.

The students might be asked to list as many meanings as they can for a multi-meaning word like *spring, play, cast, cross, school, pupil,* and *well,* then compare and discuss the meanings they have listed. After exhausting their own ideas, they might consult the dictionary for the full array of meanings.

Work with Context Clues "in Action"

READING AID 6

Live practice in identifying words through using context clues can be provided from day to day as words that appear to be unfamiliar come up in reading selections.

The instructor can guide students: "When you meet a word that seems unfamiliar, zero in on the context. There you may find clues to help you 'solve' the word. Be a clue detective! Ask yourself, 'What clues can I discover in the context?' "

A passage like the one below offers an opportunity for older students to practice with context clues "in action":

The Graduation Committee quickly selected the Senior Class gift—a juke box for the student lounge. There was complete agreement—the vote was *unanimous.*

Students who do not recognize the word *unanimous* can be encouraged to reread the passage while asking themselves, "What word makes sense here?" When they focus on the word in its context, some of the students are likely to recognize it and exclaim, "It's *unanimous*!" When they are asked, "What clues helped you solve it?" some student may point out, "Everyone agreed, so *unanimous* fits in."

As the above example suggests, when a student has misread a word or is hesitating over the word, it is often helpful—instead of diverting attention to analyzing the word's structure, breaking it into syllables, or analyzing it phonetically—*simply to ask the student to reread the passage and to think about the meaning.* As the student does so, he or she

*Idea from Olive Stafford Niles, Mildred Dougherty, and David Memory, *Reading Tactics,* B (Glenview, Ill.: Scott, Foresman and Co., 1977), p. 11.

may realize that the misreading does not fit in and may then proceed to make a correct identification. Since the students are using known words to identify words, teachers will want to consider carefully the difficulty of the reading materials. Obviously, if too many of the surrounding words are unknown, the students are not likely to make correct identifications.

Strategies for Using Context Clues in Word Attack

READING AID 7

Students who zero in on both context clues and the word's initial sound have acquired a combination of word attack techniques that will often result in correct identifications. Marksheffel (1966, p. 206) suggests the following two-pronged procedure:

> One technique is to ask a child who is having difficulty with a word, "What word would make sense in this sentence?" Such help often elicits the correct response. If the child's response is incorrect, the teacher may agree that the answer is a meaningful one but ask if the suggested word begins like the one in the book. The additional suggestion directs the child to use phonics as an additional aid for identifying the word.

READING AID 8

Students who reveal a need can be "walked through" the following strategy until it becomes their own to use independently:

1. When you are having difficulty with a word, ask yourself, "What word makes sense here?" Read the entire sentence to detect context clues.
2. If you can't identify the word or if your first impression does not make sense, give the word a closer look.
3. Look especially at the beginning sound to see if this sound starts a word that makes sense in the context.
4. Context clues are not always to be found in the sentence that contains the unfamiliar word. Clues may be in another part of the paragraph, even in another part of the selection. If clues in the sentence do not reveal the word's identity, it may help to read further. The broader context may provide the key (Dallman, 1974, p. 140).
5. If you find you need to, turn to other aids. Look for familiar word parts. Break the word into syllables. Then, if the word still defies you, reach for your dictionary.

"Assignment Words" Offer an Opportunity

READING AID 9

Teachers can search through a passage that will be assigned students for reading and locate words likely to be stumbling blocks. Then they can locate each word for the students on the page (or project the page) and work with each word to discover clues to its identity. Opportunities will also occur *after* the students have read an assignment.

More on Context Clues. Further discussion of the use of context clues will be found in Chapter 3, "Helping Students Learn the Meanings of Words." There you will find a discussion of specific types of context clues, including syntactic (or word order and function) clues and semantic (or word meaning) clues. You will also find possible ways to lift the awareness level of students concerning clues and to sharpen their context clue power.

Helping Students Attack Words through Structural Analysis

Let us consider the order of things for students when they encounter words that appear to be unfamiliar. As we have noted, context clues to a word's identity should always be tried first. Students should ask, "What word makes sense here?" Holding meaning clues in mind, they should then, if they need to, resort to other word attack tools to identify the word or to check on a tentative identification. Perhaps they will notice familiar parts. If they do, they may be able to identify the word quickly. Picking up word-part clues may eliminate the need for the slower word attack methods of dividing the word into syllables and analyzing it part by part through phonics.

Analyzing words through their meaningful parts—their roots, prefixes, suffixes, and inflectional endings—in order to identify the words, constitutes *structural analysis*. Dividing words into syllables is another aspect of structural analysis. Structural analysis is an area where middle/secondary school classroom teachers can make an especially productive contribution to their students' reading. Textbooks and other course materials contain, in abundance, words made up of prefixes, suffixes, and roots. As important words come up from day to day, teachers can call attention to frequently recurring word parts. Double dividends for students should follow: first, a firmer command of words they meet in reading for the subject, and second, a working knowledge of word parts as a lifetime tool in reading.

Teachers can develop skill in using word-part clues in these (and other) ways: 1) they can help students spot easy, familiar root words in long words that appear to be unfamiliar, and 2) they can deliberately enrich their students' working stock of common word parts.

Perhaps at this point it is appropriate to clarify the *root* of a word as the part that carries the main load of the meaning—the base of the word to which other parts (prefixes, suffixes, and inflectional endings) are added. *Prefixes* are added beginning parts that modify the meaning, and *suffixes* are added ending parts that modify the meaning.

For the teacher in search of background information on structural analysis, much help is offered in Dolores Durkin's *Strategies for Identifying Words* (Boston: Allyn and Bacon, 1976).

Help Students Spot Familiar Roots in Troublesome Words

READING AID 10

Students can be led to spot easy, familiar root words in some of the long words that come up as reading hurdles. Guiding them to do this is possible—and profitable—within the classroom. It takes only minutes of class time.

A word like *inadvisability* may seem to some students to "come by the yard." Words that have picked up a number of prefixes and suffixes may frighten students out of proportion to their difficulty. Left alone, some students come upon a word like this, glance at the first few letters, and give up, skipping over the rest. But if the word is written on the board and examined, these students can be led to spot an easy root (here it is *advise*) in the "difficult" word. Once they do so, the puzzle of the "new" word may be solved.

If *unproductively* should be a block for some readers, you might inquire, "Can you see a word within a word—a root word—in this word?" printing it on the chalkboard. With guidance, students will mentally snip off the *un-* and the *-ive* and the *-ly*, discovering *product*—and then note the effect of the suffixes and prefixes. When they mentally reassemble the parts and return to the context, they have very likely solved the word.

If the word *diplomatically* is a stumbling block, you may wish to print it on the board, asking, "Is there a part you know?" Students may respond, "Oh, diplomat!" They may now perceive the long word *diplomatically* as an easy word which has two suffixes tail-ending it. Only its length made it appear forbidding.

As other words come up as hurdles, these can go onto the chalkboard. "Can you strip this one down to its root word?" (*immunization*). "Can you see into this word—how it's built up?" (*incontestable*).

Of course, word-part analysis presupposes some familiarity with frequently recurring prefixes and suffixes. As you guide each analysis, you will be adding to your students' working stock of these word parts.

Students will see into words more quickly if, as you analyze them, you mark off the root word on the board with vertical slash marks:

im | measur | able

or highlight it with colored chalk:

im**practical**ity

re**forest**ation

Now the words may be revealed as not so difficult after all.

Students Will Need Sharp Eyes for Disguised Roots

READING AID 11

Students will need to have sharp eyes for roots that turn up "in disguise," roots that have changed their spelling and pronunciation when a suffix has been added. As they practice "seeing into" long words, they should work first with words that contain easy-to-recognize roots, words like *unenjoyable* and *unfailingly*. They should then move on to words in which the root is harder to recognize because it appears in changed form—*envy*, for example, in *unenviable*, *quote* in *quotable*, *move* in *immovableness*.

Students Can Discover the Meaning of Word Parts

READING AID 12

We have just considered ways to help students spot easy, familiar roots in words that look long and forbidding. We will also want to develop students' skill in structural analysis in another way, by increasing their working stock of "high-yield" word parts—prefixes, suffixes, and roots—word parts that appear in countless derivatives.

We can guide students to discover for themselves the meaning of a common word part. Let's suppose that young readers have been blocked by the word *misalliance* in this sentence: "Ellen's parents felt she had made a *misalliance* in marrying Ben." (Sentence from Niles et al., 1964, p. 22.)

The teacher leads the group to focus on the prefix in *misalliance:* "Do you notice a familiar prefix?" [Some students point out **mis-**.] "Can you think of other words that have that prefix?" [The students may suggest, "Misspell," "Misprint," "Misplace."] "What do you think *mis-* means?" [Some of the students will answer "wrong" or "wrongly."] "Now what do you think Ellen's parents thought?" [Perhaps a student will answer, "That she had taken a wrong step in marrying Ben."] The teacher can then help the group refine the meaning of *misalliance* to "wrong connection" or "wrong alliance."

Greek and Latin Word Parts Pay Off in Every Classroom

READING AID 13

Many of the "high-yield" word parts that students should know come from Greek and Latin. Since these parts abound in students' reading, subject area teachers can profitably work with these parts at frequent opportunities. The gains for students in word analysis should snowball.

The social studies instructor who focuses on the prefix *anti-*, meaning against, when, for example, students meet the word *antilabor,* has handed them a key that will help them in the future to unlock *antitrust, antiwar, antislavery, antipoverty,* and *anti-inflation.* The mathematics teacher who teaches the prefix *circum-*, meaning around, when, for example, the students meet *circumference,* has helped them to recognize the words *circumnavigate, circumpolar,* and others.

Nowhere do Greek and Latin word parts pay off more richly than in science, where the pronunciation of long words is a serious roadblock. The science instructor who teaches the prefix *micro-*, meaning small, when the students encounter the term *microscope* has helped them to attack and recognize, ever after, *micro-organism, microbiology, micrometeorite, microwave, microgroove,* and hosts of others in the *micro-* family.

Students May Need Further Practice

READING AID 14

Practice with word parts in live reading situations, is, of course, ideal, since here the students can observe word parts "in action." Some students, however, may need further practice. Clear, interesting explanations and practice work to use with groups or individuals or to serve as patterns for teacher-made materials can be found in Olive Stafford Niles, Mildred Dougherty, and David Memory, *Reading Tactics,* A–F (Glenview, Ill.: Scott, Foresman and Co., 1977).

Lists of Useful Word Parts for the Teacher

Which word parts will be especially useful to work with as we help students attack and identify words? Prefixes appear to be more valuable, more generative of future word identifications, than are roots and suffixes. You will find in the appendix a list of selected prefixes and roots, and a list of suffixes. Burmeister (1978, pp. 365–388) has performed a service for content area teachers by compiling a great many useful Greek and Latin roots and classifying them by subject areas.

A Word of Caution. As we conclude this section, a word of encouragement and a word of caution seem called for. For older students, structural analysis can be one of the most productive aids in word identification. As we have noted, picking up word-part clues may eliminate the need for the slower methods of syllable division and phonic analysis. Like phonics, however, structural analysis should not be overstressed. As Dallman (1974, p. 122) cautions, "If too much attention has been paid to locating root words, prefixes, and suffixes, it is possible for the reader to become inefficient because the reader approaches too many words by trying to locate word parts. . . . It is undesirable to have all 'new words' analyzed either structurally or phonetically." Work on structural analysis, then, should be in balance. Always the student should be encouraged to make first use—and *full* use—of context and later to return to context to check the identification.

Helping Students Attack Words through Syllable Division

Students often ask, "How can I learn to pronounce hard words? That's my hassle!" Teachers observe that some older students barely glance at a difficult word encountered in reading and give up. They look at the first few letters, see that the word looks unfamiliar, and slide over the rest.

Long Words Are Just Small Parts Strung Together

"Long, hard words are just a mess of letters," one student lamented to his teacher (Bragstad, 1978). We can help such students by making them aware that long words are just small parts strung together, that they can attack these words part by part all the way to the end—in short, that they can "divide and conquer."

Guidelines for Teaching Older Students Syllable Division

A few guidelines should prove helpful as we train upper level students to use syllable division, always in combination with other tools, to pronounce and identify words:

1. Where does syllable division fit into the order of things for students as they attack words in order to identify them? After scrutinizing the context for possible help, the student looks for familiar word parts and sorts out syllables, trying to work out the pronunciation syllable by syllable (Durkin, 1976, p. 75).
2. Spending hours on the learning of rules for syllabication appears to many authorities to be of doubtful value. While a few simple rules will undoubtedly be helpful, students can develop a working knowledge of syllable division in less formal ways than memorizing rules.
3. Some middle/secondary school students, as we have noted, are "half-glancers." For practical purposes they seem unaware that syllables exist. Middles and endings of words receive only slight attention. Raising the consciousness level of these students about syllables should definitely prove helpful.
4. Students need to be trained, not just told, to look all the way along the word. You will find in this section a number of possible activities to help provide this training.
5. In helping students break into syllables words that come up in their day-to-day reading, teachers will find it useful to have among their own resources a command of the rules for syllable division. Six useful rules are supplied in the appendix.

How Can We Check on Strengths and Needs in Syllable Division?

READING AID 15

How can we learn our students' strengths and needs in suitable division? Daily observation will, of course, be helpful. When we observe a student staring helplessly at a word, a word that should be easy to work out syllable by syllable, that student may be saying, "I need help with syllables!"

The McCullough Word Analysis Tests, Part 6 (see Reading Aid 1), appropriate for use from fourth grade up, tests the student's ability to apply eight rules for syllabication. Teachers can test high school students informally, in just minutes, simply by asking them to draw lines between the syllables of the following words, each of which illustrates a principle of syllabication: *culvert, nasal, nitrogen, python, unusable*, humble, freckle, laurel* (Niles, 1964, p. 32).

*The author added the word *unusable* to Dr. Niles' list in order to test the prefix-suffix principle of syllable division.

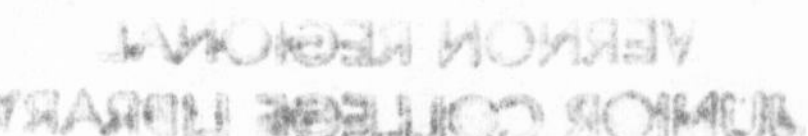

Activities for Syllable Division

The activities in the coming section suggest possible ways that teachers can teach or reinforce students' skills in using syllable division to attack and identify words.

Reducing a Word to Easy-to-Manage, Pronounceable Parts

READING AID 16

As we have noted, students need to be *trained,* not just told, to look all the way along a word. Classroom teachers are in an ideal position to provide this training as they work with words in real life situations. They can simply write on the board, preferably in context, a forbidding polysyllable the students have just met or will soon meet in reading, mark off its syllables with vertical slashes, and mark the accent(s). This takes just moments! Then the students pronounce the word part by part with the teacher. They should quickly perceive that a word that looks as if it comes by the yard can be reduced to a number of short, easy-to-manage, pronounceable parts:

en | vi′ | ron | men′ | tal | ist

As these students read silently, they should begin to break down polysyllables for themselves. Students who need initial practice in *hearing* the syllables in spoken words should profit from Reading Aids 19–21.

A Magic Index Card

READING AID 17

When reading teachers are working with students alone or in small groups, they can, of course, observe closely what these students are doing as they read the printed page. When it is apparent that a student has come to a standstill before a word that should be easy to work out syllable by syllable, some teachers use a "bit of magic"—a small index card. They walk over to the student, cover the word in the student's book with the card, then expose the word to the student syllable by syllable, while suggesting, "Attack it part by part." One high school girl looked up helplessly as she encountered the word *pandemonium*. When the word was exposed part by part and she focused on each part—pan | de | mo | ni | um—then considered the context, recognition dawned. "Oh, *pandemonium!*" Similarly, teachers can use an index card as a cover-card at the chalkboard, printing a word that has blocked students, exposing it syllable by syllable, and guiding the students to attack it part by part.

Students should now be more inclined to attack words part by part as they read alone.

Students "Chunk" Words

READING AID 18

One reading expert (Barr, 1978) teaches students practical syllabication and appropriately calls the process "chunking." She prints a long, forbidding word on the board and tells the group: "That word really looks unmanageable! Let's break it into chunks—let's 'chunk' it! Where do you think we should split off the first chunk?" The students suggest where the first break should come. Then the teacher guides the group in "chunking" the whole word.

The teacher comments: "The students may not divide the word into its parts precisely, but they come close enough. The similarity of the parts to words they already know helps them sound out each part. For a time, we spend a few minutes each day working with words that are coming up in their reading. The students are not burdened by cumbersome rules for syllabication, yet they manage to learn what makes a pronounceable chunk. Gradually, they form the habit of 'chunking' as they read on their own "

What Is a Syllable?

READING AID 19

Students in remedial classes may need to be taken back to the basic understanding of what constitutes a syllable. They can begin by listening for the syllables in spoken words. One reading teacher gives this instruction:

> Each separate part you hear in a word is a syllable. In the word *boat* you hear one part or one syllable. In the word *danger* you hear two parts or two syllables. In the word *tornado* you hear three parts or three syllables. How many parts or syllables do you hear in your first name? Your last name? A friend's name?

Tune Up Your Ears to Syllables

READING AID 20

After the students understand that each separate part they hear in a word constitutes a syllable, a remedial teacher might prepare a list of perhaps ten words, words of one, two, three, or more syllables. If the students will enjoy the challenge, the teacher can include some real "biggies." The students number from one to ten.

The teacher explains, "I'll read some words to you slowly. Please write the number of syllables you hear in each word. As you know, each part of a word that you hear separately is a syllable. Let's try a sample or two. How many syllables do you hear in *guitar? motorcycle?*" [The students respond.]

"Now I'll read the words. Please listen carefully and answer. [As the teacher pronounces each word, he or she displays a card with the printed word.]

1. camp
2. adventure
3. boating
4. hippopotamus
5. minibike.

"Now tune up your ears for some 'toughies':

6. establish
7. establishment
8. disestablishment
9. disestablishmentarian
10. antidisestablishmentarianism."

The teacher suggests, "Now check your answers with a partner. If you don't agree on an answer, ask me to pronounce the word once more. If you believe you're right, defend your answer to your partner. Battle it out with your partner until you decide!"

What Would You Like to Own?

READING AID 21

For a two-minute reinforcer, students who need practice on hearing syllables in spoken words might be asked, "Can you tell us something you would like to own? Then, can you tell us the number of syllables in its name?" The students might answer: "Guitar—two," "Stereo—three," "Kayak—two," "Jaguar—two," "Hondamatic—four," "Backpack—two," "Terrier—three," "Skateboard—two."

Moving on to Printed Words

READING AID 22

Students who need this basic work on syllables should move on from spoken syllables to printed syllables. To help students determine the number of syllables in printed words, teachers might share insights like these or elicit them from students:

> Each syllable has one vowel sound. To decide on the number of syllables in a word, think of the number of vowel sounds you hear in that word. There are as many syllables as there are sounded vowels. All you have to do to find the number of syllables in a word is to count the *sounded* vowels.
>
> What about *silent* vowels? What about the word *mile* or *same?* Would you count the *e* in such a word as forming another syllable? [The students decide.] What about a word in which there are two vowels together, a word like *boat* [*reach, shout* or *oil*]. Would you count each vowel as a separate syllable? [The students decide.] You see, *the only vowels that count* when you are deciding the number of syllables are vowels *that are sounded.* Count only the vowels you *hear—not* all those you see. (Slightly adapted from Smith, Book A, 1968, p. 79).

Five Tips for Syllable Division

READING AID 23

As you recall, many authorities question the value of spending long hours on teaching formal rules for syllabication. As they view it, students can develop a working knowledge of syllable division in less formal ways. A few simple rules, however, will undoubtedly be helpful. Since some of the rules have numbers of exceptions and since students respond to the idea of being given helpful *tips,* let us call them "tips" instead of rules.

The five tips in Figure 2–3 should prove useful when students need to break down words in day-to-day reading situations. A classroom-size placard, striking in size and color (see Figure 2–3), can be an instant reference. The students can become familiar with the tips through their continual application in class. The tips on the placard appear in short form. Unabridged tips will be found in the appendix.

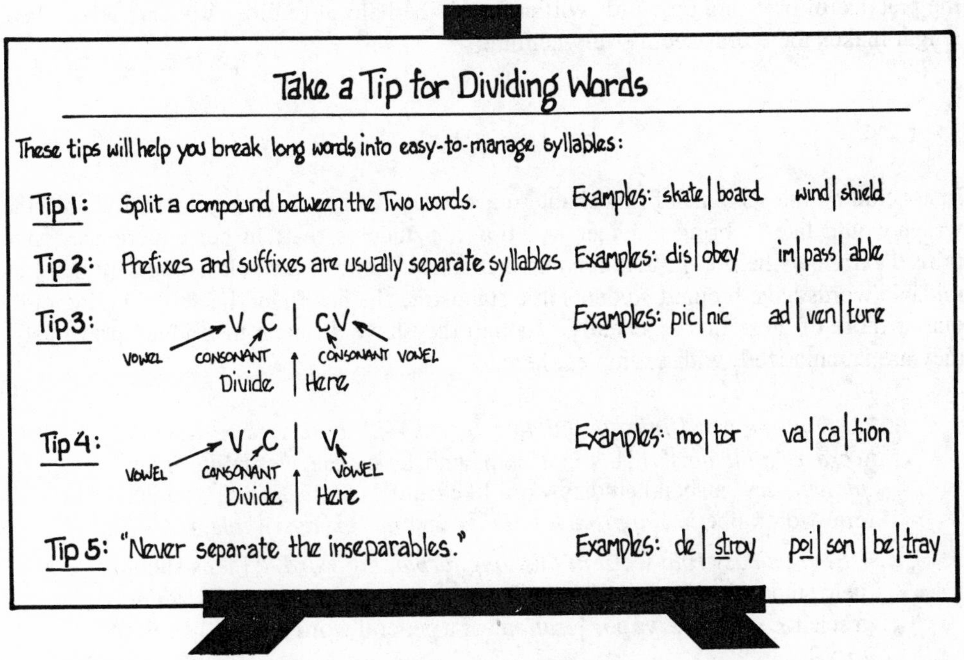

Take a Tip for Dividing Words

These tips will help you break long words into easy-to-manage syllables:

Tip 1: Split a compound between the Two words. Examples: skate | board wind | shield

Tip 2: Prefixes and suffixes are usually separate syllables Examples: dis | obey im | pass | able

Tip 3: V C | C V (vowel, consonant, consonant, vowel) Divide Here Examples: pic | nic ad | ven | ture

Tip 4: V C | V (vowel, consonant, vowel) Divide Here Examples: mo | tor va | ca | tion

Tip 5: "Never separate the inseparables." Examples: de | stroy poi | son | be | tray

A colorful stand-up placard with tips for syllable-division can be both eye-catching and mind-catching. Once prepared, it will always be on hand for instant reference.

FIGURE 2–3

Perhaps all that upper level students need will be a "booster shot" for syllable principles learned years ago, plus reminders to "look all the way along the word" and to make full use of context.

The Goal Is Not to Divide Words Precisely

The goal, as we recognize, is not to lead students to divide words with great precision—it is possible for them to work out word identities without knowing precisely where some of the breaks between the syllables fall. We should strive instead to heighten their awareness about syllables, to make them *actively* aware that it often helps in identifying words to attack them part by part.

READING AID 24

Students should appreciate the benefits—the limitations, too—of breaking down words in order to identify them. Teachers can share these understandings:

> Of course, zeroing in on the context will be your best help in identifying words. If the word still resists you, breaking it into syllables may help. Sometimes after you have tried to divide a word into syllables, it will not come out sounding like a word you know. If that happens, returning to the context may help you "solve" the word. If the context doesn't help, you have a never-failing tool—reach for your dictionary.

Syllable Division Should Not Be Overstressed

Some words of caution about work with syllable division seem to be appropriate. Like phonic analysis and structural analysis, syllable division should not be overstressed. If too much emphasis is placed on dividing words into parts, the reader may become inefficient because he or she takes this slower approach when it is not necessary. Often the reader can identify a word by using only the context combined with the initial sound. Nonetheless, the practice of breaking up words will definitely be helpful to older students when sheer length makes the words seem overwhelming.

Take a Tip!

READING AID 25

In concluding the sections of this chapter on structural analysis and syllable division, the writer would like to bring together five tips for students that, in her experience, have proved extremely helpful in both reading centers and content area classrooms. When formidable words have brought students to a standstill, she has found herself "pulling out" one or more of these tips repeatedly. Though they have all been mentioned previously, they are summarized, with examples, here:

1. "*Break the word into its building blocks—if you can. See how the word is built up!*" [This can help with a science word like *inter* | *planet* | *ary,* a social studies word like *trans* | *continent* | *al,* and general words like *in* | *approach* | *ability* and *in* | *exhaust* | *ible.*]
2. "*Find an easy root word in this long forbidding word.*" [This should help students attack a social studies word like *inter* | **national** | *ization,* a science word like **vapor** | *ization,* or a general word like *dis* | **similar** | *ity.*]
3. "*Snip off prefixes and suffixes to break the word down. Some long words are just smaller meaning units strung together. Then reassem-*

ble the words." [This can help students attack a social studies word like *un* | *constitution* | *ality,* science words like *pre* | *diagnosis* or *circum* | *polar,* and general words like *in* | *contest* | *ability* and *disput* | *acious.*]

4. "*Break the word down into easy-to-manage syllables—divide and conquer. Long words are just short syllables strung together.*" [This can help with a word in social studies or science like *en* | *vi* | *ron* | *men* | *tal* | *ist.*]
5. "*Some students glance at the first few letters and give up. Instead, examine the word syllable by syllable all the way to the end. Zero in on middles and ends, not just beginnings.*" [This tip should help with a science word like *immuno* | *reaction*—indeed, with any long and difficult word.]

Helping Students Use Accent in Attacking Words

Students need a working knowledge of accent in order to pronounce and recognize words that appear to be unfamiliar. One student, struggling with the word *catastrophe*, pronounced it *cat-ə-STROPH-ē* and was left bewildered. When, however, the student was led to consider the context and to shift the accent, there came a "click of recognition." The student exclaimed, "Oh, it's *ca-TAS-trə-phē*!"

Guidelines for Helping Older Students Use Accent

The following guidelines should be useful to reading teachers and at times to content area teachers as they help older students make full use of accent in identifying words.

1. Work with accent can and should be "live." It will take best when the student really needs to *use* an understanding of accent to identify a word.
2. Teachers who observe a student struggling over a word sometimes suggest, "Try shifting the accent." Some students look up at the teacher as if to ask, "What's *that*?" With these students, the first step is often to increase their awareness of accent. Practice work in which they are led to *hear* accent may be a needed first step.
3. Since English words are not consistent in their accent patterns and few principles of accent are "count-on-able," many authorities question the value of spending school time teaching rules for accent.
4. It is helpful to lead students to develop a "shift the accent" strategy—to place the accent first on one syllable, then on another until they arrive at a word they recognize. Some students have great difficulty in doing this. Practice in "live" situations should help these students to make correct identifications.

Some Students Need to "Meet" Accent

READING AID 26

Some students, as we have noted, are not aware of the usefulness of accent in word attack—*and hardly aware of accent at all!* We might explain accent to these students in this way:

When we pronounce a word of more than one syllable, we say at least one of those syllables with more force than the others—we say that syllable a little louder. In the word *camping,* for example, we say the *camp-* syllable harder than the *-ing* syllable. Notice the force of your breath as you say that syllable. This greater loudness or force is called *accent.* In the dictionary an accent mark (′) is used to show which syllable we stress with our voice—*camp′ing.*

READING AID 27

Tap Out the Syllables

We can help make accent clear to students by pronouncing a word like *camp′ing* or *com mu′ ni ty* syllable by syllable and at the same time tapping out the syllables with a ruler, pencil, or finger, giving a harder, louder tap to the accented syllable.

READING AID 28

Tap Out Your Name

Students might be asked, "Where is your first name accented?" . . . "Your middle name?" . . . "Your last name?"

Then they might be asked, "Can you say your first name and at the same time tap out the accent pattern with your finger, giving a louder tap to the accented syllable?" . . . "Your middle name?" . . ." Your last name?" . . . "A friend's name?"

READING AID 29

Accent Words—Wrong!

If students are having difficulty hearing the accented syllable in a word, it may help to pronounce the word and deliberately accent the wrong syllable (Gray, 1960, p. 131). They will be amused—and develop a keener ear for accent—if you ask, "Which pronunciation sounds right—*sel′ fish* or *sel fish′? cir′ cus* or *cir cus′? mot′ to* or *mot to′? Sat′ ur day* or *Sat ur′ day? syl′ la ble* or *syl lab′ le?"*

READING AID 30

Tune Up Your Ears to Accent

To "lift the consciousness level" of students for accent, one teacher cut jumbo-size accent marks from bright-colored cardboard, then glued to each accent mark a backing of sticky masking tape. These spectacular accent marks were to be placed after the stressed syllables of words on the chalkboard. On the board the teacher printed words, words in the students' sight vocabularies, leaving a little space between the syllables. The students read each word and decided which syllable should have the accent. Then a student placed a sticky accent mark on the board after that syllable. Words like the following were "decorated" with accent marks. The colorful accent marks forcefully reminded the students that accent *exists!*

A′ pril
to night′
mu se′ um
gov′ ern ment
ca tas′ tro phe

A "Shift-the-Accent" Strategy

READING AID 31

Dolores Durkin (1976, p. 302) suggests a practical alternative to giving instructional time to rules of accent—rules that cannot be counted on. The alternative is for students to "try on" the accent—first on one syllable, then on another:

> . . . Encourage children to assign stress to each syllable in an unfamiliar word (beginning with the first) until there is that "click of recognition". . . . For instance, with a word like *attention*, stress can be given to the first syllable on a trial basis, once the sound of each syllable has been worked out. Since this suggests no known word, the second can be stressed. Since this does suggest a familiar word, the trial-and-error process ends. In the long run, such a process probably will be easier and more productive than attempts at using generalizations.

The accent need not be "tried on" the syllables in a rigid one-two-three sequence. The student whose first trial does not work out may quickly shift the accent correctly, using his or her "feel" for the rhythms of English words.

READING AID 32

When we observe that a student fails to recognize a word because he or she has misplaced the accent, four magic words may lead to a correct identification: "Try shifting the accent!" A student read aloud, "Retail sales are the BAR-ometer of prosperity." When he was led to think about what made sense and to shift the accent, recognition dawned, "Oh, the baROMeter of prosperity!"

Helping Students Attack Words through Phonic Aids

As we work closely with secondary school students while they are reading, we sometimes see a student come to a standstill before a letter symbol—*au,* for instance, in the word *automatic*. It is apparent that the student has no idea what sound that symbol stands for. When assisted, the student may exclaim, "Oh, *automatic!*" At least part of this student's difficulty probably lies in not having mastered a certain phonic element.

What is phonic analysis? It is sounding out a word, analyzing the word to figure out the sounds the letters and letter combinations stand for, then blending these sounds together to form and recognize the word.

This section on phonic analysis is, of course, not for every teacher. Which teachers will want to work with skills of phonics? Teachers in middle school self-contained classrooms will be concerned to meet their students' needs. Since most secondary students have long since mastered letter-sound correspondences, the responsibility on that level will fall to the remedial teacher.

Most middle/secondary school teachers, even those with degrees in reading, do not step into their classrooms or reading centers well prepared for teaching phonics. I remember my own tremors when I was suddenly transferred from teaching English to teaching reading in my high school. I had no idea how to teach phonics—I did not know the phonic principles formally myself! I recall asking a friend, a master teacher of young children, "If I phone you every night this week, Libby, will you teach me over the telephone how to teach phonics?" She exclaimed, "Ellen, it would take me *months* to teach you how to teach phonics!" Luckily, the task did not prove to be that long or that difficult. By phoning my friend now and then in the evening and leaning on excellent published resources, I learned to teach phonics—often the night before I met my students, it is true. We who teach older students can add *a bit at a time* to our lore in phonics, then use our knowledge to give needed skills to students year after year.

Much help is available in published resources. An inviting little book that "teaches the teacher" and seems heaven-sent for the beginning teacher of phonics is Clyde Roberts'

Word Attack (New York: Harcourt Brace Jovanovich, 1978). Practice exercises, on a wide range of levels, to use with students or to serve as patterns for teacher-made materials are available in Nila Banton Smith, *Be a Better Reader Series,* Basic Skills Edition, Third Edition, Books A–G (Englewood Cliffs, N.J.: Prentice-Hall, 1977, 1978). A manageable little book intended to strengthen the background of teachers is Dolores Durkin's *Strategies for Identifying Words* (Boston: Allyn and Bacon, 1976). This book is readable and inviting, and not at all overwhelming. A programmed text intended for the same purpose is Marian A. Hull's *Phonics for the Reading Teacher* (Columbus, Ohio: Charles E. Merrill Co., 1969).

What Phonic Lore Is Basic?

What phonic lore is basic for upper level students? Shepherd (1973, p. 51) asserts that the phonic principles in the following list may need attention as we work with high school students who have special needs in phonics. To the would-be phonics teacher, this list may seem somewhat overwhelming. Many such teachers have welcomed the clear, simple explanations of these principles in Clyde Roberts' inviting little book, *Word Attack,* referred to in the previous paragraph.

1. The vowel in a syllable which ends with one or more consonants (a closed syllable) has a short sound. Examples: *as*h, c*e*ll, f*i*fth, t*o*n, b*u*d
2. A vowel which is the final letter of a syllable (an open syllable) is usually long. Examples: vill*i,* zer*o,* rati*o*
3. A syllable having two vowels, one of which is a final *e,* usually has the long sound of the first vowel with the final *e* silent. Examples: nitr*ate,*
4. The sound of a vowel followed by the letter *r* is controlled by the sound of the *r*. Specifically, *a* or *o* followed by *r* is neither long nor short. The vowels *i, e,* and *u* followed by *r* sound the same. Examples: *ar*bitrate, v*er*min, int*er*nal, f*or*ce, n*ur*ture
5. In words that contain two vowels together (digraph) such as *ai, ay, oa, ee, ea,* usually the first is long and the sound is silent. Example: impe*a*ch, br*ai*n, st*ea*m, r*ay,* st*ee*l
6. In words that contain two vowels together such as *au, aw, eu, ew, oo,* the vowel letters (digraphs) have a special sound unlike either of the vowels. Examples: *cau*stic, past*eu*rize, f*oo*d, *sew*erage
7. In words that contain two consonants together such as *sh, *wh, th, ch,* the consonant letters (digraphs) produce a single and new sound. Examples: *sh*ip, *wh*eat, *th*is, *th*ird, *ch*ange, *ch*orus, *ch*ef

   *The w is silent when followed by *o;* example: *who*
8. Some words have a blend of two or more consonants each of which retains its own sound. Examples: *bl*ood, *st*omach, *gl*and, *pro*nounce, *tr*ade, *dr*aft, *str*aw
9. Some words have a blend of two vowels (diphthongs) which produces a blended sound. Examples: c*oi*l, b*oy*cott, m*ou*th, fl*ow*ery
10. When *c* or *g* is followed by *e, i,* or *y,* each is usually soft. Examples: c*i*ty, c*e*ntury, c*y*st, g*e*ometric, g*y*roscope
11. The unaccented syllable of a word may cause the vowel to have the schwa sound (the schwa sound designated by the inverted *e* (ə) is indis-

tinct and does not give the vowel a distinctive sound). Examples: respiration, corolla, ventral, quadruped

In what order should phonics skills be taught? Since teachers of older students will often be concerned with reinforcing skills already taught rather than with the initial teaching, they will often be giving students "on the spot" phonics, skills related to the need of the moment to identify a word. For readers of this book who are interested in an instructional sequence, Heilman (1964) recommends the following order in *Phonics in Proper Perspective* (1964, p. 19).

1. Auditory-visual discrimination
2. Teaching consonant sounds
   a) Initial consonants
   b) Consonant digraphs (sh, wh, th, ch)
   c) Consonant blends (br, cl, str, etc.)
   d) Substituting initial consonant sounds
   e) Sounding consonants at end of words
   f) Consonant digraphs (nk, ng, ck, qu)
   g) Consonant irregularities
   h) Silent consonants
   i) Sight-word list—non-phonetic spellings
   j) Contractions
3. Teaching vowel sounds
   a) Short vowel sounds
   b) Long vowel sounds
   c) Teaching long and short sounds together
   d) Exceptions to vowel rules taught
   e) Diphthongs
   f) Sounds of o͞o and o͝o

Guidelines for Teaching Phonics to Older Students

The following guidelines should prove useful as we work with older students to strengthen their skills in phonics:

1. The teacher will need to be a *super*salesperson. Sounding out letters is likely to seem remote from the students' world of sports events, guitars, first cars, and blue jeans! But the teacher hears these students lament, "I don't know how to pronounce long words!" The teacher might capitalize on this interest as a selling-point: "This work will help you pronounce words, no matter how long or how difficult. College students need these skills! I need and use these skills!"

   We have mentioned a secondary school student who had not mastered the letter combination *au* in the word *automatic*. The teacher might suggest, "This word part really pays! There are *pages* and *pages* of words in the dictionary that begin with this sound! [The teacher can hold up the dictionary and turn through those pages.] Now you'll have a handle on *hundreds* of words!"

   We have spoken of using popular books on how to read in college to give "lowly" work on word attack status. As the writer works with older students on phonics, one of these books is sometimes near—right on the desk or table.* She holds it up before the group and remarks: "College students need these skills. You'll be

*Julia Florence Sherbourne, *Toward Reading Comprehension*, 2nd ed. (Lexington, Mass.: D.C. Heath and Co., 1977), pp. 482–499.

glad you have them if you go to college. Part of our work today came from this college book. Adult readers use these skills—I need and use these skills!"

2. It should help to pull out important words from selections the students are actually studying in their courses—English, science, social studies, mathematics—then to demonstrate, through examples, that phonic aids *really work*. The students may react, "Good! This will help me in my courses!"
3. Most secondary school students have, over the years, acquired a familiarity with their language and already have considerable knowledge of the basic sounds in English and the letters that represent them. The need of some students is to *make full use* of this knowledge. With older students who are not seriously disabled, we will not need to relay—slowly and laboriously—a foundation in phonics. As Dr. Ruth Strang (1965) observed: "Older students can often get at the identity of a word by pronouncing it by syllables and using what knowledge of phonics they already have. We will need to guide some students, however, in doing this."
4. Work in phonics should not be given students in large, untakeable doses. Minilessons can be related to the needs of the moment. Ideally, the practice words should be words that have just proved to be a stumbling block or words the students will need to use immediately.
5. Each phonics lesson should grow out of a contextual setting and end with a contextual setting.
6. Many reading authorities hold that phonic generalizations "take" better with students if the teacher guides them to discover the generalization instead of giving it to them in gift wrappings. In the writer's experience, however, there are practical considerations that will often lead us to teach older students deductively. Inductive teaching often proceeds slowly, and in many cases the phonic principle has already, years ago, been taught inductively. If that is the case, all the students need may be a quick *reminder* of the generalization. In that event, we may wish to proceed deductively—and more rapidly—by recalling the principle (or helping students recall it) and then provide practice applying that principle to "current" words. High school students are not very patient about spending a lot of time developing principles of phonics! Often some combination of inductive and deductive teaching will be most effective.
7. Work with students on a phonic generalization should start with *known words,* then move on to more difficult words, words the students do not recognize at sight, words challenging enough to give the students a sense of accomplishment when they have "solved" the word.
8. Students should realize that phonics generalizations are not "rules" that always work—that it isn't a matter of "See this, say that!" (Durkin, 1976, p. 285). Nevertheless, they can rest assured that "sounding out" will give them some help with the majority of words in English—indeed, with a substantial 85 percent of all words!
9. Students should understand that using a phonics aid is a starting point, that they may work out a pronunciation somewhat like, *but not exactly like,* the correct one. In that case, they may want to examine the context thoughtfully and try various shifts in pronunciation in order to recognize the word.

Students will not use their phonic skills alone but in combination with context clues, structural clues, and the dictionary. They should not feel locked into rigid procedures. Shepherd (1973, p. 50) suggests a very flexible sequence. A slightly abridged version follows. As you see, the student uses no more aids than necessary to get a breakthrough.

> At first the reader will attempt to recognize the word through clues in the context. If this works, he need go no further. However, if it doesn't, he will resort to phonic and

structural analysis . . . If he is successful, he will see if the word, as he has analyzed it, fits contextually. If it does, he will go no further. If it does not, he will consult the dictionary. Again he returns to the context to fit the appropriate meaning into the sentence. The reader in actual practice uses all of these methods, checking one against the other . . . .

When a mature reader analyzes a word, he does it quickly, using the various options open to him in combination simultaneously, not stopping to label for himself the method(s) being employed.

10. As we have noted, most students on the secondary level have long since mastered letter-sound correspondences. Students seriously deficient on that level should have the help of a remedial teacher.

How Can We Check Quickly on a Phonic Need?

READING AID 33

Suppose a teacher has observed a possible need in phonics and would like to check more carefully. The need might be the final *e* vowel principle, the sounds of letter combinations like *au, oi,* or *qu,* or the sound of the final syllable *-tion.* Ekwall (1976, p. 102) suggests this simple way of checking: "Write several nonsense words with the pattern to be tested and ask the student, 'If these were real words, how would you say them?'" For example, we might check a student's understanding of the final *e* vowel principle by asking the student to pronounce the nonsense words, *tipe, rete, sape, pune,* and *sote.* We might check mastery of the sound *qu* represents by *quif, quat, quam, quet,* and *quem.*

Teachers who wish to diagnose thoroughly a student's strengths and needs in phonics will find much practical help in Eldon Ekwall, *The Teacher Handbook of Diagnosis and Remediation in Reading* (Boston: Allyn and Bacon, 1977).

What Are Some Guidelines for Teaching a Phonics Lesson?

Teachers have asked the writer: "How can a teacher without training or experience in teaching phonics teach a phonics lesson?" Remedial reading teachers and middle school teachers who have self-contained classrooms may find useful the guidelines on the next few pages. Content area teachers will find them of less interest.

Dr. Robert Karlin (1977, pp. 147–149) suggests that a lesson should include the following phases:

1. Auditory discrimination—learning how the phonic element *sounds* and distinguishing it from other sounds
2. Visual discrimination—learning how the phonic element *appears* in a word and learning to differentiate that element from others the student will see in words
3. Word blending or building—practicing blending the sound being taught with the other sounds in the word in order to identify the word
4. Contextual application—practicing identifying in a context setting words containing the particular phonic element.

The author of this book does not intend to suggest a rigid sequence. Some students will learn more successfully if the steps are placed in a different sequence, and some can master the principle without all the phases. There is probably no one way to teach phonics —rather many ways in many situations. In no case should the lesson become a "drag" or seem to the students to have no purpose.

On the following pages you will find a word-by-word account of a possible lesson based, as you will see, on Dr. Karlin's sequence. The lesson concerns the letter combination *qu,* a phonic element that seriously handicapped high school readers have often failed to master. The writer is indebted to Dr. Karlin for ideas of his that have been worked into this lesson. As Dr. Karlin (1977, p. 147) points out, at no time is the sound of the phonic element removed from its natural surroundings—emphasis is placed upon its sound as it appears in different words. The lesson introduces the phonic element in a contextual setting and ends with contextual application.

A Lesson on the Letter Combination *Qu*

READING AID 34

Let's suppose that students have been blocked in reading because they do not know the sound the letters *qu* represent. The lesson follows soon afterward, while the need for help is still fresh in mind. The word that blocked the students is printed on the board (or on a dittoed worksheet) in the following sentence:

As election day drew near, the rivals became more *quarrelsome.*

The teacher comments, "This word [indicating *quarrelsome*] blocked you in your reading. You had trouble with the beginning sound. When you know this sound, it will help you figure out the pronunciation of *hundreds* of words!"

On the board (or on worksheets) are words the students already know at sight, each beginning with *qu.* They might be

quit
quick
quite
queen
question

The teacher says: "Please listen carefully to the beginning of each word as I pronounce it." The teacher pronounces each word slowly, emphasizing but not isolating the sound of *qu.* Different students, too, might pronounce the words. [The students are learning how the phonic element sounds. This phase of the lesson is *auditory discrimination.*]

Next, the teacher asks: "What, obviously, *looks* the same in these words?" The students answer, and someone marks off the *qu's* in the way they are marked in the following list. [This phase of the lesson is *visual discrimination.* The students are learning how the phonic element appears in a word and learning to differentiate that element from others they will see in words.]

quit
quick
quite
queen
question

The teacher goes on, "This word part really pays off! You'll find pages and pages of words in the dictionary that have this sound!" The teacher holds up the dictionary and shows the group those pages. "When you know this sound, you'll have a handle on *hundreds* of words you'll meet in reading."

"Now will *you* please pronounce these words?" The students pronounce them, emphasizing in each the sound of *qu,* [Here is more work on *auditory discrimination.* The students are distinguishing the sound of the initial letters and fixing more firmly in mind that *qu* represents the sound of *kw.*]

The teacher asks, "Now can you distinguish this sound from others that are similar? I'll read some words. Do they begin with the same sound as *quick, quit,* and *quite?* Please listen to each word and decide. [Here is further work on *auditory discrimination.* The students are having practice differentiating the sound of *qu* from other sounds. Karlin (1977, p. 148) suggests that words not containing *qu* should come toward the end of the list.] Does *quiet* contain our sound? *quaint? quality? qualify? quiver? quench? quarterback? quaver? kindle? wakening? questionnaire? culprit? guest? custom? quintet?*" [Students who answer incorrectly are revealing that they need further practice.]

"To make use of what you've learned, you'll need to be able to blend the sound of *q-u* with the other sounds in a word in order to 'solve' the word. Here are some words you know. Can you substitute our sound for the first letter(s) to build a new word? [This phase of the lesson involves *blending.*] Here's the word *shiver.* Can you take off the *sh* and put *qu* in its place to build a new word?" *Shiver* and the other words in the following list appear on the board (or on a worksheet). The teacher has printed the letters *qu* on a two-by-two-inch card and at the chalkboard covers the *sh* of *shiver* with the card. "What new word is formed? Yes, *quiver*—to tremble. Now try this one. Substitute *qu* for the *f* in *faint.* What new word is formed? Yes, *quaint.*" The teacher covers the beginning letter(s) in the words below with the *qu* card. The students blend and read aloud the new words. (If the students are using a worksheet, they cross out the original letters and write the *qu* above them.)

hitter becomes *quitter*
wake becomes *quake*
vote becomes *quote*
pack becomes *quack*
rest becomes *quest*
guilt becomes *quilt*

The lesson sequence ends with contextual application. The teacher might ask, "Can you complete these sentences with words beginning with *qu?*" Sentences like the following are on the chalkboard (or on a worksheet).

The angry students ripped up the goalposts. No one could ______________ the noisy crowd. [*quiet*]

Why do all my teachers give ______________ on the same day? [*quizzes*]

After the ______________ called the signal, the center snapped the ball to the fullback. [*quarterback*]

Our basketball ______________ battered the opposing team. [*quintet*]

Soon after, the teacher *proves* the usefulness of this new tool by spotlighting *qu* words the students are now meeting or will be meeting in their actual courses.

The teacher points out, "Here's a sentence straight from your science textbook." A sentence like this is on the board (or on a worksheet):

The astronauts, along with their moon rocks, were placed in *quarantine.*

The students sound out *quarantine,* working with it briefly. At this point the teacher is not intent on teaching the meaning (that can be supplied incidentally)—only on proving to the students that they will be meeting *qu* words in their course materials.

"You'll meet this word in social studies:

Congress set up the *quota* system and closed the gates of America to many would-be immigrants.

"Here's one you may already know from math:

A *quadrilateral* has four sides and four angles."

The students may react, "This will really help me!"

The students' newly acquired skill with a phonic element will need reinforcement. The teacher will continue to spotlight *qu* words, as they come up from day to day. In the initial lesson or later, the students should work with words (of appropriate difficulty) that contain the phonic element *within* the word—words like *equal, conquest,* and *headquarters.* As with any phonic element, the students should become aware of exceptions, in this case, words in which *qu* has the sound of *k,* among them *conquer, mosquito, etiquette,* and *antique.*

The words in the lesson just reported, it might be noted, have already been printed on the board or on a dittoed worksheet. This speeds up the lesson. It may be convenient, when thorough teaching of a phonic skill is necessary, to teach it the *day after* the students reveal a need for the skill. In between, the teacher can print the words on the board or prepare a worksheet. Worksheets have an obvious advantage in that the teacher gradually accumulates a supply of instant lesson materials. Kept on file, these can be pulled out in moments and put to work to meet the needs of future students.

The reader will find down-to-earth suggestions for phonic lessons in Lou Burmeister, *Words—From Print to Meaning* (Reading, Mass.: Addison-Wesley Publishing Co., 1975).

READING AID 35

"Quicken Your *Qu's!*"*

Most students will not need the thorough teaching of a phonic element delineated in Reading Aid 34. Often such an element can be taught or retaught through a mini-lesson in which the steps in the preceding lesson are telescoped.

Suppose students have been blocked in reading a passage by not knowing the sound *qu* represents in the word *quotable.* Clues in the context have failed to reveal the word's identity. The teacher quickly lists on the board a few easy words starting with *qu,* words in the students' sight vocabularies. The words might be *quick, queen, question, quit,* and *quite.*

The teacher asks, "What looks the same in these words?" As the students answer, someone marks off the *qu's* by drawing a long box, as they were marked off in Reading Aid 34.

Then the teacher asks, "Please pronounce these words. What *sounds* the same?" The students distinguish the sound of the initial letters and note that *qu* represents the sound of *kw.*

*Agnes Ann Pastva and Mary Owen used this catch-phrase in *Composing with Paragraphs* (New York: Cambridge Book Co. 1974), p. 153.

"Can you distinguish our sound from similar sounds? Listen to these words. Do they begin with the same sound as *quick* and *quit?*" The teacher reads words like *quiet, quiz, quake, custom, quality, kindle, wakening,* and *quiver.*

Having differentiated the sound of *qu,* the students now attack *quotable,* the word that blocked them in reading, making full use of clues in the context. This time they are successful.

A Mini-Lesson: What Is the Effect of Silent Final *E*

READING AID 36

Suppose the teacher has observed that some students need to master or review this vowel principle: the effect of final silent *e* when the word contains a vowel, then a consonant, then a final *e* in the same syllable.

The teacher comments: "This word gave you trouble, and the context didn't help." A sentence containing the word *cube* is on the board, and the teacher indicates that word.

The teacher asks the students to pronounce words like those that follow—words the students already know:

rope	line	hike	brake	date
bite	time	pale	vote	scene

Then the teacher leads the student to "discover" the effect of the silent final *e* by asking questions like these: "Do you find a silent letter in each of these words?" . . . "Which letter?" . . . "Does a consonant or a vowel precede the silent *e*?" . . . "What sound, long or short, does the first vowel have in all these words?"

The teacher continues: "This clue will help you identify *countless* words. Can you fill the blanks in this sentence?"

> When a word has a vowel, then a consonant, then a final *e* in the same syllable, the first vowel is usually (long) and the final *e* is (silent).

The students now return to the original sentence containing the word *cube* and read it successfully.

In reinforcing this vowel principle, Dr. Olive Niles (1972, p. 61) supplied students with this graphic aid:

Clue to the long sound of the vowel
VC + silent *e*
s t r i p e

Students find the following statement of the vowel principle easy to remember: "Final silent *e* tells the vowel before the single consonant to *say its name.*"

Later the students move on to apply the principle to less familiar words and to words of more than one syllable, words like *fuse, athlete, dynamite, communicate,* and *trapeze.* The students work with these words in context. The teacher spotlights final *e* words in the students' course materials.

Lively rhymelets like the one that follows concluded Dr. Niles' work with final e. The students selected words from a list to complete the rhymelets (Niles, 1972, p. 64).

> Said the old-timer, "Son, if you marry a wife,
> All your days will be nothing but trouble and (strife) !"

The mini-lesson on *qu* on the preceding pages and the one on final *e* suggest possible ways of teaching phonics to older students. These lessons are illustrative only. Handicapped readers will have many other phonic needs that teachers will wish to meet through instruction and practice.

An "Instant Word Attack Kit"

READING AID 37

The "instant word attack kit" has proved heaven-sent for teachers overwhelmed at the prospect of teaching phonics; it has been so welcome that directions for making the kit are repeated here from *Improving Reading in Every Class* 2nd ed., (Thomas and Robinson, 1977, p. 95):

> Would you like to have at your fingertips insights on how to teach phonics and other word attack skills, plus a generous supply of practice materials? Once prepared, an "instant word attack kit" can be a timesaver for you for many years.
>
> Spend an evening or two with the scissors and some phonics workbooks and you can add such a kit to your classroom resources. Cover a spacious carton with bright construction or adhesive-backed paper. Put two or three dozen manila folders in the carton.
>
> In the first folder go tests to explore the needs of students. The second is to contain charts or profiles to record the needs of groups or individuals. Next come folders, in alphabetical order, for each of many different phonic and structural elements and skills—hard and soft *c*, the diphthong *oi*, the schwa, silent consonants, syllable division, accent, diacritical marks, and many others. Each folder is stocked with practice exercises cut from workbooks on various grade levels, with each exercise coded by grade level in the upper left-hand corner. The folders of a seventh-grade English teacher, for example, were stocked with exercises on all levels from four through nine.
>
> When economy matters, the pages of a few workbooks will go a long way when classified in a file of this type. You will need two copies of each workbook so that the reverse side of each page can be included.
>
> As a timesaver, the kit is great. If a student or group is having trouble with the sounds of *c*, for example, you can find within seconds practice work on just the right level. Of course, practice work is timely when the need has just been demonstrated in a live reading situation and when the student is ready to use the skill for an immediate job. The file supplies material before motivation cools.
>
> But how can a teacher with no training or experience in teaching reading learn quickly how to teach phonics? The box itself teaches the teacher. Place the teacher's manuals for the workbooks in the box behind the manila folders. In the upper right-hand corner of each practice page from a workbook, record the initials of the corresponding manual. A teacher who doesn't know how to teach hard and soft *c* can refer to the manual from the practice exercise and receive sound instruction. To provide general background for the teacher, Marian A. Hull's *Phonics for the Reading Teacher* (Columbus, Ohio: Charles E. Merrill, 1969) might be added to the kit.
>
> When working with a group whose members have a common need, you may refer to the kit, then ditto your own practice materials; or you may wish to project a workbook page on a screen before the group. When working with an individual, you can place the practice page in a plastic envelope, and the student can write on the plastic surface with a special pen. Thus the materials are reusable.
>
> You may wish to turn to the teacher's manuals for insights, then create your own instructional materials, using subject matter of compelling interest to students. Your self-made materials can be filed in the appropriate folder, thus enriching the resources of the kit.
>
> In one English class for which a word attack kit was created, each student had an individual folder. If the teacher observed a special need, the student was likely to find a note in the folder guiding him or her to an appropriate practice exercise. Sometimes the practice exercise served as filler. A student could work on it the first time she or he

completed the class work ahead of the others. Since students were accustomed to working in laboratory-type kits, no stigma was attached.

If you plan to stock such a file, you may wish to consider appropriate levels of the following books and workbooks. Pages that look juvenile can be rejected.

Useful Books and Workbooks

Boning, Richard A. *Working with Sounds* booklets of the *Specific Skills Series*. Baldwin, N.Y.: Barnell Loft, 1976–1978.

Hargrave, Rowena, and Leila Armstrong. *Building Reading Skills*. New York: McCormick-Mathers Publishing Co., 1970–1971.

Kottmeyer, William, and Kay Ware. *Conquests in Reading*. St. Louis: Webster Publishing Co., 1968.

Kottmeyer, William, and Kay Ware. *The Magic World of Dr. Spello*, 2nd ed. St. Louis: Webster Publishing Co., 1968.

Monroe, Marion, A. Sterl Artley, and Helen M. Robinson. *Basic Reading Skills*, 2nd ed. Glenview, Ill.: Scott, Foresman and Co., 1970.

Roberts, Clyde. *Word Attack*. New York: Harcourt Brace Jovanovich, 1978.

Rudd, Josephine. *Word Attack Manual*. Cambridge, Mass.: Educators Publishing Service, 1962.

Smith, Nila Banton. *Be a Better Reader*, Basic Skills Edition, 3rd ed., Books A–G. Englewood Cliffs, N.J.: Prentice-Hall, 1977, 1978.

Wolfe, Josephine B. *Merrill Phonics Skilltext*. Columbus: Charles E. Merrill Co., 1973.

A teacher inexperienced in teaching phonics may be at a loss as to how to label the manila folders with all the essential phonic and structural skills. The workbooks just enumerated, or their teacher's manuals, offer lists of skills.

With an instant word attack kit, the task of learning to teach phonics need not be overwhelming. By following the simple, clearly stated, this-is-how-to-do-it procedures in the teacher's manuals, you can add one skill at a time to your word attack lore.

Fun Fare for Phonics

On the pages that follow, you will find a variety of activities to reinforce mastery of skills of phonics. Using a few "sample" principles, we will suggest how phonics skills can be reviewed in fresh, lively, lighthearted ways. In selecting the principles, the writer has been influenced by Burmeister's list (1975, pp. 51–92) of special needs she has observed in middle school and high school students. These needs include hard and soft *c* and *g;* the diphthongs *oi, oy, ou, ow;* the digraphs *au, aw;* the consonantizing of *i* in final syllables *(-tion, -sion, -cious, -tial, -cial)*; and, already covered in this chapter, the determination of syllable and syllabication generalization.

Students often benefit from a change of pace as they work on basic skills. After spending a few minutes in a "fun-break," they are more willing to dig into work-type practice. Most of the activities suggested here should take only a few minutes of class time.

All the activities are intended to supplement a well-structured program in word attack. All have a definite learning purpose; always the student should understand that purpose. None of the activities is intended as busywork—the teacher will be on hand guiding and checking.

Some of the activities require dittoed materials, workboards, and gameboards. If these are laminated or covered with plastic, they become permanently reusable classroom resources. Students can write on the plastic surface—later the writing can be erased for the next student. Care should be taken in choosing a marker for plastic. The pen should make a fine, clear line, and the ink should be water soluble.* Time and thought are invested in the preparation of materials like these. Then, once prepared, they become permanent time-savers for the teacher.

Work on phonics, as we have noted, should begin and end with meaningful context. The need for the skill practiced in the activity should have been demonstrated in context. And the activity should be followed by practicing the skill in context.

As with other areas of word attack, activities will be especially meaningful for the students if they work with words they are now meeting, or will soon meet, in readings for their actual courses.

Why create materials when ready-made materials can easily be purchased? Materials the teacher creates can focus in on the particular needs of the student. They can also focus on the words of the moment, words the student needs to identify in order to read current selections. Then, too, the usual phonics workbooks may be symbols of past failure to the under-par student. Hopefully, this will not be the case with activities pulled out of the teacher's "fun-kit."

Play Phonics Tic-Tac-Toe

READING AID 38

Phonics Tic-Tac-Toe (Swenson, 1960) is easy to prepare and fun to play. After students have worked with a certain phonic element and need reinforcement—it might be the letter combination *au*—they are supplied with a tic-tac-toe grille. In the spaces on the grille are written words beginning with or containing *au,* words of appropriate difficulty, in a snatch of context. Each player has several markers, Xs or Os cut from cardboard. The player may place the marker on a space, provided he or she can pronounce correctly the word printed on that space. Three in a row wins, as usual. M&M candies make popular prizes!

Teachers can draw the tic-tac-toe framework on a sheet of paper or on the chalkboard. Or they can make permanent plastic-covered gameboards. With gameboards, the tasks for the student can be written on the plastic surface with a marking pen for plastic and later erased, so that the gameboards can be put to many different uses. A tic-tac-toe gameboard looks like the one in Figure 2–4.

To help underconfident readers experience success and to increase the value of the practice, teachers may wish to give the students time before they play to look over the gameboard and work out the pronunciations.

It is desirable that the words on the gameboard really require sounding out—that they should not already be in the students' sight vocabularies. If the students recognize the words at sight, they will gain no practice using the phonic element in attacking the word on the space.

SEE MASTER COPY PAGE 1

Some teachers fill a looseleaf notebook with tic-tac-toe grilles, devoting each page to one of many different phonic elements. The pages can be laminated or slipped into plastic protectors. You will find a tic-tac-toe grille ready to be filled in with appropriate tasks on Master Copy Page 1.

Use Context Close to the Students

READING AID 39

As we have stressed previously, an activity like tic-tac-toe should begin and end with meaningful context.

After working with the *au* sound, the teacher might write on the board (or on a ditto) several sentences with blanks to be filled in with *au* words. The sentences might be on

*A Sanford Vis-à-Vis pen writes exceptionally well on a plastic surface. The writing can be erased with a damp sponge or facial tissue.

cautious driver	launch a boat	famous author
haul a load	leaky faucet	applaud loudly
large auditorium	autumn leaves	win the pole vault

FIGURE 2–4

The game of tic-tac-toe can help to reinforce the skills of phonics—here the sound that **au** ***represents.***

timely topics—something the students are thinking about and caring about that day. The students read the sentences and fill in the *au* word.

Examples:

The popular ______________ of *Boy Gets Car* will speak at school today. *(author)*

He will speak in the ______________. *(auditorium)*

Students may ask for his ______________. *(autograph)*

Students like to read about a fascinating subject—themselves! Suppose likable, irrepressible young Tommy needs to reinforce his understanding that the two letters *ow* usually sound as they do in the word *cow*. Tommy's teacher might create practice sentences like these—*for* Tommy and *about* Tommy: "You, Tommy, are our class *clown*. Why do you sometimes make your teacher *frown!*"

It's a Favor to Ask Students!

READING AID 40

Student assistants can enrich the resources of classrooms and reading centers by preparing materials like the tic-tac-toe boards. A reading consultant (Bragstad, 1978) shares her views on this:

> It's a favor to young people to ask them to help. They need the experience of giving service. Many view being asked to take responsibility as a vote of confidence. When students in our school were asked the question, "What has made you feel good about yourself in our school?" many students mentioned being asked to help as evidence that the teacher cared about them. National Honor Societies and Future Teachers groups are

a possible source of volunteers. Sometimes I go into a study hall and find students who are doing nothing. When I ask, "Do you have half an hour to help?" five or six say yes. Quiet students who are seldom asked to contribute may benefit most.

READING AID 41

Scribble Your Friend a Note!

After students have studied a certain phonic element, they might take a five-minute fun break to send a friend a "scribble-gram."* The teacher writes on the board several words that contain, for example, the letter combination *qu*, and asks the students: "Can you write a note to a friend of yours using some words that contain *qu?* Load your note with *qu* words, if you can! You may think up your own words, or help yourself to words on the board."

The students come up with notes like the one in Figure 2–5. They enjoy reading aloud their "scribble-grams."

Words for the "loaded" notes might include final silent *e, au, aw, oi, oy, ou, ow, eu;* hard and soft *c* or *g;* the final syllables *-tion, -cious,* and others; consonant blends and digraphs, and other phonic elements.

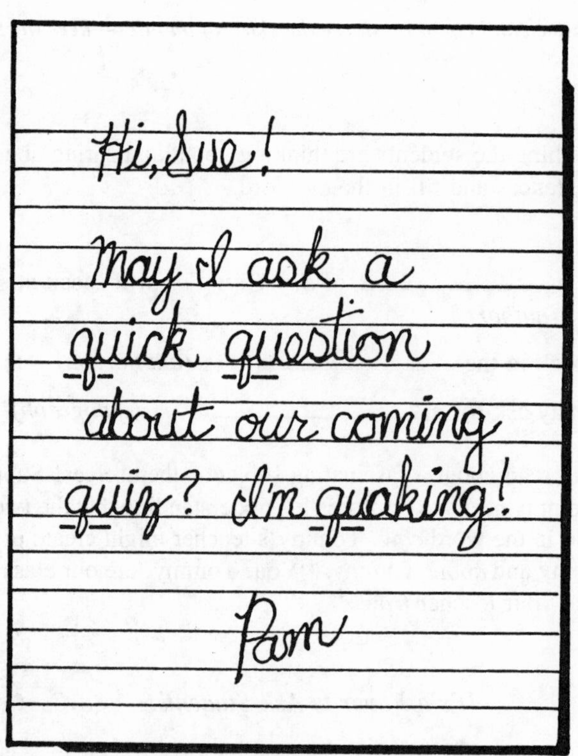

FIGURE 2–5

Students practice phonic elements by sending a "scribble-gram" to a friend. Here is one loaded with* qu *words.

*Robert Potter coined the word "scribble-gram" and used it in *Writing Sense* (New York: Globe Book Co., 1975), p. 25.

Phonics "I Spy!"

READING AID 42

On a day when younger students need to reinforce certain skills of phonics, the teacher might use this two-minute activity. The teacher might plant near the students objects or pictures of objects that start with those sounds. The students are asked, "Can you spot something near that starts with soft *c?*" A bright shiny cent might be nearby. "Can you spot something near that starts with hard *c?*" A picture of a Corvette might be nearby. For soft *g,* it might be the gem in a student's ring; for hard *g,* a stick of gum; for *qu,* the queen from a deck of cards; for *ph,* a photograph; for *au,* a picture of an automobile or some autumn leaves or a picture of these leaves. Now the students are bringing their visual learning channel to bear.

Fill the Blank!

READING AID 43

Upper level students may need only a quick "call back" of certain phonic skills. In that case, no slow discovery process should be necessary.

Suppose certain students need to review the diphthongs *oi* and *oy.* It is economical to teach these together since their sounds are identical. A stand-up placard like the one in Figure 2–6 might be displayed. On it appear eye-catching pictures of an oil can and an oyster!

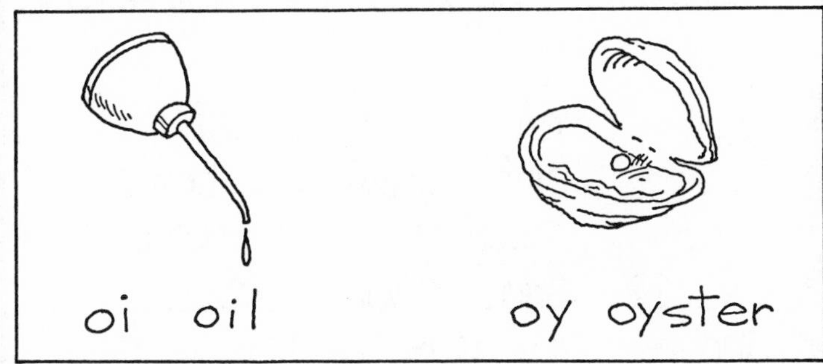

***An eye-catching oil can and oyster can help teach the diphthongs* oi *and* oy!**

FIGURE 2–6

On the companion placards shown in Figure 2–7 (or perhaps on the chalkboard) appear words, each of which contains a blank to be filled in with *oi* or *oy.* A small cardboard square with the letters *oi* and another with *oy* are attached to the placard with a string, as shown in the figure. In a quick practice intended as reinforcement, the student places the square in each blank, thus completing the word—then blends and arrives at the word. The placard with the oil can and the oyster stands close by as a strong reminder. The teacher, at hand to prevent frustration, listens as the student reads the words.

The teacher can select for the placard words that advance roughly in difficulty, making it possible to discontinue the practice at the point where the words become too difficult for the student or the group involved. Students seem to like manipulating the card on the string.

Here again, and in the following reading aids, the activity should begin with a demonstrated need in a context setting and should be followed with contextual application.

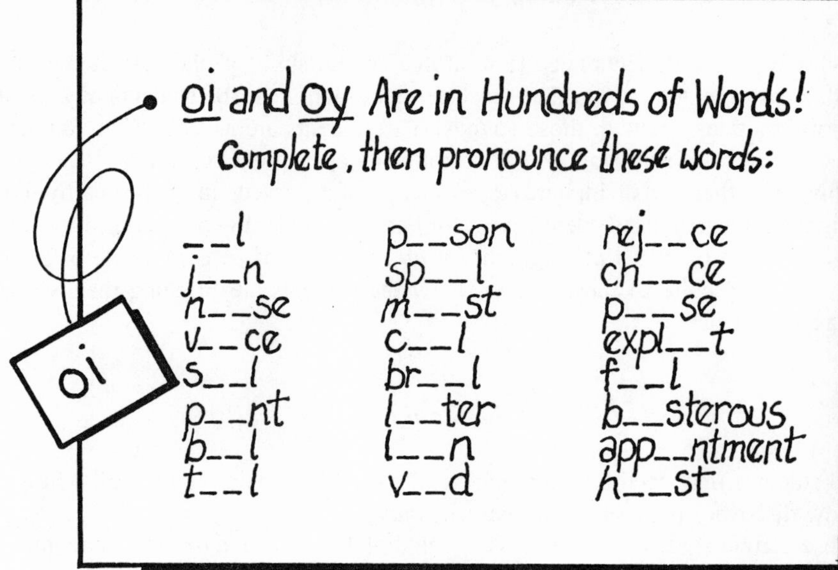

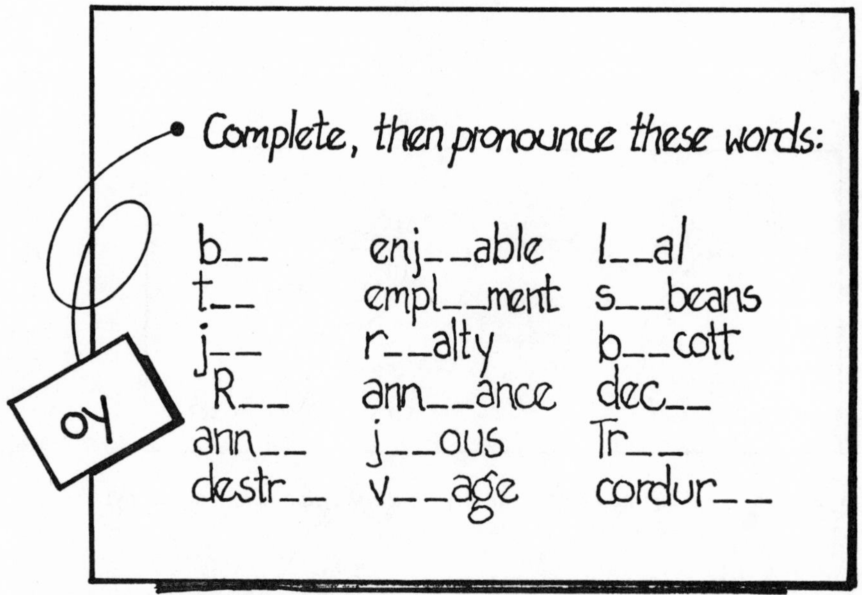

FIGURE 2–7

Students fill the blank with the letters on the end of the string, then blend and arrive at each word.

READING AID 44

*Climb the Rope Ladder!**

Students scurry up rope "ladders" in the school gym. Why not scurry up *word*-ladders? For reinforcement of a certain phonic element, words or words in a snatch of context can be printed on the rungs of a word-ladder (see Figure 2–8). The students pronounce the words, which roughly advance in difficulty. The easy words on the lower rungs are in-

*Evelyn Spache shares the idea of climbing a ladder in *Reading Activities for Child Involvement* (Boston: Allyn and Bacon, 1972), p. 84.

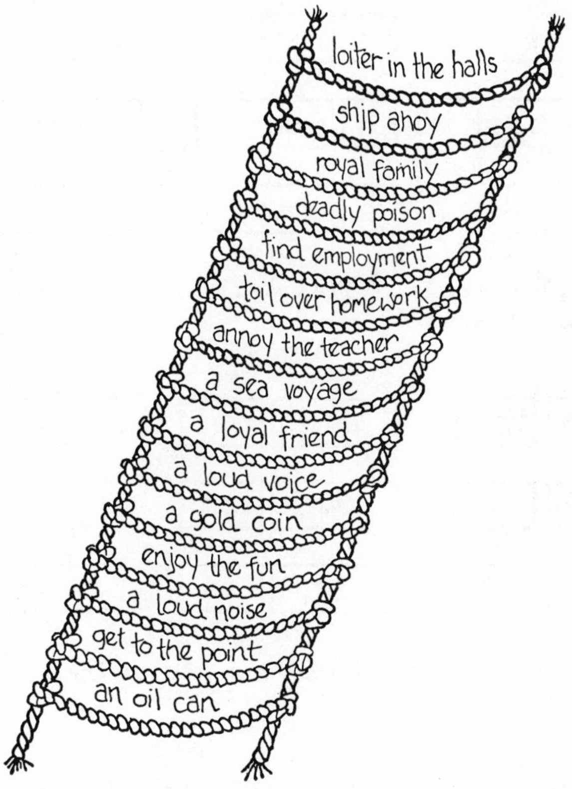

FIGURE 2–8

***Students climb the word-ladder to higher and harder rungs as they pronounce words containing the diphthongs* oi *or* oy.**

tended to make success probable as the student begins the climb. After being given time for preparation, the student pronounces the words for the teacher.

Again, the ladder should include words not already in the students' sight vocabularies. If the students recognize all the words at sight, they will have no practice using *oi* and *oy* in word attack. Meanings can be supplied incidentally if needed. After the student has pronounced *hoist* for example, the teacher can add, "Yes, *hoist*—to lift or pull something up."

Teachers might fill a looseleaf notebook with word ladders, devoting each page to one of many different phonic elements. You will find a "word ladder" ready to be filled in with tasks appropriate for the students on Master Copy Page 2.

SEE MASTER COPY PAGE 2

Spill a Word!

READING AID 45

When a student has been having trouble with a certain letter combination, words beginning with that combination—*ph,* for example—can be printed on cards, then the cards can be cut in two so that the beginning letters are on a separate card. The parts are placed in an envelope labeled *ph.* The student spills the parts out onto a desk or table, assembles the words, then practices pronouncing each word (see Figure 2–9). Of course, the words will be appropriate in difficulty.

In listing special needs she has observed in middle school and secondary school students, Burmeister (1975, p. 81) includes a command of final syllables in which the letter *i* becomes a consonant. Among these syllables she lists *-tion* (pronounced *shŭn*); *-sion* (pronounced *shŭn* or sometimes *zhŭn*); *-cious* (pronounced *shŭs*); and *-tial* and *-cial* (both

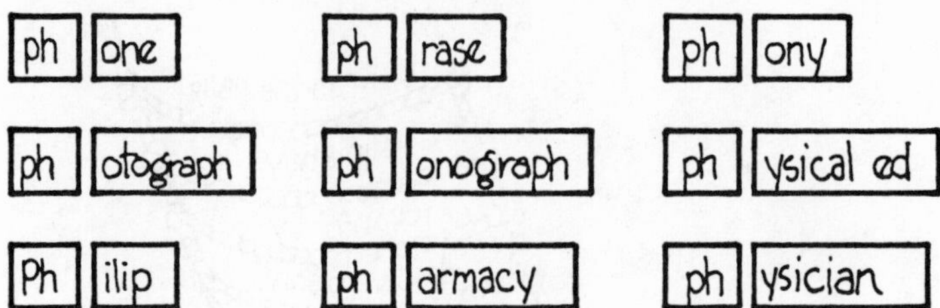

FIGURE 2–9

These word cards have been cut in two. The student practices the sound of* ph *by assembling and pronouncing the words.

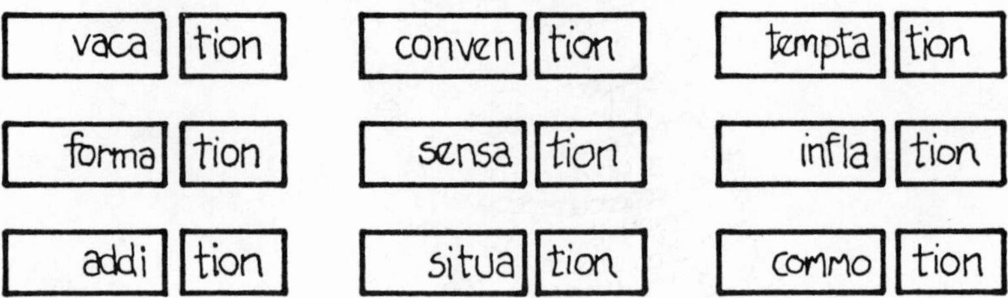

FIGURE 2–10

Words with the tricky final syllable* -tion *have been cut apart. The student assembles and pronounces each word.

pronounced *shăl*). Words with these final syllables can be printed on cards, cut in two, and placed in envelopes, a separate envelope for the group of words that end with each final syllable. The student scatters the cards on the table, then assembles and pronounces each word (see Figure 2–10).

Again, activities like this will be more meaningful for students if some of the words are words they are now meeting or will soon be meeting in reading assignments for their actual courses.

Race the Clock!

READING AID 46

When a student has been having difficulty with a certain phonic principle, the teacher can list words that illustrate that principle, words the student should recognize instantly—then let the student practice sounding out the words until he or she has mastered them at sight. When the student is *confident of this mastery,* he or she announces, "I'm ready to be timed!" At that point, the teacher times the student with a stopwatch as the words are pronounced.

Now the student *can definitely see progress*. The teacher comments: "A little while ago you were having trouble with that sound. Now you've pronounced those words in a few seconds!" Practices like this help to move words the students had to attack phonetically into their sight vocabularies.

Confident students might race each other. M&Ms make popular prizes. Of course, *time pressure is inappropriate with many students*. Insecure readers do not react well to having the stopwatch tick away the moments.

G as in This Stick of Gum!

READING AID 47

Sometimes, as we have noted, all that older students need is a quick "call back" of phonic principles they have learned in the past. In that case, no slow process of discovering the principle is necessary.

One teacher repeatedly observed older students having difficulty with the two sounds of the consonant *g*. What could be done to make those sounds "stick"? The teacher prepared two eye-catching, mind-catching stand-up placards. On the soft *g* placard appeared a real "gem," a ten-cent-store diamond flashing brilliantly! On the hard *g* placard was glued some real sticks of gum! The printing, done with broad felt-tip pens, was in bright colors. (See Figure 2–11.)

The teacher comments, "*G* is a tricky consonant. It has two different sounds. Do you remember those sounds?" Some of the students probably recall them. "The tricky part is to decide *when to use each sound.* Can you remember two clues?" Either the students remember, or the "spectacular" placards remind them.

After reviewing the principle, the students work with words containing hard and soft *g's* on dittoed worksheets or on pages from a commercial workbook. They mark the *g's* in each word hard or soft, then practice pronouncing the words.

The "tricky consonant *g*" troubles many upperlevel readers. For small remedial groups, teachers have made colorful, inviting workboards (a permanent resource to use through the years), on which students work with the sounds of *g* (see Figure 2–12). A large sheet of heavy poster paper is covered with plastic. Then a bright-colored pocket is glued to the lower corner and stocked with words, on varying levels of difficulty, containing *g*. In small boxes in the upper corner, small squares printed *H* for hard and *S* for soft are ready for use as markers.

The teacher selects from the pocket words appropriate in difficulty for the individual student, then arranges these on the workboard.* The student marks the *g* in each word hard or soft and works out the pronunciation. The placards with the flashing gem and the sticks of gum stand close by as powerful reminders. The teacher, at hand to prevent frustration, listens as the student reads the words.

The pocket, well-stocked with words on varying levels of difficulty, offers a real advantage. Appropriate cards are ready to pull out and match to the individual student.

The teacher follows up this practice by working with *g* words in context—sometimes words the students are meeting or will be meeting in their courses. The teacher points out, "See! This tool you have is really helping!"

When students repeatedly experienced difficulty with the two sounds of the "tricky consonant *c*," the same teacher prepared more placards. On the stand-up placard for hard *c* was a colorful picture of a car—a Corvette, high in teen appeal. On the placard for soft *c* were glued some actual bright, shiny cents. A companion workboard was prepared and used in the same way as the *g* board described in Reading Aid 47.

Work on Phonics Should Not Be Overstressed. Some concluding thoughts seem appropriate for this section on helping students attack words through phonic analysis. We have devoted considerable space to this section because teachers often say, "I don't know how to teach phonics." In the total reading program, work on phonics should not be overstressed. Instruction should be provided for under-par readers who have demonstrated a

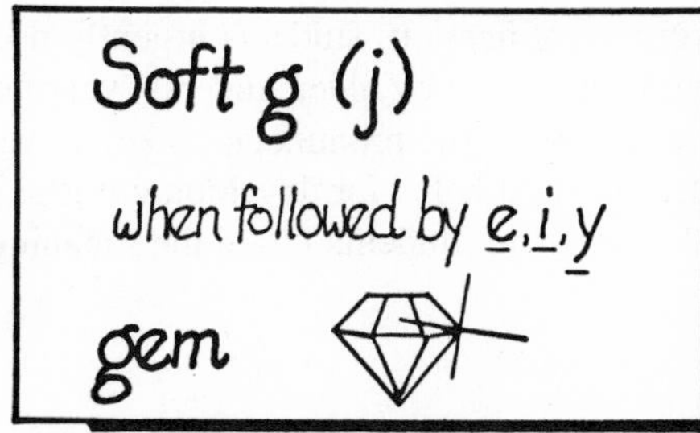

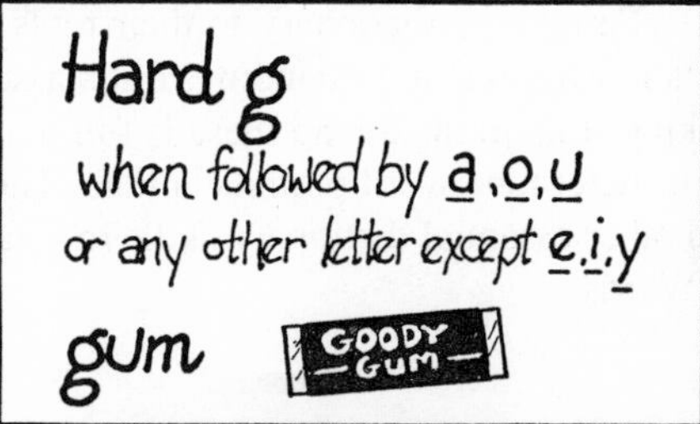

Soft g *as in this flashing gem! Hard* g *as in this stick of gum! These stand up placards are lively reminders.*

FIGURE 2–11

*The words on the "tricky consonant *g*" board are taken from Olive Stafford Niles et al., *Guidebook for Tactics in Reading I* (Glenview, Ill.: Scott, Foresman and Co., 1961), p. 32.

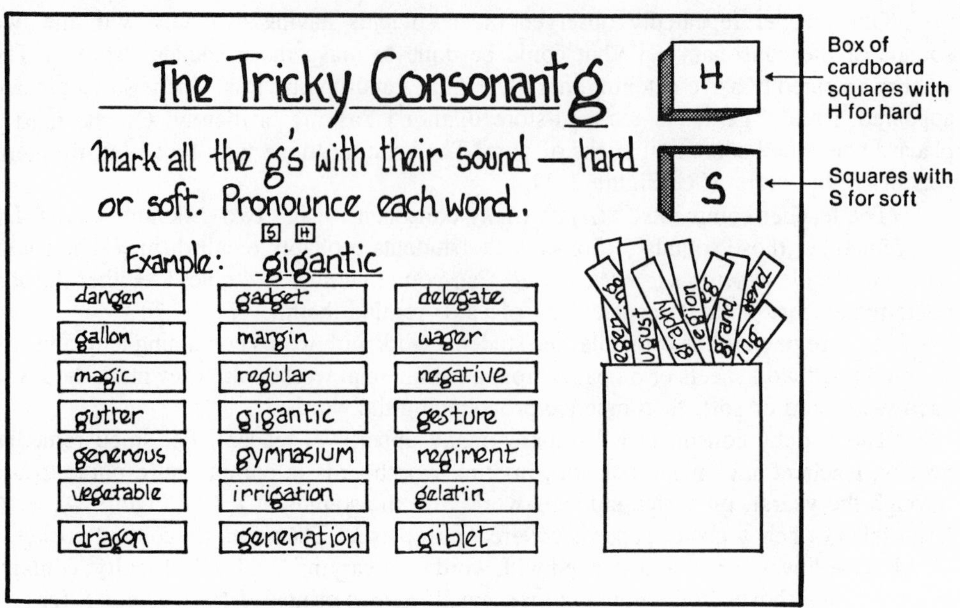

FIGURE 2–12

The student marks the tricky* g's *in each word hard or soft, then pronounces the word.

need. With these students, work on phonics should proceed hand in hand with work on vocabulary, comprehension, speed, study skills, critical reading, reading for personal enjoyment, and other areas essential to the students' total reading progress. With developmental students on the secondary level, phonics is an area that will require little or no attention.

Helping Students Use the Dictionary in Identifying Words

We began this chapter on how to help students attack unfamiliar words by defining word attack. We defined it as working on a word in order to recognize it in one or more of these ways: 1) through clues in the context, 2) through phonic analysis, 3) through structural analysis, 4) through use of the dictionary, or 5) through a combination of these methods.

In the preceding list, reaching for the dictionary comes, as you see, not first but last in the sequence. It is economy of effort for students to try to work out a word's identity for themselves *first* and to resort to the dictionary only if the other strategies do not prove successful.

To add the dictionary to their tools for word identification, students urgently need certain skills and understandings often assumed to be mastered by older students, yet often lacking. Important among these is full mastery of the use of the pronunciation key to verify or determine word pronunciations. The reader will find helps for developing this skill and other essential dictionary skills in Chapter 3, "Helping Students Learn the Meanings of Words."

A Five-Part Strategy for Word Attack

READING AID 49

Here is a five-part strategy for students as they attack and thus identify words. It sums up the four components of word attack covered in this chapter:

A Five-Part Strategy for Word Attack

1. *Launch your attack by searching the word's context for clues.*
Crack down on the word instead of reading right on past it without a try. Context is likely to be your most important single aid.
2. *Look for word-part clues.*
Take the word apart if you can. Do you recognize any part—a prefix? a suffix? an inflectional ending? a root? Words that at first look difficult can often be broken down into well-known building blocks. Considering the context again do you now recognize the word?
3. *Work through the word, syllable by syllable. "Divide and conquer."*
Try to sound out the word by easy-to-manage syllables. A long word is simply short syllables strung together. Is it familiar after all? Recalling context, have you now "solved" the word?
4. *Try a shift in pronunciation.*
If you have not yet arrived at a word you know, attack it again by seeing if a change—perhaps in syllable division or accent—gives you a breakthrough. Again, does the word you have worked out click with the context?
5. *Reach for the dictionary.*
If after Steps 1–4 the word still defies you, you have a never-failing tool. Now is the time to turn to your dictionary.

The skillful reader does not click off these steps one at a time in the order given. Steps 2 and 3 are not sequential but "all mixed in." It may be desirable to use any combination of the first four steps almost simultaneously. If one method fails to work, the reader attacks with another. Students should feel free to skip as many steps as they can as long as they arrive at the essential goal—an understanding of meaning (Durkin, 1976, p. 54).

Beware of "Word-Attack-itis"!

A chapter on helping students attack words should perhaps close with a caution—beware of "Word-attack-itis"! Word analysis should not be stressed to the point where the focus ceases to be on meaning. Always the student should make first use—and full use—of context.

In the secondary developmental reading program, as we have noted, word attack is the area that will require the least attention. Work on word attack should be provided for readers who have demonstrated a need. It should then proceed hand in hand with work on vocabulary, comprehension, speed, study skills, critical reading, reading for personal enjoyment, and other areas essential to the student's total reading progress.

Helping Students Develop Their Sight Vocabularies

In this chapter we have discussed equipping students with the various tools they need for working on words in order to make correct identification. A student's sight vocabulary, on the other hand, is made up of the words the student can recognize instantly without using these tools. Our ultimate goal is to develop the sight vocabularies of our students to the point where they do not have to puzzle out a word's identity through word attack, but, recognizing great numbers of words at sight, they can concentrate their full attention on the flow of ideas in the passage. Our goal, then, is to eliminate, to a considerable extent, the need for skills of word attack.

Words move gradually from the stage at which they must be "worked on" through word attack tools into the stage at which the student can recognize them instantly. Of course, this transfer into the student's stock of sight words comes with repeated exposures, each exposure strengthening the form-meaning association obviously essential for sight recognition.

READING AID 50

Wide Reading—One of the Best Sight Vocabulary Builders

Where can students meet words again and again? Wide reading—in school and out of school—is one of the most effective sight vocabulary builders. When we guide students to books that are right for them in difficulty and interest, they spend many hours in the world of printed words. Held to the task by interest, they figure out silently unfamiliar words they meet; as they do so, they are practicing their skills of word attack. As they meet the same words again and again, they gradually build them into their sight vocabularies. The right books, then, can be "silent reading teachers," offering students practice in word attack and, as time goes on, helping to put word attack skills out of a job.

READING AID 51

Giving Words a "Push" into the Student's Stock of Sight Words

Students enrolled in the remedial reading program may need the direct teaching of basic sight words. Suppose a remedial teacher, through day-to-day observation of a group (or an individual student), has compiled a list of several words these students should be able to—but cannot—recognize instantly. How might this teacher give these words a "push" into the students' stock of sight words through a group sight-word lesson?

Let's suppose the teacher has selected six words, words definitely in the students' speaking-listening vocabularies. Most of them do not contain parts that help in working out their identities. With these particular words, the teacher does not wish to stress sounding out. The words should be recognized without phonic analysis, and some of them show little relationship between the way they are spelled and the way they are pronounced. Some are words the students *want* to learn to read—the teacher has included these to heighten interest. All are high-frequency words, words important for the students to know for any material they will be reading. The teacher wishes to teach these words directly. Suppose the words are *through, friendship, weather, together, thought,* and *loyalty.*

You will find below a possible sequence of steps for teaching whole words to groups of students. During this sequence, all possible sensory learning channels can be brought into play—visual, auditory, kinesthetic, tactile—to strengthen the association between the form of the word and its meaning and to help make recognition instant. Children differ greatly in the speed with which they learn to recognize words at sight. Some can move through the steps quickly and/or omit certain steps. Others, however, may need all the steps, plus additional reinforcement.

1. The teacher explains the *why* of the lesson: "Here are six high-frequency words—words you'll meet *often* as you read and study. You can learn to recognize words like this at sight *in a split second!* Sight words will help you read better and faster!"
2. Using manuscript printing, the teacher has placed on the board a sentence containing one of the target words and has underlined the word. The teacher introduces the word in this sentence.
3. Next, the teacher spotlights the word by printing it on the board separately, taking the word out of context so that the details of its form will stand out. The teacher points to the word and pronounces it clearly.

4. The teacher asks, "Now will *you* please pronounce the word. *Look at it carefully* as you say it."
5. To focus attention on the visual characteristics of the word, the teacher might now suggest, especially with younger children: "Now take a picture of the word in your mind. Shut your eyes and 'see' the word." . . . "Now open your eyes and compare your mind picture with the word on the board." (This step can often be omitted.)
6. Thus far, the students have been learning through their visual and auditory channels. They can now add kinesthetic reinforcement. To encourage close attention to the form of the entire word, the teacher asks, "Please look again carefully at the word on the board. Then look away and try to print the word as you remember it." The students print the word, then compare their word with the model on the board, taking careful note of any parts they did not reproduce correctly. Those who made errors repeat the prccess. They continue trying until they can print the word correctly.
7. The other five words are taught by a similar procedure.
8. The six words now appear on the board in a different order. The teacher comments: "Here are our words—in a scrambled order. Please practice reading them silently." In a moment the teacher calls on different students to read aloud, pointing to the words in random order. If the students respond rapidly, the teacher has *proof* that they have learned to read the words at sight—though further reinforcement may still be needed.
9. Soon afterward, the students meet the same words in meaningful, interesting context.

Many students can be taught sight vocabulary through a quick procedure in which the steps in the preceding lesson are telescoped. The student sees the word on the printed page—the teacher tells the student what it says—the student pronounces the word a time or two—then the student writes the word correctly from memory.

Students Can Practice Quick Recognition with Flash Cards

READING AID 52

A simple way to provide further practice in quick recognition is to use flash cards on which sight words previously taught have been printed in manuscript. Each student has a packet of cards on which the words have been printed with a black felt-tip marker. Five-by-eight-inch index cards, cut lengthwise into thirds, make a convenient size. The teacher has a packet of cards large enough to display before the group. The flash cards can be used in the ways shown in the following list. The students seem to like manipulating their pack of flash cards.

1. The teacher asks, "Please spread your cards out in front of you. I am going to flash one of your words. Quickly find the word I show and hold it up." A student is then called on to read the word. The teacher flashes the rest of the words.
2. The teacher asks, "When I pronounce a word, quickly hold up your card for that word." The teacher quickly goes through all the words.
3. The teacher holds up a phrase card or a sentence card with a blank to be filled in. The teacher asks, "Please hold up the word that makes

sense in this blank." A student is then called on to read the phrase or sentence.

4. The teacher asks, "Now shuffle your word cards and spread them out before you. Please practice reading them silently. In a minute you'll have a chance to read your words aloud just as fast as you can." Responding rapidly is evidence that the students can now read the words at sight—though some may still need further reinforcement.

Lively Activities Can Reinforce Mastery of Sight Words

Students who have been taught sight words as suggested in Reading Aid 51 may need additional practice. In that case, lively reinforcement can be provided in a great variety of ways. Activities, including games, that afford the students practice recognizing the words in isolation should, of course, be followed by their reading the words in context.

READING AID 53

A "Grab Bag" of Troublesome Words. Often, as Durkin (1976, p. 264) reminds us, small embellishments are all it takes to spark interest. To a teacher who was struggling with two boys who seemingly couldn't care less about sight vocabulary, Durkin suggested a "grab bag." Short phrases that included troublesome words were printed on the board with each phrase numbered, and small cards with corresponding numbers were placed in a bag. The boys took turns reaching into the grab bag for a number, then reading the corresponding phrase on the board. If the child read the phrase correctly, he could keep the card—if incorrectly, the card was returned to the grab bag. At the end, the child who had more cards was pronounced the winner. Eager to win, the boys worked diligently, before the game began, reviewing the words on the board. "A good time was had by all"—*plus* productive practice.

READING AID 54

A "Tailored-to-the-Student" Tachistoscope. Teachers can make a hand tachistoscope (a quick-flash device by means of which sight words are exposed for a fraction of a second through a slot) for a younger student and tailor it to some strong personal interest of the student. For Tommy, whose interest is touch football, the t-scope might take the form of a football. For other students, t-scopes might appear in the guise of baseballs, bats, airplanes, and race cars! (Idea from Durrell, 1956, p. 216)

To make a football for t-scope practice, use heavy paper to cut out a 6½-by-9½-inch football. Draw the lacing and stitching. Near the center, cut out—*across* the football—a ½-by-2-inch exposure slot. Print previously taught sight words on a long, narrow strip of paper at double-spaced intervals, words the right size to be exposed through the slot—these are to be revealed through the window one at a time. Place a four-by-six-inch index card across the football as backing behind the exposure slot, and glue this card to the football at each end, leaving the top, bottom, and center of the card free.

When the time comes for practice, insert the long strip of words between this backing and the paper football and draw the strip through at a steady pace so that each word is exposed for the student for about one-third of a second.

A teacher who created personalized t-scopes comments: "Spotlighting a child's interest can help develop rapport and form a closer relationship. Magazine illustrations of airplanes, automobiles, boats, and the like, can be mounted on poster paper to form the t-scopes. I keep my homemade t-scopes in a growing collection to use with future students."

More Aids for Developing Students' Sight Vocabularies. The word analysis behaviors already discussed in this chapter contribute to the development of students' sight vocabularies. Furthermore, many of the reading aids offered in Chapter 3, "Helping Students Learn the Meanings of Words," strengthen the form-meaning association and will be of interest in this connection. Teachers help to develop sight vocabulary as they pre-teach "stopper" words before students read a selection (Reading Aids 73–75), as they help students break words into parts and analyze them through their structure (Reading Aids 89–92, 95–97), as they help students develop independent word-learning techniques (Reading Aids 112–114, 118, 119), and as they arrange stimulating, fun-to-do activities that require their students to be involved creatively with words (Reading Aids 121, 122, 124, 126).

References

Barr, Rebecca, reading consultant for the University of Chicago Laboratory School, in remarks to the writer, July 1978.

Bragstad, Bernice, reading consultant of La Follette Senior High School, Madison, Wisconsin, in remarks to the writer, March 1978.

Burmeister, Lou. *Reading Strategies for Secondary School Teachers,* 2nd ed. Reading, Mass.: Addison-Wesley Publishing Co., 1978.

Burmeister, Lou. *Words—From Print to Meaning: Classroom Activities for Building Sight Vocabulary, for Using Context Clues, Morphology, and Phonics.* Reading, Mass.: Addison-Wesley Publishing Co., 1975.

Carner, Richard L. "Diagnosis of Reading Difficulties," in *Handbook for the Volunteer Tutor,* edited by Sidney J. Rauch. Newark, Del.: International Reading Assoc., 1969.

Dallman, Martha, Roger L. Rouch, Lynette Y. C. Chang, John J. De Boer. *The Teaching of Reading,* 4th ed. New York: Holt, Rinehart and Winston, 1974.

Durkin, Dolores. *Strategies for Identifying Words.* Boston: Allyn and Bacon, 1976.

———. *Teaching Young Children to Read,* 2nd ed. Boston: Allyn and Bacon, 1976.

Durrell, Donald D. *Improving Reading Instruction.* New York: Harcourt, Brace and World, 1956.

Ekwall, Eldon E. *Diagnosis and Remediation of the Disabled Reader.* Boston: Allyn and Bacon, 1976.

———. *Teacher's Handbook on Diagnosis and Remediation in Reading.* Boston: Allyn and Bacon, 1977.

Gray, William S. *On Their Own in Reading.* Glenview, Ill.: Scott, Foresman and Co., 1960.

Heilman, Arthur W. *Phonics in Proper Perspective.* Columbus, Ohio: Charles E. Merrill Publishing Co., 1964.

Karlin, Robert. *Teaching Reading in High School.* Indianapolis: Bobbs-Merrill Co., 1964; 3rd ed., 1977.

Marksheffel, Ned D. *Better Reading in Secondary School.* New York: Ronald Press Co., 1966.

Niles, Olive Stafford, Dorothy Kendall Bracken, Mildred A. Dougherty, and Robert Farrar Kinder. *Guidebook for Tactics in Reading,* Level I and II (two vols.). Glenview, Ill.: Scott, Foresman and Co., 1961, 1964.

Niles, Olive S., Elsie Katterjohn, and Mildred A. Dougherty. *Tactics in Reading, A and B.* Glenview, Ill.: Scott, Foresman and Co., 1972, 1973.

Pauk, Walter. *How To Study in College,* 2nd ed. Boston: Houghton Mifflin Co., 1974.

Roberts, Clyde. *Word Attack: A Way To Better Reading.* New York: Harcourt Brace Jovanovich, 1978.

Rudd, Josephine. *Word Attack Manual.* Cambridge, Mass.: Educators Publishing Service, 1962.

Shepherd, David L. *Comprehensive High School Reading Methods.* Columbus, Ohio: Charles E. Merrill Publishing Co., 1973.

Spache, Evelyn B. *Reading Activities for Child Involvement.* Boston: Allyn and Bacon, 1972.

Spache, George D. and Paul C. Berg. *The Art of Efficient Reading.* New York: Macmillan Publishing Co., 1955; 2nd ed., 1966.

Stauffer, Russell G. *Teaching Reading as a Thinking Process.* New York: Harper and Row, 1969.

Strang, Ruth, in class lecture on the teaching of secondary school reading, University of Chicago, Summer 1965.

Swenson, Dorothy, reading clinician of Glenoak School, St. Petersburg, Florida, in remarks to the author, October 1960.

Thomas, Ellen Lamar, and H. Alan Robinson, *Improving Reading in Every Class,* 2nd ed. Boston: Allyn and Bacon, 1977.

3

Helping Students Learn the Meanings of Words

Teachers in every classroom will want students to master the "official" vocabulary of their courses and to grow in general vocabulary as well. You will find in this chapter scores of practical ways to help your students turn on word power.

If you are a subject matter teacher and not a reading specialist, you may have little idea of what an important contribution you can make to improving the reading of your students. And in no area of reading are you likely to be more effective than in vocabulary.

You can give your students self-help techniques for improving their vocabularies through your regular class instruction—and you need not take undue additional time. You can help them master new terms for their immediate course work and at the same time grow in reading ability. You need not have a day of formal training in the teaching of reading in order to do this.

How important is word power to reading power in content area courses and in general reading? If the student cannot understand the words on the page, surely that student cannot comprehend the ideas accurately and—most assuredly—cannot read faster. Comprehension, speed of comprehension, and, accordingly, *reading success* rest solidly on the foundation of word power.

Research supports the day-to-day observation of teachers that word power is the "first story" of the reading structure. In an investigation of the factors involved in comprehension, Davis (1968, p. 544) identified knowledge of word meanings as *one of the most important factors* involved in comprehension. After investigating factors affecting the school performance of disadvantaged children, Becker (1977, p. 540) concluded that deficiency in vocabulary-concept knowledge constitutes *the most important factor*. Referring to words and their referents as "among the most important building blocks for intelligent functioning," he pled for programs engineered to teach vocabulary-concept knowledge in a systematic way throughout the school years.

What would be the plight of students if they should "go it alone" in handling the technical vocabulary of their courses? Without teacher guidance, word blocks would very likely soon obstruct their learning. In leafing through the pages of a widely used high school mathematics textbook, the writer found on those pages—in just moments—the terms *coefficient, associative, commutative, coordinate, distributive, irrational, variable, factor, finite, infinite, power,* and *exponent.* The students' confusion may be compounded, as Karlin (1977, p. 113) points out, because they know the meaning of "balance of *power*" and "*exponent* of jazz," but must now learn quite new, different, and specialized meanings for those familiar words! In turning through the pages of a popular science textbook, the writer found—again in just moments—the terms *spirogyra, conjugation, alternation of generations, zygote, pistil, stamens, ovules,* and *pollination.* In examining a social studies textbook, the writer discovered not only difficult concrete words but also terms high on the rungs of the abstraction ladder—words like *laissez-faire, exploitation,* and *conflict of interest.*

What about courses sometimes considered "non-reading"—homemaking, fine arts, technical courses? Here, too, new specialized terms pile up into a heavy vocabulary load. In industrial arts, for example, difficult technical terms crowd the pages of textbooks and job sheets. A precise working understanding is often crucial. Not knowing the difference between *drilling* and *counterdrilling* can mean disaster for that bookcase the student is building as his special project in shop!

What a good gift we give students when we help them develop their general vocabularies! Beyond the walls of our own classrooms, we are helping them succeed in the broader school situation. A student's vocabulary strength constitutes one of the most reliable predictors of academic success. At the University of Illinois, entering freshmen were given a twenty-nine-word vocabulary test. Their scores proved highly useful in predicting how well they would fare through their four college years! And we are also contributing to our students' on-the-job success, for, according to investigations, vocabulary is closely related to success on the job. Why is this so? In addition to the part that word power plays in on-the-job learning, we *do our thinking* with words—*get our thoughts inside the minds of others* with words—*influence others* with words.

You will find on the coming pages some possible answers to the following questions—answers practical enough, the writer hopes, to try out in your classroom tomorrow:

1. How can you learn your students' strengths and needs in vocabulary—including the specific words that will need your special attention?
2. What are some possible ways to help your students *want* to grow in vocabulary?
3. How can you invest new words with meaning through experience?
4. How can you encourage vocabulary growth through personal reading?
5. How can you take down the obstacle course by pre-teaching "stopper" words?
6. How can students learn to make full use of context to help them get at word meanings?
7. How can students get vocabulary increments through analyzing word parts?
8. How can you work with word origins to fix meanings in mind?
9. What dictionary competencies are essential? How can students develop these competencies?
10. How can you give students on-their-own techniques for learning and retaining words?
11. How should students "crack down" on a new word?

12. What are some lively activities for motivating students and enriching vocabulary study?

How do the contents of the present chapter differ from those of Chapter 2, "Helping Students to Attack Words"? In that chapter we discussed word attack as an aid in *recognizing* on the printed page a word already in the student's speaking-listening vocabulary, a word whose meaning is already known to the student. In the present chapter we will discuss learning a word *whose meaning is unknown.*

Readers who desire further discussion of each of the aspects of vocabulary development considered in this chapter may wish to refer to Chapter 2, "Building Vocabulary and Word Attack Skills," in the companion volume (Thomas and Robinson, *Improving Reading in Every Class: A Sourcebook for Teachers,* 2nd ed., 1977).

Learning about Vocabulary Strengths and Weaknesses

Learning something about the vocabulary strengths and needs of our students not only helps us plan appropriate vocabulary activities for those students—but it also helps us place appropriate reading materials in their hands.

Standardized Reading Tests Offer Some Information

READING AID 55

Your school may have on file recent standardized reading survey test scores—scores that are yours for the asking. These provide rough insights into the achievements and needs of students in general vocabulary. If recent scores are not available, you may wish to give your students such a test. The Gates-MacGinitie Reading Test is widely used for survey purposes.

> *Gates-MacGinitie Reading Test* (Boston: Houghton Mifflin Co., 1978), Level D, intended for grades 4–6, three forms; Level E, for grades 7–9, three forms; Level F, for grades 10–12, two forms. This test offers sub-scores in general vocabulary, comprehension, and speed combined with accuracy.

If you are a content area teacher, you may wish to gain insights into vocabulary strength in your particular subject area. *The Diagnostic Reading Test, Section 1: Vocabulary* offers information about the student's vocabulary in a number of subject fields.

> *Diagnostic Reading Test, Section 1: Vocabulary* (Mountain Home, N.C.: The Committee on Diagnostic Reading Test, 1967), intended for grades 7–13; two forms, A and B. This test yields scores in four subject fields: English, mathematics, science, and social studies. There are 200 words in all, 50 in each area. The complete test takes 40 minutes; each subject area, 10 minutes. Since the time limit may "contaminate" the vocabulary score with a speed factor, for some students and in certain circumstances, it may be advisable to impose no time limit. Of course, disregarding the time limit converts the test into an informal diagnostic device as the norming of the test included the time factor.

Which Do the Students Need—Work on Meaning Vocabulary or on Word Recognition?

READING AID 56

When a student scores poorly on the vocabulary section of a standardized test, we are left with an important question unanswered: Is the student's problem *meaning vocabulary,* or is the problem *word recognition?* Is it the *meanings* of the words that the student does not know, or does the student *fail to recognize* in printed form words he/she can already say or can understand upon hearing them? Ted may, for example, know the meaning of the word *authentic* when he hears it yet miss it on a vocabulary test. He may not know how the symbols *au* are sounded or how to "divide and conquer" the word by syllables. In the same way, he may be fully aware of the meaning of the spoken word *unanimous* yet be unaware that the letters on the page before him form the word he knows.

We can reuse the vocabulary section of a standardized test to reveal the real problem of students like Ted—to "separate out" students who have word recognition problems. When students score low on the vocabulary section, we can have them retake that section *as a listening test*. This time, as Ted for example follows along in the test booklet, the teacher *pronounces* each word along with each of the multiple choices, and Ted selects an answer. If his score now improves markedly, we have evidence that Ted actually knows the meaning of more words than he appeared to know—he simply did not recognize these words in their printed form.

Remedial work on attacking words in order to identify them is now indicated for Ted, and the teacher will want to find out more about his specific needs in word attack. Possible ways to diagnose and meet students' needs in word attack will be found in Chapter 2, "Helping Students To Attack Words."

How Can We Know Which Words We Need to Teach?

Classroom teachers sometimes ask, "How can I know which words and concepts my students do not already know—which ones I need to teach so that they can learn successfully from my course materials?" *This question is crucial for vocabulary progress.* Some practical helps will follow in Reading Aids 57–62.

READING AID 57

General Guidelines for Selecting Words. A teacher might ask the following questions (based on suggestions of Hill (1979, p. 248) as an aid in identifying those words and concepts that need to be taught:

1. How crucial is the word or concept to my students' understanding of current reading selections or content-learning materials?
2. How often will the word appear in reading materials in school and in life?
3. What special difficulty does the word currently hold for my students?
4. Because of the role that interest plays in learning, what special interest does the word hold for my students?

READING AID 58

Teachers Can Use Their Intuition in Selecting Words—Then Test That Intuition. The teacher can simply cull a selection before his or her students read it and, following intuition, try to identify specific words that may need to be taught. The less experienced teacher will then do well to check up on that intuition by testing the students on the words selected. The students' books can be open, and the words listed on the board, together with the page and the line where each word can be located. The students are asked, "Do you know—or can you puzzle out—what these words mean as they are used in this passage?" By giving such a test periodically, the teacher will, of course, sharpen his or her perception of words the students do and do not know. With time, the teacher's "feel" for selecting words may become extremely accurate. (Idea from Ryder, 1978, p. 35)

READING AID 59

"What Does This Concept Mean to You?" Estes and Vaughn (1979, pp. 99, 101) point out that as we diagnose our students' vocabulary knowledge, we must also determine whether they understand the concepts associated with the words. They maintain that one of the best "pretests" possible at the beginning of a unit is to ask students: "What is your understanding of the following concepts which we are going to study? In a few words, tell what each one means to you." The students' answers will reveal to the teacher much about what they understand and in what terms they understand it.

READING AID 60

Reference Books Can Help Teachers Decide Which Words to Teach. Are reference books available to give teachers insights concerning which words are likely to be unknown? *The Living Word Vocabulary* (Dale and O'Rourke, 1976) provides just such a reference. In each of 43,000 entries, the authors have listed a word, a meaning, and the grade level at which between 67 and 84 percent of students tested in their investigations knew the word with that particular meaning. By turning to this reference, the teacher can get some idea, in an instant, whether a particular word-meaning combination will be unknown to students.

How often will students encounter a specific word in their general reading? The answer to this question will, of course, influence a teacher's decision about what words to teach. For insights about word frequency, the teacher may wish to consult the *American Heritage Word Frequency Book* (Carroll, Davies, and Richman, 1971). This list helpfully ranks each of 86,000 words from most frequent to least frequent and estimates the frequency with which the word is likely to appear in general reading.

READING AID 61

The Students Themselves Can "Nominate" Words to Be Taught. The students themselves can assist in identifying words that should be taught. The teacher can ask a few students (or perhaps a class) to scan a chapter or selection and identify the key words and concepts that will, in their opinion, be "stoppers" to comprehension. Obviously, the students doing the "nominating" should represent a broad range in reading ability. Hill (1979, p. 251) suggests that the students work individually to make their selections, then form a composite list of words.

One caution may be in order (Graves, 1979). You may find that students differ greatly in the accuracy with which they select words that need attention! Your superior readers may select many more words than your poorest readers do! Before drawing up a final list, the teacher will do well to test the students' "intuition," as suggested in Reading Aid 58.

Student Questionnaires Can Be Revealing

READING AID 62

Students *live* with their own vocabularies—daily they experience their own strengths and shortcomings. Their answers to the following questions will provide more insights into the tools students have already acquired and the tools they lack for enriching their word resources:

1. What do you do when you're studying an assignment and meet an important word you don't know?
2. Have you ever consciously done anything to build your vocabulary? If so, what methods have you used?
3. Are you using any of the methods at the present time? If so, which method(s)?
4. Do you feel that, as you read and study, you often need help in understanding the meanings of words?
5. Would you like to be introduced to some of the most effective ways to acquire a superior vocabulary?

Students are likely to answer "yes" to question 5. Then all through the year, their response is likely to be positive when the teacher prefaces vocabulary work with: "We're having this vocabulary work because you requested it." In the writer's experience, students tend to take advantage of help they themselves have "ordered." A further dividend is the rapport that comes from "hearing" students and caring about their requests. Of course, students do not always appraise their own needs accurately. Their answers should be combined with other insights.

Helping Students Want to Grow in Vocabulary

Since growth in general vocabulary is a long-term, do-it-yourself process, our hope of success is for the students themselves to *want* to expand their vocabularies. Possible ways to help motivate growth in both the technical vocabulary of content area courses and in general vocabulary are suggested on the next few pages. Others are shared in the companion volume (Thomas and Robinson, *Improving Reading in Every Class,* unabridged 2nd ed., 1977), pp. 17–20.

Technical Terms are Precision Tools for Grasping Knowledge

Our students' mastery of the specialized vocabulary in content area courses is, of course, related to interest. When interest runs high, students sometimes develop a fantastic affinity for the vocabulary of the subject. The impressive technical vocabularies we often observe, even in handicapped readers, on the subject of their motorcycles, their cars, their transistors, and their stereos attest to the power of interest!

READING AID 63

Teachers of subjects in which difficult new terms and concepts abound can lead their students to these understandings:

> As you begin to study this subject seriously, it may seem as if you're learning a foreign language! Difficult and unfamiliar terms come crowding! Once an unfamiliar term is defined, the author will use it again and again—assuming ever after that you understand it.
>
> Rote memory is not enough. You must acquire a "working understanding"—learn to use the new word tools rigorously and intelligently. Pass over these new terms lightly, and word blocks will obstruct your learning; your reading will become an obstacle course. Learn the new terms thoroughly at the time they're introduced, and you'll have precision tools for grasping essential new knowledge to the last day of the course—and beyond. Clearly, your vocabulary competencies now become a tremendous asset!

Hurdles Fall Down!

READING AID 64

In one reading improvement class, a classroom-size poster pictures unknown words as reading "hurdles" (see Figure 3–1). A similar poster has been used in classes as diverse as mathematics and music theory. The teacher helps drive home the message:

> Words you do not know are hurdles! They block your comprehension! They may bring your speed to a standstill! Each word you learn *speeds up your reading indirectly!* As we work on words in class today, these hurdles will fall down!

The words on the poster can easily be changed to fit the particular lesson at hand. Vertical slits at the right and left of the bars of the hurdle enable the teacher to slip in cards with words being studied currently—the "words of the day."

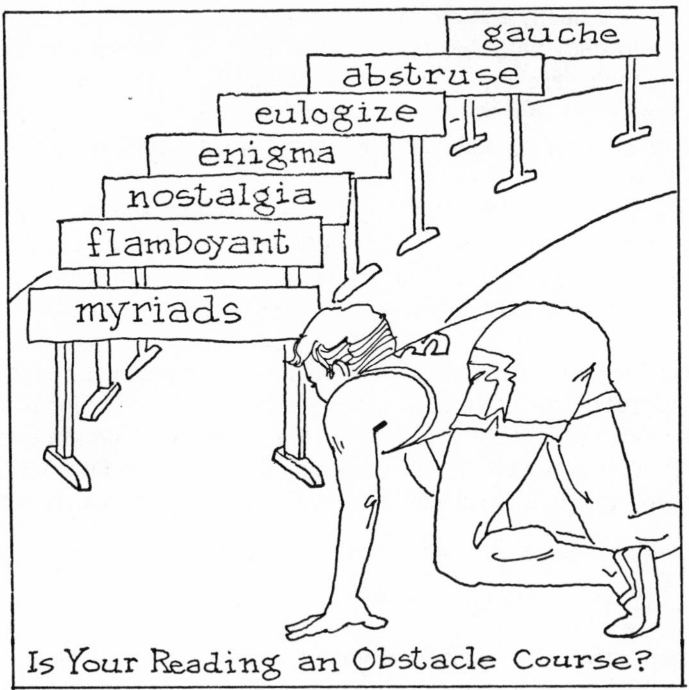

A classroom-size poster can challenge students to master new words and remove the "hurdles."

Figure 3–1

"Look at All the Words You've Learned!"

READING AID 65

Research strongly suggests that planned instruction in general vocabulary is superior to a casual or incidental approach. Being aware of this, English and reading teachers may wish to make a direct attack on carefully selected words through periodic vocabulary lessons.

SEE MASTER COPY PAGE 3

A teacher of small reading improvement classes reports how students were motivated to enthusiastic effort, partly through a before-and-after graph that provided proof of progress. You will find this graph on Master Copy Page 3. A high final test score gave the student solid evidence of progress on an individual lesson, and a row of high scores across the page became a source of even greater satisfaction.

The pretest was an essential—and soon became a routine—part of each lesson. Without a pretest on the words to be studied, students tend to be overconfident. Having a vague familiarity with the words in the lesson, they react, "Oh, I already know those words!" Often they do *not* know the correct or the exact meaning. It took just moments for the students to obtain their score on the pretest—they were simply asked to write the meanings of five (or so) sample words that the teacher had selected from the coming lesson. The teacher walked around the small group and graded the papers quickly.

The spirit of the pretest was forward-looking. Low scores did not become a source of discouragement. The teacher commented: "Of course you're not expected to know the words on the pretest. We don't want to spend our time on words you already know! Watch your scores *skyrocket* on the final test!" To give heart to less confident students, the teacher had saved the graphs of former students whose *pre* and *post* scores were in dramatic contrast—often star athletes or V.I.P.'s at school, *not* all good students—and showed the class these graphs.

In the lesson itself, the words were introduced to the students in context, usually in interesting teacher-made or commercial vocabulary lessons. The students were introduced to—then put into practice—the retention techniques suggested in Reading Aid 113. Because the groups were small, the time spent in study could be individualized. The students were encouraged to study until they felt that they had mastered the words in the lesson, then to announce to the teacher, "I'm ready for my test." Word play activities often enlivened the lessons.* The adjustment of study time to fit the individual, the powerful techniques for retention, plus the vocabulary "fun fare" brought gratifying final test scores to almost all the students.

The following commercial vocabulary books proved to be useful resources—often as a source of appropriate words for teacher-made lessons and at times as a source of already prepared lessons: Ward S. Miller, *Word Wealth,* intended for grades 9–12, and *Word Wealth Junior,* intended for grades 7–9 (New York: Holt, Rinehart and Winston, 1967).

Teachers who use the before-and-after graph on the master copy page may wish to "erase" the words at the top of the page with white typewriter correction fluid and substitute words appropriate in difficulty and interest for their immediate students.

Singer (1969, p. 49) suggests a simple graph like the one in Figure 3–2, kept up to date from week to week, to give students evidence of their growing vocabulary resources.

"Try to Get Along without Words!"

READING AID 66

In this brief "fun activity," students in reading or English class volunteer to try to communicate *without using words* something they have done that day—before they left home that morning, on their way to school, before their first period class, in one of their classes, in the halls, during their lunch hour. The class tries to guess what the student is attempting to communicate. Both actors and audience may develop a new and deeper appreciation for words!

Lively, Lighthearted Activities

Vocabulary study, especially in English and reading classes, offers a special opportunity for involvement in activities intended to create a sense of excitement about words and to motivate vocabulary learning. You will find suggestions for fun activities here and there throughout this chapter and at its close.

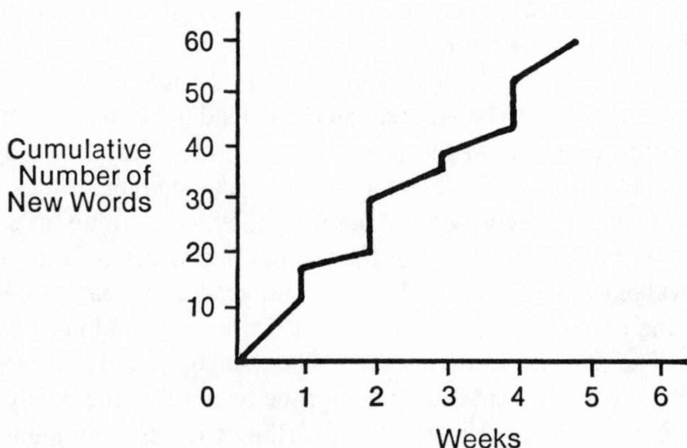

Figure 3–2

A simple graph like this can remind students that the new words they have mastered are adding up to an impressive total.

*Possible word play activities are suggested later in this chapter and in the companion volume (Thomas and Robinson, 1977), pp. 359–373.

Using, Providing, or Enriching Background Experience

At times deficiencies in life experience may make it difficult for the student to attach any meaning to the printed symbols on the page. Suppose, as one writer suggested, Paul has never seen skis or a picture of a skier—has never, in fact, seen snow. How difficult for those little marks—*s-k-i-i-n-g*—on the page before him to have meaning! The teacher might be able to patch together some meaning for Paul because Paul has seen hills, he has seen long, narrow boards, and he has experienced slipping in the mud. But what a shortcut for Paul to see a film of a skier speeding down a mountainside! (Johnson, 1965)

What the student *brings to* those little ink marks on the page enables them to spring to life. The Reading Aids that follow will suggest possible ways to give students direct and indirect experience and thus invest new words with meaning.

Excursions Can Enlarge Vocabularies

READING AID 67

Excursions beyond the school walls can enlarge students' vocabularies and richly invest new words with meaning. A field trip to an airport for a class studying transportation can give real meaning to terms like *runway, control tower, beacon, flight dispatcher, traffic controller, meteorologist, ramp, hangar, conveyor belt,* and *terminal building*. But the excursion alone will not be enough. For maximum benefits, teachers will want to *introduce* important words before the excursion—*use* them, when possible, during the excursion—then *reinforce* them after the excursion.

Indirect experience—films, film strips, projected pictures, records, tape recordings, interviews, and classroom visitors—these, too, can bring new words to life.

Realia Can Speed and Strengthen Learning

READING AID 68

Models and other realia can help students "experience" new terms and concepts. A science teacher might help students to quickly grasp *bilateral symmetry* by showing them a mounted specimen of a luna moth with its symmetrical wings outspread. A social studies teacher might make *artifact* more meaningful by showing the class, as the term is introduced, arrowheads, spearpoints, and axes shaped by primitive Indians who roamed the region long ago.

A biology teacher (Weir, 1979) in the Canal Zone used an exciting bit of realia most of us cannot match in our classrooms—"Oscar," a living boa constrictor! Oscar, who had been captured in a Panamanian rain forest, now lived in a cage in the classroom. With Oscar removed from his cage and placed on a laboratory table as a living example, the teacher taught concepts like *constriction, protective coloration, vestigial* limbs, and—since Oscar was a rainbow boa constrictor—even *iridescence*.

In one reading class, after the students had met the word *accolade* in a selection, the teacher invited the students to bring accolades of their own to class. On the next day, varsity football letters, blue ribbons from horse shows, swimming medals, and certificates won in music contests arrived in class with their proud owners and gave powerful reinforcement to the meaning of *accolade*.

Bring Words Close to the Lives of Young People

READING AID 69

Words brought close to the lives of young people should take on meaning for them more quickly. A business education teacher (Haehn, 1979) who was teaching a group of college-bound seniors, wanted her students to master the terms *signature loan, delinquent account, graduated account, graduated repayments, default,* and *security*. She related each term to an experience that was a real prospect for many of these seniors—applying for a student loan to see them through college. A mathematics teacher (Muelder, 1979) who wanted his students to grasp the concept of ratio related it, the day after a big football victory over an old rival, to the number of yards their team had gained and the number of times the ball had been carried. He also related the concept of ratio to the relationship between the number of boys to girls present that day in the classroom.

Junior girls who had just taken their Scholastic Aptitude Tests returned to school and told their reading teacher: "We forgot words we had studied by ourselves on long lists in the S.A.T. practice books, but we remembered the ones we had talked about in class and studied in sentences close to our lives." Perhaps they were recalling sentences like this one:

> You care about someone—then you don't see him anymore. Later when something, like a popular song, brings back memories you shared together, you feel *poignant* emotions.

*Build Your Own "Picto-cabulary" Collection**

READING AID 70

Students can "experience" new terms and concepts through pictures. As younger students begin a study of Switzerland, a bulletin board with conspicuously labeled, colorful pictures can help them grasp the meaning of words they will soon be meeting, words like *chalet, Alps, avalanche,* and *glacier* (Dallman, 1974, p. 200). Students should be able to grasp the meaning of *facade* quickly when their teacher holds up and explains a close-to-home example—a yearbook picture of the facade of their own school. With scissors in hand, teachers can be on the lookout for suitable pictures as they turn through magazines in their own personal reading. A growing word-through-pictures collection, kept on call in file folders, is an easy-to-acquire, no-cost, very useful vocabulary resource.

Happenings in Class Can Bring Words to Life

READING AID 71

Classroom teachers, especially English and reading teachers with their special interest in general vocabulary, can take advantage of happenings in class to bring new words to life. One day in English class, Ann and Terri, who were close friends, suddenly became convulsed with the giggles. The teacher snatched the moment and, with living examples, taught the class the word *paroxysm.* In the same school the signal for a fire drill was a harsh, grating, ear-splitting blast. Immediately after a fire drill, the teacher grabbed the opportunity to teach honors students the word *cacophonous.* The Greek parts *kakos,* meaning bad, and *phone,* meaning sound, helped to reinforce the meaning.

Wide Reading Builds Word Power

Students with no personal reading interests usually have limited vocabularies. And the reverse is true—those with far-ranging reading interests usually have rich vocabularies (McCallister, 1957).

READING AID 72

We can help students enrich their vocabularies by encouraging them to read widely for their own enjoyment and information. If we succeed, they will spend many hours in the

*The writer borrowed the word *picto-cabulary* from Richard A. Boning, who uses it in his *Picto-cabulary Series,* designed for levels 4–6 and 5–9. This outstanding vocabulary program is designed to plant indelible word images through a pictorial approach. The publisher is Barnell Loft, Ltd., Baldwin, N.Y., 1972–1976.

world of words. They will meet words repeatedly in similar and different settings—perhaps with a little increment of meaning at each encounter—and gradually incorporate some of them into their vocabularies.

To help not-so-able readers grow in vocabulary through personal reading, we must get into their hands books appropriate in difficulty. The book must be difficult enough, of course, to confront the reader with some unknown words. But it must not contain too many of these or the student will become frustrated, comprehension will break down, and the hope of vocabulary growth will be defeated. A rule of thumb often suggested is to select material with two or three words new to the student per hundred running words.

Dozens of possible ways to win students to personal reading are offered in Reading Aids 268–298 in Chapter 7, "Turn Your Students into Readers—for Life."

Pre-Teaching "Stopper" Words

As we sit down to plan a reading assignment, we might ask ourselves these questions: "Which words are likely to block my students? Should I remove some of these blocks before they begin reading? If so, which ones?"

Teachers Can Do Advance Teaching of Carefully Selected Words

READING AID 73

Teachers can help take down the obstacle course by pre-teaching "stopper" words. As the chill is taken off the reading, discouraged readers may take heart. Teachers will not want to pre-teach so many words, however, that the pre-teaching runs away with the lesson. The words should be few and thoughtfully selected—real "stoppers."

This is triple-duty instruction! By teaching "stopper" words, teachers in every classroom can make a contribution to 1) *vocabulary learning,* 2) *facility in reading the selection assigned,* and 3) *subject-matter learning,* at the very same moment! A homemaking teacher removes the word-block *colander* just before the class reads the recipe for spaghetti. A mathematics teacher removes the obstacle of *equidistant* as he assigns the class a passage on the perpendicular bisector theorem. An English teacher helps bring the *Odyssey* within reach by pre-teaching about the *imperturbable* Odysseus, the *strategem* of the wooden horse, and the like—at the same time catching interest through intriguing glimpses of plot. A social studies teacher clarifies *indulgence* before students read about the Reformation.

The following guidelines for pre-teaching "stopper" words have proved useful to teachers in content area classrooms:

1. ***Introduce the new word in context.*** You might locate the word for the students in the coming passage, write it on the board in context, or possibly project the page on a screen with an opaque projector. Lead students to make full use of any context clues to help them reason out the meaning.
2. ***Spotlight an easy root word within a long, forbidding word.*** An extremely important service to students is simply to make them aware that long, forbidding words have parts. Left alone, some students meet a word like *imperturbable,* glance at the first few letters, and skip over the rest. It often helps to spotlight an easy root word—here *perturb*—within a difficult word. With *commutative,* mathematics teachers might ask, "What does *commuter* mean?" With *exponential,* they might ask, "Can you see a part you already know—one you've used many times?" A social studies teacher could direct attention to *total* in *totalitarian.* A science teacher can focus on the building blocks in *interplanetary.* A music teacher might point out *recite* in *recitative.*

Students will "see into" words quickly if, as they analyze words, you mark off root words on the board with vertical lines or highlight them with colored chalk.

extra | territorial | ity
inter**change**able

Now the words may be revealed as not so difficult after all.

3. ***Reduce difficult polysyllables to easy-to-manage syllables.*** As numerous teachers will substantiate, many students slide over new and difficult words. How easily do you think you could learn *platyhelminthes* for biology class if you had not examined it syllable by syllable all the way to the end? For practical purposes some students seem unaware that syllables exist. They tend to glance at the first few letters of a difficult word and give up. Middles and endings of words thus receive only slight attention. Words of more than two or three syllables are, as one student expressed it, "just a mess of letters" (Bragstad, 1975).

   But a long, formidable polysyllable can be put on the board with its syllables marked off by vertical slashes, with accent marks, and perhaps with its phonetic spelling. The group can pronounce the word part by part with the teacher. They soon see that a word which looks as if it comes by the yard can be reduced to a number of short, easy-to-manage, pronounceable parts:

   plat′ | ē | hel | min′ | thēz
   an′ | thro | po | log′ | i | cal
   en | vi′ | ron | men′ | tal | ist

4. ***Call attention to accented syllables.*** It will often be helpful to mark the stressed syllables with conspicuous accent marks. As you lead students through the pronunciation of a word, you can sharpen their awareness of the force of these marks.

   As teachers follow guidelines 2–4, their students are learning to divide and conquer—to examine a difficult word for meaningful parts and to work through it syllable by syllable all the way to the end. As teachers direct attention to parts, they are helping to change the habits of those who did not really focus on new and difficult words.

5. ***Tap teen experience.*** Some new words or terms are made to order for tapping the experiences of teenagers. For example, a topic close to many young people is buying a first car. A teacher of typewriting relates new words to this experience as the terms *promissory note* and *collateral loan* are pre-taught. Now the new terms are likely to stick in mind (Haehn, 1979).

6. ***Pre-teach multi-meaning terms.*** Some words take off one meaning and put on another as students walk across the doorsill of a classroom! *Law* does so as they walk into science class, *between* and *point* as they walk into geometry, *role* as they walk into social studies. *Culture* can refer to an appreciation of the arts in English class and to tiny-celled organisms swimming around in a petri dish in biology! Such words often call for pre-teaching since the student may react, "That's easy; I already know that word!" Often, however, this student does not know the precise meaning called for in the particular field.

7. ***Help ensure retention.*** Students should be helped to use all possible senses and strategies in attempting to retain new words. A mathematics teacher observes, "As a key word is pre-taught, my students see the word, say it, hear it, repeat it, and review it. Then in class sessions that follow, I use the word again and again—avoiding the use of pronouns."

8. ***Help students move toward independence.*** On all levels teachers will want to give appropriate assistance with difficult terms, then gradually move their students in the direction of independence. How to equip students with long-term *self-help* methods for dealing with difficult words is the subject of much of the rest of this chapter.

Breaking the Concept Barrier

READING AID 74

Classroom teachers will often need to teach words for which their students do not have an available concept in their cognitive storehouse. Here, of course, our task is more difficult than teaching new words which represent concepts the students have already formed.

Let's take a look at the difference. Suppose students need to know the meaning of the new word *neophyte*. Of course, they have already formed the concept of *beginner*. We can teach those students *neophyte* quickly simply by providing a close synonym like *beginner* or *novice*. On the other hand, suppose the students need to know the meaning of the concept *laissez-faire,* which, for those students, is an entirely new concept. In this situation we must teach the students the new term *by building a basic understanding of the concept*.

One writer (Boettcher, 1979, p. 5) points up the contrast in the difficulty of those two tasks: "Very simply, when students are presented with a synonym for a word for which they have already formed an available concept, they say, 'Oh,' and are able to continue on. . . . When, on the other hand, students are presented with a synonym for a word for which they have no available concept, they are likely to say, 'Huh?' "

The ten procedures that follow may prove suggestive in breaking the concept barrier.* *They are not intended as a lock-step sequence or even necessarily as a sequence.* Instead, they are procedures that may be useful *somewhere along the line*—before reading, along with reading, or during activities and discussions—after students are motivated and always in natural situations. Of course, not every procedure will be called for with every concept:

1. The instructor uses the term for the concept (let's suppose it's *iridescence*) and perhaps asks the students to repeat it, stressing the pronunciation if necessary.
2. Ask yourself, "Is there a way to use *show* along with *tell* in teaching this concept?" In military and industrial training, models, filmstrips, drawings, diagrams, and charts as well as direct observation are effective in teaching concepts. Suppose we try to *tell* students about iridescence: "Iridescence is an interplay of rainbow colors." How much more quickly students will grasp this concept if we show them a handful of "live" iridescent sequins!
3. One way or another—through having the students read, listen, or view an object or a representation—the teacher elicits or conveys the information, "This is an example of (*the concept*)," and, "This is also an example." The students are likely to name as examples of the concept of iridescence mother of pearl, a soap bubble in the sun, and feathers from a peacock's tail.

*Jack R. Fraenkel offers a table for attaining concepts. We have used it to guide our thinking and have incorporated, adapted, and elaborated some of the steps for teaching concepts that he suggests in *Helping Students Think and Value: Strategies for Teaching the Social Studies* (Englewood Cliffs, N.J.: Prentice-Hall, 1973), pp. 198–204. Fraenkel, in turn, adapted the table from Hilda Taba, Mary C. Durkin, Jack R. Fraenkel, and Anthony H. McNaughton, *A Teacher's Handbook to Elementary Social Studies: An Inductive Approach* (Reading, Mass.: Addison-Wesley Publishing Co., 1971), p. 71.

4. One way or another—again, through having students read, listen, or view an object or a representation—the teacher conveys or elicits the information. "This is *not* an example," and "This is *not* an example either." *Non*-examples of iridescence might include ribbon streamers of rainbow colors and the rainbow itself—both non-examples, of course, because they lack the "play" of shifting colors. As a general rule, negative examples should follow a number of positive examples and should be fewer. Now the students are sharpening their awareness of the essential elements which all the examples of the concept have in common but which the non-examples lack.
5. At some point the teacher might ask, "What characteristics does (*the concept*) have that make it possible for you to identify it?" Now the class can try to identify the major characteristics that all the examples have in common. These might be written on the board for all to see.
6. The teacher might ask, "Now can you explain what (*the concept*) is?" Now the students analyze the meaning of the concept, working out a definition that includes its essential attributes. The teacher has formulated a good definition in advance and has in mind the major attributes. With *iridescence,* the definition might be "rainbow colors that seem to move and shift when viewed from different angles and in different lights."
7. A concept more readily springs to life when, as students discuss the concept, the examples are close to their own lives. The concept of *subsidy,* for instance, may come alive when one example cited is the student activity fund's subsidizing their school newspaper. The concept *constitution* becomes more real when a copy of the Student Government Constitution is brought into class and examined.
8. With difficult concepts, in order to broaden and deepen their students' understanding, instructors can later spotlight more complex or unusual examples. They might ask, "Is *this* an example of *civil disobedience?*" These later examples will involve new attributes that expand the definition.
9. If this reinforcement is needed, the teacher asks at an appropriate time, "Can you find examples of your own?" Now the students might search out and bring to class their own examples.
10. With difficult concepts, the instructor will wish to avoid concentrating the learning of a concept into a single, short, intensive session. Spaced-out learning will result in firmer learning and retention.

In the sequence above, the learning proceeds inductively. Students examine examples and non-examples of the concept, then discover for themselves the defining characteristics. If teachers prefer to work deductively, they provide students with the definition of the concept and its key attributes at the outset. Then as examples and non-examples come up (at first mostly examples), they raise the question: "Is this an example of *conflict of interest?* Why or why not?" Later the students suggest their own examples.

For more detailed procedures for teaching words for which students have not yet developed a concept, the reader may wish to consult the companion volume (Thomas and Robinson, *Improving Reading in Every Class,* unabridged 2nd ed., 1977), pp. 311–314.

READING AID 75

Printed Aids Can Help Remove Obstacles

Printed vocabulary aids supplied to students before they read an assignment can help remove word blocks and, at the same time, help the students grow in vocabulary. Some teachers supply on a study guide a list of crucial terms together with easy-to-grasp definitions plus the page and the line where the words can be located in context. Some list on the study guide words that are to become the special responsibility of the students. Some supply a handout with key terms and their meanings to accompany a movie or a film strip. Some supply a glossary of important terms as a review sheet. Some, when they ditto reading selections for students, supply the definitions for difficult terms in footnotes. Seniors in American Problems who were assigned a rigorous selection on alienation, for example, were glad to find in a footnote a definition of the formidable "stopper" word, *entelechy!*

The Right Textbook Can Help

READING AID 76

To the extent that choice is possible, school systems and teachers should select textbooks that give maximum help with the development of vocabulary. They should, as Hill (1979, p. 250) reminds us, examine books for careful pacing in introducing new terms, for the extent and the care with which words are defined and reinforced in context, and for the provision of word-learning aids. Difficult new concepts should not come crowding upon the students—they should be introduced with careful pacing, they should be defined, and they should be clarified by examples and perhaps non-examples, then reinforced. Other textbook features that contribute to the development of a strong vocabulary include aids for pronouncing and accenting difficult words (supplied in parentheses each time a difficult new "official" term is introduced), a pronunciation key to help students interpret those aids, lists at the beginning or end of each chapter of words that should be mastered, a glossary with clear, easy-to-grasp definitions, and a complete and accurate index.

Helping Students Use Context Clues as an Aid in Reasoning Out Meanings

In the preceding chapter we discussed context as the most important aid for students in recognizing in printed form words whose meanings they already know. Context is also *the* major aid for students in the development of their meaning vocabularies. In the experience of many teachers, few students, even superior readers, make full use of clues in the surrounding language to get at the meanings of words they do not know.

A high school reading teacher, year after year, asked this question of students, including upperclassmen, who were starting a course in developmental reading: "What do you do when you're reading and you encounter an unfamiliar word?" Some of the students answered, "I look it up in the dictionary." Some answered, "I skip it." A few mentioned making use of the context. Almost none revealed any familiarity at all with different types of context clues.

"A Reading Detective's Paradise of Clues"

One writer calls the printed page "a reading detective's paradise of clues" for readers in their search for meaning (Stauffer, 1969, p. 304). We will discuss on the coming pages two categories of context clues: 1) syntactic (word order and function) clues; and 2) semantic (or meaning) clues.

READING AID 77

Clues in the Syntax Can Delimit Choices. Students should become consciously aware that syntax—the arrangement, relationship, and function of words in sentences—can aid them as they try to reason out the meaning of words they do not know. The reader of this book can appreciate the significance of syntax by contrasting the meaning of *a day off* with *an off day!* (Durkin, 1976, p. 8) While the help that syntax offers students does not directly illuminate the meaning, it often eliminates a host of improbable meanings.

The following example (Robinson, 1978, pp. 91–92) illustrates this narrowing of possible choices:

> His *truculent* criticism of your painting betrayed some jealousy.
>
> Let's assume that a given learner understood the message above with the exception of the word *truculent.* Before attempting to apply any other strategies in figuring out the word, he or she knows that the word is not the name of something (noun or subject) or an action word (verb) just by its position in the sentence. By its position, it must be describing the subject *criticism* and hence is an adjective. Now the choices of meaning have been, at least, grossly delimited.
>
> It is not necessary for learners to have to label parts of speech and proceed formally as above, but it is useful to help them realize that they know much more about the unknown language unit than they suspect at first glance.

The use of syntactic clues in the student's reasoning-out process is "all mixed together" with another type of clue, the semantic or meaning clue. Let us turn now to semantic clues.

READING AID 78

Specific Types of Semantic Clues Can "Raise the Consciousness Level" of Students. A semantic clue, or meaning clue, is a help which known words in the surrounding context offer readers as they seek to arrive at the meaning of an unknown word.

Students sharpen their context clue power when they learn to ask as they meet a strange word, "What meaning clues can I discover in the context?" We can "raise their consciousness levels" about the usefulness of context clues by making them aware of specific *types* of meaning clues.

Explanations of ten different types of meaning clues, together with examples, follow.* They should be suggestive to teachers as they clarify these clues for students, work with words encountered in actual course materials, or develop their own practice exercises, using words of appropriate difficulty. In practice exercises, students can make a try at the meaning of the stimulus word in sentences like the ones that follow, then compare and discuss their tries. Students who arrived at the correct meaning can point out for other students the clues they found to be revealing.

Students *need not memorize the types of clues*—their names are not important. The purpose is only to convince students that context clues abound to help them in their reading and to turn them into day-to-day context clue users. Overlap will be noted; clues rarely exist in pure form.

1. ***Direct Explanation Clue***—Here the writer supplies an outright explanation of a word the reader may not know:

   > An *ecologist,* a scientist who specializes in the relationship between living things and their environment, is likely to have authoritative opinions on the problem of pollution versus man's survival.
   >
   > The development of the *laser*—that is, a device which concentrates high energies from radiation into a narrow, sharply focused beam of light—has practical applications in medicine.
   >
   > Perhaps someday every home will have a *robot.* This man-like machine that operates automatically may perform for us many routine and unexciting jobs. (Niles, 1977, p. 18)

*Most of the types of context clues explained on these pages were first identified by McCullough (1945, pp. 1–5). Others have arrived at somewhat different classifications of contextual aids. The reader may wish to refer to Ames's broad classification (1966) and Quealy's summary (1969) of the classification schemes of major investigators.

2. ***Experience Clue***—From your own life experience (or indirect experience from reading, TV, and the like), you know how people and things react in a given situation.

   Finally the moment of leaving home arrives. The unexplored world of college lies ahead. Almost every entering college student approaches life on campus with some *trepidation*.

3. ***Comparison or Contrast Clue***—Here you can get some suggestion of the new word's meaning because you compare or contrast it with an idea expressed in familiar words nearby.

   When the light brightens, the pupils of the eyes contract; when it grows darker, they *dilate*.

   Peggy excels in basketball, photography, and music, and her older brother is even more *versatile*.

4. ***Explanation Through Example Clue***—Here you find near the unknown word an example that throws light on the meaning.

   In the course of evolutionary development, certain human organs have *atrophied*. The appendix, for example, has wasted away from disuse.

   President Lincoln's attitude toward the fallen South was *magnanimous*—"with malice toward none, with charity for all."

   An occasional *respite* during a long evening of study is desirable. Ginnie often took a short breather between chapters or between assignments.

   While the player raced across the line for the winning touchdown, *pandemonium* broke loose in the stands. The happy rooters yelled, screamed, rang cow bells, blew horns, and made every kind of noise imaginable to show their joy and enthusiasm. (Evans, 1972)

5. ***Mood or Tone Clue***—Here the writer sets a mood—for example, happy, somber, frightening, eerie. The meaning of the unknown word must harmonize.

   The *lugubrious* wails of the gypsies matched the dreary whistling of the wind in the all-but-deserted cemetery. (Strang, McCullough, and Traxler, 1967, p. 231)

6. ***Summary or Restatement Clue***—Here the new word appears to wrap up the situation. You know the circumstances the new word is summing up.

   Pete Littlefield, our center, stands six feet three inches in his stocking feet and weighs an even 210 pounds. His teammates call him "Runt," an obvious *misnomer*. (Evans, 1972)

   The greatest effect of the Renaissance on education was a growing *secularization* in schools. More school curricula focused on man's expression of feelings toward the world in which he lived. Schools became interested in teaching about affairs of the world, not only about religious matters.

7. ***Synonym Clue***—Here you learn something about the meaning of the unknown word because it repeats an idea expressed in words you know nearby.

Flooded with spotlights—the focus of all attention—the newly crowned prom queen began her reign. She was the *cynosure* of all eyes for the rest of the evening.

Louis XIV kept his nobles constantly involved in rites and ceremonies and certain ways of doing things. Such *protocol* permitted him to keep them busily engaged while he ruled France without interference.

8. ***Familiar Expression or Language Experience Clue***—Here your familiarity with common language patterns—expressions you hear every day—helps you. In the example below, you are familiar with the expression *took upon himself*. So you have a strong clue to the meaning of *appropriated*.

   He took upon himself—yes, he *appropriated*—the entire responsibility for raising money for the class gift.

9. ***Words in a Series Clue***—Here you know the general nature of the items or ideas being enumerated. So you get some idea of the meaning of the unknown word.

   The apples had their places all around the room. They were *codlins,* and golden pippins, brown russets and scarlet crabs, *biffins,* nonpareils and queanings, big green bakers, pearmains, and red streaks. (Seibert and Crocker, 1958, p. 52)

10. ***Inference Clue***—Here you infer, or reason out, the meaning of the new word from the clues that are at hand. Of course, this type of clue overlaps all the other types except direct explanation.

    While driving his father's new car, Mike had a serious collision. Luckily, bystanders *corroborated* his statement that he had been driving carefully.

    We freshmen envied the *aplomb* of the self-possessed seniors who seemed to be oozing self-confidence.

Some instructors prefer a simpler classification, referring to semantic, or meaning, clues simply as either *direct* or *indirect* clues. They use the term *direct* to designate the direct explanation type of clue and the term *indirect* to refer to all the other types.

Students should understand that the examples above have exceptionally revealing context clues and have been contrived to clarify the different types of meaning clues. They should move on from contrived sentences to work with clues in "real life" reading, where context clues, while definitely helpful, do not often reveal meaning so neatly.

Semantic Clues Can Be Missing or Misleading

READING AID 79

Students should become aware that context sometimes has little to reveal concerning a word's meaning. In the sentence below, the subject the college students "rapped" about all night might be any one of many possibilities!

> In our dorm we had "talkathons" far into the night. Just after our prof in psych class lectured on *determinism,* we argued about it until three o'clock in the morning!

Students should also become aware that context is occasionally a real "fooler." In the example below, both the context of *restive* and the word's structure might lead the reader to conclude that Sharon was at peace or at rest. But Sharon was just the opposite—she was *restive* or restless!

Alone with her thoughts in the complete solitude of the quiet woodland, Sharon felt *restive*.

Students Need Do's and Don'ts for Using Context

READING AID 80

Teachers want students to become aware as they work with context clues that context often supplies at least a hint of a word's meaning. On the other hand, they hope that students will realize that the meaning they arrive at through context is usually tentative or general and *that the dictionary is indispensable* and should usually be consulted to verify or reject a context guess that may have significance for further reading. Teachers will wish to emphasize frequently and strongly that no single context revelation will illuminate all future encounters with the word. They should help students recognize that many situations require the utmost precision of meaning, while for others a general meaning is sufficient, and they should guide their students in making the distinction. Students should not gain the impression that context clues will be found only in the immediate sentence. They should become aware of clues remote from the word to be defined—in another part of the paragraph, even in another part of the selection.

Students may wish to arrive at their own guidelines for using context clues. The following table shows in capsule form a few that have already been generated.

Do's and Don'ts for Using Context

Do Rely on Context Clues

1. When you have an "unmissable clue"—a direct explanation.
2. When you have highly revealing clues and the meaning you arrive at definitely "clicks" with the rest of the passage.
3. When, in view of your purpose for reading the selection, you need only a general sense of the meaning.

Don't Rely on Context Clues (Turn to Your Dictionary)

1. When you require a precise meaning. It usually takes the dictionary to pin the meaning down.
2. When the word is a key word, one crucial to your understanding, and full comprehension is important to you.
3. When the clues suggest several possibilities—the meaning might be one of several—and you don't know which.
4. When you don't know the nearby words.
5. When you have encountered the word a number of times, realize that it is a common, useful one which you will meet again, and will want to master thoroughly for future reading.

Using Context Clues to Figure Out Assignment Words

READING AID 81

The students' day-to-day course materials offer a source of meaningful practice in using context clues as an aid in reasoning out meanings. Here is one way a teacher might guide such practice:

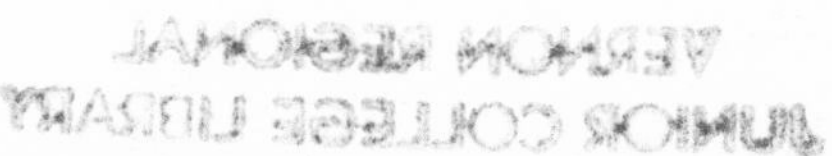

The teacher has searched through a passage that has been assigned and has selected words, most of which have fairly revealing context. The teacher asks the students, who have their books open: "Find the word ________ one-third of the way down page ___. Can you puzzle out its meaning from the context?" The students offer their tries, which are often successful. When the teacher probes, "What led you to the meaning?" the students point out the clues that were revealing. The dictionary comes into play to verify or reject the tries, to determine the nuance of meaning, to disclose the meaning when the context refuses to yield clues, and to check pronunciation.

Let Students Prove Their Mastery on a Test

READING AID 82

After skill with context clues has been taught and practiced, emphasize the importance of using context clues by including a context clue question on a unit test. Provide a passage in which a challenging word appears in fairly revealing context. Ask the students to reason out the meaning of the word, then to list the clues they used in order to arrive at the meaning.

Students will take skill development *much* more seriously if they are checked in a regular testing situation. They will realize how important their teachers consider the skill. (Bragstad, 1979)

Students Should Learn that Context Exerts Control in Figurative Expressions

READING AID 83

Figurative expressions, which *abound* on the pages of readings in English and social studies, may be stumbling blocks for some readers. Their teachers, mature readers themselves, grasp these expressions so easily that they may be unaware of their students' bewilderment. Students should learn that they will frequently meet language that is figurative—language that has an intended meaning often *quite different from what is literally said.*

Students may know the meanings of *all* the individual words in a figurative expression yet have no idea of the expression's meaning. In expressions like the following, students who take in what the words actually *say* are lost: "the senator has strong *grass-roots* support," "they *took* the ship out of *mothballs,*" "the way the political *wind is blowing,*" "*ride roughshod over* a veto," "*blind* justice," "*tongues* in tress," "we have *given our hearts away,* a sordid boon," "forever *chasing rainbows,*" "a *shrinking violet,*" "he *lost face.*"

Consider the plight of students in social studies class who try to interpret the expression "our country, a melting pot" literally! Let's imagine that they consult their teacher, who comes to their rescue: "You're reading how millions of immigrants—Italians, Irish, Germans, Poles—left their homelands to come to America and, after a generation or two, learned new ways and became Americanized. Why do you think the author uses the expression 'a great melting pot'? What happens when different ingredients—like butter, solid chocolate, and sugar—are put into a pot and heated?" Some student is likely to answer: "They'll melt and mix together." The teacher goes on: "Why do you think the author calls our country 'a great melting pot'?" One of the students may suggest: "All these different people, like the different things in the pot, blended together and became Americans." The teacher continues: "Then just what is a melting pot?" Perhaps some student will answer: "A place where a mixing of different nationalities is taking place—where they're melting into one."

In reading situations that come up from day to day, teachers can alert students to the control that context exerts over the meaning of individual words in figurative expressions, guide them *not* to interpret these expressions literally, make them aware that they will frequently meet language that is figurative, alert them to the writer's purpose of adding vividness, clarity, and/or beauty.

Students Might Analyze Figurative Expressions in Student Writing

READING AID 84

In English and reading class, we can bring figurative language closer to students by examining examples in the students' own writing or in the writing of their schoolmates. As Hillocks, McCabe, and McCampbell (1971, p. 213) suggest: "If the school has a literary magazine, it is usually possible to find two or three poems [or essays] in back issues that offer good examples for analysis. Using student materials has the decided advantage of making figurative language appear less esoteric and of encouraging students to use it in their own writing. . . . After the students have examined the effects of figurative language, it will seem sensible to name the different kinds of figures (metaphor, simile, hyperbole, and personification are the most common) and discriminate among them."

Students Might Analyze Figurative Language in Their Own "Teen Talk"

READING AID 85

Students might work with figurative expressions heard every day in their own "teen talk," contrasting what the words literally say with the meaning the speaker or writer actually intends. Expressions like these might be analyzed: *the top banana, the pits, my car's a lemon, a hot potato, come unglued, hang loose, blow your mind, apple polish.*

"Now" Practice with Context Clues

READING AID 86

It is often possible, especially in English and reading classes, where teachers are working to enrich general vocabulary, to relate words to some timely topic—something the students are thinking and caring about that day. In one class, on a November day when football was in the air, the students worked with *stentorian* and reasoned it out in this context: "The *stentorian* voice of the head cheerleader boomed over the loudspeaker: 'Everybody up for the kickoff!' " (Evans, 1972) On a day when many students in the class had just taken part in an assembly program by the school choir, the students puzzled out the italicized words in sentences about a fascinating subject, *themselves:* "You were all decked out in the *regalia* of the school choir." . . . "You sang your opening number with *verve*." . . . "The tones of your last number were *dulcet*." . . . "All of you are *devotees* of choral music!"

Special days offer opportunities for "now" practice, as the students reason out timely words: "On the community Christmas tree are *myriads* of colored lights." . . . "Would you like to have your birthday *coincide* with Christmas?"

Students Can Reason Out the "Word Champ"!

READING AID 87

Students who like verbal fun enjoy meeting the "word champs" of the English language in English or reading class. Words that break records for length are listed in the *Guinness Book of World Records*. A husky "champ" of twenty-nine letters, the longest word in *The Oxford English Dictionary,* is *floccinaucinihilipilification*.

Students who have become context clue hunters will experience satisfaction when they find that they can reason out the meaning of this forbidding-looking word. The "champ" might be written on the board in the following sentence:

What turns me off about that senior is his constant *floccinaucinihilipilification* of freshmen!

The students will quickly infer from the context that the word means "belittling" or "putting down." They will feel well pleased with themselves when they learn that they have come very close to the dictionary meaning, "The action of estimating someone as worthless."

The reader will find further discussion of developing context clue power in the companion volume (Thomas and Robinson, *Improving Reading in Every Class,* unabridged 2nd ed., 1977), pp. 24–38 and 359–361. There you will find an informal procedure for testing students' facility in using context clues, practice exercises intended to help students become eager context clue hunters, and fun activities for students to supplement the solid fare on how to utilize context revelation.

Learning Word Meanings through Structural Analysis

In Chapter 2 we discussed analyzing the structure of words as an aid to recognizing in printed form words already in the student's speaking-listening vocabulary. In the present chapter we will consider structural analysis as an important help in learning the *meanings of unknown words*.

As you may recall from Chapter 2, *structural analysis* consists of analyzing words through their meaningful parts—their roots, prefixes, suffixes, and inflectional endings. We stressed in that chapter that structural analysis is an area where middle/secondary classroom teachers can make an especially productive contribution to their students' reading. Since the readings we assign students *abound* in word parts that can be used to unlock meanings, we will do well to seize many opportunities to work with these parts. As we do so, we will be giving our students double dividends: first, a firmer command of words in their current readings, and, second, a working knowledge of word parts to use in reasoning out meanings in all their future reading. Science teachers report that work with Greek and Latin word parts pays off richly in science, where a concentration of awesome polysyllables contributes to the difficulty of the reading.

Again recalling the chapter on word attack, we can develop skill with word-part clues in the following ways: 1) we can help students spot easy *familiar* root words in long words that appear to be unfamiliar, and 2) we can deliberately enrich our students' working stock of frequently recurring word parts—prefixes, suffixes, and roots—word parts that appear in countless English derivatives.

Probing Each Student's Knowledge of Word Parts

READING AID 88

For an easy-to-make, easy-to-take informal test, list ten or so Greek or Latin prefixes and/or roots appropriate for your students' level. Use word parts that, according to your observation, should be part of their standard equipment for word analysis—parts, if you are a content area teacher, that recur in your assigned readings, especially current readings. Ask the students simply to write the meanings. The results may reveal surprising lacks. You will find in the appendix a list of common Greek and Latin prefixes and roots, roughly classified by grade levels.

Day-to-day observation is a great—and sometimes a dismaying—revealer. The writer of this book has been surprised—and impelled into action—when not one student in a group of capable upperclassmen working to improve their general vocabularies could give the meaning of a common Greek or Latin word part—like *pseudo-*, *omni-*, and *tele-*,—any one of which would have helped those students to unlock a far-flung family of related English words!

Open Students' Eyes to Familiar Word Parts

READING AID 89

As we have noted, one way to develop skill with structural analysis is to open students' eyes to easy, familiar parts in words that look long and forbidding. Practice in live reading situations is, of course, ideal. There the students observe word parts "in action."

> Suppose students are reading and come upon a word that looks forbidding—*antiremilitarization,* for example in this headline:
>
> SPEAKER AT ANTIREMILITARIZATION RALLY ATTACKS PROPOSED BUDGET*
>
> The teacher might write the word on the board, then ask, "Can you break this long word into its building blocks—do you see parts you already know?" The students snip off the *anti-*, the *re-*, and the *-ation,* and spotlight the root, *militarize*. Then, with guidance, they note the effect of the prefixes and the suffix. When they mentally reassemble the building blocks and return to the context, they have solved a "difficult" word. They now know that the rally in the headline was "against arming again with military forces."

Students will need sharp eyes for roots that turn up "in disguise"—in words like *divisive* (divide), *requisition* (require), and *discontinuity* (discontinue).

Enriching Students' Working Stock of Word Parts

READING AID 90

A second way to sharpen skill in structural analysis is to deliberately enrich our students' working stock of high-yield prefixes and roots as an aid in reasoning out word meanings. When students use this aid, they are doing *not* additive—one-word-at-a-time—learning, but *generative* learning. They learn a common prefix or root, then use that word part as a tool to *generate* the learning of new words. In the writer's experience, prefixes prove especially valuable to students in generating new learning.

Teachers may want to use an inductive approach through which students "discover" the meaning of Greek and Latin word parts as unknown words confront them in reading.

> When the phrase, "a self-pitying malcontent," confronted an English class, the teacher saw an opportunity to teach a productive prefix. The teacher commented: "The prefix *mal-* occurs in scores of words. Can you think of other words with *mal-?*" The students suggested "malpractice," "maladjusted," and "maltreat," and these words were written on the board. A student observed, "All those words mean something about bad or wrong." With the aid of the context, the group concluded that *malcontent* means a "badly contented," hence a discontented person.

When science students come upon the suffix *-lysis* in words like *analysis, hydrolysis,* and *electrolysis,* the stage is set for learning a high-yield word part. They discover, "all those words mean 'breaking up' in some way." Now they have a handle on hosts of other words, among them *photolysis, thermolysis, autolysis,* and *biolysis.*

It's Easy to "Sell" Greek and Latin Parts

READING AID 91

Teachers should have little difficulty "selling" students the value of Greek and Latin word parts. Suppose a group has just met the word *automatic* in a reading passage and, in

*The writer is indebted to Olive S. Niles, Mildred A. Dougherty, and Elsie Katterjohn, *Tactics in Reading,* Book D (Glenview, Ill.: Scott, Foresman and Co., 1977), p. 42, for the headline and the idea of breaking down the challenging word *antiremilitarization.*

working with this word, has learned that *auto-* is a prefix meaning *self.* These comments by the teacher should be persuasive:

> You've just made a stride ahead in vocabulary! Look at all the *auto-* words in this dictionary! [The teacher holds up a dictionary and runs a finger down the columns.] Here are dozens and dozens of words that start with *auto-*! Now you have a handle on all those words!

The students themselves are quick to see their gains. As they learn productive parts like *auto-, anti-, multi-, circum-,* and *micro-,* they suddenly notice that these parts are turning up often in their reading and that they can use them as "pass keys" to unlock words. One student exclaimed, "This is neat! Those parts are popping up all over!"

A New Word Part in Thirty Seconds!

READING AID 92

When a word containing a productive Greek or Latin word part comes up in reading, time is not always available for a "discovery" lesson. In that case, a teacher might take just a few seconds to write the word on the board—let's say its *pseudoscience* to underline the Greek or Latin part, and to write the meaning of the part on the board (see Figure 3–3). The teacher then comments on the meaning of *pseudo-* and on the meaning of the word. If the writing is not erased for a few days, the word part may "teach itself"! The students' learning can be reinforced when they encounter *pseudo-* on other occasions—in words like *pseudonym, pseudointellectual,* and *pseudosophisticated.* The students perceive that they now have a key to unlock scores of words containing *pseudo-*. Again they may react, "That's neat!"

Let Students Collect Dividends on a Test!

READING AID 93

Show that you consider skill in structural analysis a really important vocabulary tool by including on a unit test a question that demands this skill. Do this after your students have practiced unlocking meanings and after their working stock of word parts has been enriched with high-yield parts. Include on the test a sentence that includes a challenging word whose meaning can be unlocked through the use of newly acquired word parts. Ask the students to try to reason out the meaning.

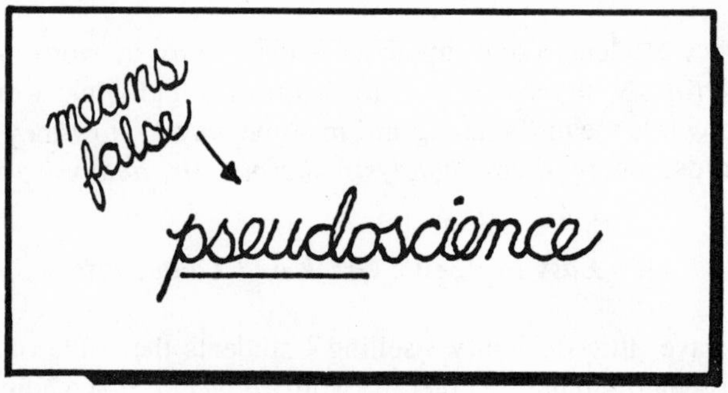

FIGURE 3-3

A Greek or Latin word part left on the chalkboard for a few days may "teach itself" to a class.

In one developmental reading class, upperclassmen who had learned the word parts *dys* meaning bad, *chrom* meaning color, and *op* meaning sight, were challenged on a test by the formidable-looking word, *dyschromatopsia:*

Bob was rejected as a commercial pilot because of *dyschromatopsia*.

Almost every student came up with the right answer—*colorblindness!*

But Using Word Parts Has Limitations!

READING AID 94

Students should definitely experience the *limitations* of reasoning out meanings through word parts. Those who are not aware of limitations might work on *lackadaisical* in this way: Does *lackadaisical* have anything to do with a missing daisy? Or a missing day? Is it anything like *dazed* or a *day's cycle?* (Palmer, 1979, p. 22) What a convincing reminder to the student to check out a possible meaning with the context!

Students should be prepared for deceptive combinations of letters, combinations that are "foolers" because they resemble a Greek or Latin word part but are completely unrelated. The students who worked with the Latin prefix *mal-* in Reading Aid 90 learned that this prefix often means bad or wrong.They should also learn that the letters *m-a-l* sometimes occur when they do not form a Latin part—that there's nothing necessarily bad, for example, about a chocolate *malt,* a *male,* or a *mallard* duck! The root *opt* means sight and helps students reason out *optician, optics*—even *ophthalmologist.* But *optimist* and *option* are not their cousins! (Gainsburg, 1967, 3, p. 115) The Latin root *am* or *ama* means like or love and serves the students well with *amorous, amour,* and *enamored.* But love has little to do with an ambush or ambergris! Students can be given this suggestion: "Ask yourself: Does the meaning of the Greek or Latin part click with the rest of the sentence? *Try out a possible meaning in the surrounding context. Reject it if you can't tune it in!*"

A fuller discussion of structural analysis, including its limitations, will be found in the companion volume (Thomas and Robinson, *Improving Reading in Every Class,* unabridged 2nd ed., 1977), pp. 39–55.

Lists of Useful Word Parts for the Teacher

The reader will find in the appendix of this book a list of commonly recurring Greek and Latin prefixes and roots, roughly classified by grade levels. David Shepherd's useful list of common suffixes (1973, pp. 64–66) is also made available in the appendix, with the generous permission of the publishers. Burmeister (1974, pp. 299–308) has performed a real service for teachers by compiling a great many frequently recurring Greek and Latin word parts and conveniently classifying them according to subject areas. By referring to this list, classroom teachers can become familiar with the word parts their students are likely to be meeting constantly in reading materials in their particular field.

Activities to Enliven Work with Word Parts

Class activities to sharpen up—and liven up—the use of word parts, activities especially appropriate in English or reading class, are shared in the following section. Others can be found in the companion volume (Thomas and Robinson, *Improving Reading in Every Class,* unabridged 2nd ed., 1977), pp. 39–49, 361–363.

READING AID 95

*"Instant" Vocabulary**

Students can be intrigued by the idea that they are gaining "instant" vocabulary—that when they learn a high-yield word part, *in that very instant* they have acquired a hold on a *family* of related words. Those, for instance, who have just learned the prefix *mal-* , meaning bad, in the word *malcontent* in Reading Aid 90, will be delighted to learn that they now have a handle on *malign, malodorous, malefactor,malevolent, malediction, malady, malaise, malfeasance, maladroit,* and even the formidable *malapropism*. Those who have just learned the prefix *a-*(also *an-*), meaning without, in the word *amoral,* for example, will be impressed with the usefulness of Greek and Latin parts when they realize that they have instantly acquired *atypical, asocial, asymmetrical, asexual, arhythmic,* and *apetalous,* as well as others. Those who have just met *-cide,* meaning killing, in the word *homicide* will be impressed if the teacher points out their instant dividends in *pesticide, germicide, insecticide, tyrannocide, fratricide, matricide,* and *patricide*.

College-bound students, those who have their S.A.T.'s ahead, can become quick converts to the use of Greek and Latin word parts as a source of relatively rapid vocabulary growth.

READING AID 96

Prefix-and-Root Card Game

Prefixes and/or roots to which students have already been introduced are printed on cards. The card pack is shuffled, then placed face down on the table. Two players take turns turning up the top card. If the player can give a derivative that contains the word part on the card, he or she may keep the card. If not, the other player tries to supply the derivative. If that player fails, the teacher or another student is asked to supply the derivative, and the card is returned to the bottom of the pack. The player with the greater number of cards when all the cards have been taken wins.

For maximum learning value, the players can be invited to study the cards before the game starts and "arm" themselves with derivatives.

READING AID 97

Fill in the Spokes of a "Word Wheel"

Students draw on a sheet of paper, or on the board, the hub of a "word wheel" and spokes radiating from it. They write on the hub a productive word part—*multi-,* meaning many, for example. Who in the class can fill in the most spokes with derivatives of *multi-*? It's fair to consult a student dictionary. Soon words like these are radiating in all directions from the hub: *multitude, multiply, multimillionaire, multicellular, multicolored, multiform, multilingual,* and perhaps even *multitudinous*.

READING AID 98

"Doctor Up" Your Vocabulary!

"Doctoring up" one's vocabulary, in the way suggested on Master Copy Pages 4–6, should appeal to advanced students who are seriously bent on expanding their vocabularies. The lively lesson on the master copy is intended for capable high school upperclassmen.†

*Ida L. Ehrlich used this catch-phrase as the title of a book on building vocabulary through Greek and Latin word parts. The book is *Instant Vocabulary* (New York: Pocketbooks, 1968).

†The chapter, "How to Talk About Doctors," in Norman Lewis, *Word Power Made Easy*, suggested this exercise (Garden City, N.Y.: Doubleday and Co., Permabooks, 1953), pp. 45–72.

SEE MASTER COPY PAGES 4-6

The names of medical specialists are derived from Greek and Latin and, in many cases, have within their names productive Greek and Latin roots–*psych,* meaning mind, in *psychiatrist; cardi,* meaning heart, in *cardiologist; gyn,* meaning woman, in *gynocologist.* In the lesson on the master copy, the students "doctor up" their vocabularies by learning—and using—roots like these as a key to unlocking other English words.

Students can *see*—and be impressed with —their quick vocabulary growth through a lesson like this. And there's a fun element in it, too!

The lesson on the master copy may suggest to readers their own original ways of providing practice with word parts. They will want to match the difficulty of the word parts and of the derived words to the students in the groups most carefully. A number of other possible formats for practice exercises are suggested in the companion volume (Thomas and Robinson, *Improving Reading in Every Class,* unabridged 2nd ed., 1977), pp. 41–48.

Teasers

READING AID 99

After students have studied the word parts (mostly Greek and Latin) that are involved in the words, they might try to puzzle out the following teasers. These particular teasers were used in upperclass honors groups:

> Mr. Chubbs, five feet tall and five feet around, was nicknamed "Mr. Five-by-Five." Was this a *misnomer?*
>
> You open your billfold and find just the *centesimal* part of a dollar. How much do you have?
>
> If you are *prescient,* are you a sharp second-guesser?
>
> Your teacher calls on you, and you answer in *circumlocutions.* Do you go straight to the point?
>
> Would you have a good time in a sailboat with *mal de mer?*
>
> Is "the man on the flying trapeze" likely to be an *acrophobe?*
>
> The scholar was completely misled by some *pseudepigrapha* supposed to have been written by the English poetess, Christina Rossetti. What does *pseudepigrapha* mean? (Note the Latin root *graph,* which means write.)
>
> In our class have you learned some impressive *polysyllabic neologisms?*

A Sesquipedalian "Fun-Break"

READING AID 100

Capable upperclassmen who enjoy verbal fun might like to puzzle out the meaning of the expression, a *sesquipedalian word.* With guidance, they can reason out the meaning of this "fun" word from the Latin parts, *ped,* meaning foot, and *sesqui,* meaning one-and-a-half. They will enjoy learning that the present-day meaning of *sesquipedalian* is "extremely long" (it refers to long words), that *sesquipedalian* itself is a *sesquipedalian* or "foot-and-a-half-long" word, and that if they use long words, they themselves are *sesquipedalianists!*

The following "word champ" with its forty-five letters, the longest word listed in *Webster's New Third International,* is not for the faint-hearted: *pneumonoultramicroscopicsilicovolcanokoniosis.* With guidance, students can probably arrive at the pronunciation. Again with help, they can break the word into parts and probably arrive at this fairly close meaning: a [miner's] disease of the lungs caused by ultramicroscopic particles of silicate dust from volcanic rock. (Students will need a helping hand with *koni,* meaning dust, and *osis,* meaning disease.) Some sharp student will probably exclaim, "It's the same as silicosis!"

According to the *Guinness Book of World Records,* the longest word in common use in English is *disproportionableness* with its mere twenty-one letters (also found in *The Oxford English Dictionary).* Sharp "word analysts" will figure out that it means the state of being unable to be in proportion!

Learning New Words through Word Origins

Working with the origins of selected words, incidentally, as students meet them in reading or in planned activities, can have important values.

A Not-to-Be-Forgotten Story Can Fix the Meaning in Mind

READING AID 101

The romance and excitement of word origins can help create word enthusiasts. And interesting derivations can become "memory pegs" for students as they work to retain meanings. Dorothy Piercey (1976, p. 10) suggests how this might easily happen with the word *mnemonic:*

> If you did not know the word *mnemonic,* would it help if you were told this story? Mnemon was a companion of Achilles, the man with the vulnerable heel who supposedly also had a memory problem. The main reason Achilles kept Mnemon around was to be his memory. Mnemon, in fact, means mind or memory, thus our word *mnemonic* [meaning helping the memory or a memory helper].
>
> Hopefully you would be reminded of this story when you saw the visual stimulus *mnemonic* and would pull the story from your storehouse and be reminded that *mnemonic* means memory helper.

The word *preposterous,* too, has a lively story. Within this word, *pre* and *post,* meaning before and after, stand side by side—are juxtaposed. This is obviously "contrary to reason, absurd, ridiculous"!

A Word's Story Can Enrich the Meaning

READING AID 102

The story of the word *excruciating* creates a vivid and lasting picture and gives the word rich overtones. The ancestor of the word *excruciating* is the Latin root *crux* or *cruc,* meaning cross. The word means intense pain or anguish, pain as agonizing as if you were dying—nailed to a cross! All of that agony is caught in the word *excruciating!* Students who have learned this story are more likely to feel the power of the word and to interpret and use the word with precision.

Students should learn *where* in their dictionary they can locate information about a word's derivation—they will find it enclosed in brackets in the dictionary entry. Those who learn to note and use this often curious and fascinating information have acquired one more permanently usable tool for vocabulary expansion.

A list of fascinating source books useful to teachers as they plan work on word origins will be found in the companion volume (Thomas and Robinson, *Improving Reading in Every Class,* unabridged 2nd ed., 1977), p. 57.

Developing Dictionary Competence—A Must

The "ideal product" of the vocabulary program runs to the dictionary for the fun of learning about a word. When students learn to make appropriate, frequent, and enthusiastic use of the dictionary, they have a tool to keep their vocabularies growing—for life.

In order to use the dictionary efficiently, students will need the following skills and understandings, often—many times not justifiably—taken for granted:

1. The dictionary is the students' check on a meaning and pronunciation they have tentatively arrived at through their vocabulary and word attack skills. And it is the place to turn if, after applying these skills, the meaning of the word still resists them.
2. Students should be able to *find* the word they want quickly—to open the dictionary to the appropriate section and to use their knowledge of the alphabet to arrive at the word.
3. They should be able to use guide words as "speed devices" for locating the word.
4. Students should understand that inflected word forms will not ordinarily be found as dictionary entries. They should be able to analyze inflected forms and to identify the root word that *will appear* as the dictionary entry.
5. The dictionary usually offers students their choice of a number of definitions. They should not select the first one their eyes light upon, as students are likely to do—or the easiest—or the shortest—but they should search for the best fit in view of the context. Day-to-day practice, tied in with live reading situations, is usually required before students habitually select the meaning that fits into the context setting.

A more complete enumeration of essential dictionary skills will be found in the companion volume (Thomas and Robinson, *Improving Reading in Every Class,* unabridged 2nd ed., 1977), p. 59.

Simplified Dictionaries Should Be Standard Equipment

READING AID 103

A supply of multilevel dictionaries within a classroom is highly desirable in vocabulary development. Many middle school and high school students become lost in adult dictionaries—in the writer's experience, student dictionaries are far more useful for all except capable upperclassmen. What is gained if a seventh-grader who is deficient in vocabulary looks up the word *renunciation* and finds the meaning given as the *act of repudiating*? This student should be guided to an appropriate student dictionary. Many student dictionaries offer an added advantage—they provide clear model sentences that help the students *use* their new words with precision.

A list of simplified dictionaries intended for students is included in the companion volume (Thomas and Robinson, *Improving Reading in Every Class,* unabridged 2nd ed., 1977), p. 59. Two widely used dictionaries from that list are:

Thorndike-Barnhart Intermediate Dictionary, 2nd ed. Glenview, Ill.: Scott, Foresman and Co., 1975. Grades 4–8.

Thorndike-Barnhart Advanced Dictionary, 2nd ed. Glenview, Ill.: Scott, Foresman and Co., 1974. Grades 9–12.

Since the dictionary is a lifetime tool for growth in reading, and since group work is sometimes desirable, schools should do their utmost to provide sets of student dictionaries for English and reading classrooms—if sets for each room are unobtainable, at least one set that can be moved from classroom to classroom.

"Find What You're After–Fast!"

READING AID 104

Teachers who see their students turning idly through countless dictionary pages "on their way to" a word can help to make those students dictionary speedsters. Brief mini-lessons should help:

> Can you locate the word you're after—*fast*? Can you open your dictionary close to the very page you want?
>
> You'll find words faster if you divide your dictionary into fourths. What letters of the alphabet do you think you'll find in the beginning quarter? [After examining the dictionary, the students may decide on *a* through *d*.] What letters in the second quarter? [The students may decide on *e* through *l*.] The third quarter? [*m* through *r*.] The last quarter? [*s* through *z*.] You'll find words faster if you memorize the letters that begin these quarters—*e* and *m* and *s*.

Josephine Rudd (1962, p. 130) suggests follow-up practice like this:

> In which part of the dictionary would you look for each of the following words? Write the number 1, 2, 3 or 4 on the line beside each word to show the quarter of the dictionary in which the word may be found:

_______ twirl	_______ marlin
_______ chalk	_______ damage
_______ glamor	_______ nomad
_______ unleash	_______ lunge
_______ knack	_______ gesture
_______ wriggle	_______ ogre
_______ overcast	_______ degree

Classroom sets of dictionaries open up opportunities for live—and lively—practice with actual dictionaries. Students can record their speed, or compete in speed, as they try to open their dictionaries directly to the proper section and make full use of guide words to locate the word they're after.

ABCs–To Find Words Quickly

READING AID 105

Some students need to sharpen their alphabet skills to the point where they can use alphabetical order—even to the fourth or fifth letter—to locate a word quickly. They might practice alphabetizing words in which they must work with the second and third letters, then move on to practice that involves even finer discriminations (Rudd, 1962, p. 130):

> The four words in each row across begin with the same three, four, or even five letters. Number the four words in each row to show the order in which they appear in the dictionary:

_______ quite	_______ quilt	_______ quit	_______ quiet
_______ initiate	_______ initial	_______ initiative	_______ iniquity
_______ magnificent	_______ magnolia	_______ magneto	_______ magnify
_______ retreat	_______ retrench	_______ retract	_______ retroactive

The practice words above are just "samples." Practice with more than a few words may be called for.

Are You A Dictionary Dawdler?

READING AID 106

After opening the dictionary, many high school students dawdle on their way to a word. Some fail to make any use at all of guide words. A mini-lesson can increase the speed of "dictionary dawdlers":

> Are you a dictionary dawdler? Or can you find the word you're after—*fast?* What aids does your dictionary provide to speed you? [Some students suggest the guide words.] Why does a word appear in heavy print at the upper left of the page? At the upper right? [For some students it is a revelation that these words represent the first and the last word on the dictionary page.]
>
> How are these words a speed device? [Some student might answer: "You skim until you find the two that your word falls between, according to the alphabet. These guide words will flag you."]
>
> Yes, some guide words tell you, "Speed right on past these pages." Others tell you, "This is the page you're after." In that case, flash your eyes down the page to find the word you want.

Again, if classroom sets of dictionaries are available, groups can have live practice. Students might record their speed or compete in dictionary races as they make full use of guide words to find what they're after—*fast.*

If a classroom set of dictionaries is not available, practice with guide words can, as Shepherd (1973, p. 75) suggests, be simulated:

> Under line the words in Column B which would be found on the page of the dictionary indicated by the guide words in Column A.

Column A		*Column B*		
1. come	—command	comedy	companion	comfort
2. frank	—free	fret	freckle	fraud
3. spread	—sputnik	sprout	squat	sport
4. hinder	—historic	Hindu	hoist	hitch
5. plan	—plaster	plasma	plantation	plane

These again are just a few sample questions. Additional practice may be called for.

"Why, It's Not in the Dictionary!"

READING AID 107

Students sometimes run to their teacher and exclaim, "Why, the dictionary doesn't have this word! I just looked it up, and it isn't there!" They have probably looked for an inflected word as a main entry. Apparently they have no idea that they can locate the word under another form. Since reading selections *abound* in inflected forms, these students will often be blocked in using the dictionary unless they have these basic understandings:

1. The form in which they meet a word in reading may not be the form in which they will find it in the dictionary.
2. Inflected forms (forms ending in *-s, -es, -'s, -ed, -ing, -er, -est)* will not ordinarily appear as first entries in the dictionary. Neither will some forms with suffixes.
3. Students will need to analyze the inflected form, or the form with the suffix, and *identify the root word that will be found as a first entry.*

Students should understand, for example, that *dories* will not be a dictionary entry, but *dory* will; that *jostling* will not, but *jostle* will; that *parried* will not, but *parry* will; that *agilely* probably will not, but *agile* will; *muggiest* will not, but *muggy* will; *surliness* may not, but *surly* will. They should know that in working out the meaning of a word like *ultrasophisticated,* they will need to distinguish the two parts *ultra-* and *sophisticated,* look up the meaning of the prefix *ultra-,* then mentally combine the meanings of *ultra-* and *sophisticated.*

Practice in which the student identifies the root word in words that come up in natural reading situations, then actually locates the word in the dictionary will be meaningful and useful. Now there should be fewer "lost words"!

Can You Tune in on the Right Meaning?

READING AID 108

Students often lose their way among the confusing array of meanings the dictionary offers for a word they have encountered. Frequent opportunities occur in classrooms to help them "tune in" on the right meaning.

An example that holds a surprise for the students can drive home the importance of "tuning in":

> Although Mr. Grimes was handsome, brilliant, and wealthy, he was the most simple, *homely* person we know.*

The student wonders, "How can Dr. Grimes possibly be both handsome and homely at the same time?" But when they "tune in" on meaning number three below, they are no longer puzzled:†

> **home ly** (hōm′lē), *adj.*, **-li er, -li est. 1** not good-looking; having ordinary appearance or features: plain. See **ugly** for synonym study. **2** suited to home life: simple; everyday: *homely pleasures. homely food.* **3** of plain manners: unpretentious: *a simple, homely man.* —**home′li ness,** *n.*

Even more striking evidence for the need for "tuning in" on the right meaning is found in this classic example:

Mother was found in a bottle.

Of course, this particular mother was found in a vinegar bottle!

Practicing "Fine Tuning" with Dictionary Meanings in Content Subjects

READING AID 109

Teachers of content area courses sometimes see students blocked in comprehending passages when familiar words turn up with completely new meanings—specialized meanings in that particular subject field. *Belt,* for example, turns up with a new meaning for geography students in the phrase "belt of vegetation." Teachers will want to seize every opportunity to help students use the dictionary to remove such blocks.

*Sentence adapted from Richard Corbin, Marguerite Blough, and Howard Vander Beek, *Guide to Modern English for Grade Nine* (Glenview, Ill.: Scott, Foresman and Co., 1960), p. 99.

†Dictionary entry from *Thorndike-Barnhart Advanced Dictionary* by E. L. Thorndike and Clarence L. Barnhart. Copyright © 1974 by Scott, Foresman and Co. Reprinted by permission.

One teacher introduced students to the concept of "fine tuning" with dictionary meanings when the word *host* turned up in biology in this sentence: "The oak tree is *host* to the mistletoe."

> Demonstrating with the dictionary, the teacher pointed out: "You see that in your dictionary the meanings for each word are numbered: 1, 2, 3, 4, 5, and so on. Just how can you select the right meaning from among all those?" The students suggest, "Choose the meaning that fits in with the thought."
>
> The teacher goes on: "Yes, you tune one of those numbered dictionary meanings into the context. It's like *doing fine tuning on your radio dial.* You move the 'pointer' along the dial, turning it carefully to the different numbers until one number brings in what you want exactly right."
>
> In their classroom dictionary the students now examine the numbered meanings for *host* until they "tune in" on meaning number three, which is just right for the context: "a living animal or plant that provides nourishment or lodging to a parasite."

Students may need to do "fine tuning" in sewing class for the word *nap* in the phrase "the *nap* of the fabric"; for *reduce* in mathematics in "*reduce* the fraction"; for *passing* in music in *passing note;* for *foot* in English in *poetic foot.*

"What Is Your P.Q.?"

READING AID 110

Many students—even top readers—do not know how to use the dictionary's pronunciation key. Many use it carelessly or not at all. In every classroom, teachers will find natural situations that are just right for helping students acquire this essential skill.

When students are having difficulty pronouncing new words, one classroom teacher of juniors prepares a ditto with the heading, "What Is Your P.Q.?" (Pronounciation Quotient). Then the teacher sets out to send that "P.Q." upward:

> "We've all felt embarrassed when, in a conversation, we've groped for a word, then faltered and trailed off because we couldn't pronounce it. Where can you find help in pronouncing a word that has a surprise twist in it—for instance, *d-e-v-o-t-e-e?"* (The word is printed on the ditto in a snatch of context.) The students, classroom dictionaries ready, respond that the pronounciation is "fenced in" by parentheses just after the word in the dictionary.
>
> "Please copy on your paper all the signs and marks that tell you how to pronounce *d-e-v-o-t-e-e*." The students record after the word on the ditto the phonetic entry:
>
> a *devotee* of sports (dev′ ə tē′)
>
> "How can you be *positive* about how to pronounce each sound?" The students suggest the pronunciation key. Then the teacher "walks them through" the process of sounding out each syllable.
>
> Many students are likely to need help with the schwa sound (ə). The teacher points out, "This is one of the most frequent sounds in English—it occurs in *thousands* of words. Learn it, and you'll save yourself countless future trips to the pronunciation key."
>
> Students, surprisingly, may not understand the force of accent. Then they need an explanation: "Stress *most* strongly the syllable with the heavy accent mark. Stress *less* strongly—but still stress—the syllable with the lighter accent mark." Now the students try to pronounce *devotee*, accenting the syllables correctly. They might tap out the syllables on their desks with a pencil, the teacher explaining: "It's like a drumbeat—the heavy beat on the syllable with the heavy accent, and the lighter beat on the syllable with

the lighter accent." Finally, they blend the syllables together into a whole word with the correct accents. The teacher suggests, "Now say it again and again until you're comfortable forming the sounds."

All this for the word *devotee!* But now the students have an important new vocabulary tool, one that will enable them to pronounce difficult new words always. More "handle-with-care" words follow on the ditto, words whose pronunciation may be a surprise—words like *circuitous, scion, respite.*

Students should understand that the symbols in pronunciation keys differ from one dictionary to another and they should definitely have practice using dictionaries with different sets of symbols.

Students Should Learn to Remove the Blocks of Unfamiliar Allusions

READING AID 111

Students will encounter allusions to mythology, to Biblical passages, to characters in literature, to events in history—allusions with which they are completely unfamiliar. What a block to comprehension an allusion to the bed of Procrustes, to the prodigal son, or to meeting one's Waterloo will be to some students!

As we teach students to remove these obstacles for themselves, we might move from much support to less support. We might suggest: "You'll find a reference to the witches' Sabbath in your reading for tomorrow and one to the Eumenides. An unabridged dictionary or *Brewer's Dictionary of Phrase and Fable* will make these clear."

Students move toward independence in solving their "allusion" problems when they habitually consult an unabridged dictionary, *Brewer's Dictionary of Phrase and Fable,* the *Larousse Encyclopedia of Mythology,* and/or the *Oxford Classical Dictionary*—all "gold mines" to help them understand allusions.

Students Need On-Their-Own Techniques for Learning and Retaining Words

In this chapter, we have considered a number of methods that students can use to expand and enrich their vocabularies—making full use of context as an aid in reasoning out meanings, using structural analysis to unlock meanings, using word origins to "fix" and enrich meanings, turning to the dictionary as a lifelong tool. Of course, maturing readers should gradually move closer to independence in mastering new words. Let us now consider other ways through which students can promote their own long-term vocabulary growth and ways by which they can retain their newly acquired words permanently.

Key Terms Should be "Collector's Items"

READING AID 112

Teachers in subject classrooms want students to develop on-their-own competence in mastering the key technical terms of the course. They will wish to alert students, early in the course, to the way the authors of their textbooks alert them to important "official" terms, to the fact that authors usually flag students with a conspicuous signal and that the signal may be heavy black, or boldface, type—or it may be italics or color. One way to alert students to the signals used in their own textbook is suggested in Reading Aid 216. Guidelines to place in the hand of students for mastering "official" vocabulary will be found on Master Copy Page 32.

Teachers in subject classrooms may want to encourage students to make a record of important terms for special study—to write selected words and their meanings on small vocabulary slips, in a notebook, or perhaps on a "divided-page." A simple word slip like the one shown in Figure 3–4 is a handy means of recording terms for special study. Another handy device is the "divided-page," which appears on Master Copy Page 7. Both vocabulary slips and the "divided-page" invite the student to put to use "the most powerful study technique"—self-recitation (Pauk, p. 25). The student exposes the term and conceals the meaning while self-reciting the meaning, not by rote but with full appreciation of the content. Mastery will be faster and firmer if the student puts into practice the retention techniques offered in Reading Aid 113.

SEE MASTER COPY PAGE 7.

Give Students Do-It-Yourself Retention Techniques

READING AID 113

Students exclaim to their teachers, "I study new words and then forget them! How can I retain the meanings?" Let us consider some powerful do-it-yourself retention strategies.

Some students, as they attempt to master new words, passively reread the words and their definitions. They will do firmer, faster learning if they not only read but also *say* and *write* the new words and their meanings. According to Ekwall (1977, p. 45), research done by the Socony Vacuum Oil Company suggests that we tend to remember an impressive 90 percent of what we say as we *do* a thing, 70 percent of what we say as we *talk* and reinforce our learning, 50 percent of what we *see and also hear,* and only 10 percent of what we simply *read or hear*. While individuals differ in the strengths of their various sensory learning channels, the message for most learners is "See it! Say it! Hear it! Draw or write it!" (Dudycha, p. 96)

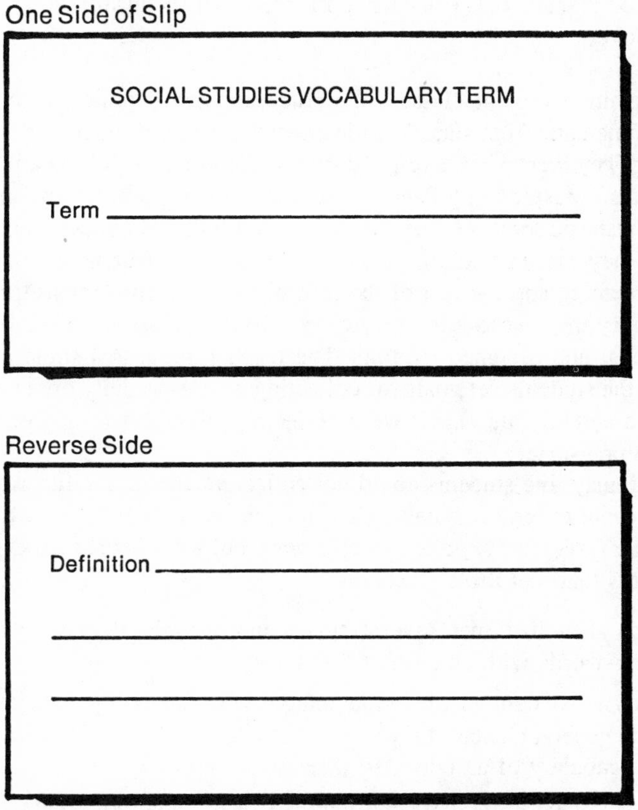

One Side of Slip

SOCIAL STUDIES VOCABULARY TERM

Term ______________________________

Reverse Side

Definition ______________________________

____

____

FIGURE 3–4

Vocabulary slips encourage "do-it-yourself" mastery of important terms.

Students can be introduced to the powerful V.A.K. technique:

> You can put new words on instant call through powerful retention techniques. Why not use triple-strength learning? If you learn words with your eyes alone, you're using just one-third of your possible learning channels. Why not employ all-out V.A.K. learning—*V*isual, *A*uditory, and *K*inesthetic?
>
> 1. Use your eyes as you *see* and reread the word and definition.
> 2. *Say* the word—aloud or whisper. This is powerful reinforcement. And *saying* the word helps it slide into your speaking and writing.
> 3. Strengthen learning with your ears as you *hear* yourself say it.
> 4. Add kinesthetic (muscular) learning as you *write* out the word and definition with, perhaps, an illustrative sentence.
>
> This is no longer relatively weak learning, through the channel of your eyes alone—it is *all-out, fully active, multi-sensory learning*. "See it! Say it! Hear it! Draw or write it!" is four-way reinforcement. The change of pace—eyes, voice, ears, pencil—keeps you alert and increases your "intake."

Personal Word-Collections Can Catch On

READING AID 114

A vocabulary program should help students become self-motivated, self-guided, and self-directed—knowing ways to help themselves and assuming responsibility for their own progress. Otherwise, they are left dependent, and their vocabulary growth will probably come to a standstill after high school and college. Let us now turn to a do-it-yourself vocabulary method that students can carry on for themselves during school days and after school days are over.

SEE MASTER COPY PAGE 8

In small reading improvement classes, the students were supplied with a word-kit in school colors (homemade from small manila envelopes) and trimmed with a sticker of the school pennant. They were also given a starter supply of colorful vocabulary slips (see Figure 3–5 and also Master Copy Page 8) printed on blue, pink, green, and canary ditto paper. In an enthusiastic send-off, the students were invited to collect on the slips important new words they met in reading (and from lectures, conversations, and television), then fill in the meaning and the rest of the information at a convenient time. They were encouraged to carry their word-kits everywhere—to their classes, to the library, to their homes for personal and assigned reading. The teacher suggested some exciting starter words. Some of the students set goals for collecting words—a daily quota or a number to be collected by a certain date. Their word-collecting, though strongly encouraged, was voluntary not compulsory.

Since, obviously, the students could not collect *all* the unfamiliar words they met, the group worked out criteria for making a selection. As a general rule, they would not collect rarities like *syzygy, zyzzogeton,* or *xylotomy,* but would consider as good "collector's items" words that met these standards:

1. Words they had met several times and thought they would meet again—words with an aura of familiarity;
2. Words in live contexts, in books, magazines, and newspapers intended for the general reader—they would know that these words should be in the vocabulary of an educated person;
3. Words related to their special interests or to their future careers;
4. Vivid, expressive words to give life to their conversation and writing.

The teacher stressed that filling in a word slip need not take undue time. The students would fill in the word's pronunciation *only if* it gave them trouble and the derivation *only if* it would help them remember the meaning. They would fill in their own example of the use of the word if they wanted the word to become part of their *active* vocabularies. Of course, they would *always* fill in the context in which they had found the word used and a careful statement of the meaning. To facilitate review of their new words, the students would print the word alone on the reverse side of the slip.

During the next few days the students brought in their finds and shared them. The teacher, too, brought "gifts" of exciting words for the collections. Part of the chalkboard became a colorful "wall of words." Here the students sometimes wrote in colored chalk a favorite word and taught it to the class, personalizing their contribution with their initials. At times the students were asked to give a password at the door—a new word and its meaning. A popular senior class president visited class and exhibited his own personal word-collection, which had reached shoebox proportions. The teacher often brought to class words from her own personal collection, an overflowing shoe box, thus suggesting to the students that educated adults keep their vocabularies growing. She often shared her excitement: "Here's a new word I've found!"

Our students put intense personal effort into trying for sports awards—why not for "words awards"? A teacher of summer reading improvement classes offered a prize to the student who, at the end of the session, had made the best personal word-collection. The prize was a popular paperback on developing a powerful vocabulary. Many years later a distinguished-looking gentleman walked up to this teacher in the lobby of a hotel in a great city: "I'm John B_____. You taught me one summer years and years ago! I won the prize for the best word-collection!"

Dr. Ruth Strang (1964) commented: "Some teachers report disappointing results from personal word-collecting. This should not happen if the students are taught how to use their collections." Most students will need to have their enthusiasm periodically re-kindled. An English teacher remarked: "When I make a big deal of the collections, the students do, too!"

One teacher reports: "I have seen students snatch another student's vocabulary slip and eagerly copy the information for their own collections." Nothing succeeds like the teacher's enthusiasm!

VOCABULARY SLIP

New word CAMARADERIE

Pronunciation kä′ mə rä′ də rē

Sentence in which you found it used The dorm was warm and friendly with a camaraderie among the students.

Derivation (if helpful) from French, camarade, meaning comrade.

Meaning the friendly spirit among comrades

Your example of its use There was a camaraderie around the campfire at night.

Students are invited to collect important new words on vocabulary slips like this one. Some of the students' word collections reach shoebox proportions.

FIGURE 3–5

The "No-Limit" Vocabulary Method

READING AID 115

A teacher of developmental reading classes aroused interest by printing on the chalkboard:

COMING SOON: THE "ABSOLUTELY-NO-LIMIT" VOCABULARY METHOD
LIFT YOUR VOCABULARY
TO ANY LEVEL YOU WANT!

When the day arrived, she gave an enthusiastic send-off to the method of personal word-collecting discussed in Reading Aid 114. Then she asked the class if they could point out some of the *pluses* of this vocabulary method. Here are the advantages the students suggested:

1. It's a personal method—*you* decide the words you want and need. It's a "perfect fit" for *you*—you can collect words related to your interests.
2. You can use your collection of word slips to self-recite and insure retention.
3. It makes you independent in vocabulary growth. You don't need commercial materials or a teacher. It's a lifetime method.
4. There's no limit—you can lift your vocabulary to any level you want!

"Use Bookmarks to Jot Down Words"

READING AID 116

SEE MASTER COPY PAGE 9

Students who enjoy reading for pleasure and like to become lost in a book may be "turned off" at the thought of interrupting their reading to fill out a word slip. Their teacher might suggest: "If you don't want to break your train of thought, check the word in the margin of your book or make a light pencil dot and record it on a word slip later. If you don't own the book, you might use a bookmark to jot down words you plan to work on later, together with the page locations where you can return and find the words in context." The reader will find inviting bookmarks on Master Copy Page 9.

A popular physics teacher (Kimmel, 1975), one with a broad personal interest in students, observed in his classes a need for general vocabulary improvement. So he designed an attractive bookmark as a stimulus. He suggested: "Just jot the new word on one of the spaces on the bookmark, together with its page location. Your writing 'page 9¼,' for example, would mean that you can find the word later on page nine, one-fourth of the way down the page. Then work on the word later—whenever you want to." Another class designed its own original bookmark, with space for both the words and their meanings.

Students' Word Slips Will Need Correcting

READING AID 117

As the students begin to collect words, their word slips are likely to contain errors. Teachers will want to correct the word slips and, if possible, prevent these errors. They will want to stress the importance of spelling the word entry correctly and of recording the context in which the students found the word and *enough* of that context. They may need to stress the fact that the brackets in the word's entry in the dictionary hold the word's derivation, *not a definition*. They will want to guide the students to record the definition *that fits the context*. They will want the students to become aware that a semicolon, not a comma, marks the end of a definition in the dictionary; otherwise the students may record just a fragment of a definition. When the students write original sentences on their word slips, the new words will often be used imprecisely. How to give students "secrets" of using difficult new words with precision is suggested in Reading Aid 119. The task of correcting the word slips need not be overwhelming. Correct for each student a few slips that contain representative errors.

"Play Word Solitaire!"

READING AID 118

Students can be invited to "play solitaire" with their word slips:

> It takes reviews to clinch retention. You've printed the new word at the top of the slip. Now play solitaire! Working with perhaps ten slips at a time, cover the meaning and look at the word. Ask yourself the meaning. Try to express it not by rote but with full appreciation of the content. Or test yourself the other way—by covering the word and looking at the meaning. Ask yourself the new word. Separate your word slips into an I-do-know pile and an I-don't-know pile. Gradually move the words into your I-do-know pile.
>
> Now do self-testing. Pull out a few slips and give yourself a test, using as "test questions" the words printed alone on the reverse side of your slips. Write the meanings and perhaps an illustrative sentence.
>
> Carry your word slips with you for odd-moment review—anywhere. You can have imaginary conversations with yourself—waiting for a friend, walking down the street—conversations in which you practice using each new word.

"How Can I Use This New Word?"

READING AID 119

When students practice using their new words in original sentences, they are strengthening their retention of the word and its meaning. And as they practice *actually using* their "finds," they become more fluent in speaking and writing. But it is often *extremely* difficult for young people to use their new words with precision. Often they ask their teachers, "Can you help me put this word into a sentence?"

Suppose Kerri has met the new word *trite* and knows vaguely that it means *overworked* or *worn out*. She wonders, "Can I use *trite* in a sentence about being overworked with too much homework?" Kerri needs to be given some rescue techniques. Her teacher can share these understandings:

> How can you be sure how to use a new word? Can you use *trite* to describe overworked students with a hundred math problems to do? You have two rescue techniques. First, use the clear, model sentences in your dictionary. [Kerri and her teacher look up *trite* and discover this sentence: " 'Busy as a bee' is a trite expression." They agree that here *trite* means overworked, yes, but that here it refers to a *verbal expression* that has lost its freshness.]
>
> You have another rescue technique when you are lost trying to use a new word. It's the signal in dark type, *syn.*, in your dictionary that guides you to the word's *shade* of meaning. [Kerri and her teacher find the *syn.* signal and examine the explanation for *trite* in the dictionary entry below:*

> **trite** (trīt), ***adj.*** [**TRITER** (-ẽr), **TRITEST** (-ist)], [L. *tritus*, pp. of *terere*, to rub, **wear** out], **worn** out by constant use; no longer having **freshness, originality**, or novelty; hackneyed; **stale: as, "busy as a bee" is** a *trite* expression.
> ***SYN.***—**trite** is applied to something, **especially an expression** or idea, which through **repeated use or application has lost its** original **freshness and** impressive force (e.g., "**like a bolt from** the blue"); **hackneyed** refers to such **expressions which through** constant use have become virtually meaningless (e.g., "last but not least"); **stereotyped** applies to those fixed expressions which seem invariably to be called up in certain situations (e.g. "I point with pride" in a political oration); **commonplace** is used of any obvious or conventional remark or idea (e.g., "it isn't the heat, it's the humidity"). —***ANT.*** original, fresh.

*With permission. From *Webster's New World Dictionary*, College Edition. Copyright © 1962 by The World Publishing Company.

Here Kerri finds confirmation that *trite* refers especially to a verbal expression that is worn out, *not* to worn-out students!]

Now Kerri has her answer. And she has acquired an important new vocabulary tool, one that will help her use difficult new words with precision always.

How to Crack Down on a Word

In this chapter we have considered a number of procedures for vocabulary improvement: using context clues, unlocking new words through Greek and Latin word parts, associating the current meaning with the derivation, consulting the dictionary, recording and reviewing words through a personal word collection. A student might ask, ''With which of these procedures should I react when I meet an unfamiliar word? Under what circumstances? In what order?''

READING AID 120

The following strategy suggests a sequence:

How to Crack Down on a Word

Crack down on an unknown word that blocks your comprehension instead of reading right on past the word without a try.

1. *Always search the context for clues first.*
   Through the context, you may catch overtones of meaning. As you do so, you develop a psychological ''set'' toward the word—you have ''laid'' the first layer of cement for fixing the term in your vocabulary.''
2. *Examine the word for familiar parts.*
   Take the word apart if you can. It may help to sound it out as best you can. Do you recognize any part? Guess all you can from any part you recognize. When you do discover a familiar part, your gain is usually great. Now you have a ''handle'' to take hold of the new word.
3. *Reach for the dictionary,* if Steps 1 and 2 haven't yielded all the meaning you want. Now here is where your vocabulary can improve dramatically. Recall any guess you made from context. Now verify or reject your guess. This order of things gives you full benefit of the mental set you created by previously trying to deduce the meaning. ''The more correct your guess proves to be, the more likely you are to remember the meaning. Nevertheless, if your guess is ridiculously wrong, you may find yourself less likely to forget the word than if you had not guessed at all.'' As you learn the meaning, try to associate the word with its derivation. The derivation is often rich with unforgettable associations.
4. *Record the word,* if it is one you wish to collect to work on further, on a word slip or in your vocabulary notebook. Space out reviews as needed. Now the new word should be yours—to stay.

The quoted material is from Shaw (1955, pp. 290–300.)

It should be noted that Steps 1 and 2 in the above sequence often overlap. Context clues and word part clues often impinge upon the student's understanding simultaneously.

Lively, Lighthearted Activities with Words

Vocabulary work offers an opportunity for a variety of lively, lighthearted activities, especially in English and reading class. Such activities create excitement about words and help to turn students into dedicated word collectors. Both troubled readers and top readers seem to respond to this lighter approach. The teacher's own enthusiasm for words has a chance to come through during all this fun fare. Activities from the teacher's "fun kit" offer a welcome change of pace.

"Pen Pals"

READING AID 121

Students select two or three words from those in a current lesson and write a "scribble-gram" to a classmate who sits nearby, working the new words into the note.* Such a note appears in Figure 3–5.

It's "fun fare" when the notes are read aloud and students are called on to try to give the meaning of each new word.

Word in the Spotlight

READING AID 122

Now and then a word might be spotlighted as the Word of the Day, a word especially timely at school on that particular day:

WORD IN THE SPOTLIGHT

accolade

Today in the Awards Assembly many students will receive *accolades.*

On "yearbook day" the word in the spotlight might be *memorabilia*: "Yearbooks are out today! On the pages you will find *memorabilia* of your years in high school."

Future Bernhardts Pantomime Words!

READING AID 123

After new words have had initial study, student volunteers can reinforce the meanings of certain ones through pantomimes. Students who have dramatic talent and can do this well are likely to volunteer. In reading classes, students have vividly pantomimed "a senior looking at a freshman with a *supercilious* expression," "a *regal* bearing," "*loquacious* students," "a *morose* expression," "a *lackadaisical* manner," "a *paroxysm* of giggles," "a *pugnacious* stance," "a hula-dancer's *sinuous* movements." After performing, the pantomine artist calls on a classmate to identify the word being pantomimed.

*Robert Potter coined the word "scribble-gram" and used it in *Writing Sense* (New York: Globe Book Co., 1975), p. 25.

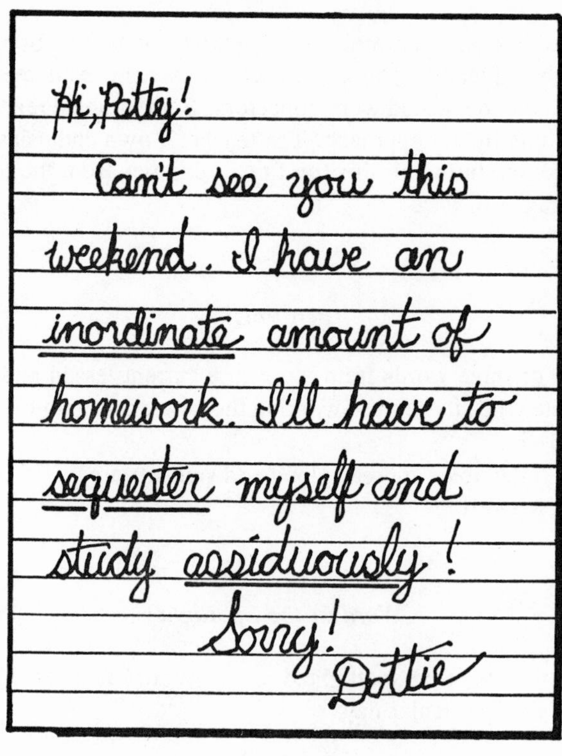
Hi, Patty!
Can't see you this weekend. I have an inordinate amount of homework. I'll have to sequester myself and study assiduously!
Sorry!
Dottie

FIGURE 3-6

Students can practice using their new words by writing a "scribble-gram" to a friend.

READING AID 124

"Mrs. Malaprop, How Could You!"

Capable upperclassmen are informed that Mrs. Malaprop in Sheridan's comedy, *The Rivals,* wanted her wealthy niece, Lydia Languish, to make the right marriage—also that Mrs. Malaprop is world famous for her blunders with words. These blunders are *malapropisms,* errors in which one word is mistaken for another similar in sound.

The teacher asks: "Can you correct Mrs. Malaprop's blunder? This is what she said:

'I don't want any daughter of mine to be a *progeny*!'
'This very day I have *interceded* another letter from her secret lover!'
'Alas, my *affluence* over my niece is small!'
'*Illiterate* your lover, Lydia, from your memory!' "

The students and the teacher might enjoy making up some malapropisms of their own: "Oh, how could you make such an *amphibious* statement!" "An *allegory* that had been sunning itself on a log splashed into the swamp." "At the wedding I wished them a long life of *martial* bliss!"

READING AID 125

"Would Your Ego Be Deflated?"

Using some of the words in the following list (or other descriptive words), upperclass honors groups are asked: Would your ego be inflated or deflated if someone described you in this way? Why?

cantankerous?	veracious?	obdurate?
sapient?	versatile?	indomitable?
supercilious?	scintillating?	articulate?
odious?	unctuous?	sagacious?
garrulous?	lackadaisical?	empathic?
beneficent?	scurrilous?	charismatic?

Of course, learning occurs during the discussion—very often lively learning.

"Try to Read My Mind!"

READING AID 126

This "mind reading" is really context clue reading. Using words from a group already studied, each student makes up a sentence, leaving a blank where one of the new words is to be inserted. Here is one student's sentence: "Diving into the swimming pool with your track shoes on would be ________________." The word in mind is *incongruous*. The student reads the sentence, then calls on a classmate to supply the word. If that student succeeds in filling the blank correctly, it becomes his or her turn to offer a sentence.

Here are some typical students' sentences:

Dave is a miracle shooting baskets. Our ________________ for him is "Mr. Magic." (*epithet*)

For lunch I had a ________________ double-burger, fries, and a coke. (*succulent*)

Diane ________________ Farrah Fawcett. (*emulates*)

Some students like to load their sentences with several new words and try to overwhelm their classmates.

Teachers Are People!

READING AID 127

The writer has included the following activity to share with the reader three thoughts: 1) We can create high-interest situations in which students practice reasoning out words from context clues; 2) An interesting bit of realia can help students retain the meaning of a difficult word; 3) A warm, close relationship with students can develop when teachers reveal themselves as people.

The writer brought to English class a bit of very personal realia, a Sigma Chi fraternity pin, and used it to help students discover the meaning of the "college prep" word *esoteric*. She showed the class the pin and commented: "The meaning of this pin is *esoteric*. Though it was a gift to me, I can never know its meaning! Only the Sigma Chis know the meaning of the white cross and the Greek letters. No one outside the fraternity can ever know! Again, the meaning of this pin is *esoteric*. Now can you puzzle out the meaning of *esoteric?*" Some of the students suggested, "Secret." Others suggested, "Known only to those who are 'in.' " The latter were delighted to find that the meaning that they had reasoned out was right on target—that the meaning in their classroom dictionaries for *esoteric* in this particular context was "known only to the inner circle."

Again, in the writer's experience, a warm, close relationship with students can develop when the teacher shares appropriate parts of his or her personal life, revealing the teacher as a person. Another *plus* is interest. The students in the example just given are almost sure to take interest in this very personal bit of information—a Sigma Chi had cared about their teacher!

References

Ames, W.S. "The Development of a Classification Scheme of Contextual Aids." *Reading Research Quarterly,* 2 (Fall 1966): 57–82.

Becker, Wesley C. "Teaching Reading and Language to the Disadvantaged—What We Have Learned from Field Research." *Harvard Educational Review,* 47, no. 4 (1977): 518–543.

Boettcher, Judith A. "New Concept Vocabulary: What Is It, and What Do I Do with It When I Find It?", unpublished manuscript, May 1979.

Bragstad, Bernice, reading consultant at LaFollette High School, Madison, Wisconsin, in remarks to the writer, May 1975.

Carroll, John B., Peter Davis, and Barry Richman. *American Heritage Word Frequency Book.* Boston: Houghton Mifflin Co., 1971.

Dale, Edgar, and Joseph O'Rourke. *The Living Word Vocabulary.* Elgin, Ill.: Dome, 1976.

Dallman, Martha, Roger L. Rouch, Lynette Y.C. Chang, and John J. De Boer. *The Teaching of Reading,* 4th ed. New York: Holt, Rinehart and Winston, 1974.

Davis, Frederick B. "Research in Comprehension in Reading." *Reading Research Quarterly,* 3, no. 4 (1968): 499–545.

Dudycha, George J. *Learn More with Less Effort.* New York: Harper and Row, 1957.

Durkin, Dolores. *Strategies for Identifying Words.* Boston: Allyn and Bacon, 1976.

Ekwall, Eldon. *Teacher's Handbook on Diagnosis and Remediation in Reading.* Boston: Allyn and Bacon, 1977.

Evans, Edna H., former English teacher at Phoenix College. Sentence contributed from vocabulary materials created for teenagers, 1972.

Gainsburg, Joseph C. *Advanced Skills in Reading,* Books 1, 2, 3. Teacher's annotated edition. New York: Macmillan Co., 1967.

Graves, Michael F., Department of Curriculum and Instruction, University of Minnesota, in conversation with the writer, April 1979.

Haehn, Faynelle, business education teacher at the University of Chicago Laboratory School, in remarks to the writer, January 1979.

Hill, Walter R. *Secondary School Reading: Process, Program, Procedure.* Boston: Allyn and Bacon, 1979.

Hillocks, George, Bernard J. McCabe, and James F. McCampbell. *The Dynamics of English Instruction, Grades 7–12.* New York: Random House, 1971.

Johnson, Harry. The writer found this vivid example in notes she took years ago on readings about vocabulary. Can anyone write her the source so that credit can be given in the next edition? The date is approximate.

Karlin, Robert. *Teaching Reading in High School,* 3rd ed. Indianapolis: Bobbs-Merrill Co., 1977.

Kimmel, Richard, former physics teacher at the University of Chicago Laboratory School, in remarks to the writer, July 1975.

Lynch, Elizabeth K., former social studies teacher at Neshaminy Langhorne High School, Langhorne, Pennsylvania, in remarks to the writer, January 1978.

McCallister, James A., in remarks to the writer, July 1957.

McCullough, Constance. "The Recognition of Context Clues in Reading." *Elementary English Review,* 22 (January 1945): 1–5.

Muelder, Richard, mathematics teacher at the University of Chicago Laboratory School, in remarks to the writer, January 1979.

Niles, Olive Stafford, Mildred Dougherty, and David Memory. *Reading Tactics A.* Glenview, Ill.: Scott, Foresman and Co., 1977.

Pauk, Walter. *How to Study in College.* Boston: Houghton Mifflin Co., 1952.

Piercey, Dorothy. *Reading Activities in Content Areas.* Boston: Allyn and Bacon, 1976.

Quealy, Roger J. "Senior High School Students' Use of Contextual Aids in Reading." *Reading Research Quarterly,* 4 (Summer 1969): 512–533.

Robinson, H. Alan. *Teaching Reading and Study Strategies: The Content Areas,* 2nd ed. Boston: Allyn and Bacon, 1978.

Ryder, Randall J. "Teaching New Meanings for Words." *Minnesota English Journal,* 9 (Fall 1978): 29–41.

Shaw, Philip B. *Effective Reading and Learning.* New York: Thomas Y. Crowell Co., 1955.

Singer, Harry. "Teaching Word Recognition Skills." In *Handbook for the Volunteer Tutor,* edited by Sidney J. Rauch. Newark, Del.: International Reading Association, 1969. Graph reprinted with permission of Harry Singer and the International Reading Association.

Stauffer, Russell G. *Teaching Reading as a Thinking Process.* New York: Harper and Row, 1969.

Strang, Ruth, in lecture to class in the teaching of secondary school reading, University of Chicago, summer 1965.

Strang, Ruth, Constance M. McCullough, and Arthur E. Traxler. *The Improvement of Reading,* 4th ed. New York: McGraw-Hill Book Co., 1967.

Thomas, Ellen Lamar, and H. Alan Robinson. *Improving Reading in Every Class,* 2nd ed. Boston: Allyn and Bacon, 1977.

Weir, Marie C., former biology teacher at Balboa High School, Balboa, Canal Zone, in remarks to the writer, January 1979.

Improving Comprehension

Some Ways to Help Your Students Comprehend

Must troubled readers face one failure after another—day after day? Must top readers mark time in comprehension? Here are some possible ways to help both your best and poorest readers comprehend more effectively in your classroom tomorrow.

What happens when, day after day, Danny, a troubled reader, tries his assignments, then puts the book down with "Too hard for me"? There may be a chain reaction: anxiety that makes it difficult to concentrate—fear of being exposed as a poor reader—fear of even trying—losing out on practice and dropping even farther behind—feeling the disapproval of parents—feeling himself a failure in the eyes of his teachers and classmates—developing a negative self-concept—regarding school as a place where he will always fail. What, on the other hand, may happen when a teacher helps Danny toward reading success? With time, some of his anxiety may drop away, discouragement may give way to hope. He may take hold, try once more, and begin to grow in reading. As his sense of failure begins to fade, he may develop a more positive self-concept. He may decide that there is something to value between the covers of a book, and he may succeed better in the broader school situation.

Bringing solid improvement to students like Danny will, most assuredly, not be easy. But suppose *all* his classroom teachers, and the remedial reading teacher, deliberately plan for Danny day-to-day experiences of success and approval in and through reading. Their combined efforts should, with time, bring worthwhile reading progress.

How can a classroom teacher, untrained formally in teaching reading, come to the aid of students like Danny? This chapter shares ways classroom teachers have found useful in helping troubled readers comprehend more effectively, ways that do not require special expertise in teaching reading.

The activities shared on the coming pages are, for the most part, straight-from-the-classroom examples, and the students involved are flesh-and-blood students. The writer hopes that you find some of the ideas suggestive as you generate your own effective ways to help your troubled readers. You will find much overlapping of types of reading aids.

Of course, when top readers are confronted with extremely difficult reading, they, too, become "troubled." The procedures that follow will help your gifted readers, too, to stretch their comprehension and handle successfully material that would otherwise have been beyond them.

Under-par readers are often blocked by deficiencies in the areas of word attack and vocabulary. Helps for readers who have these deficiencies have been offered in the preceding chapters.

On the pages that follow, you will notice an emphasis on *pre*-reading activities. According to the writer's observation, a number of teachers may not fully realize the advantages to be gained from helping students *before* they read a difficult selection. Carefully planned *pre*-reading activities can be of special value because they help *develop* comprehension. Many *post*-reading activities merely *check* comprehension.

Not all of these types of activities should be part of all assignments for all readers, and, of course, students should not become overly dependent on their teacher. The goal is to accommodate students' reading abilities and facilitate their success in reading while gradually leading them from dependence on the teacher to *independence*. (Graves, Palmer, and Furniss, 1976, p. 3)

Finding Out about Their Reading

What are your students' strengths in reading and the blocks in their way?

Standardized Test Scores May Be Yours for the Asking

READING AID 128

Your school may already have on file recent standardized reading test scores which, as school opens in the fall, are yours for the asking. These can give you rough initial insights about each student's comprehension and suggest the range in reading strengths you have among your students. A classroom teacher suggests jotting these scores in your class record book "as a first step in getting acquainted" (Flickinger, 1969). You will, however, wish to supplement—and often supplant—the impression given by standardized test scores with more helpful information.

Teachers may wish to do their own testing when recent scores are not available. The Gates-MacGinitie Reading Test is widely used by middle schools and high schools, and the Cooperative Reading Test by high schools and junior colleges:

> Gates-MacGinitie Reading Test (Houghton Mifflin Company): Level D intended for grades 4–6, three forms; Level E for grades 7–9, three forms; Level F for grades 10–12, two forms. *This test offers scores in vocabulary, in comprehension, and in speed and accuracy.*
>
> The Cooperative Reading Test (Cooperative Test Division, Educational Testing Service): Lower Level intended for grades 9–12; Upper Level intended for superior students in grades 11 and 12 and for college freshmen and sophomores; two forms. *This test offers subscores in vocabulary, level (power) of comprehension, and speed of comprehension. The content is fairly difficult study-type material.*

But How Well Can Your Students Read Their Actual Course Materials?

READING AID 129

But how well can your students handle the materials you will actually assign them? How well can they answer questions on their reading of the type you will expect them to answer all year? You are not at all certain from the standardized test score—your course assignments will differ so greatly from the content on the test!

Why not let your students complete a typical reading assignment right in class, where you can observe them at work, and test their comprehension? Once constructed, your "homemade" test may be usable for several years.

Select for your test a passage from your actual course materials, ideally of the difficulty and length that you will be assigning students for reading on their own outside of class. If the students cannot complete that much within a class period, select for your test just a section of such an assignment—1,000 words should provide an adequate sample. If all of your students have the book, you will not even need to duplicate the passage. Your students can be asked simply to turn to a certain page and begin when you give the signal.

You might give directions something like these: "We'll use the information we get today to help you have a good year. Please study this passage right here in class as if it were an assignment for our class. When you've finished, you will have some questions. You may make notes as you study, and you may use your notes as you answer the questions. Raise your hand as soon as you finish, and I'll bring you the questions."

As the students raise their hands, jot down their names, inconspicuously, in the order in which they finish. In this way you will have a list that suggests which students in the class may be the more rapid readers, the average readers, and the slower readers. Obviously, you do not have an index of "pure" speed of reading since the students spent some of their time making notes. (If you wish to know each student's rate in words per minute, you can obtain it as suggested in Reading Aid 237.)

Your checkup on your students' comprehension might begin with one free response question: "What, in the main, did the author say?" or "Just write a summary of the main points." Add questions, perhaps short-answer questions, that call for skills you know will be important for your reading assignments all through the year—skills like finding the main idea, grasping directly stated details, seeing relationships, making inferences and generalizations, understanding character portrayal, recognizing the writer's tone and bias, and other competencies needed to achieve in your course. (If you want to assess recall as well as comprehension, you will ask your students to answer these questions without referring back to the selection and you will not have them take notes.) If you wish to explore vocabulary strengths, you can list key words together with their page locations and ask: "What do these words mean *as they are used in the passage?*" Here, of course, the student is permitted to refer back to the selection.

Care must be taken lest students regard this important diagnostic test as "just another quiz." They should feel that their teacher is sincerely interested and eager to help. The purpose of the test should be made quite clear: "We'll use this information to help you have a good year."

Observe your students while they are working. If Tim, as he tackles the assignment, moves his lips and head as he reads and appears to be struggling with many of the words, you have learned something about his reading ability. If Melinda reads for awhile, then stops several times to gaze out the window, you have acquired insights about her "study techniques." (Robinson, 1978, p. 37)

All the students should hand in their notes. The quality of the jottings in their notes, their answers to your questions, the time it took them to complete the task, plus your observations while they are studying should provide you with some useful insights:

1. Can individual students discriminate between main ideas and subordinate material?
2. Can they take notes effectively?
3. Can they summarize their reading?
4. How well can they handle factual questions?
5. How well can they handle inferential questions?

6. How rapidly did they study the material?
7. Are the students' vocabularies equal to the passage?
8. Can they handle material of this difficulty, or does it appear to be beyond them? How much pre-reading instruction should they have from you in order to handle it?

Test papers can be returned to the students and used as a springboard for sessions on how to read and study. It is probably best not to assign a grade to these papers but simply to note strengths and needs. Students who performed well can be asked to share their "success secrets."

Teachers in search of patterns to follow in making informal tests for assessing students' abilities to succeed in their actual courses will find these in abundance in Ruth J. Viox, *Evaluating Reading and Study Skills in the Secondary Classroom* (Newark, Del.: International Reading Association, 1968). Ralph C. Preston and his colleagues offer practical suggestions in *Guiding the Social Studies Reading of High School Students* (Washington, D.C.: National Council for the Social Studies, 1963). A reading specialist may be available to assist less experienced teachers in preparing and interpreting teacher-made tests.

What dividends can you gain from finding out about your students' reading? *Insights to help you plan for their greater reading success* all through the year. Let us turn now to a number of ways to improve your students reading comprehension—and their learning in your subject as well.

Students Should "Meet Their Textbook"

Today's publishers are providing students with textbooks that have superior aids for reading and study. Many of these aids, however, will be lost on students. There is evidence that even superior students do not make good use of such aids unless they are given special instruction (Robinson, 1961, p. 30).

Students Should Learn to Use a Yearlong "Tool"

READING AID 130

Early in their courses, many teachers give time and thought to helping students use the physical tools of the course. In science class, we could not conceive of letting them use the tools of the laboratory without special training. We train them to use balances, micrometers, and centrifuges with precision. In contrast, in a number of classrooms, students are given little guidance in using that yearlong tool of learning—their textbook. Yet they may spend more hours over their textbook during a year than they will in the laboratory!

Time spent early in the year on a "meet your textbook" session—and throughout the year, as specific study aids are needed—should upgrade students' use of this important tool of learning and the caliber of their independent study—all through the year.

Students should come to know and *use* these study helps, when they are present, in their new textbooks:

- The table of contents, with its concise, sequential listing of major topics covered
- Preface, explaining the *why* of the book, its special viewpoint
- Introductory questions, when present, leading into the chapter
- Large-size or boldface headings that announce the content of a section

- Italics, boldface, or color used to signal "official" terms
- Italics, boldface, or color used to call attention to concepts, rules, or principles that should be learned and to flag these for easy reference
- Typographical danger signals of pitfalls to avoid
- Aids for pronouncing and accenting difficult new terms (if these aids are present)
- Graphic aids—pictures, graphs, charts, diagrams, maps, time-lines
- Lists of important concepts or terms to remember
- Chapter summaries that wrap up big ideas
- Self-check tests at the close of chapters and/or throughout chapters
- Suggested additional readings at the ends of chapters
- Glossary
- Index

Students should meet the following more specialized study aids, and others, when they are present in the textbooks of specific subjects: boxed excerpts from documents in social studies; biographical and anecdotal vignettes in science, social studies, and other courses; list of symbols for easy reference in mathematics.

Once these study aids have been pointed out to students in connection with a single chapter, the students should have them more readily at their command for *all* the chapters.

Students Can Experience some "Aid-less" Pages

READING AID 131

To dramatize the value of textbook aids to study, one teacher projected on a screen pages with all these aids removed. *Missing* from the page were signals of "official" terms, boldface headings, and so on. The class reacted to this "aidless" page. One boy commented: "It isn't friendly. It doesn't talk to you. It doesn't come to help you. You have to fight with it to get what's important." (Haehn 1979)

Good grades are powerful persuaders for students! Give one group of students an "aidless" selection to study, one you have duplicated with the study aids removed; give a second group the same selection with the study aids present. Time the reading, and give a test that reflects information highlighted by the aids. The results may "sell" textbook aids to students! As another possibility, simply tell the students that 50 percent of their test questions will reflect terms, concepts, and generalizations that are spotlighted by the reading-study aids in the chapter. (Ideas from Hill, 1979, p. 136)

Remove Roadblocks before Students Read

READING AID 132

As we sit down at our desks to plan a reading assignment, we might imagine ourselves as one of our own students, with the reading power, the background of school courses, and the life experiences of that student. Our thoughts might run like this:

> What are the "unmissable" learnings—those the students simply *must* take away from this reading? . . . What blocks will stand in their way? . . . What background do they lack? What gaps should I fill in? . . . This part will be obscure. How can I help them get through it? Would some guiding questions help? . . . What new concepts and terms are likely to block them? Should I remove some of these blocks before they

begin reading? . . . How can I give them something to look for as they read instead of turning them loose without a target?

This is high payoff instruction! We are helping discouraged readers take heart and preventing reading difficulties before they happen! It may very well be that time spent in *getting ready to read* is the most potent means of improving comprehension (Robinson, 1978, p. 84).

Help Students Step into Their Reading with a Mini-Preview

In today's literature on teaching reading, we often meet the term *advance organizer*. Psychologist David Ausubel (1960), who originated the term, asked himself, "What happens when students read a 'prestructuring' statement before they read a long passage?" To answer the question, he used a controlled study in which one group had the advantage of first reading a short introductory passage (500 words) that "ideationally organized" a longer passage (2500 words). The short statement mobilized relevant concepts already in the learner's mind, served as an anchoring focus for the reception of the new material, and made the new material more familiar and meaningful. What happened as a result? For many students, the use of advance organizers definitely upgraded student comprehension of principles, facts, and application—and aided retention, too. Few textbooks, Ausubel observed, come to the aid of students by providing prestructuring statements, and too few teachers provide advance organizers as they assign reading selections.

Let us now consider how we can help students "step into" their readings through our own creative organizers—how we can mobilize relevant material in the learner's mind and provide "an anchoring focus for the reception of the new material." Since advance organizers need not take much time, let us call them mini-previews.

A Simple Preview Can Upgrade Comprehension and Retention

READING AID 133

A simple preview of a coming unit or part of a unit—one that takes just a few minutes—can be a helpful advance organizer. Students read at a disadvantage when new work is simply taken up detail by detail with little thought of relating those details to the structure of the whole. Through a preview, the students can see the main concepts and principles in their relations to each other and to previous reading. The preview can take the form of a well-organized talk by the instructor—in most cases, it need not be a long talk (Butler and Wren, 1965, p. 134). In addition to helping the class view the total picture, the preview provides background understandings, and these, too, make for more effective reading.

A reading teacher who was helping social studies students comprehend a chapter on the making of the United States Constitution gave the class this advance organizer:

> The year was 1787. Kings were crushing the common man all over the world. Nowhere on earth was there a government "of the people." Thirteen little American colonies had amazed the world—they had won the Revolution. Then they had banded together under a loose government, the Articles of Confederation. Now there was almost chaos! The weak government was powerless to solve the nation's problems!
>
> A convention was called to strengthen the Articles of Confederation. It was a meeting of giants, Washington, Madison, Hamilton, Franklin. Clashes soon followed—small states against large states—slave states against free states. Knotty questions arose: How much power should the central government have? The states? How should the government be organized? What if one branch should become too powerful?
>
> Two opposing plans for the new government developed—the New Jersey Plan and the Virginia Plan. There was a clash over these plans—then a deadlock. Would the

Constitution *ever* become a reality? Would thirteen jealous states give up enough of their power so that a strong central government could be formed? This is the story of the birth of the only constitution in the world that starts "We the people."

Students Can Share Their Experiences to Form a Mini-Preview

READING AID 134

Students and their teacher can "brainstorm" about a subject they are to read about, reporting and sharing their personal experiences. Their pooled information can, like a more formal advance organizer, provide "an anchoring focus for the reception of the new material."

Karlin (1977, p. 119) offers the following suggestion for preparing science students for reading what is assigned in their science textbook on the subject of "Why Airplanes Fly":

> The students discuss take-offs and landings they have observed on visits to an airport. Those who have flown are encouraged to describe the aircraft and their flight briefly. The teacher may share some personal experiences.
>
> The teacher introduces a model airplane and demonstrates what happens when it is released, then challenges the students to try to explain the flight. The students respond on the basis of their experiences.

Dr. Karlin (1977, p. 118) suggests this time allotment—if the lesson is to be forty-five minutes long, perhaps five to ten minutes should be devoted to readiness.

A Preview of a "Coming Attraction"

READING AID 135

Television networks catch interest in coming attractions with intriguing previews. We might borrow this technique to catch students' interest in their coming readings.

Suppose a teacher realizes that the not-so-able readers will have difficulty getting into the exciting but fairly difficult adventure story, "Leiningen and the Ants." The teacher might catch up interest in the plot and have the students meet the characters and setting in an "advance organizer" something like the one that follows.

This mini-preview—it takes little more than a minute and a half to give it for a class—should send students into the story with a "set" to read better and faster (Graves, Palmer, and Furness, 1976, p. 14):

> You may have heard about the vicious killer bees which have been frightening South American natives. We're going to be reading about another South American menace, armies of flesh-eating ants. These ants plunder the countryside, devouring all vegetation and wildlife in their path. In just minutes after their attack, only bare bones and dead earth are left.
>
> In the story you'll read, one plantation owner, Leiningen, decides he can outwit the marauding ants and stop their seemingly inevitable onslaught. Leiningen has prepared for some time for the arrival of this terror. His plantation is entirely surrounded by water. Leiningen has ordered that all trees on both sides of the water barrier be cut down. Most of the people on his plantation are removed to remoter ground. Everything seems to be tipped in Leiningen's favor. Then Leiningen receives word that the ants are closing in on the tiny, water-surrounded enclosure. Leiningen rides out to take a firsthand look at his enemy. In the distance is a giant, black, crawling mass moving slowly and steadily toward the island sanctuary. For one day and a night Leiningen and his workers heroically keep the ants at bay. But on the afternoon of the second day, the ants break through and begin to cross the channel toward the helpless defenders. Find out how the ants were able to make the crossing and what happened to the defenders when you read "Leiningen and the Ants."

Previewing Can Help Students Step into a Difficult Novel

READING AID 136

Most high school students would have to stretch to comprehend the first few chapters of *Tess of the D'Urbervilles.* Let us look in on a class where the dialect barriers in *Tess* and the detailed description of the Vale of Blackmoor, a setting far away and long ago, might have created listless or lost readers. To create *momentum,* the teacher brought the theme of a brooding fate close to the lives of the students:

> In this novel Hardy concerns himself with fate and its dark influence over lives. What *is* fate? [The students share their thoughts.] Do you believe that fate controls *your* life? Do you believe that fate controls the grade you make in this course? Whether you will find the right man or the right girl? Whether you will find happiness in life or heartbreak? Do you believe that fate decrees the moment and the manner of your death—determines when "your hour has come"? Or do you believe that you, through your free will, rule your own destiny? [Classes can become quite excited talking this over.]

After a few minutes, the teacher turns to the opening of the novel with this mini-preview:

> In the opening chapters, we meet Tess, the heroine—a pretty country lass. There is a soft femininity and an air of trustfulness and innocence about Tess. At a May Day dance she attracts the eye and the lingering thoughts of a young student who is on a walking tour through the valley. Somehow he cannot forget this shy country girl in her soft white gown!
>
> Now in a novel by Thomas Hardy, fate is brooding. Suddenly Tess's father, a laborer, learns that he is descended from the noble family of D'Urbervilles! A high-born D'Urberville should not demean himself to work! Soon Tess's parents and her brothers and sisters are almost starving.
>
> Close to despair, Tess's mother remembers Tess and her beauty. She will send Tess to claim kinship with some wealthy D'Urbervilles in a nearby town. Perhaps Tess's beauty will attract a wealthy husband and save the family!
>
> But Tess's beauty and her innocence prove to be her ruin. Tess cannot escape a relentless Fate—it strikes one tragic blow after another.

The teacher reads aloud the opening chapter or two expressively, snipping away slow passages, then quickly weaving the parts together by telling the story. She closes with exciting questions—questions to *impel* the students to read on: "What character, whom you will soon meet, will be 'the tragic mischief' of Tess's life? What young man you have already met fleetingly will play a leading role? What will be the first cruel stroke of Fate?"

Students who are likely to become discouraged as they read on alone are offered these tips:

1. You're likely to encounter parts you do not understand. Keep reading! Chances are you'll understand again soon.
2. When you encounter dialect expressions, try to get the drift from the context. In passages with dialect the drift will be enough.
3. If you do not understand a part you think will be important, mark it to ask your teacher in class tomorrow.
4. Though some passages will seem difficult, push right on. You can probably get the drift of the story.

Suppose classes try *Tess of the D'Urbervilles* without this "advance organizing" and with only their teacher's directions: "Read the first two chapters." They may drudge through these chapters and close the book, turned off by *Tess of the D'Urbervilles* and, by contagion, turned off when they are assigned a similar classic. With an advance organizer, which requires just a class hour or two, the students are far better prepared to step into this difficult novel and read it on their own. The momentum created helps to take the students past the barriers. Now what might have seemed to be a musty, dusty tome from long ago promises a thought-provoking and a very human story.

Previewing, a "Must" for Documents

READING AID 137

Mini-previews are crucial in social studies when the readings at hand are primary sources. Presenting a document in its historical setting is, in Dr. Krug's view (1969, pp. 55–56), *the most important condition for the use of the document.* Some students have been given only this instruction: "For tomorrow read the Gettysburg Address." That's all! In contrast, other students have read this address after a sensitive teacher has taken them back more than a century—touched on Lincoln's anguish at the bloodshed he declared was "eating out his life"—pictured him hesitantly trying out his address on a colored servant, a friend in the White House, then making last-minute revisions on the train to Gettysburg—conveyed his deep desire to express his sincere belief in democracy, to inspire devotion to carry on the cause—pictured him stepping forward on the platform in his black suit and tall hat, his kind eyes on the cold, weary people—helped the students hear his slow, clear tones as he spoke of a "new birth of freedom," hear the polite but slight applause—made them aware of his conviction that his address had been a failure—and of the final verdict of history.

Building Bridges to Students' Concerns

What are young people caring about? How can we build bridges from reading to their close concerns and thus strongly *motivate* their comprehension?

We Can Build Bridges to Students' Emotional Experiences

One constant to fall back on, especially in English class, as we "build bridges," is the emotional experience of young people. "No matter how slow the class," observes a supervisor of student teachers, "the students will have some experience with hate, with fear, with loneliness: some bent . . . toward honor, toward courage, toward love." (Farrell, 1966, p. 44)

READING AID 138

In the following example, the teacher built a bridge to an emotional experience young people know well:

> The grade was 12; the time was anytime. Students were asked to define *love* in 5 minutes. . . . They were asked to jot down all ideas that came to them. Then they were asked to define lovers—in 3 minutes. The variety of responses, ranging from "an itch that can't be scratched" to "understanding each other in every possible way," intrigued the class. The examples of lovers ranged from peer couples to Romeo and Juliet. "West Side Story" was then discussed, and from there they proceeded to the reading of *Romeo and Juliet.* (Robinson, 1978, p. 69)

The reading teacher in the following example built a bridge to another emotional experience young people know well.

> High school juniors enrolled with the reading teacher for help walked into class one day discouraged. In English they had been assigned a group of poems, among them Shakespeare's sonnet that starts "When in disgrace with fortune." One boy exclaimed, "I don't know what it's saying!"

The teacher built the following bridge to the sonnet: "Emotional depths are part of our day-to-day living. We cannot escape them, nor could the world's greatest writer, Shakespeare. Think quietly about this: How do you feel when *you* are depressed? What dark thoughts come to your mind? Now please think about this: What, if anything, lifts you out of a mood of depression?"

Now the stage was set for Shakespeare's sharing of his deep depression—and the solace he found—in Sonnet 29. With guidance, the students now read the sonnet with comprehension. Now they felt a closeness to the poet. He, too, had felt alienated—had longed for someone else's appearance and talents—had almost despised himself—had found a valued human relationship his solace.

We Can Throw Students into Roles to which They Can Relate

READING AID 139

We can sometimes build a bridge by putting students inside the shoes and skin of one of the characters in a story or of a historical character, thus throwing them into a role, perhaps a dilemma, then asking the provocative question, "What would you do if *you* were in this situation?" An English teacher pondered this question: How to build a bridge that would span two thousand years from teenagers in blue jeans to Brutus in his agony of indecision about assassinating Caesar. In a high school where entering a top college was a first value, she posed this choice between what is right in terms of the larger good and personal loyalty to a friend who is about to harm others because of his ambition.

> Think quietly about this. Before you hear anyone else's answer, jot down your own personal reaction. Imagine you are a senior. You and your friends are going to college—it's important to you to go to college. Everyone has to take an exam—an exam crucial for you to enter the college you want, in fact to enter college at all, and it's graded on the curve. You've discovered that your best friend has secured the answers. If he cheats, it will definitely affect you and all the others in the class. If you report your friend, it's obviously going to affect him greatly. *What will you do and why?* [There is a lively exchange of "solutions." The students feel the torment Brutus is feeling.]
>
> In the coming play Brutus will face a similar dilemma—an even more painful dilemma because it involves the death of his friend. (McCampbell, 1979)

We Can Relate Reading to Things Cared About

READING AID 140

What are young people caring about? Their deepest concerns are expressed in "their" music—in sensitive and beautiful rock/pop lyrics: the generation gap—recurrent war—the agony of loneliness, of personal insecurity—the groping for solutions—the enigma of love (Larrick, 1971, p. 187). In remedial reading classes, students who shy away from print have listened to recordings of popular songs and, at the same time, followed, with deeply personal reaction, the lyrics on a page dittoed by their teacher.* Many such lyrics, as Ann Williamson (1977, p. 84) points out, provoke serious thought. For black groups or groups interested in black culture, lyrics like James Brown's "I'm Black and I'm Proud" and Nina Simone's "To Be Young, Gifted and Black" stir both thought and emotion. Many of John Denver's lyrics stimulate serious thinking about ecology and the beauty of nature. Lyrics that are passionately political catch interest and generate thoughtful reaction and discussion. Returning to the lyrics alone after the students have listened to the music, the teacher can use this immensely popular subject matter to ask questions that cover almost the full range of comprehension skills. Even a "dull" lesson on reading skills can take on

*The following book may be a revelation of the poetic quality of some of the lyrics: *Grandfather Rock: The New Poetry and the Old,* edited by David Morse (New York. Dell Publishing Co., 1972).

life with this approach (Larrick, 1971, p. 187). Most importantly, reading is now in the Things-We-Care-About Department.

Use that Wonder-Worker—Interest

What is the power of interest as a factor that helps toward comprehension? When groups of teenagers were asked, "What makes reading easy?" many answered, "Interest." (Strange, 1965)

In one investigation (Bernstein, 1955, p. 283), ninth-graders who were slightly retarded in reading were asked to read two selections well matched in reading difficulty but differing greatly in interest. These students read the more interesting selection *with greater comprehension and greater speed as well.* What role does interest play in the comprehension of students in everyday reading activities? According to Estes and Vaughan (1973, p. 150), higher interest has been shown to be concomitant with superior comprehension except for children reading well below their grade level.

Witness the power of interest in driver education! Just let not-so-able readers set their hearts on passing their driver's test. Give them the highway department's handbook with information crucial for those who wish to secure their first license. Some who seem unable to read textbook chapters assigned at school manage to pull out the essential information! (Schnayer, 1969, p. 698)

While interest alone will not solve the problems of seriously below-grade readers, and while materials matched to the reading reach of students are of very great importance, a message comes through loud and clear. When we excite the interest of students before they read a selection, when we provide opportunities for them to read in areas of already strong interests, and, importantly, when we help them expand those interests, we create situations conducive to more effective comprehension. Certainly our students will sometimes read in non-interest areas. In that case, another message comes through to us—we should then guide their reading more carefully.

Fully aware, then, of the power of interest, we might ask as we plan an assignment, "How can I capture my students' interest before they begin the reading, pull them into the reading, help them really *want* to read?" You will find on the following pages a few suggestions. Imaginative teachers will devise many more ways to spark interest.

Make Dramatic Assignments

READING AID 141

"Read the next chapter for tomorrow," students are sometimes told. They may drudge through the chapter, their motivation only to get the reading over with—if indeed they read the pages at all. In contrast, teachers can sometimes pull out something striking or dramatic from the assigned pages and play this up as they introduce the assignment.

"Do the problems on page 37," mathematics students are sometimes told. "And, by the way, read the two or three pages just before the problems." Contrast their reading with that of students whose mathematics teacher (Muelder, 1970) spotlights this "believe it or not" problem:

> "What is the probability that among you twenty-five people in the class two have the same birthday?" To the surprise of the class, the teacher then proves that there is an even chance that two have the same birthday. Next he adds another class and works with fifty students. He proves that it is statistically certain that two have the same birthday. Now the minds of many students are alive with questions: "How can we calculate the probability that a certain event will occur?" "What are the reasons behind this type of calculation?" "Just what is meant by statistical certainty?" As they leave class the teacher reminds them, "You'll find all the answers in your reading for tomorrow."

Even students who are not mathematics oriented sometimes dig into this assignment.

Live Issues Can Involve Students

READING AID 142

Issues students are seeing in today's headlines and hearing hotly debated can ignite their interest. Here is a way any live issue can quickly come alive in the classroom. A class public opinion poll is conducted on the issue—it might be a heated election campaign or the part we should play in solving the world's food problems. Through the poll, each student is instantly involved in a problem-solving situation. Here's how such a poll might work out in science class:

> Suppose a poll is taken on the question: Should the restraints in the U.S. on research with test tube babies be lifted? The teacher might ask provocative questions: ''Do the *pros* of giving hope to millions of childless couples outweigh the dangers?'' . . . ''What if this leads to baby farms—to mass produced, tailor-made babies whose genes have been altered in the test tube?'' . . . ''What about the dangers to the family?'' . . . ''Should a well-to-do woman who does not want to be bothered with being pregnant be able to advertise: 'Wanted for nine months: one surrogate mother who will rent out her womb and carry my child for me'?''

The students consider, ''What do we need to find out?'' and set up an outline of what they want to look for. The teacher has on hand materials that span the students' reading levels—easy newspaper material, general magazine material, general science magazine material, more learned science magazine material, and scholarly journal material. The students read, then discuss their findings, to arrive at a more informed opinion. A follow-up poll is taken to find out how many have changed their opinions.

Interviewing relatives and friends is exciting, especially when the issue is explosive. Vehement opinions may send students into reading:

> Ask adults you know—relatives, neighbors, friends—what they think when they hear (''safe' nuclear power plants,'' ''handgun control,'' ''Proposition 13,'' ''E.R.A.''; when they hear someone urging engineering man's heredity in laboratories, spending billions on space shots; or when they hear comments about some other controversial issue or figure.) They will probably respond with sharply conflicting views. What information do you need in order to make up your mind intelligently? Read to arrive at an informed opinion.

Is This Myth or Fact?

READING AID 143

Interest can sometimes be stirred by the question: Is this *myth* or *fact?* The students are given statements, some of them ''inflammables,'' and are asked to label each on the basis of their present impression as myth or fact. In one class statements on the controversial welfare system, for example, included:

1. The welfare rolls are full of able-bodied loafers!
2. Once on welfare, always on welfare!
3. Most welfare children are illegitimate.

The students' clashing impressions led them to ask, ''How can we be *sure?*'' They turned to reading, and to other sources, to obtain more solid information. (Lynch 1978)

Visitors–Including Clashing Visitors–Can Turn on Interest

READING AID 144

Visitors to the classroom can set the stage for reading. A group of reading "holdouts" responded to these send-offs (Social Studies Department, La Follette High School, Madison, Wisconsin):

> A parole officer and some young ex-prisoners under his guidance visited the class. They talked about the influences that lead young people to crime, about whether the penal system discourages crime or fosters it, and about the need for change as they saw it. Their visit touched off questions—and weeks of reading about young people and crime. Teacher and librarian filled book shelves and tables with reading matter on a diversity of levels.
>
> Members of minority groups in the community—an Indian, a Puerto Rican, a black—were invited to talk about what it means to be in their minority group in America today. They touched off extensive reading by the students, who now saw the problems in human terms and cared about finding solutions.

A teacher might make an assignment with only these words: "Read about pollution in the next chapter." And the students might (or they might not!) dutifully drudge through the assigned reading. Two visitors, though, whose views are in head-on collision, will more likely turn the students into excited learners:

> The public relations representative of a public utility company, one charged with polluting the community's land, air, and water, visits the class and presents his viewpoint. Then the spokesman for a militant environmentalist group takes "equal time" to present his view. The students ask: "Can I decide this question until I get more information?" Materials are available to span the reading range within the class. The students read to try to determine what position the facts support.

"Fasten-Your-Seat-Belt" Tape Recordings Can Excite Interest

READING AID 145

Tape recordings of the opening pages of "fasten-your-seat-belt" fiction can excite interest and can sometimes serve as enablers for "I-can't readers."

To lure her reading holdouts, reading specialist Laura Johnson (1973, p. 129) prepares read-along cassettes. The student is offered a cassette player, earphones, a tape, and a paperback so shiny and colorful a student can't resist reaching for it. Carl, long a holdout, is caught by the picture of motorcycle and boy on the cover of *The Wild One*. "In nothing flat," Mrs. Johnson writes, "motorcycles win out . . ., and he marches off to an empty carrel where he can listen to *The Wild One* in peace and quiet."

Turned on by an exciting opening, the students sometimes read on to the last page by themselves. For those who cannot or do not, Mrs. Johnson records entire paperbacks—fast-paced ones—as read-along books. Now the "non-print" students are held captive for hours in a world of printed words. As they follow along, their eyes on the book, they hear a word at the same time as they see it and may come to associate the heard word with the printed symbol. Thus they gradually assimilate some words for future use in reading. Psychological barriers may begin to fall as they have a reading experience without failure. Perhaps for the first time in their lives, they experience an entire book, and this experience belongs in the Fun Department! Here, indeed, is strong motivation for them to learn to read! (Bragstad, 1979)

It should be noted that students who listen to read-along tapes should clearly understand the why of keeping their eyes on the book and should be strongly urged to do this. Students who are engrossed in listening to an exciting recording with their heads on their desks are having the fun part of the read-along experience without collecting the dividends in growth in reading!

Course Work the Students Have "Ordered" Helps Sustain Interest

READING AID 146

Ideally, motivation should of course be more than momentary, and interest, a long-term sustaining force. During the opening days of school, students can sometimes be given an active part in planning the course. Students tend to respond well to their own "self-assignments."

The first week of school, seniors enrolled in a course on Problems of Democracy were asked to list the ten most crucial problems that America faces, problems that threaten the quality of American life. Class members nominated serious problems, then compiled a master list of those named the most often. The teacher then revealed the ten problems facing America that eminent social scientists had named as most crucial, and the students compared these with their own nominations. Then, by class vote, they decided which problems they would spend the year investigating. Now the students approached the year's study to answer their own "big questions." Both classroom and school library were well stocked with multi-level materials on America's problems. (Lynch, 1978)

*When this "Character" Talks, Students Listen–and Read!**

READING AID 147

Interest-catchers can vary from something as simple as making a striking statement related to the assignment (see Reading Aid 153) to something like the real "spectacular" described here—a fascinating character from long ago who steps into the classroom! Such a "spectacular" might be planned by a department to serve a number of classrooms in that department, by a district supervisor to serve a district, or perhaps by a creative classroom teacher.

A character from long ago who steps into the classroom can *turn on interest—turn on questions—turn students on to the library*. What if Emily Dickinson in her flowing white gown suddenly appeared in your English classroom? Charles Darwin in your biology class? Such a "happening" occurs quite often in Evanston (Illinois) classrooms:

> He marches into the classroom as Col. Obediah La Raus, colonial firebrand inflamed against British oppression and a soldier in the American Revolution. He is clad in colonial garb and armed with a musket from Revolutionary days. He carries a big black suitcase full of fascinating artifacts from the period. "My name is Obediah," he tells the surprised students. "It may sound funny to you, but it's a common name to us. Most of you step into horseless carriages, but that's not the way it was with me."
>
> Not really. His real name is Roger La Raus. He sometimes appears in classes as black-suited Lawful La Raus, a pilgrim; as Civil War General ("Ultimate Surrender") La Raus; as Comrade La Rausovich, who, with a Russian accent, expounds on totalitarianism; even as Romulus Lazarus, a Roman legionary who survived Pompeii. In his real life role, he's the social studies supervisor for Evanston's elementary schools. He takes this repertoire of characters "on the road" in Evanston classrooms.
>
> Dr. La Raus believes in making history more realistic and generating excitement in classrooms. He impersonates historical figures to bring the past to life.
>
> "You really need something to motivate the students, " Dr. La Raus explains. "I march into a classroom and give an overview after the students are into a unit and

*The writer is indebted to the *Chicago Tribune* for May 28, 1978, for this heading (adapted) and to that publication and the *Cedar Rapids Gazette* for July 2, 1978, for some of the facts and phrasings in this report.

already know a little something about the period. I want to leave the teacher with a class of excited students full of questions. It works! When the teacher mentions a related book, the kids jump to read it. Librarians are alerted and ready for excited learners.

"This costume cost me 26 cents, and that's *with* tax," Dr. La Raus commented, fingering the buttons on a black uniform coat picked up at a second-hand store. "My artifacts—a powder horn, a bayonet, an adz, an early flag from Virginia—all cost less than a dollar. I found most of them at garage sales."

In his presentation, Dr. La Raus tells colorful stories—historically accurate—to grip attention, to give students a perspective not often available in textbooks, to stimulate their thinking. "I hope to turn students on to the library. After a visit many dig into reading about the period.

"Characters from literature—from science—from history can step into classrooms from long ago. You might think it takes a great flair for drama, but it doesn't," Dr. La Raus maintains. "All it takes is a good teacher with the lore of the period, a bit of ingenuity in throwing together a costume, and a desire to light the fire!"

The reader is likely to recognize Dr. La Raus's one-man show as an especially creative "advance organizer."

Tie Reading in with Exciting Doing

Students are unlikely to read "just to get it over with"—or not to read at all—if we tie the reading in with tasks they find exciting, then make available reading matter to match the reach of every reader. Obviously, teachers will want to devise activities that are "their own thing." The examples that follow will perhaps serve as a stimulus to the teacher's own creative thinking.

READING AID 148

A teacher can sometimes plan "exciting doing" that is somewhat different from the usual classroom fare: this inner-city class caught fire (as reported on the ABC TV program "Make a Wish," April 27, 1975):

> The students redesigned their own community as the ideal community of the future. They transformed its residences, recreational centers, transportation—even set up its government. They "tried on" roles like building inspector and mayor. They "plugged in" to reading to find solutions to problems. They emerged with important insights: "Environment happens because people make it that way," and "Each individual has a responsibility toward his city to make it what it should be."

READING AID 149

A challenge to debate the teacher can send students into reading. When students in Spanish class were reading the epic *Araucana,* their teacher took on the class in a debate:

> For tomorrow you'll be reading how the conquistadores enslaved the Incas and put to death their great chief Atahualpa. Which side was in the right? Tomorrow I'll take the side of the conquistadores. You come prepared to plead the case of the Incas. As you read, look for evidence that the Incas suffered great wrongs.

Now reading the epic becomes an active search for debate points rather than an aimless drifting down the page. (La Porte, 1970)

READING AID 150

Combine live issues in the community with "live" student involvement and reading becomes more active and part of the current scene.

> A teacher of Environmental Studies tapped the social concern of students. When the County Commissioners called a hearing about a recycling program being considered

for the county, the class named a student spokesman to attend the meeting and take a stand. Then the whole class dug into the research in order to arm their spokesman. Several community members, all the rest adults, addressed that meeting. The teenager alone was applauded—with a burst of applause!

Students in Problems of Democracy class *lived* citizenship. All year they could earn a "test-size" *A* by attending community meetings—meetings about the environment, appearances of political candidates, meetings of county commissioners, Common Cause meetings. Their social studies classroom overflowed with related readings on a wide range of reading levels. Some students read beforehand to be armed at the meetings, then afterward because of the interest the meeting had generated. (Lynch, 1978)

READING AID 151

With contagious enthusiasm, Sartain (1973, p. 47) takes an enthusiastic look at "purposeful projects"—the launching of a project close to the students, the planning of sources of information, the reading, the climax of completing the project:

You can lead students to reading, but you can't make them read? Many students in today's schools are not convinced that book learning has much value for them. But there is *one* subject that appeals to *all* students. What is this miraculous motivator? Why, driver education, of course! Here instead of purposeless readings and busy work, the assigned readings contribute directly to the attainment of competencies the students know to be immediately useful.

We can make students just as enthusiastic—well, almost as enthusiastic—about reading in other subject fields as they are in driver education. We can do so if we break away from the pedantically subject-centered approach to secondary teaching and adopt a *purposeful project involvement approach.*

We need first to observe what is important in the everyday lives of our young people, to observe their behaviors and listen to their conversations to determine their major frustrations, their strongest desires, their peer values, their social activities, and their family concerns. Consider what these young people would do with their time if they were not required to attend school. Then make a list of projects that can be carried out in school to satisfy some of their needs as growing human beings. You may find them almost as eager to engage in a community survey of opinions or conditions or in trying to solve the problems of an area of economic blight as they are to take driver training.

Launch the project in some striking way—a bulletin board with captioned illustrations, a film, a class discussion, a field trip. As interest intensifies, ask whether the students would like to engage in a related activity, or wait until the project idea comes from them. Engage the youngsters in step-by-step planning of what they want to do. Invite them to itemize types of information they need. This can lead to the listing of sources—people and references—followed by individual and committee efforts to locate, read, share, and use the information. *Voilà!* Your students are purposefully involved in reading in order to complete a project that is *important to them*. Plan with the class the form the final project will take—a display; a program at school; a publication for students, parents, interested citizens, or community leaders; a radio or TV program; a program at a shopping center. Divide the class into committees to work on parts of the investigation. Guide the students to reading materials they are comfortable with. Introduce the reading and study skills they need to gain the information they must have for their activity. Arrange and carry out the final presentation as planned.

Young people, Sartain comments, learn what they *want* to learn. Then he reminds us: "Our reading involvement projects will be successful only if we steer individuals or small groups to reading materials at their comfortable developmental levels."

READING AID 152

A teacher's use of exciting realia can sometimes "tie reading in with exciting doing." The science teacher in the following example outdid himself in providing spectacular realia—he brought about a real scurry of reading:

Anything can happen in biology class! Students walked in one day to find skulls of man and his ancestors—plaster casts, that is—spread out on a table. Neanderthal Man, Australopithecus, Cro-Magnon Man, and others—spanning a million years or more—were all present! The teacher raised these questions: "How would you arrange these skulls in evolutionary sequence?" . . . Then: "What is the primary characteristic that determines how high an organism is in the evolutionary sequence?" . . . "What other characteristics will you consider?"

Interest engaged, the students read from a variety of multi-level sources, shared information, and succeeded in placing the skulls according to the march of time. Some read far *beyond* the immediate topic to learn more about the fascinating ancestors of man. (Hozinsky, 1979)

Help Students Read with Purpose through Questions

Suppose students go into a reading assignment with no purpose. They have seen, written on the chalkboard, only these directions: "Read pages 496–524 for tomorrow." They may comply by running their eyes aimlessly over the page, their purpose to "get the reading over with" and close the book as quickly as possible.

READING AID 153

As we sit at our desks planning a reading assignment, we might ask ourselves, "What are the not-to-be-missed learnings?" and then, "What purpose question(s) will guide the students unerringly to these?" Suppose not-so-able readers are to read Langston Hughes' poignant poem, "Dreams Deferred." It takes only moments to provide them with a purpose for reading:

> "This poem is about some dreams of people in Harlem that have not yet come true. Please read the poem and write down each person's dream" (Cuban and Roden, 1975, p. 38). For any of these dreamers has the American Dream of equal opportunity come true?"

With this "set" for the reading, the students are likely to become more active, searching, comprehending readers.

Suppose capable readers are to read "The Lovesong of J. Alfred Prufrock," a difficult poem even for advanced readers. The following question, posed before reading, sets purpose and should help them stretch their comprehension:

> J. Alfred Prufrock is not satisfied with his life. How would you feel if your life was as J. Alfred described it? (Graves, Palmer, and Furniss, 1974, p. 17.)

The following question gives students a clearcut purpose for reading Dylan Thomas's poem, "Do Not Go Gentle into That Good Night":

> The author feels that one should not just gently accept death. Note the advice he gives to wise men, good men, wild men, grave men, and finally, his father. Do you agree with his advice? (Graves, Palmer, and Furniss, 1974, p. 17.)

Each of the following questions gives students a real, immediate, and clearcut purpose. In addition, each question has "you" appeal:

> Why might you, a boy or girl in the 1980s, be dissatisfied with the type of education you would have had in ancient Sparta? (Association of Teachers of Social Studies, 1977, p. 57)

If you have ever had a Pyrrhic victory, tell about it. (Association of Teachers of Social Studies, 1977, p. 57)

If you had lived in the 1850s, would you have considered John Brown a hero or a murderer? (Association of Teachers of Social Studies, 1977, p. 60)

If in 1939 you were a citizen of Nazi, Germany, would you have supported the policies of Adolf Hitler? (Association of Teachers of Social Studies, 1977, p. 40).

Striking statements can *ask* for analysis, inviting purposeful reading to find out more. This question in science has puzzle appeal:

A heart cell in a tiny embryo "knows" it's going to become a cell in your heart instead of ending up in your eye! How does it "know"? (Hozinsky, 1979)

READING AID 154

Of course, the life need of students will be to formulate their own purposes for reading, then read to accomplish those purposes. Being told what to look for is not the way a person learns in adulthood. So we will want to move our students in the direction of formulating their own purpose-questions. As a step in this direction, we can place students in situations that stimulate these questions.

A teacher might write on the board, "Read about Lapland, pages 105–108." But let's suppose that, instead, the teacher takes young readers on an imaginary airplane trip across the Arctic region, drops them into frozen Lapland, then encourages them to "start living there." With guidance and the stimulus of pictures, the students ask: "Where would we live?" "What would we eat?" "What would our fathers do to earn a living?" "What fun would we have?" Now the students have a reading target—to find out how they will live in their "new home." (Slightly adapted from Kenworthy, 1969, p. 89)

One instructor (Podendorf, 1970) took some young science students out into the school grounds to see a crabapple tree in bloom. Around the trunk close to the ground was a conspicuous scar. The teacher asked, "What do you think caused that scar?" The students thought this over. "A dog chewed it!" "Insects ate it!" "A wire was too tight!" The teacher remarked, "I happen to know that that tree has roots of one variety and the trunk, branches, and leaves of another!" The class had heard of grafting. Perhaps it was that! One student commented, "I've seen a tree with two different kinds of apples!" The instructor added, "I've seen one with seven different kinds!" The students were full of questions: "Are there different kinds of grafting?" "How are these done?" "What determines the success or failure of grafting?"

When the students returned to the classroom, these questions went up on the chalkboard and became the master list. The class had now made their own assignment, which was dittoed and given to each student. Then the students planned how they would locate information to answer their questions.

Our focus in Reading Aid 154 was on involving students in formulating their own questions as an aid to reading comprehension. But there are other, far-reaching implications. When we place a premium on the inert, receptive mind in students, that is precisely what we will get. When, on the other hand, the students themselves raise the questions, they are no longer passive, receiving truth and knowledge from the teacher—instead, they are becoming actively involved in their own learning. A social scientist with deep social concerns (Banks, 1976, p. xii–xiv) sees implications far beyond the classroom. Students who are searching, involved learners, Banks maintains, will be more likely to contribute, when they become adult citizens, to the resolution of the momentous problems we face in the world community, to the improvement of the human condition, and to the salvation of our imperiled planet.

We might ask the following questions to check whether students are becoming actively involved in their own learning: Do I as the teacher come across as the "star performer"? Or are the students raising more and more of the questions and taking more and more responsibility for their own learning?

Study Guides Can Turn on Reading Power

READING AID 155

Study guides can help students manage "unmanageable" reading assignments. Teachers can build solid reading assistance right into the study guide. Here are ten tips for creating guides for less-than-able readers:

1. First, take advantage of two wonder-workers. First, *let the task before the students be one that they want to perform*. Second, *see that they understand clearly what they are to know and be able to do when they complete the reading.*
2. Add a touch of novelty, if you can. One teacher typed interesting questions on the movement of the pioneers westward against the background of a dittoed map.
3. When possible, keep the questions few but important.
4. Consider arranging the questions from easy to difficult. When underconfident readers cannot answer a question that appears early on the study guide, they may become "drop outs" from the assignment. Simply placing the easier questions first provides them with some support.
5. Generally, questions that call for information directly stated in the black-and-white print will be easier than those that require reasoning beyond the print. Since most higher-level thinking rests on a basis of factual information, teachers may want to devise questions to help students pull out the underlying facts and then move on to questions that call for inferential reading.
6. Consider supplying some students with "direction-finders." You can provide support by arranging the questions in the order in which the answers are located in the passage. You can provide even stronger support, when this is appropriate, by citing the page, column, paragraph, even the line where the answer will be found. This support may "save" an assignment for handicapped readers. Although they may skim to find the answers, perhaps that much reading practice is preferable to no reading practice at all. You can discourage skimming for bits and pieces, if you wish, by asking broad synthesis questions.
7. If you need to break the vocabulary barrier, you might list on the study guide "stopper words" and supply simple, clear definitions, or you might list on the guide important words whose mastery is to become the special responsibility of the students.
8. Consider a study guide consisting of Part I, easier questions probing for the most essential content, and Part II, more difficult questions. Students for whom both parts would be overwhelming might be held responsible only for Part I. You might modify the assignment for those students with a quiet word, the final decision being left up to the student: "If you complete Part I, you'll have the basic information. Try as much of Part II as you like, but this is optional for you."
9. See that students for whom assignments are modified do not view themselves as second-class citizens. Perhaps they will not feel "second-class" if, from the first week of school in September, assignments have been matched to groups and individuals. It can become routine in a classroom to adjust assignments in the light of considerations other than the students' reading levels—their personal interests, choices, and point of view, for example, or some special contribution they can make to the class.

10. It may be helpful to divide the assignment into a series of intermediate steps and to make shorter, "divide-and-conquer" assignments (Hill, 1979, p. 125). Placing a study guide that looks manageable in the hands of an under-par reader can help give that student heart.

A "How-to-Study" Study Guide

READING AID 156

The study guide just described helps students to identify in the reading assignment information that they should master. A second type of study guide, appropriate with especially difficult passages, not only guides the student to essential information but also *tells the student how to read and study* in order to acquire that information. (Idea from Karlin, 1977, p. 127)

A how-to-study, or process, study guide can consist of a duplicated reading selection with study helps that appear in the margin, helps that direct the students' attention to the way they should read and study this particular passage. Study helps like the following might appear in the margin:

> "Slow down and read this page very carefully. Do not read on until you are sure of the answer to this question: ____ ____."
>
> "Is this statement [an arrow points to the statement] a sound conclusion? Can you find solid evidence to support it in the passage?"
>
> "Where is the context clue to the meaning of this word?"
>
> "Read on to find the three examples."

Instead of duplicating the passage, the teacher might simply duplicate the study helps on strips of paper which the students are to place alongside their textbooks. The study helps would align perfectly with the corresponding lines of the textbook. (Karlin, 1977, p. 130)

With certain readings, it may be helpful for the study guide to ask the student to read the chapter in manageable parts, to stop at designated points, and to answer a question or two at each stopping point before reading on. (Aulls, 1978, p. 68)

Utilize or Provide Background Experience

READING AID 157

Enriching students' background experience for the coming reading or relating that reading to their previous experience is another force of comprehension. The more students bring *to* the printed page, the more they take *from* it. Paradoxically, we can use "non-reading" to strengthen reading—talks by classroom visitors, television, films, filmstrips, projected pictures, records and tape recordings, models, interviews, and away-from-school excursions.

As for visitors, we can find "gold in our own backyard" in our own student body. In English class, a visitor—a senior who has been to mountain climbing school—might share the dangers and the lure of mountain climbing and enrich the students' background for reading *Annapurna*. As for films to strengthen background, in social studies *The Twisted Cross* (1956) or *The Rise and Fall of the Third Reich* Series (1972) can make difficult readings on Hitler's Germany more comprehensible. The students have front seats at dramatic events; they hear voices and meet people from this period of the past. In industrial arts, a fascinating film on how a car is born might serve as a "lead-in" for reading about mass production. With every increment in background, the reading process is eased!

Difficult key terms and concepts can sometimes be handled more easily after the students have met them through a non-verbal experience. Superb slide sets on the drama of evolution, *Three Billion Years of Life* (1976), for example, can help remove such barriers. Through these slides, terms like *vestigal forms, homologous structures,* and *organic molecules,* which could easily have been lifeless letters on the page, come alive with meaning.

We can maximize the dividends from these non-verbal experiences through discussion beforehand, through assigning questions to be held in mind and answered during the experience, and through followup.

Since slide sets, film strips and films vary in quality, teachers will want to evaluate these aids in advance most carefully.

Excursions away from school, when these are practical, can be used to strengthen students' background. In the following paragraph, a science teacher reports how a carefully planned excursion to an exciting Sleep Laboratory led to a flurry of reading:

> In the Sleep Laboratory at the University of Chicago, scientists are carrying on exciting investigations of the phenomena of sleep. Before the class visited the lab, I made two visits myself to gather background information. This I shared with the class before the trip. Talk about serendipities! That week the *Tribune* started a series of articles on sleep, and *Science News* ran an article. And the students brought in readings. Interest pulled them into these readings—and far beyond. What might have been halfhearted reading became interested, involved, and thoughtful reading. (Hozinsky, 1979)

Walk Students through the Opening

READING AID 158

Troubled readers often try a few paragraphs or pages, then close the book with "Too hard for me!" Those opening pages are often "stoppers." We can create a force for comprehension—again, we can create momentum—by walking students through the opening of a selection.

In social studies, when the reading assignment is primary source material, the teacher can place the document in its historical setting, as we have noted, making it exciting fare. Perhaps the teacher will want to read the opening aloud expressively, leading the students to make interpretations, breaking the "bygone days" barrier by making archaic expressions more familiar. Then the teacher can raise key questions to be kept in mind as the students read on alone.

A high school English teacher (Ravin, 1979), working with students on the opening pages of a difficult short story, removes an impassable barrier. The protagonist is a drunken seaman. A narrator sometimes intrudes and gives stage directions, then suddenly climbs into the skin of the drunken seaman. The shifts are bewildering—there are no punctuation signals. But before the students attempt to read this difficult story, their teacher points out to them where the narrator is detached as a narrator and where he is speaking through the mouth of the seaman. She has them observe how the language differs—the narrator literate, almost poetic, the seaman, crude and illiterate. Then the students look through the story and identify a "sample" passage where each one is speaking. In just a few minutes, the teacher has turned students who would surely have been lost readers into comprehending readers.

We have already suggested (in Reading Aid 136) how a teacher might walk students through the opening of *Tess of the D'Urbervilles* as the students meet the characters, become at home in a faraway setting, pick up the first threads of plot, become familiar with a recurring theme, are left to read on alone with exciting questions in mind.

Reading the opening together can *actually build reading power.* It strengthens background for the rest of the passage, a facilitating force for comprehension. There is a tremendous psychological advantage for discouraged readers in that they already "into it." Once their teacher has walked them through the opening, they are better able to walk on alone.

Of course, the right moment to break off is when the student is "caught." It is good timing with "The Diamond Necklace" if, as the bell rings at the close of the hour, Madame Loisel is left in grief and despair, the fabulous diamond necklace borrowed from her wealthy friend mysteriously missing. (Donham, 1975)

Open Book Lessons Can Develop Skills

READING AID 159

Especially with troubled readers, time in class will often be well spent with their books open on the desks before them. Guided open-book practice in which the students analyze how to arrive at the answer to a question can be a highly rewarding practice. "Let's turn to the passage and . . ." can be a frequent suggestion of teachers. (Kenworthy, 1966, p. 104)

Often teachers can profitably have the students' books open as higher-level comprehension skills are developed. The students can search the passage for the answers to questions that demand reasoning *beyond* the print. In science class, such a question might be: "Does the evidence in the passage *really* justify this conclusion?" In English class, it might be: "How does Telemakhos show in Book 1 of the *Odyssey* that he is beginning to grow up?" Questions asking, "What do you predict?" may lend themselves to open-book work. A question like this might be posed: "Who will stand the strain of guilt better—Macbeth or Lady Macbeth?" Referring to the text, the students might discuss the facts and inferences that led them to their decisions.

Open-book work can be extremely helpful as students are learning to read pictorial aids, maps, diagrams, and charts. Without this guided practice many students seem to regard these as blank spaces on the page where they can "rest their eyes"!

Books can be opened when the students' recent reading of a passage has been a disaster. Now the stage is set for an open-book lesson on how you *should have read the passage*. (Moulton, 1969)

Read Aloud—and Build Reading Power

READING AID 160

Reading aloud to students can capture a class. And it can *actually build reading power*. The least successful reader in the class can reap these benefits.

A dramatic oral reading can generate edge-of-chair listening. It can give a class the experience of *sharing* the enjoyment of reading. It can prove to "tuned-out" readers that there is something to enjoy between book covers. It can intrigue students about what lies ahead in a selection. Reading aloud the opening may offer underconfident readers hope of completing the assignment. As we have noted, there is a tremendous psychological advantage in that they are already "into it." The oral reading creates *momentum* so that less confident readers may be able to read on silently alone.

Along with the benefits just mentioned, reading aloud by the teacher can bring a number of other benefits:

1. Students are accustomed to the color, the arresting sound effects, and the dramatic acting on television. Expressive oral reading can bring print "lying flat on the page" to life. Classes can become lost in a sensitive, dramatic oral reading.
2. Reading aloud can build word power. Oral readers can promote the growth of meaning vocabulary by quickly supplying the meanings for unknown words or leading students to figure out meanings.

3. Classes need not be passive while you are reading to them. Pausing, you can lead students to paraphrase difficult passages, thus strengthening their ability to interpret.
4. While reading aloud, ask questions that elicit important skills of comprehension. These questions can lead students to focus on—and dig the meaning out of—the lines that yield the answers.
5. Some instructors encourage edge-of-the-chair listening by writing on the board two or three intriguing questions. The class is told, "Raise your hands when you think I have read the answer to the first question." Hands wave as students find the answers, which often call for between-the-lines reading.
6. Reading aloud the opening of a selection may act as a speed device. It strengthens the students' background for the selection and generates concentration—and along with these may come increased speed.
7. You can constantly stir interest by leading students to anticipate—to try to predict—what lies ahead. You can close your reading with exciting questions—questions to impel the students to read on. Having understood and enjoyed your reading, underconfident readers may make a genuine effort to do this. They will be more likely to succeed if they are given class time to begin their silent reading.
8. Your oral reading need not be the only reading. Questions can require the students to return to the passage. Students can be asked to verify points, to locate passages that support statements, to make interpretations. Now with a more positive mind-set, discouraged readers may work their way through the selection. Thus the oral reading becomes an enabler. It has not taken the place of silent reading—it has made that silent reading possible.

Of course, instructors will avoid making students overly dependent on oral reading and will help gradually maturing readers advance along the road to independence.

Students Can Become "Special Investigators"

READING AID 161

Teachers sometimes excuse the poorest readers in the class from a reading assignment that is beyond their reach and substitute an assignment that does not call for reading—understandably, they want the student to experience greatly needed success. Perhaps they ask the student to make a model, a drawing, or a poster. Such a project, well done, undoubtedly gives the student a sense of accomplishment, but it may not contribute materially to the student's growth in reading.

Suppose, instead, that when the core of readings assigned the class is well beyond the poorest readers, the teacher invites those students to become "special investigators." The class is science, and the unit is evolution. The teacher makes certain that there "happens to be" a need for special investigations of related topics—an exploration, for instance, of the fascinating evolution of the horse or a study of fossils as keys to the mysteries of ancient life. The topics chosen are high in interest for the handicapped readers, who are guided in conference to references they can handle. They share their findings with the class. Through class discussions, slides, and the opaque projector, the "special investigators" get some of the information they missed through not completing the assigned readings. They do not feel that they are second-class citizens. Instead, they seem to like being exempt from the regular assignment in order to pursue a bit of original "research." Particularly good readers, too, are used as "specialists." Specialists may be either short term or continuing. Knowing that they are to serve as resource persons for the class, both good and poor readers may read *far* beyond their teacher's expectations in order to make themselves the "teacher of the moment." Why should one-assignment-for-all be sacrosanct when adjusting the assignment will contribute to a young person's reading growth and personal adjustment? (Idea from Fallers, 1970)

Have a "Silent Reading Teacher" in Your Classroom

We have shared in this chapter a number of devices for arousing the interest of students. More than just motivators, they should help young people overleap some of their barriers. *This momentum may be lost, however, if as the students begin to study, they open books that confront them with insurmountable difficulties*. Let us now consider bringing the right reading matter and the motivated student close together.

READING AID 162

As a high school teacher looks out over a classroom, Ted, who can barely handle materials on the sixth-grade level, may be sitting next to Dave, who can easily handle college-level reading. If Ted is assigned tasks far beyond him, he simply cannot cope, is deprived of the opportunity to practice reading, and may fall farther, even hopelessly, behind. If "college reader" Dave is not given reading tasks he has to stretch to, he may mark time in reading all year.

Research suggests that a mismatch between students like Ted and Dave and their assigned reading materials is quite prevalent. A more careful matching should bring immediate gains in interpretation of reading material and in content area learning. In time, the indirect dividends will include growth in reading ability, a stronger motivation to complete reading assignments, and a more positive attitude toward the content area course. (Hill, 1979, p. 118)

You can have a "silent reading teacher" in your classroom. This "silent teacher" is a collection of reading resources right for the reading levels and interests of your students.

How can the right reading resources be "a silent reading teacher"? When we guide students to reading right for them in difficulty and interest, even poor readers may spend many hours in the world of printed words. As they read, they meet and gradually learn new words in a pleasant way. They enrich their background information, in itself a facilitator for their future reading. The reading practice tends to strengthen their comprehension. Easy, exciting readings "pull them along" quickly and tend to increase their speed.

Many of the activities suggested in this chapter offer opportunities for a roomful of students to pursue the same subject using materials on a diversity of reading levels. With such activities a collection of the right reading resources will build silently and daily toward reading success.

In certain units, teachers may consider a core of assigned readings for the class essential for commonality; this core is almost sure to be beyond the reach of some of the students. Yet no matter how diverse the reading levels within the group, the teacher can often get the right reading matter into the hands of the student *through supplementary materials*.

What can a classroom collection of reading resources include? It can include a "clipping bank" of mounted course-related newspaper and magazine clippings, clippings that cost the teacher just a few dabs of paste! It can include attractive multi-level trade books related to the work of the course, trundled into the classroom from the library—supplementary textbooks with easier-to-read explanations for the less able readers and more challenging ones for the gifted—outstanding writings authored by the students themselves, dramatizations, interviews, reviews of books. It can include pamphlets and brochures that have come free or at low cost—indeed, almost "gift-wrapped"—from the Government Printing Office. In the periodical department, it can include course-related journals and popular magazines as well as newspapers. The latter can range in difficulty from *You and Your World* (Columbus, Ohio: Xerox Education Publications), designed for readers on third- to fifth-grade reading levels, to the *New York Times!* You will find a highly selective annotated list of newspapers and magazines for under-par readers in Reading Aid 288.

Such a collection of reading resources is built up over a period of time—one item and then another. A single added item can mean a successful reading experience for some troubled reader. With time, the reading collection the teacher has worked for will be *working for the teacher*—to give students successful reading experiences year after year.

How can teachers estimate the difficulty of reading materials and match these materials to individual students? You will find specific procedures for "Operation Matching" in Reading Aids 264–267. Further help is offered in the companion volume (Thomas and Robinson, *Improving Reading in Every Class,* unabridged 2nd ed., 1977), pp. 304–305.

Teachers sometimes ask, "How can poor readers be guided to easier materials in such a way that they do not appear different from the other students?" Possible ways to give sensitive guidance are offered in the companion volume on pages 134 and 135.

Of course, little is gained—in fact, much harm may result for students—by supplying poor readers with easy materials and leaving them on that level, so that they never stretch their reading power. It is desirable to challenge students with more difficult reading as rapidly as possible. *The goal is a sequence of increasingly difficult reading experiences with the students held to all they can do.* Teachers should experience deep satisfaction when, as time passes, poor readers advance to more difficult materials.

In many of the Reading Aids in this section, we have emphasized the power of interest and purpose as forces toward comprehension. Perhaps it bears repeating that interest cannot insure success *without reading materials matched to the reach of the students.* Neither interest nor well-matched materials are likely to be fully effective without the other. Together, they can be a potent force for comprehension.

Further suggestions for matching book and reader are offered in the companion volume (Thomas and Robinson, *Improving Reading in Every Class,* unabridged 2nd ed., 1977), pp. 296–310.

School Librarians Can Be Right-Hand Angels

READING AID 163

Suppose a class is to research this question: What are the major theories about the origin of the solar system? All too often classes rush through doors of the school library, where the librarians are unaware what they have come for. The first students through the doors grab off the shelves whatever books on the subject are easily available. The rest of the students find nothing and are discouraged and frustrated before they begin. The librarian has no opportunity to come to the rescue of the troubled readers with suitable materials. (Marantz, 1969, pp. 123–125)

Suppose, instead, the teacher and the librarian work together to do advance planning for the assignment. Working with the span of reading levels in the class in mind, they talk over what the students can use to solve the problem. The librarian makes a special search for easier-to-read materials in order to have enough for not-so-able readers. The teacher and the librarian may find it appropriate to provide some filmstrips, slides, or other non-print materials for these less verbally oriented students. Top readers are not overlooked—materials are there for them to "stretch to."

Perhaps the teacher and the librarian decide to bring the materials into the classroom where the teacher or the librarian can work with the students individually to guide them to their best sources. Perhaps a special collection is assembled in the library for this particular assignment. Now when the students rush through the library doors, they find a well stocked and suitably stocked reserve shelf. (Marantz, 1969, pp. 123–125)

Librarians will want to use their knowledge of individual students to *hold students to all they can do.* As has been noted, little is gained—in fact, much harm may be done—by supplying poor readers with easy materials and leaving them there, so that they never advance in reading power. The goal, as time passes, is a sequence of increasingly difficult readings.

READING AID 164

School librarians can be "right-hand angels" in preparing supplementary booklists. Suppose, again, that the subject for a class to investigate is the origin of the solar system. The teacher shares with the librarian the reading range within the class, and the librarian prepares a matching bibliography for the students to use. This includes annotations on what the materials cover and also such key words as *readable, highly interesting, popular treatment, average difficulty, mature presentation, scholarly, academic,* and *highly technical* to help the students find books on their levels. Such difficulty labels provide built-in reading guidance and greatly enhance the value of booklists librarians prepare for teachers and students.

Arrange Readings in an Easier-to-Harder Sequence

READING AID 165

Students can sometimes handle difficult reading if we guide them to easier reading on the subject first. Suppose you were confronted with having to read a rigorous article on creating human clones through binary fission! How helpful to read some popular articles on cloning human beings first!

Students should come to appreciate a quality encyclopedia as a possible starting point; sometimes that is the ideal starting point in making an investigation. They should be aware that it may offer a quick overview of the subject they are investigating and that they can often base more thorough study on this helpful orientation. They should understand that once they have strengthened their background through this general introduction, they may be able to advance to and comprehend more difficult, more technical material.

Suppose a freshman boy who is reading a little below the others in his class is assigned these questions: "What causes tornadoes? Can anyone predict when and where tornadoes will form? What protections do we have against tornadoes?" He might do well to turn first to *The New Book of Knowledge, The World Book Encyclopedia,* or *Compton's Encyclopedia.* With his background thus strengthened, he might advance to the "in-between" encyclopedias, *Collier's* and the *Encyclopedia International,* more advanced than the "juvenile" encyclopedias but less advanced than the *Americana* or the *Britannica.*

Magazine articles can be similarly sequenced. A student might first read a popular article in *Science Digest,* then go on, if the student can handle it, to a more learned and technical article in *Scientific American* or *Science.*

A biology teacher (Hozinsky, 1979) suggests how an easy-to-harder sequence may serve as an "enabler" for students in their textbook reading.

> Although a single textbook may be prescribed for students in a class, they need not necessarily feel locked into this one book. We keep a number of easier-to-read textbooks on a reserve shelf in the school library. Students who are thrown by the explanation of mitosis in a more advanced textbook, *Modern Cell Biology* by William D. McElroy and Carl P. Swanson (Englewood Cliffs, N.J.: Prentice-Hall, 1976), may be able to grasp the simpler explanation in *Biological Science: An Ecological Approach,* BSCS Green Version (Chicago: Rand McNally, 1973). Now, having acquired some background understandings of the terms and processes, perhaps they can extend themselves and digest the corresponding passage in their own textbooks. If not, they are still ahead in what they have learned about mitosis from the easier book.

Capable readers in English class have put down William Faulkner's *The Sound and the Fury,* sighing "Oh, *what* is it saying?" The writer has found the Monarch commercial study guides, when used with guidance, invaluable for conscientious students who need support in reading difficult books. *Masterpieces of World Literature* (originally titled Masterplots: Magill, 1952–1969), with its short plots, offers an orientation to the world's great fiction. The thread of plot which this work offers has marked the way out of the labyrinth for students struggling with Joyce's *Ulysses* and *Portrait of the Artist as a Young Man.*

In the following paragraphs, teachers report how simplified versions of *Great Expectations* and the *Illiad* "saved" these classics for high school readers:

> Debbie, a freshman, would have been a lost reader in the opening chapters of *Great Expectations.* Her teacher guided her to a well-written simplified edition. At the dramatic point where Pip rings hesitatingly at Miss Havisham's gate, is admitted by the haughty Estella, is led by her candle along the dark passage, and discovers Miss Havisham's secret, Debbie "graduated" to Dickens' classic. The simplified edition had not taken the place of the classic—it had *made its reading possible.* (McCampbell, 1979). I watched a student struggling over the *Illiad* the other day. At first he was lost trying to work his way through the page-long Homeric similes, the obscure references to myths, the galaxies of major and minor gods and goddesses. Then he was guided to a first-quality simplified *Iliad.* After becoming acquainted with the gods and heroes in the simplified version, picking up the plot threads, and being captured by dramatic situations, the student could now return to the original *Iliad* and work his way through.

The students themselves should come to understand that enriching their background can be a force for the comprehension of difficult materials. They should be encouraged—until it becomes second nature—to arrange their own easier-to-harder reading sequences.

Teachers Can Turn Author

READING AID 166

When published materials are not what you want for your troubled readers, you may wish to turn author and create materials exactly to your liking. The task of rewriting need not be long and formidable.

At times, you may need only to select and bring together a few parts of a passage that originally was too long and complex for your students. At other times, you may wish to write a short, easy-to-read digest of crucial points in a unit and supply this as alternate reading to far-below-average readers. Or you may occasionally wish to simplify an entire article or chapter. At La Follette High School (Madison, Wisconsin), three teachers of the course in western civilization shared and thereby lightened the task of rewriting materials. All wished to use some eyewitness accounts of the Nuremberg trials from Davidson's *Trial of the Germans.* They divided up the accounts, and each rewrote a share, lowering the reading level.

A reading consultant may be available to help less experienced teachers lower the reading level appropriately. Practical helps can also be found in E. R. Hennefrund, "Writing for the Reluctant Reader," an article which appeared in the *Writer's Digest* 58 August, 1978, 30–35. Background information concerning factors likely to facilitate comprehension, learning, and retention will be found in George R. Klare, *The Measurement of Readability* (Ames, Iowa: The Iowa State University Press, 1963).

We Should Move Students Closer to Independence

We have offered in this section a variety of ways to help troubled readers comprehend more effectively. Of course, hand in hand with these, there will be an additional help for students—gradually *moving them from more guidance to less, then on closer to independence in reading difficult selections.* In the meantime, reading guidance appropriate to the learner, the learning situation, and the difficulty of the materials will be a *shortcut* to that destination.

The reader may wish to turn elsewhere in this book for additional material on improving comprehension. Chapter 5, "How to Streamline Your Study," offers a number of aids to comprehension. Especially useful among these are the preview strategy (Reading Aids 195–205) and the question strategy (Reading Aids 206–211). The OK5R approach, a package of strategies for mastering a textbook chapter, is examined in Reading Aid 234. The selection "Helping Students Find the Main Idea" (Reading Aids 167–186) shares methods and materials for developing one specific comprehension skill, skill in differentiating the main idea of a paragraph from the supporting material. Teachers can also "turn on" comprehension power through the everyday classroom activity of asking questions. You will find a section "Questions Can Develop Comprehension" in the companion volume (Thomas and Robinson, *Improving Reading in Every Class,* unabridged 2nd ed., 1977), pp. 169–183.

References

Association of Teachers of Social Studies in the City of New York. *A Handbook for the Teaching of Social Studies*. Boston: Allyn and Bacon, 1967, 1977.

Aulls, Mark W. *Developmental and Remedial Reading in the Middle Grades.* Boston: Allyn and Bacon, 1978.

Banks, James A., in his foreword to Francis P. Hunkins, *Involving Students in Questioning.* Boston: Allyn and Bacon, 1976.

Bernstein, Margery R. "Relationship Between Interest and Reading Comprehension." *Journal of Educational Research,* 49, no. 4 (December 1955): 283–288.

Bragstad, Bernice, reading consultant at La Follette High School, Madison, Wisconsin, in remarks to the writer, January 1979.

Butler, Charles H., and F. Lynwood Wren. *The Teaching of Secondary School Mathematics.* New York: McGraw-Hill Book Co., 1965.

Cuban, Larry, and Philip Roden. *Promise of America: The Starting Line.* Glenview, Ill.: Scott, Foresman and Co., 1975.

Donham, Virginia, former teacher at New Trier High School, Winnetka, Illinois, in remarks to the writer, July 1975.

Estes, Thomas H., and Joseph L. Vaughan, Jr. "Reading Interest and Comprehension Implications." *The Reading Teacher,* 27, no. 2 (November 1973): 149–153.

Fallers, Margaret, former University of Chicago Laboratory School social studies teacher, in remarks to the writer, April 1970.

Farrell, Edmund J. "Listen My Children, and You Shall Read." *English Journal,* 55, no. 1 (1966): 43–45.

Flickinger, Alice, former University of Chicago Laboratory School social studies teacher, in remarks to the writer, October 1969.

Graves, Michael F., Rebecca J. Palmer, and David W. Furniss. *Structuring Reading Activities for English Classes.* Urbana, Ill.: National Council of Teachers of English, 1976. Copyright © 1976 by ERIC/RCS and NCTE. Reprinted with permission.

Haehn, Faynelle, University of Chicago Laboratory School typewriting teacher, in conversation with the writer, May 1979.

Hill, Walter R. *Secondary School Reading: Process, Program, Procedure.* Boston: Allyn and Bacon, 1979.

Hozinsky, Murray. University of Chicago Laboratory School biology teacher, in remarks to the writer, January 1979.

Hunkins, Francis P. *Involving Students in Questioning.* Boston: Allyn and Bacon, 1976.

Johnson, Laura S. "Cool It, Teach! and Tape All of It!" *Journal of Reading,* 17, no. 2 (1973): 129–131.

Johnson, Laura S., reading specialist at Evanston Township High School, Evanston, Illinois, in remarks to the writer, November 1974.

Kenworthy, Leonard S. *Social Studies for the Seventies.* Waltham, Mass.: Blaisdell Publishing Co., 1969.

Krug, Mark M. "Primary Sources: Their Nature and Use in the Teaching of History." In *A New Look at Reading in the Social Studies.* Edited by Ralph C. Preston. Perspectives in Reading Series, No. 12. Newark, Del.: International Reading Association, 1969.

La Porte, Emma, former Spanish teacher at New Trier High School, Winnetka, Illinois, in remarks to the writer, May 1970.

Larrick, Nancy. "Pop/Rock Lyrics, Poetry and Reading, "*Journal of Reading,* 15, no. 3 (1971): 187.

Lynch, Elizabeth K., former social studies teacher, Neshaminy Langhorne High School, Langhorne, Pennsylvania, in remarks to the writer, January 1978.

Marantz, Sylvia. "A Hot Issue for a Cool Librarian." In *Fusing Reading Skills and Content.* Edited by H. Alan Robinson and Ellen Lamar Thomas. Newark, Del.: International Reading Association, 1969.

McCampbell, Darlene, Chairman of the English Department at the University of Chicago Laboratory School, in remarks to the writer, January 1979.

Moulton, Paul, former University of Chicago Laboratory School mathematics teacher, in remarks to the writer, May 1969.

Muelder, Richard H., University of Chicago Laboratory School mathematics teacher, in remarks to the writer, June 1970.

Niles, Olive Stafford. "Improvement of Basic Comprehension Skills: An Attainable Goal in Secondary School," a Scott Foresman monograph on education (Glenview, Ill.: Scott, Foresman and Co., 1964).

Podendorf, Illa, former University of Chicago Laboratory School science teacher, in remarks to the writer, May 1970.

Ravin, Sophie, University of Chicago Laboratory School English teacher, in remarks to the writer, January 1979.

Rise and Fall of the Third Reich. Wilmette, Ill.: Films, Inc., 1972.

Robinson, Francis P. "Study Skills for Superior Students in Secondary School." *The Reading Teacher,* 15 (September 1961).

Robinson, H. Alan. *Teaching Reading and Study Strategies,* 2nd ed. Boston: Allyn and Bacon, 1978.

Sartain, Harry W. "Content Reading—They'll Like It." *Journal of Reading,* 17 (October 1973): 47–51. Reprinted with permission of Harry W. Sartain and the International Reading Association.

Shnayer, Sidney W. "Relationships Between Reading Interest and Reading Comprehension." In *Reading and Realism.* Edited by J. Allen Figurel. Newark, Del.: International Reading Association, 1969.

Strang, Ruth, in lecture to class in the teaching of secondary school reading. University of Chicago, summer 1965.

Thomas, Ellen Lamar, and H. Alan Robinson. *Improving Reading in Every Class,* 2nd ed. Boston: Allyn and Bacon, 1977.

Three Billion Years of Life: The Drama of Evolution, slide set. White Plains, N.Y.: Science and Mankind, Inc., 1976.

Twisted Cross, The, NBC film. Champaign, Ill.: Visual Aids, University of Illinois, 1956.

Williamson, Ann P. "Affective Strategies at the Secondary Level." In *Classroom Practice in Reading.* Edited by Richard A. Earle. Newark, Del.: International Reading Association, 1977.

Helping Students Pull Out the Main Ideas from Paragraphs

If students cannot pull out the main ideas as they do close study of an informational passage, everything on the page seems of equal importance. Since they have no means of selecting, the task of study must seem overwhelming! We give students a major aid to study when we help them pull out the main ideas of paragraphs.

What is the plight of students who cannot pull out the main ideas from informational reading? The chapter before them is a blur—they cannot distinguish what is important from what is less important. They are at a loss to mark or underline the chapter, to make notes on the chapter, or to make an outline. And, of course, they cannot summarize the chapter.

To students who cannot select and discard, a chapter in their science or social studies textbook is a welter of facts and concepts—there may be as many as 400 in a chapter assigned for study on the high school level! How unmanageable the task of study must appear to these students!

Teachers Will Want to Work on Paragraph Patterns that Students Will Meet in Their Courses

You will find on the coming pages possible procedures for teaching students to find the main ideas in paragraphs. As illustrative materials, the writer has selected ten paragraph patterns, patterns that in her experience students encountered quite often in readings for their courses. You will find suggestions as to what a teacher might do and say in working with students on each of these ten patterns. You will also find, on the master copy pages, a pictorial aid for each paragraph pattern, a diagram that can be reproduced in quantities for students or projected on a screen before the class.

Of course, teachers will want to concentrate on the paragraph patterns that students will most often meet in the work of their particular courses. Accordingly, they will probably wish to create their own lesson materials for those particular patterns. They will also wish to work with paragraphs appropriate for the age levels and the reading reach of their students. The paragraphs on the master copies were prepared for use with high school students enrolled in developmental reading classes.

Suggestions for initial, basic work on finding the main idea for younger students, together with worksheets, are offered in the companion volume (Thomas and Robinson, *Improving Reading in Every Class,* unabridged 2nd ed., 1977), pp. 184–189. Instructional materials intended for more advanced students, including college students, will be found in James McCallister, "Using Paragraph Clues as Aids to Understanding," *Journal of Reading,* 8, no. 1 (October 1964): 11–16.

After students have developed competence in identifying the main ideas of paragraphs, it is desirable to move on to finding the main ideas of longer selections. Since subpoints that fall under main points are important in close study, students should also move on to identifying important details in paragraphs.

The writer has prepared this section in the hope that you will find the idea of paragraph placards as useful as she has found them in working with groups of students and in conferences with individual students who need help in singling out important information. The appropriate placard can be "whisked out" at the moment of need to clarify the structure of a paragraph with which a student is struggling. Again, teachers will do well to examine the reading materials they are assigning, learn what patterns occur frequently in those materials, then match their procedures and pictorial aids to those recurring patterns.

Finding the Main Idea, Just One of the Skills of Comprehension

The pages that follow offer an example of procedures for developing *one* of the skills of comprehension. Teachers will want to plan strategies and collect or create materials for developing *a broad range of comprehension skills*. Important among these are grasping important details, grasping implied meanings and drawing inferences, recognizing the author's tone, mood, and intent, drawing conclusions and making generalizations, and other processes involved in comprehension.

Students Respond Well to Work They Themselves Have "Ordered"

READING AID 167

Students respond well to being asked to tell their teacher what they feel they need in the way of study helps and to make requests about the content of the coming course. A teacher of high school developmental reading classes asked her students early in the year to mark a simple checklist. These were among the items:*

- ☐ I need to be able to find the main points when I am reading informational material.
- ☐ I need to be able to tell the difference between what is important and what is unimportant as I am reading.
- ☐ I should like to have help in taking notes when I read an assignment.
- ☐ I need help in retaining what is important.

In group after group, many students checked all four! Here was a clear message to work with finding main ideas, a skill basic to meeting all four requests. As the weeks passed, the students' own requests for help were used as motivators. The teacher would preface a lesson: "We're having this work with main ideas because you requested it." In the writer's experience, students tend to take advantage of help they themselves have "ordered." And there is an extra dividend for the teacher—the rapport that comes with caring about students' requests.

Students Come Up with Their Own "Whys"

READING AID 168

Let us suppose that a teacher whose students have responded to the checklist in Reading Aid 167, is introducing a lesson on how to find the main idea. The teacher might begin: "Almost all of you requested work on finding the main points of reading assignments. *Why* did you ask for this? *How* can it help you?"

In three or four minutes the students come up with some of the reasons. With guidance and some additions by the teacher, they generate the following list of "whys."

Why Learn to Find the Main Idea

1. When you can spot the main ideas in a passage, you'll probably *know better what to study* for tests and exams.
2. You'll *retain better!* A single textbook chapter may include a staggering number of facts and ideas—struggling to retain all these is hopeless! The first step in retention is to be able to select what's *important* to remember.
3. You'll *retain more easily.* Once you've grasped the main idea, the details fall into place in relation to it. Seen in relation to each other, both main ideas and details are far more easily remembered.
4. You'll need to spot the main points or you can't take effective school or college notes.
5. You'll sometimes be instructed: "Write a summary of this selection." Obviously, in order to summarize, you'll need to select the main points.
6. Colleges consider finding main ideas *an important "college prep" skill.* You'll find this question recurring on your S.A.T.'s: "What is the main idea of this passage?" When you take your S.A.T.'s, you'll think, "Good! I practiced that in class!"

*Such a checklist will be found in the companion volume (Thomas and Robinson, *Improving Reading in Every Class,* unabridged 2nd ed., 1977), p. 281.

7. When you can spot the main ideas, you've acquired a *speed technique*. When fast skimming is appropriate, you can skim for the main ideas.

READING AID 169

The Paragraph, the Building Block of Written Discourse

Students should understand why the unit they are working with is the paragraph. Insights like these, shared with classes by their teacher, can serve as motivators for work with paragraphs:

> What unit makes up almost all the material you'll read for information? That *building block of written discourse—the paragraph*. Almost everything you'll read at school is made up of paragraphs! Your informational reading after school years are over will be made up of paragraphs! You'll have a major tool for school and lifelong learning when you learn to "crack" a *paragraph* for its important content!

READING AID 170

What Is the Main Idea?

As we consider possible procedures for helping students find the main idea of paragraphs, let's picture the students as high school sophomores enrolled in developmental reading classes. Somewhere along the line most of them have gained some familiarity with the concept of the main idea.

The teacher asks: "*Just what is this main idea* we're after? We can find it better if we define it." The students contribute ideas and the teacher adds and elaborates to arrive at these pointers: "The main idea is the central thought the paragraph expresses. All the other sentences help to explain or support this central thought." . . . "The main idea is the point the paragraph makes—the point the author wants to leave with you." . . . "The main idea is a general statement. It is more general, broader, and covers more than any of the details that support it."

READING AID 171

Paragraph Pattern 1—Main Idea Sentence Placed First

With each of the paragraph patterns that follow, the teacher will need to make a decision whether to teach the pattern deductively or inductively. Practical considerations may lead to the decision to teach certain patterns deductively. Many older students have already acquired some familiarity with paragraph patterns. All they may need is a quick "call back" into active use of what they have learned in the past. In the writer's experience, older students are not very patient spending a lot of time "discovering" what is already familiar! Often some combination of inductive and deductive teaching will be most effective.

Paragraph Pattern 1 will be found on Master Copy Page 10. Teachers who decide to teach this paragraph pattern deductively will wish to supply the students with copies of the pattern or project the master copy on a screen. The teachers can then read the paragraph aloud while they point out—or elicit from students—the salient features of this most frequent of all paragraph patterns.

SEE MASTER COPY PAGE 10

Teachers who prefer to teach this pattern inductively might (after reading the paragraph aloud) guide students in some such way as this: "Can you find six ideas that stand out in this paragraph?" As the students suggest ideas, the teacher quickly jots them, much abbreviated, on the board. The teacher then asks: "Does one idea sum up the others?". . . . "Does one sentence *stand out* as expressing the overall or main idea?" The students select the first sentence. If the paragraph on the master copy is used and the teaching is inductive, retyping will, of course, be necessary so that the explanation on the master copy is eliminated and the students can make their own "discovery." Perhaps in reviewing, the teacher will wish to use the master copy, supplying the students with copies or projecting the master copy on a screen to help clinch their understanding of this pattern.

After spotlighting Paragraph Pattern 1, the teacher may wish to add: "A little later when you practice identifying different paragraph patterns, your symbol for this type will be the inverted pyramid.* It suggests that the most solid thought is at the top and the details come after that."

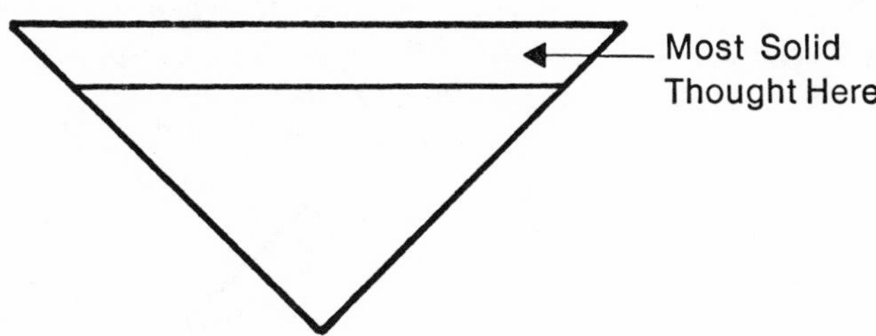

Teachers may wish to conclude the discussion of Paragraph Pattern 1 with comments like these: "Is it *always* this easy? Far from it! We should never take for granted that main idea first will be the pattern. If we do, we'll often be misled! Writers like variety—they build their paragraphs in different ways.

"Let's go on now to the second most frequent way of building paragraphs—Paragraph Pattern 2."

Note to Teachers about the Master Copies

If teachers find the master copies offered here appropriate for the age and the reading level of their students, they may wish to slip them into protective covers of clear plastic to insure long use. Paragraphs projected on a screen will be more striking if the teacher underlines the main idea sentence in red with a felt-tip pen and accents in red the arrows that lead the student's eye to the supporting details. Teachers will probably want to select from among the paragraph patterns those that suit their immediate purposes. In that case, they may wish to eliminate the numerals on the master copies with white typewriting correction fluid and then to print in the adjusted numerals.

As teachers work with students on paragraph patterns, they will want to cover only so much in a single lesson as seems manageable.

Paragraph Pattern 2—Main Idea Sentence Placed Last

READING AID 172

As with Paragraph Pattern 1, some teachers will wish to teach Paragraph Pattern 2 deductively. In that case, Master Copy Page 11 might be projected on a screen while the teacher simply points out—or elicits from students—the salient features.

SEE MASTER COPY PAGE 11

Other teachers will prefer to teach this pattern inductively, leading the class to "discover," with guidance, the main idea: "This paragraph contains a number of ideas. As I read it aloud, see if one idea stands out. We know that the main idea is the point the

*The useful paragraph symbols in this lesson have been borrowed from Doris Wilcox Gilbert, *Breaking the Reading Barrier* (Englewood Cliffs, N.J.: Prentice-Hall, 1959), pp. 46–47.

paragraph makes—the point the writer wants, most of all, to leave with you. What is the writer's message to you here?''

The students decide that the point of the whole thing is that any ''tool'' can be used for both good or evil. The teacher points out: ''Can you perceive the pattern—details first, then the sentence that sums them up last? That makes sense! Writers sometimes present a line of argument or a chain of reasoning, then the point they hope they've driven home. Their last sentence expresses the conclusion they hope you'll draw from the details that they have given.'' If the paragraph on the master copy is used, retyping will, of course, be necessary if the students are to make their own ''discovery.''

The teacher may wish to add: ''A little later when you practice identifying different paragraph patterns, your symbol for this type of paragraph will be the pyramid—details first, most solid thought at the bottom.''

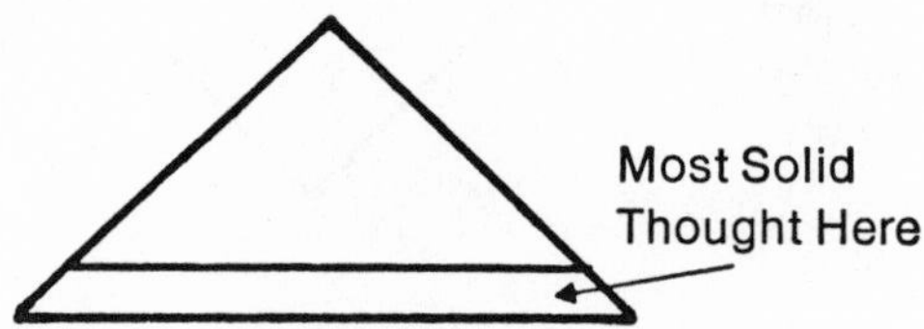

This may be an appropriate time for students to do practice work with paragraphs that fit Patterns 1 and 2. The students decide which pattern each paragraph follows, identify the main idea sentence, and label each paragraph with the appropriate symbol: either

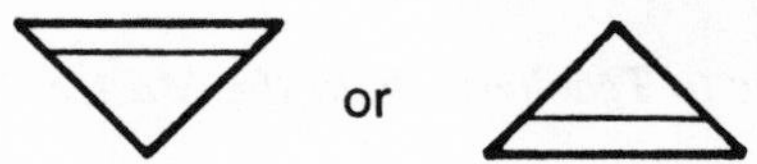

Paragraph Pattern 3—Main Idea Sentence In Between

READING AID 173

SEE MASTER COPY PAGE 12

The group moves on to Paragraph Pattern 3, which appears on Master Copy Page 12: ''We have just worked with main ideas placed first, then last in paragraphs. What about Paragraph Pattern 3?'' The teacher reads aloud the paragraph, then proceeds deductively or inductively as he or she prefers.

The students perceive that here the third sentence is the main idea sentence and learn, or perhaps recall from past instruction, that the main idea sentence may be first, last, or *anywhere in between.*

The teacher may wish to add: ''A little later when you do practice work with paragraphs and identify the different patterns, the symbol for the main idea 'anywhere in between' will be a diamond.''

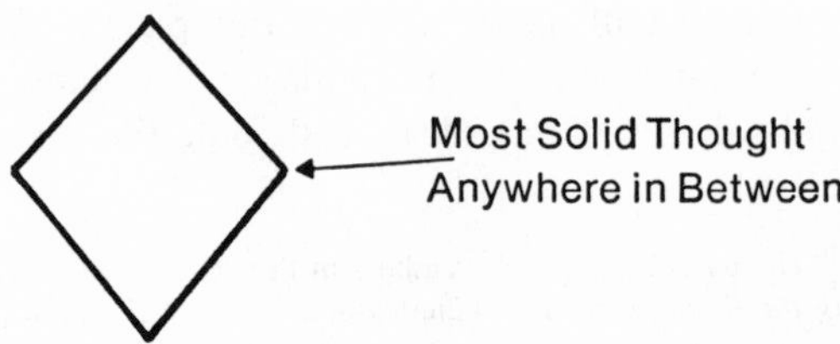

Practice with Paragraphs from Subject Areas

READING AID 174

The students have now been introduced to three paragraph patterns in which the main idea is directly stated and is found in various positions: 1) main idea first, 2) main idea last, and 3) main idea anywhere in between. The students can now complete practice exercises in which they identify the main idea sentence and perhaps assign each paragraph one of the three symbols:

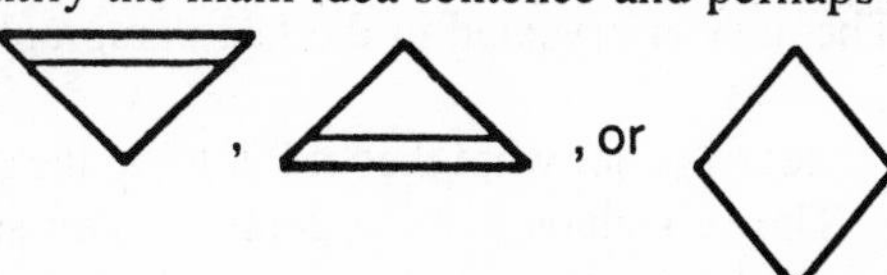

Practice work will be especially meaningful if paragraphs from the students' current course materials are analyzed. The students can work in their actual textbooks, or typical paragraphs can be duplicated or projected.

Paragraph Pattern 4—A "Split" Main Idea

READING AID 175

The paragraph that illustrates a "split" main idea appears on Master Copy Page 13. The teacher may proceed deductively or inductively.

SEE MASTER COPY PAGE 13

If the choice is deductive, the master copy might be projected on a screen or copies supplied to the students while the teacher points out—or elicits from the group—the salient features.

If the choice is inductive, the teacher might proceed: "Let's look at this paragraph. What is the main idea? Take care!" The teacher reads aloud the paragraph. (Again, if the paragraph on the master copy page is used and the students are to make their own "discovery," retyping without the explanation will be necessary.)

The students may be undecided. With discussion and guidance they perceive that here is a "split" main idea—part expressed in one sentence and part in another—and that to convey the main idea accurately, they must synthesize the two parts. The teacher elicits these understandings: "At first we might think that the first sentence expresses the main idea. But although the second and third sentences support this idea, the last sentence definitely does not. That atomic test scheduled for May 10 didn't happen! To convey the thought of the paragraph accurately, we must combine the first and last sentences: 'The atomic test was scheduled for May 10, but it was postponed.'"

The teacher will want to stress: "You will not necessarily find the parts of the 'split' main idea in the first and last sentences. You may find them in *any* of the sentences. Combine the parts essential to the main idea no matter where in the paragraph those parts are found."

The teacher may wish to add: "When you do practice work, this will be the symbol for the 'split' main idea":

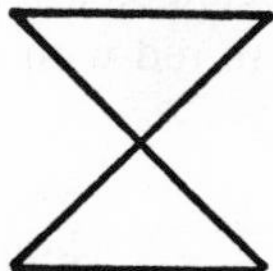

Paragraph Pattern 5—Main Idea Not Stated

READING AID 176

Again the teacher may proceed deductively or inductively, according to preference. A paragraph in which the main idea is not stated appears on Master Copy Page 14.

SEE MASTER COPY PAGE 14

If the choice is inductive, the teacher might proceed: "Can you find the main idea sentence in this paragraph?" The students cannot find one—no one sentence stands out. They conclude that there is no *stated* main idea. "What can you do then?" Some of the students suggest: "Reason it out for yourself."

The teacher comments: "In this paragraph no sentence 'takes the lead' as the main idea sentence. Each sentence supports a certain *unwritten* thought. Can you reason out or *infer* that unwritten thought?" (The answer revealed in the last paragraph on the placard has been covered.)

The students jot down on a sheet of paper what they think to be the main idea. Then they share and discuss their ideas. They conclude that the details—poor soil, unfavorable climate, and lack of trained workers—all support an "unwritten" main idea, which runs something like this: "This coastal area, for several reasons, is not favorable for growing oranges."

The teacher may wish to add: "Later when you do practice work with paragraphs and identify the different patterns, your symbol for this type of paragraph will be a square—no one idea standing out":

Paragraph Pattern 6—Is the Main Idea Always the Broadest Idea?

READING AID 177

The teacher proceeds deductively or inductively, according to preference. If the choice is deductive, the teacher shares insights like those on Master Copy Page 15.

SEE MASTER COPY PAGE 15

If the choice is inductive, the teacher might offer this guidance: "Like all paragraphs, this one holds several ideas. Which one of these is the *main* one—supported by the details in the paragraph? Take care!" The teacher reads aloud the paragraph.

Disagreement will probably follow as some students select the idea expressed in the first sentence and some select the idea in the second. The teacher helps them decide: "Which idea is built up—elaborated—in the paragraph? Which has the most said about it—the most space devoted to it?" Some students suggest the idea in the second sentence. The teacher agrees: "That political candidates use several methods is mentioned, yes; but that idea is not elaborated in the paragraph. *Only one method* is discussed. So we see that it's not always the broadest statement that expresses the main idea. It's the statement, often a conclusion, that the other ideas in the paragraph support." Again, if the master copy offered in this book is being projected on a screen, the main idea sentence will stand out conspicuously if it is underscored in red with a felt-tip pen.

Paragraph Pattern 7—A Seeming Contradiction

READING AID 178

The teacher proceeds deductively or inductively, according to preference. If the choice is deductive, the teacher shares insights like those on Master Copy Page 16.

SEE MASTER COPY PAGE 16

If the choice is inductive, the teacher might comment: "This paragraph can be a 'fooler'! Here the author expresses two contradictory ideas. Which is the main idea? Which idea is the writer advocating?" The teacher reads the paragraph aloud.

The teacher guides the discussion: "Is the first sentence the main idea sentence?" Most of the students don't think so. "Then why isn't it?" Some of the students suggest: "The rest of the paragraph doesn't support the idea that money is not super-important. Instead, the paragraph argues that making money *has great advantages*. Since the second sentence states that thought, it's the main idea sentence."

Paragraph Pattern 8—Main Idea Clarified by an Anecdote

READING AID 179

The teacher makes a choice of proceeding deductively or inductively. If the choice is deductive, the teacher shares insights like those on Master Copy Page 17.

SEE MASTER COPY PAGE 17

If the choice is inductive, the teacher can guide the group: "Please look at this paragraph. This, too, can be a 'fooler.' What is the main idea here?" The teacher reads aloud the paragraph.

The students express their ideas. Some say the main idea is that fear stops the digestive juices; others, that it is the way prisoners were once "tried" for crimes in India. With guidance, all see that the main point is expressed in the first sentence, which states that fear stops the digestive juices, and that the rest of the paragraph is an anecdote, or little story, told solely for the purpose of clarifying that main point.

The teacher cautions: "There's danger in a paragraph like this one! The story of the unusual trial of the prisoner is 'spectacular' and catches our attention—we might easily conclude that *it* is the main idea. But the story is told only to support the idea that *fear stops the flow of the digestive juices*. That idea, then, is the message of the paragraph."

Paragraph Pattern 9—Main Idea Supported by an Example

READING AID 180

If the teacher proceeds deductively, the teacher shares—or elicits—insights like those on Master Copy Page 18.

SEE MASTER COPY PAGE 18

If the choice is inductive, the teacher might offer this guidance: "This paragraph, too, can be a 'fooler.' Sometimes the author makes a main idea clear by illustrating it with one or more examples. Then take care! Danger arises because the example may be more interesting than the main idea and thus attracts our attention. We may confuse the example, which is intended only to illustrate, with the main point.

"What idea is being driven home in the paragraph?" The teacher reads the paragraph aloud. The students share their ideas. With guidance, they perceive that while the canoe example is "spectacular" and catches attention, it is *not* the main idea. It is *just an example* to demonstrate that people in a small Ohio town made many of the things they desired. The teacher comments: "Skillful readers carefully differentiate between the author's main points and supporting examples."

Paragraph Pattern 10—Main Idea in Part of a Sentence

READING AID 181

The insight shared with students through Paragraph Pattern 10 (on Master Copy 19) seems to lend itself to inductive teaching. The students quickly see that only part of the main idea sentence is supported by the details and that that part alone holds the main idea.

SEE MASTER COPY PAGE 19

What Tips Would You Give Another Student?

READING AID 182

During or after practice work, students might be led, through the following question, to pool useful pointers for finding this sometimes elusive main idea. The teacher might

SEE MASTER COPY PAGE 20

suggest: "Suppose another student told you: 'I don't know how to find the main ideas in paragraphs.' What tips could you give that student?" With guidance and some additions from the teacher, the students might generate the helps that appear on Master Copy Page 20.

Assigned Readings Offer Materials for Practice

READING AID 183

Practice work will be especially meaningful if the students work with paragraphs from their actual subject area textbooks and other assigned readings. As we have noted, teachers should do their "homework" in examining the materials they are assigning and in selecting paragraph patterns their students will encounter frequently. The students can use their actual textbooks, or selected paragraphs can be duplicated on practice worksheets. If worksheets are used, the students can be asked to bracket or underline the main idea sentence if the main idea is stated directly or to write out the main idea if they must infer it. The students are likely to react, "This work we're having will really help me get at the important points when I study my assignments."

Details May Be Important, Too. Reading Aids 167–183 have strongly stressed the importance of identifying the main ideas in paragraphs. Students should not leave such activities, however, with the impression that *only* the main idea is important. They should understand that subpoints under main points are often important, too, and that they will soon move on to work with identifying the important *details* in paragraphs.

Let Students Prove Mastery on a Test

READING AID 184

After students have had instruction and practice in finding the main idea in paragraphs, the teacher might give them the opportunity to *prove* their command of this skill by including a main idea question on a unit test. A paragraph or two that are excerpts from the students' actual textbooks can become the question material. The students can *prove* their skill by bracketing or underlining the main idea sentence if the main idea is expressed or by expressing the main idea for themselves if it must be inferred. As with vocabulary development, students will take skill development in paragraph comprehension much more seriously if they are checked in a regular testing situation. They will realize how important their teachers consider the skill.

Students Should Consider Why a Particular Assignment Was Made

READING AID 185

The students' proficiency in analyzing paragraphs will serve them best when they are called upon to do close reading and to single out and retain the important content. Often, however, the teacher has a special purpose in mind in assigning certain reading. The teacher might suggest, for example: "This book offers a point of view about large corporations quite different from that in your textbook." Then the student will want to approach the reading with the question, "Just what *is* this different viewpoint?" and they will want to single out *this particular content*. The teacher will wish to strongly emphasize for students:

> In making a reading assignment, your teacher may have made some comments on the *why* of that assignment. He or she may have helped you set a special purpose for that particular reading. In that case *your teacher's comments will influence your decision about what to regard as important, and fulfilling that purpose is likely to be your overriding consideration as you are reading.*

Students Should Understand the Limitations of Studying Paragraph Patterns

READING AID 186

Students who work with paragraph patterns like those just presented should understand that these prototypes have been made clearcut in organization—deliberately—to drive home the nature of the pattern. They should be made aware that many paragraphs in the actual prose they will be reading will not mirror these organizational patterns. They should further understand that gifted writers, especially, seek variety in the paragraphs they create and tend to depart from rigid patterns. They should appreciate, nonetheless, that writers of textbooks and other well-organized expository prose do, indeed, often follow such patterns. They should further appreciate that it is of great value for them to realize that everything they read is definitely *not of equal importance* on the pages they study and to be on sharp lookout for the main ideas.

It should also be pointed out to students that different readers may interpret a paragraph differently, express the main idea differently, even identify the main idea differently—that often we cannot say with great finality, "This—and this only—is the main idea."

Work on Main Ideas of Paragraphs Just One Important Step

The work with main ideas discussed on the preceding pages is just *one* important step in helping students single out what is important as they read and study. Having worked with main points, they will now need to learn to recognize important subpoints and to differentiate these from content that may be disregarded as they study a selection. And they should definitely move on to work with identifying the main idea of a longer selection.

Students will also profit from learning about three types of paragraphs that are classified according to the purposes they fulfill within a longer selection—paragraphs of *introduction,* of *summary,* and of *transition.* Students will be able to unlock ideas in their readings in science more successfully if they have met the major patterns of writing in science: *enumeration, classification, generalization, problem solution, comparison or contrast,* and *sequence.* They will learn more successfully from their reading materials in social studies if they have met and developed strategies for reading these major patterns of writing in social studies: *topic development, enumeration, generalization, sequence, comparison or contrast, effect-cause,* and *question-answer.* (Robinson, 1975, p. 166, p. 203)

Teachers who are searching for practical ideas for instructing students in these areas and for patterns for creating their own practice materials should find the following sources especially helpful:

Gilbert, Doris Wilcox. *Breaking the Reading Barrier.* Englewood Cliffs, N.J.: Prentice-Hall, 1959.

Judson, Horace. *The Techniques of Reading,* 3rd ed. New York: Harcourt, Brace and World, 1972.

Karlin, Robert. *Teaching Reading in High School: Improving Reading in Content Areas,* 3rd ed. Indianapolis: Bobbs-Merrill, 1977.

McCallister, James. "Using Paragraph Clues as Aids to Understanding." *Journal of Reading,* 8, no. 1 (October 1964): 11–16.

Robinson, H. Alan. *Teaching Reading and Study Strategies: The Content Areas,* 2nd ed. Boston: Allyn and Bacon, 1978.

Shepherd, David L. *Comprehensive High School Reading Methods.* Columbus, Ohio: Charles E. Merrill, 1973.

Sherbourne, Julia Florence. *Toward Reading Comprehension,* 2nd ed. Lexington, Mass.: D.C. Heath and Co., 1977.

Smith, Nila Banton. *Be a Better Reader Series,* Basic Skills Edition, 3rd ed. Englewood Cliffs, N.J.: Prentice-Hall, 1977.

What have we accomplished when we have worked successfully with students on identifying the main ideas? We have made an important addition to their study skills tool kit. As we have noted, they should now be better able to select important points when making notes on their reading, to outline a passage, and to underline or mark the main points in their books. They have now taken a long step toward the important study skill of summarizing a longer selection. In order to do this, they will need to single out important ideas from successive paragraphs and weave the most important of these into a summary.

As has been stressed, being able to identify important details in paragraphs is also essential for students who are doing close reading of informational material. Let us now move on to helping students identify major subpoints.

Helping Students Identify Important Details in Paragraphs

Students should not gain the impression that only the main idea is important in a paragraph. They should understand that subpoints under main points can be very important, too. They will benefit from guidance in identifying important subpoints.

In order to grasp the important content of informational writing, the student should move on from finding the main ideas in paragraphs to identifying the important details.

As students do this, a possible order of things is spotting these details, first, when they are marked by "full signals," next, when they are marked by "half signals," and, finally, when they are marked by no signals. The students should learn to differentiate details that are important from those that are only unnecessary repetition or elaboration. Work like this can, with real advantage to the students, be tied in with the essential study skill of notemaking.

On the pages that follow, you will find possible procedures for helping students recognize important details. Obviously, teachers will wish to work with paragraphs appropriate for the age levels and the reading levels of their students. The paragraphs in the activities that follow were prepared for high school students enrolled in classes in developmental reading. Because space in this book is limited, much has been telescoped into the next few pages. Teachers will want to divide their instruction into manageable segments, to provide appropriate follow-up practice, and to reinforce and review as needed.

In working with students on identifying what is important in informational writing, the teacher will want to stress this point strongly: "In making a reading assignment, your teacher may have in mind a special *why* for that assignment. He or she may have helped you set a special purpose for that particular reading. In that case, your teacher's comments will influence your decision about what to regard as important, and fulfilling this purpose is likely to be your overriding consideration as you are reading."

Spotting Details with "Full Signals"

READING AID 187

Let's imagine that we are looking in on a class of high school sophomores who are enrolled in developmental reading.

The teacher comments: "We have practiced finding the main ideas of paragraphs. Details, too, are often important. How can you recognize important details? And how can you have some idea which details to disregard?

"Today's work should sharpen up some important study skills. When you can spot the main ideas and the major details, you can *retain* better. As we know, a single textbook chapter may hold more than 400 facts and ideas! The struggle to retain these would be overwhelming! The first step in retention, then, is to select what's *important* to remember. When you know how to select, you can get the important points down in notes on your reading, or underline or mark them, and of course you can study for tests and exams more successfully.

"Writers often use signal words in paragraphs. These often signal important details. We'll practice spotting details first with 'full signals,' then with 'half signals,' and finally with no signals."*

The students are supplied with copies of the list of signal words that appears on Master Copy Pages 21 and 22. The teacher spends a few moments going over the list of "full signals." Each student has a duplicated work sheet with paragraphs to be used for practice.

"Let's look at paragraph one on your worksheet. Do you see how 'full signals' make the structure of this paragraph instantly clear? Do you see how the main point and important subpoints almost jump out from the page?" The students quickly spot these points—the main point and the subpoints marked with the "full signals," *first, second,* and *third.*

SEE MASTER COPY PAGES 21–22

> There are three reasons why you should strive to increase your vocabulary. The first is that words are the tools of thought. Can you imagine yourself thinking without words? The second is that you need words to tell your thoughts to others. If you say, "I know what I mean, but I can't say it," then you need more words in your speaking vocabulary. The third reason is that you cannot fully understand others unless you understand the words they use.†

"How would you take brief notes on this paragraph?" The teacher quickly jots on the board the notes the students suggest, using dotted vertical lines to drive home levels of subordination and using a "personal shorthand." See Figure 4–1. To attract students to simple, not too time consuming notemaking, the teacher uses—and encourages students to use—a quick, labor-saving "personal shorthand," as in Figure 4–1. The students are encouraged to write only the basic thought of the main idea sentence in as few words as possible and to note the details in as short form as possible.

The students now move on to more difficult practice with "full signals."

READING AID 188

What Details Can Be Disregarded?

After moving on to more difficult practice work with "full signals," the teacher goes on: "You have asked: 'When there are so many facts in a reading assignment, how can I decide between what is important and what is unimportant?' What kinds of details do you think can sometimes be disregarded as you study? As you know, your teacher may have given the class a special *why* for reading a certain assignment. If this is the case, that purpose will, of course, influence your decision about what to select as important. If you are on your own to make the selection, here are some guidelines that may prove useful. You can often disregard: 1) sentences that repeat a point you have already thoroughly grasped, 2) sentences that give an unimportant example or illustration of a point you have already grasped (however, it is often important to remember at least one example), 3) sentences that make a detour in thought to give interesting but unnecessary detail, 4) sen-

*For the concept of "full signal," "half signals," and no signals, the writer is indebted to Rachel Salisbury, *Better Work Habits* (Glenview, Ill.: Scott Foresman and Co., 1932), pp. 199–202.

†Reprinted by permission of the publisher from Julia Florence Sherbourne: *Toward Reading Comprehension* (Lexington, Mass.: D. C. Heath and Co., 1958), p. 81.

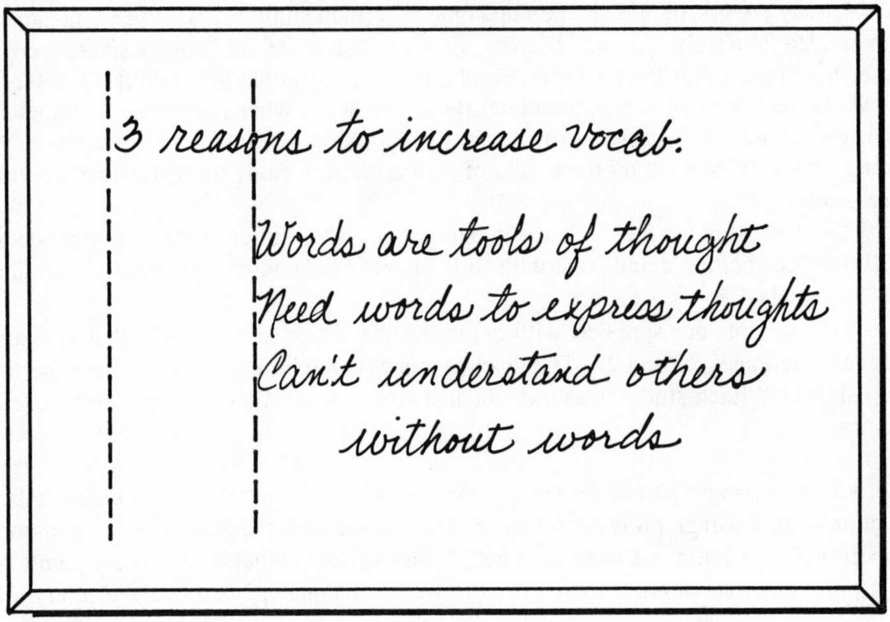

3 reasons to increase vocab.

Words are tools of thought
Need words to express thoughts
Can't understand others
without words

FIGURE 4–1

Work on finding the main points and important subpoints can be tied in with the essential study skill of notemaking.

tences that offer unimportant elaboration, and, of course, 5) content unrelated to your present purpose.*

''Let's look at Paragraph 2 on your worksheet. Among the first four sentences, can you find one that is mere elaboration?'' The students suggest the third sentence, which merely elaborates the thought just expressed in the second sentence—that the student must concentrate.

> Students find it very important to know how to learn from an address or a lecture that can be heard but once. First, the student must concentrate upon what is being said. He cannot fix his thoughts upon plans for the evening, or upon clothes, or upon any social affairs. Second, he must learn how to recognize the important points of the discussion when he hears them, so that he will not be stressing details and illustrations and overlooking the important facts. Third, he must learn and practice some system of taking notes. This is one of the most important skills used in study, and is a habit that carries over into afterlife to great advantage. Fourth, he must write up his notes soon after the lecture, when the facts as he heard them are still in his mind to supplement or correct any faulty note-taking. Fifth, he should reflect on the ideas in the lecture, and compare them with books on the same subject. Finally, he must organize his notes by making a clear outline, intelligible to himself and to others at a later date, and have this in permanent form for reference and review before examinations. The student who trains himself to take these six steps intelligently will be sure of doing work satisfactory both to the teacher and to himself.**

''Now, using 'full signals,' can you jot down quick notes on this paragraph, using the dotted lines? Use your 'personal shorthand.' '' To tie up this work with notemaking,

*Ideas 3 and 4 from Rachel Salisbury, *Better Work Habits* (Glenview, Ill.: Scott, Foresman and Co. 1932), pp. 201–202.

**From *Better Work Habits* by Rachel Salisbury. Copyright 1932 by Scott, Foresman and Co., p. 44. Reprinted by permission.

the students have been encouraged to draw two vertical dotted lines near the left edge of their paper, about three-quarters of an inch apart and running the length of the paper. As the lesson moves along, the students pull out the main point from the practice paragraph and write this flush with the dotted line to the left, as in the following example. Then they pull out important subpoints and set these in under the main point. Of course, the double lines drive home the concept of levels of subordination.

Again, the students are encouraged to strip the author's expression of the main idea and the details down to the few words that are the "kernel." The students' notes look something like those in Figure 4–2.

The teacher calls on one student to read his notes aloud, then asks: "What 'full signals' did you spot?" The students point out "First," "Second," "Third," "Fourth," "Fifth," and "Finally."

"Did you find anything more that is mere elaboration?" The students suggest sentence 6, which is just elaboration about note taking.

Spotting Details with "Half Signals"

READING AID 189

Later the students move on to find details when they are marked by "half signals." The teacher comments: "Please look at your list of signal words again (see Master Copy Pages 21 and 22). Sometimes writers mark details with just 'half signals.' Now the puzzle becomes harder." The teacher takes a few moments to go over the list of "half signals."

"Please look at the paragraph on your worksheet. Signal words, you remember, often signal important details. Will you please read this paragraph to yourselves, spotting the 'half signals' as you read and letting them guide you to the important details? Take quick notes in 'personal shorthand' again, using your dotted lines."

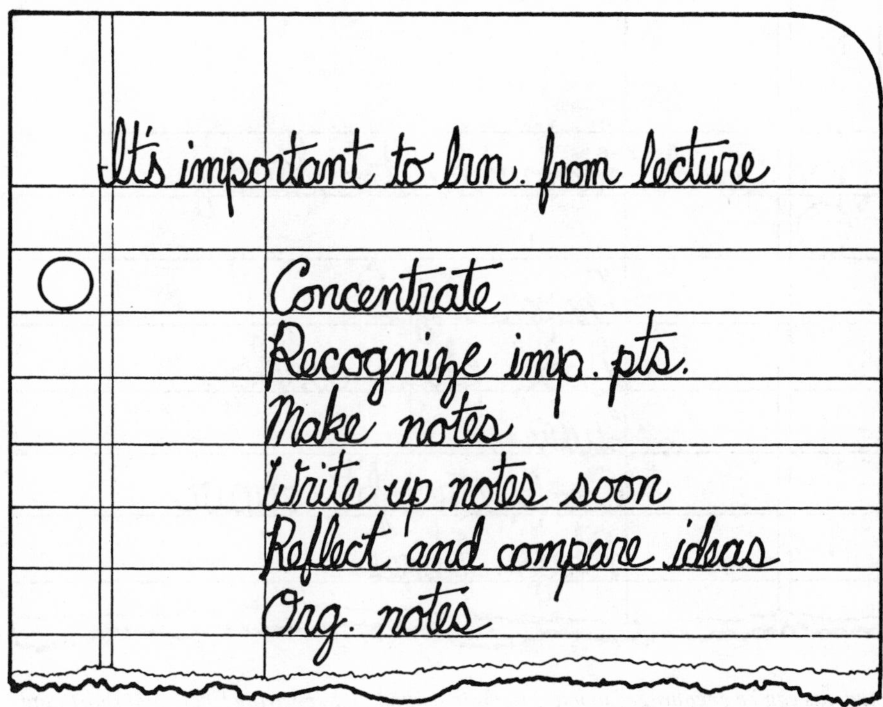

FIGURE 4–2

The double lines drive home for the student the concept of levels of subordination.

> Whether you study at home or at school, you should give attention to certain conditions favorable to study. One of the most important conditions for good study is that of proper light. Never study with the light shining directly in your eyes, or by dim light. Next, see that the physical conditions in the room are normal, that the room is properly heated and ventilated, and that there are no drafts. A room warmer than 70 degrees is not conducive to alertness. Then secure quietness. This should be easier to do at school than at home, but with a little ingenuity and planning, it can be accomplished at home. Your study hours must be as free as possible from distractions. Also provide yourself with an ordinary, comfortable, straight-backed chair, for you cannot do vigorous work while lounging about. Last, keep yourself physically fit. Give proper attention to food, sleep, and exercise, so that your study will bring maximum results.*

One of the students reads his notes to the group. They resemble those in Figure 4–3. He points out as "half signals" the words "One," "Next," "Then," "Also," and "Last."

"Let's go on to the next paragraph on your worksheet. In this paragraph, the 'half signals' are italicized. Each one says, 'Here comes an important detail!' How quickly can you pick up the main idea and four major details and jot them on your sheet with the dotted lines?"

> If you wish to be a successful teacher you must possess four characteristics. It is *of great importance* that you enjoy learning. What you learn becomes your stock in trade. It is *also important* that you wish to impart your learning to others. It is not enough to know; you must be able to pass on what you know. But, even though you can make the complex appear simple and the obscure plain, you must possess *still another* charac-

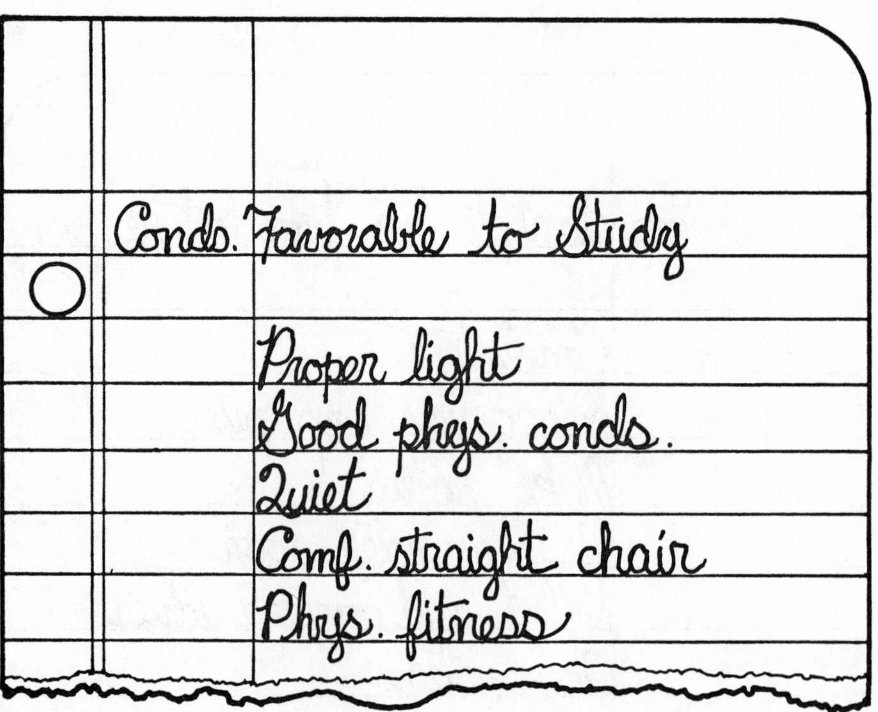

FIGURE 4–3 ***Students can be encouraged to make notes in a quick, labor-saving "personal shorthand."***

*From *Better Work Habits* by Rachel Salisbury. Copyright 1932 by Scott, Foresman and Co., p. 44. Reprinted by permission.

teristic; you must be able to inspire your students to learn. After all, you cannot make them learn anything they do not want, in some degree at least, to learn. And if you arouse their curiosity sufficiently, nothing and no one—not even you—can keep them from learning. *Finally* you must have patience. This patience is not, however, a meek, passive sort of thing. It is a determined patience which finally has its way. It is the patience of water wearing away a stone.*

The students find those points quickly and express them in as short form as possible. Their notes look something like those in Figure 4–4.

The students now go on to more difficult practice with "half signals."

Moving on to No Signals

READING AID 190

When the time is right, the students move on to recognizing important details with *no* signals. The teacher comments: "We'll go on now from 'full signals' and 'half signals' to *no* signals. We'll pull out important details with no signals at all. You will encounter many, many paragraphs that contain no signals.

"Let's look at the next paragraph on your worksheet. This paragraph informs you that there are two ways to own a book. One way is marked in the paragraph by the signal word *first*. But there is no signal at all for the second way. What is the second way?"

There are two ways in which one can own a book. The *first* is the property right you establish by paying for it, just as you pay for clothes and furniture. But this act of purchase is only the prelude to possession. Full ownership comes only when you have made it a part of yourself, and the best way to make yourself a part of it is by writing in

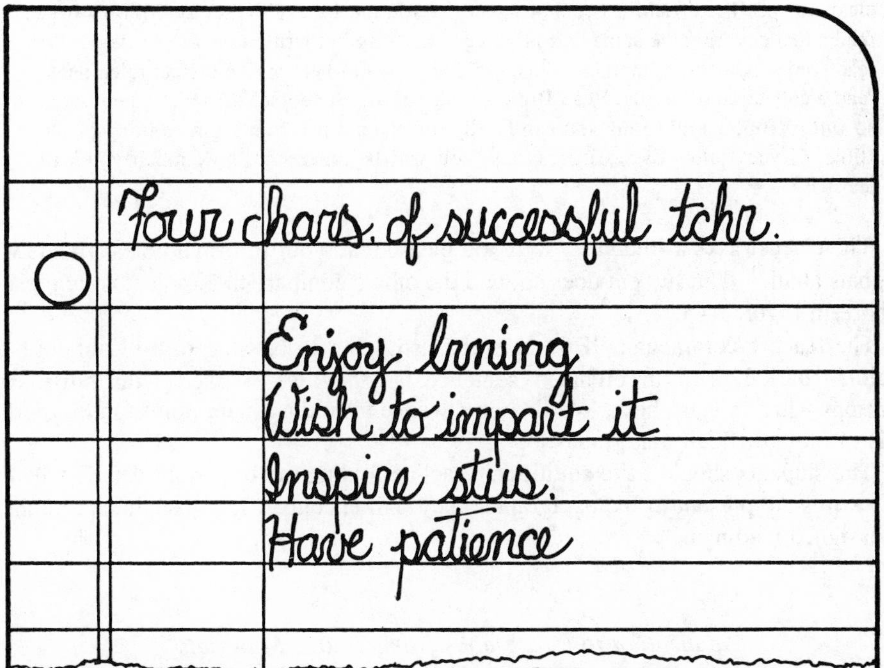

Four chars. of successful tchr.

Enjoy lrning
Wish to impart it
Inspire stus.
Have patience

FIGURE 4–4

Students strip the main idea and the major details down to the few words that are the "kernel" of thought.

*Reprinted by permission of the publisher from Julia Florence Sherbourne: *Toward Reading Comprehension* (Lexington, Mass.: D.C. Heath and Co., 1977), p. 236.

> it. An illustration may make the point clear. You buy a beefsteak and transfer it from the butcher's icebox to your own. But you do not own the beefsteak in the most important sense until you consume it and get it into your bloodstream. I am arguing that books, too, must be absorbed in your bloodstream to do you any good.*

The students read the paragraph, then report that the second way is to make the book a part of yourself by writing in it.

The teacher continues: "What kind of details can you often disregard in study-reading?" The students recall that you can disregard unnecessary repetition and elaboration. "In this paragraph [above] can you find three or four sentences in a row that are interesting but not necessary—that are unimportant elaboration?" The students point out the comparison between the book that has been assimilated and the beefsteak that has been consumed.

"Let's go on to the next paragraph on your worksheet. With *no signals at all,* can you make informal notes on this paragraph? Can you write the main idea on your paper [with the dotted lines] and indent four important subpoints?"

> Your reading can increase your background knowledge if you heed the following suggestions. Read a great deal more than you have in the past. You don't have time? Try carrying a book or a magazine with you so that you can read it at odd moments. Take your book out on trains and buses and while you wait for friends. Open it while you wait to be served in a restaurant—even while you are standing in line at the Student Union. To enrich your knowledge, read in a wide variety of fields of interest. Select readings about baseball and other sports—about music—about industry. Don't read only in one field you think you're interested in. Read various types of literature—poetry, short stories, novels, plays, essays, and articles. Read books, magazines, and at least one good newspaper. To further expand your knowledge, read to clear up specific difficulties. For instance, if you are having difficulty with history, read a text covering the same period you are studying but written on a lower level. Or read some popular biographies or historical novels. For help with classical references, read a collection of myths. Read Bible stories, or the Bible itself. English literature is so full of Biblical allusions you can hardly understand it if you know nothing of the Bible. If you follow these suggestions, you will be amazed at how much you will learn.†

The teacher asks a student: "Will you please read your informal notes—made with no signals at all?" The student does so, and the others compare their notes, which resemble those in Figure 4–5.

The teacher comments: "How useful in studying to be able to pull out four big subpoints—buried deep in eighteen sentences! Today we worked with fairly easy paragraphs—just to learn how. We'll soon advance to finding main points and important details in more difficult paragraphs."

The students should have additional practice finding the important details when no signal words are present in the paragraph. They will encounter many such paragraphs in their assigned readings.

Application to Paragraphs from Course Materials

READING AID 191

Teachers can guide students who have been introduced to finding main points and important subpoints to apply their newly acquired skills to their course materials. The students

*Mortimer J. Adler, "How to Mark A Book," *Saturday Review of Literature*, 22, no. 11 (July 6, 1940): 11. Reprinted by permission of the author.

†Reprinted by permission of the publisher from Julia Florence Sherbourne: *Toward Reading Comprehension* (Lexington, Mass.: D.C. Heath and Co., 1958), p. 80. Slightly adapted.

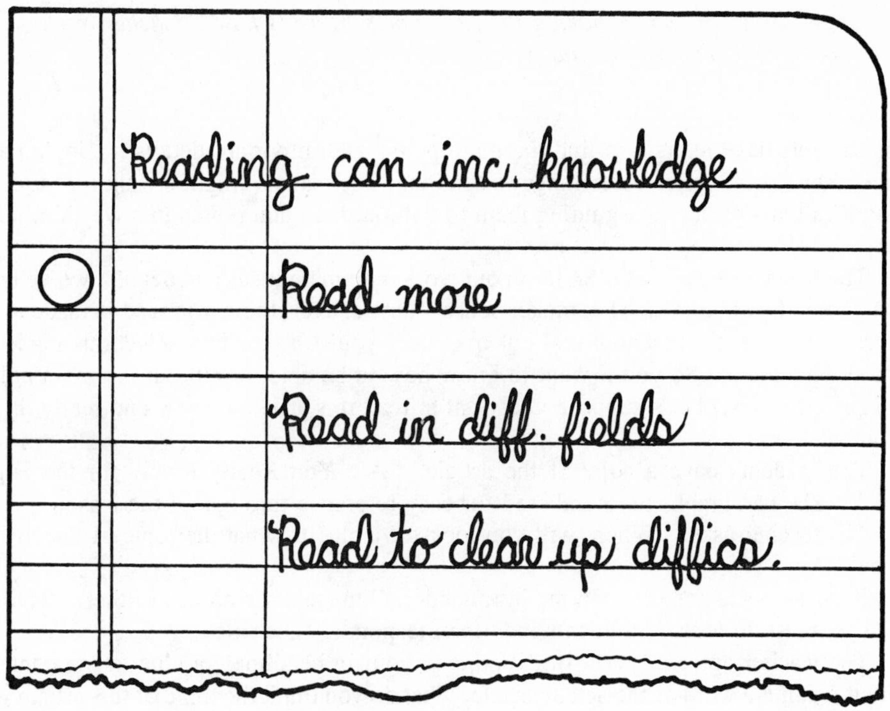

Students learn to pull out the main point and the major subpoints although they are "buried" deep in eighteen sentences.

FIGURE 4–5

can work with paragraphs in their actual textbooks, or paragraphs selected by the teacher might be duplicated on worksheets.

Can You "Crack" This Paragraph for Important Points?

READING AID 192

Why not let students *prove* on a unit test that they can find the main point and the major subpoints of a paragraph? A paragraph excerpted from the students' actual textbooks in the course can provide the question material. The students can be given directions something like this: "Can you 'crack' this paragraph? Can you pull out the main point and important subpoints and jot them down in brief notes? Be sure to show levels of subordination. Use your personal shorthand."

As we have noted, students will take work on skill development *much* more seriously if they are checked in a regular testing situation. They will realize that their teachers consider the skill really important.

Students Should Now Have More Study Power. What have we given students through this work on identifying main points and important subpoints? Hopefully, we have given them more "study power." The notes they make on their reading—and their outlines and summaries—should now include more significant information. As we have observed, they should now mark or underline their books more accurately. They should also have a useful tool to put to work as they listen to lectures or talks in class. From these they should now be better able to select the key points and to get them down in notes for future study.

Helping Students Pull Out the Main Content of a Longer Selection

After working with the main ideas and important details in paragraphs, students should have guidance in "selecting out" the important content from a longer selection and in making informal notes. Here is how a teacher might walk students through such a process.

READING AID 193

After students have learned to find the main points and important details in single paragraphs, they should move on to longer selections. The teacher might "walk the students through" a longer selection, guiding them to pull out the main points in a way similar to this.

The teacher comments: "So far in our work with main ideas and details, we've been practicing with paragraphs. That makes sense—almost everything you read is made up of paragraphs! But both in school and out of school you'll be reading selections made up of *many* paragraphs. So you'll want to know how to be able to pull out the main points of longer selections. Let's suppose you want to read this article closely and really digest its content."

The students have a copy of the article, "Are You Really Ready for the Highways?"* The paragraphs are numbered for easy reference throughout the lesson.

The teacher asks: "Where will you look for a clue to what the topic of this article will be?"

If the students answer, "In the introduction," the teacher probes further, "Is there somewhere else to look?" Students may then respond, "The title."

The teacher agrees: "Yes, titles *shout* to you, in headlines, a clue to the content. Without reading a word of the actual article, what do you think the topic of this article will be?"

The students answer: "Something about getting ready for highway driving."

The teacher then asks: "How can we become more certain what the topic is?"

Students: "Read the introduction."

The teacher suggests: "Please read silently into the article far enough so that you are *sure* of the topic."

After the students have read a few paragraphs, one of them suggests: "The topic is *not* that the grandfather would have been frightened on a superhighway. You realize that as you read on."

The teacher agrees: "The writer meant that only as an interest-catcher. Introductions often include interest-catchers."

One student suggests: "Paragraph three suggests that the topic might be the *difficulties* of superhighway driving or it might be *advice* to highway drivers."

The teacher inquires: "How can you know which it is?"

A student helps out: "If you glance through the rest of the article, you'll learn it's *advice* to drivers."

Another student: "That fits in with the title, too—'Are You Really Ready for the Highways?'"

On the chalkboard is a framework for informal notes. The students, working as a group, proceed to fill it in. They fill in the introduction part as follows:

Are You Really Ready for the Highways?

Main Idea of the Selection According to the Introduction	I. Authorities have advice for drivers on superhighways.

*This article by Norman Richards is reproduced on page 149 with the generous permission of the Marathon Oil Company from *Marathon World,* Vol. 9, No. 1, 1972. The article has been abridged and adapted.

II.

A.

B.

etc.

The teacher comments: "Now we have a purpose-setter—to learn the advice for drivers. Let's read on, paragraph by paragraph, to learn that advice. Where in each paragraph will you expect to find the main idea?" The students recall that the main idea may be first, last, or anywhere in the paragraph, that it may be "split" between two or three parts of the paragraph, or that it may not be stated at all, in which case they must infer it.

The teacher anticipates a problem: "Sometimes a writer uses a sequence of two or more paragraphs to present *one* main point. In this article, be on the lookout for some paragraphs where an important idea runs across more than one paragraph." Also: "You may find a paragraph that adds some detail that is not really 'important idea' material. You will not need to make any notes on such a paragraph."

The students work part way through the article, paragraph by paragraph, pulling out main points and important details, just as they did in their practice work with single paragraphs. They use the notemaking framework on the chalkboard flexibly, filling it in something like this:

I. Authorities have advice for drivers on superhighways.

II. Don't forget you're traveling at great speeds.
   A. Reflexes are slow.
   B. Tailgate collisions are a danger.

III. Plan trip ahead
   A. Check roadmap before entering expressway.
   B. Know number and distance of exit.

IV. Watch for dangers changing lanes and passing.
   A. Use directional signals.
   B. Scan traffic far ahead.

V. Avoid fatigue, drowsiness, eyestrain.
   A. Superhighways are hypnotic.
   B. It's safer to drive by day.

VI. Check medicines for side effects.
  A. Ask doctor.
  B. Read labels.

VII. Avoid heavy meals that cause drowsiness.
  A. Light snacks give needed energy.
  B. Coffee breaks help.
  C. Fresh air is important.

VIII. Be aware of driver fatigue.
  A. Set realistic mileage goals.
  B. Keep children from distracting driver.

When the students finish paragraph 10, the teacher reminds them: "As you know, a writer sometimes uses two or three paragraphs to develop *one* important point. Can you find a group of paragraphs coming soon that will all deal with the same point?"

The students point out that paragraphs 11, 12, and 13 are related—that they all deal with breakdowns on the highways and thus belong together as a group. After some thought they conclude that the main idea running across these paragraphs is this: *Avoid dangers from breakdowns.* They decide that they need not make notes on paragraph 12—that its reassurance that there is "little cause for alarm" is not crucial to the theme of advice to motorists who are doing high-speed driving. The students perceive that this time they should indent their notes to the third level (see below). They outline paragraphs 11–13 like this:

IX. Avoid dangers from breakdowns.
  1 A. Prevent them through check-up.
    1. Check tires
    2. Check brakes, steering, windshield wipers.
  B. Get car off pavement.
    1. Use flasher lights; raise hood.
    2. Or display white handkerchief.

The students work their way through the rest of the article. They make notes on paragraph 14 similar to this:

X. Government has failed to make uniform traffic laws.
  A. Laws differ from state to state.
  B. Check them out before a trip.

The teacher asks: ''What does a writer often do in the conclusion?'' The students suggest that the writer ''wraps up'' the discussion and may drive home what he or she wants most of all to leave with the reader. They recognize paragraph 15 as the conclusion.

They make notes on the concluding paragraph like this:

XI. Adaptation to conditions brings safety.
A. Check your car!
B. Check yourself!

The teacher makes these concluding comments: ''Now you have moved on from single paragraphs to longer selections. You'll encounter *countless* longer selections as you read and study. The study strategies you have just met should help you select and really digest the crucial content.''

A selection shorter than the one used for illustrative purposes in this section may be appropriate, or the selection used here may be further abridged.

ARE YOU REALLY READY FOR THE HIGHWAYS?

Before a Long, High-Speed Trip, Check Your Car—and Yourself

Norman Richards

1. My grandfather never drove on a modern interstate superhighway, and he probably would have been scared to death if he had. He would have considered it foolhardy to drive at the dizzying speed of 70 miles an hour with other traffic on the road, and unwise to risk a mechanical breakdown on a bleak highway, miles from help. Yet in the past 25 years, due to the greatest road building effort in world history, most Americans have become accustomed to at least an occasional high-speed trip on a freeway, turnpike, or expressway.

2. Superhighway driving *is* different, of course, from the kind of short-haul, in-town driving that most of us do on a daily basis. The average motorist puts a very small percentage of his annual mileage on the high-speed thoroughfares. When he does venture onto them for a vacation trip or other special journey, he's faced with a different set of conditions. How well he adapts to them determines his degree of safe—and pleasurable—traveling.

3. What are the most common difficulties in adjusting to superhighway driving? What advice do authorities give motorists for better traveling on the high-speed thoroughfares? In seeking the answers to these questions, I talked to state police officers, driver education authorities, members of state highway safety commissions, and officials of the American Automobile Association and the Automobile Legal Association. I also sought advice in the literature available to the motoring public.

4. ''One of the main causes of expressway accidents is slow reflexes,'' an Illinois state policeman told me. ''People just seem to forget they're traveling at much greater speeds on these roads. A driver takes his eyes off the road to light a cigarette or glance at a road map. He looks up again and he's on top of the car in front of him. This is what causes so many tailgate collisions.''

5. Plan your trip in advance, say safety authorities. You can save yourself a lot

of anxiety and risk if you check a road map before you get on an expressway. Know the number of your exit and the number of miles to it, and have a passenger watch for the exit signs, too. And, of course, if you miss your exit, don't back up, but continue on to the next one and double back.

6. Most of us are aware of the coordination required to change lanes and pass another car at high speed, but too many drivers neglect to use their directional signals when doing it. Those signals help drivers several car-lengths behind to assess the situation. AAA officials recommend scanning the traffic ahead as far as you can see, rather than keeping your eyes only on the car in front of you. This technique helps drivers avoid getting trapped behind slow-moving vehicles, and it gives them warning of drivers to watch out for: cars that are weaving from lane to lane and ones that straddle the line dividing the lanes.

7. State highway safety commissions rate fatigue and drowsiness among the most important causes of superhighway accidents. Superhighways have a hypnotic quality and dull the senses during long trips. It's always better to drive in daylight hours when visibility is good, and you're not likely to be tired. Physicians point out that eyestrain is a big factor, too: The glare of oncoming headlights and limited visibility at night can strain a driver's eyes.

8. If you're taking any kind of medicine or drugs before an expressway or turnpike trip, you'd do well to check their side effects with your doctor or read the label for warnings. Even such over-the-counter remedies as decongestants and certain cough syrups should be avoided, as well as prolonged use of aspirin. Other obvious medicines to avoid are pep pills and tranquilizers.

9. Doctors and safety officials warn against eating heavy meals before or during a lengthy trip. They point out that too much food—especially hard-to-digest fried foods like hamburgers and french fries—relaxes, dulls the senses, and causes drowsiness. Soup and frequent light snacks have a better effect and provide all the energy a driver needs. Coffee breaks relieve drowsiness, of course, and one driver training instructor told me he always chews gum on a long trip—it requires him to move his jaws and facial muscles enough to keep him alert. Another important consideration is the frequent circulation of fresh air in the car, even in winter when it may be temporarily uncomfortable.

10. On long trips, driver fatigue may loom as one of the greatest dangers. Set realistic mileage goals in advance—300 to 400 miles a day is considered a safe figure. Monotony may not be as great a safety menace as fatigue, but if it affects children on a family trip, it can result in frayed nerves and distraction for the driver. To break the monotony, it's good to keep the children's interest alive with games and such.

11. What about the business of having a breakdown, miles from the nearest service station? Police and highway commissioners are aware of these problems and can even predict the approximate number of breakdowns per year on various highways. "The obvious way to avoid breakdowns is to check the car before starting a trip," says a Missouri state trooper. "Tires are most important. So are brakes, steering, windshield wipers."

12. Suppose you have checked to be certain your car is in good working order, and you still have a breakdown. There's nothing bleaker than the feeling of being abandoned on a lonely stretch of road with no help in sight. But there's really little cause for alarm. Most highways are well patrolled by police cars and emergency vehicles. Their schedules are arranged so that no stretch of the highway goes unnoticed for a long time.

13. Police say the important thing to do when a car breaks down is to get it completely off the pavement, even if it means driving on a flat tire for a distance. The standard distress signals in all states, of course, are emergency flasher lights and a raised hood. Drivers without flasher lights should display a white handkerchief on the left side of the car and turn off all lights at night. Safety officials say many a parked car has been hit when an oncoming motorist followed a pair of taillights in the dark without realizing they weren't moving.
14. Although pressure by the federal government has spurred the introduction of automotive safety equipment in recent years, the government has failed in one important safety area: the establishment of uniform national traffic laws. Superhighway drivers should be aware that such practices as passing on the right are legal in some states but not in others. At present, 44 states allow passing on the right on multilane highways, but few of them have made it mandatory for cars to be equipped with mirrors on the right side, which most safety experts consider essential. Efforts are being made to establish a uniform national system of highway traffic laws, but until this is achieved, the best advice to the motorist is to keep in mind the inconsistencies among state traffic laws and to check the legal regulations before he takes to the superhighways.
15. In spite of the hazards of high-speed trips, the gloomy predictions of wholesale highway slaughter by a few early critics have been refuted by national statistics. One of the keys to this superior safety record has been driver adaptation to the greater speed and other special conditions of traveling on superhighways. Before a long, high-speed trip, check your car—and yourself!

5

Helping Students Streamline Their Study

In classrooms the nation over, the assignment that confronts older students most often is probably "Read this textbook chapter and master its contents." On the pages that follow, students are offered ten strategies for textbook reading. Teachers with no training or experience in teaching reading can upgrade their students' reading through these ten strategies.

Students often ask, "How can I study my textbook better and faster?" And their teachers ask, "How can I help my students to get more out of their textbooks?"

To facilitate efficient textbook study, almost every book on how to study includes the SQ3R approach to a textbook chapter, or some variation of this approach, designed by Francis P. Robinson and based on years of experimentation with effective study methods. The steps in Dr. Robinson's approach are Survey, Question, Read, Recite, Review. Other reading authorities have developed variations of SQ3R, among them OK5R, PQRST, QUEST, and POINT.

While some teachers report real success "selling" SQ3R, others report difficulty convincing students to adopt it as a coordinated system. They suggest as one possible reason that SQ3R, when introduced all at once, seems overwhelming. The part-by-part introduction to the ten study strategies suggested on the coming pages offers a possible alternative for these teachers. The study strategies are introduced to the students in "manageable" installments. Then *later* the students are offered the opportunity to coordinate the ten strategies into a smoothly operating system.

A second possible reason for resistance to SQ3R is that some students shy away from what appears to them to be a lockstep procedure for study. These students, however, may be responsive to a take-your-choice approach. In the writer's experience, students respond well to comments like these: "Try out these strategies, then study in the way that suits your learning style." . . . "Adapt these strategies to your own needs and preferences, and add effective ways of your own."

On the master copy pages in this section, you will find guidesheets written directly to students and intended to be placed in their hands. Here the procedures involved in SQ3R, and other study strategies, are served up in a take-your-choice format. Then, in a *postscript* to the guidesheets, the students are offered a procedure for combining the separate strategies into a smoothly operating system.

A high school science instructor accented freedom of choice as he offered students study guidance just after they received their new textbooks in September: (Hozinsky, 1976)

> Starting today we will use our textbook as a major aid. We'll be doing not just "everyday" reading but *extremely close* reading. You'll be offered some strategies to help you do this close reading. Try these—then use whatever ways best suit your learning style.
>
> A few weeks ago I had to digest a difficult book that contained thousands of facts. The task looked overwhelming! But when I used some of these strategies, it became manageable—whole chapters shrank! Of course, the strategies that I chose may not be the ones that you will choose.
>
> When you first turn through the chapter just assigned, it may look overwhelming. These strategies, though, will shrink it for you!

Teachers may wish to *select* from the student guidesheets—from time to time at moment of need—those that fit the course at hand and the needs of their immediate students. In that case, the numerals on the ten strategies can easily be "erased" with white typewriter correction fluid and the strategies can be re-numbered. Teachers may wish to use *just parts* of the student guidesheets, to add parts of their own devising, to revise the guidesheets to meet special needs, to reduce them to outlines. They have the publisher's permission to make these adjustments. If the master copies were reproduced consecutively, they would form a how-to-study booklet or a how-to-study section to be kept permanently in students' looseleaf notebooks. In the role of reading consultant, the writer, year after year, prepared such booklets at the request of classroom teachers. Together the classroom teacher and the consultant tailored the study guidance to the course at hand, and the consultant served it up in an attractive booklet with its cover in school colors. Some teachers may prefer to use the master copies mainly as a source of ideas for their own in-class instruction. Certainly take-home printed guidelines are not a "must" for study guidance.

For what grade levels are the master copies in this section intended? They were developed for use with capable high school sophomores and upperclassmen, but the pointers offered are appropriate on a wide range of levels. Teachers may wish to use the *principles* on the guidesheets but simplify the *presentation* for younger or less capable readers.

The printed guidesheets for students offered here are intended as a supplement for something of first importance—*thorough instruction in their application by the classroom teacher*. Teachers will want to devote time and attention—systematically—to teaching the study strategies. They will want to go *all out* selling these strategies. They will want to testify to the students that *they themselves* use the strategies. They will want to work out demonstrations in which the students see a striking before-and-after contrast—their results *before* using and *after* using a certain strategy. (Graves, 1979)

The guidelines offered here are intended as reinforcement for in-class instruction, as a permanent reference for students, and as a reminder to students to *practice* from day to day the strategies they find effective.

While the illustrative excerpts on the guidesheets have been drawn from textbooks in science and social studies, the ten strategies are applicable to textbooks in almost any subject and to articles in periodicals. In the concluding section of the guidesheets, an introduction to a variation of the SQ3R study system, the writer has entitled the operation OK5R, a name Dr. Walter Pauk originated at the Cornell University Reading-Study Center and one that students find appealing.

You will find on the student guidesheets a number of references to college study. These are deliberate. In the writer's experience, high school students respond well to such references. They react, "This is something new and promising—this is college stuff!"

The writer expresses appreciation to three former colleagues who helped with the selection of the ten strategies—Richard Boyajian and Murray Hozinsky, biology teachers in the University of Chicago Laboratory School, and Wayne Brasler, journalism teacher.

Activities for Teaching and Practicing the Ten Strategies

Teachers will want to motivate students to streamline their study. They will find possible motivational material on Master Copy Pages 23 and 24.

READING AID 194

They will then want to guide students in trying out the ten strategies while they are doing their current assignments, to instruct them so that good results are assured, and to help them become efficiency experts in the job of study. Possible ways to work with the ten strategies are suggested below. The choice is wide in the hope that the teacher will find possibilities to his or her liking. Nothing succeeds like the teacher's enthusiasm—it makes activities like the ones that follow come alive!

SEE MASTER COPY PAGES 23–24

If further suggestions are desired, the reader is referred to Chapter 3, "You Can Upgrade Students' Textbook Reading," in the companion volume (Thomas and Robinson, *Improving Reading in Every Class,* unabridged 2nd ed., 1977), pp. 136–168.

Strategy 1: Overview—To Save Time

Detailed guidesheets introducing students to the strategy of overviewing appear on Master Copy Pages 25 through 27. These guidesheets offer students *why-do-its* and *how-to-do-its* for Strategy 1.

READING AID 195

In the introduction to the guidesheets, President Kennedy's deft overviewing is spotlighted as a "speed secret." Teachers, too, will want to stress overviewing as a *time saver.* Unless we do this, students may view it as a hindrance instead of a help, reacting, "It will take too long to study the chapter!" Through guided practice we can *demonstrate* for students that a chapter can be overviewed in just a few minutes. The time required will, of course, vary with the difficulty and the organization of the chapter, and students should understand this.

SEE MASTER COPY PAGES 25–27

READING AID 196

Students Can Discover for Themselves How to Overview

The teacher can guide students to make their own discoveries about the techniques and values of overviewing by asking questions like these about a chapter just assigned: "How do the authors help you learn in just minutes what this chapter will contain? What are all the different means they use to clue you in quickly on what you'll find in the chapter?" . . . "Can you suggest a technique for overviewing based on the authors' clues?" . . . "What are some advantages of making an advance survey?" Next the teacher can reveal how reading experts answer these same questions. Finally, the class can combine their own suggestions with those of the experts to develop a step-by-step overviewing procedure.

READING AID 197

Assignment Time Right for Overview Practice

READING AID 198

One instructor selects a chapter ideally structured to practice overviewing and suggests, "Let's practice the overview technique on the chapter assigned for tonight's reading. When you've finished, you should be able to answer these two questions: What, in general, is the content of the chapter? and What big points will be discussed? You may need about ______ minutes." (As students are first introduced to the overview technique, time allotments should be generous and flexible.) This framework is on the blackboard:

What, in general, will the subject of this chapter be?

____

____

What important aspects of the subject will be discussed?

____

____

____

____

____

____

____

As the students finish their examination of the chapter, the instructor asks, "What did you find to be the general subject matter?" or "What broad problems will be explored?" Then the teacher asks, "What aspects of the subject will be discussed? Can you possibly give them in order?" As the students name the big topics they have gleaned from major chapter division headings and subheadings, the teacher records these on the chalkboard, indenting to indicate levels of subordination and revealing to the class that in this well-structured chapter they have neatly discovered the author's "hidden" outline. The students perceive that they now have a map to guide them during their thorough reading.

It should be noted that many of the chapters students will need to overview are not so well structured as those a teacher would select during this instructional step. It is desirable to practice later with materials that present real difficulties and to convince students that through flexible skimming they can still get the gist of the chapter.

It will be ideal if, at the time assignments are made, the teacher guides the class in briefly previewing chapters until the students take on the task automatically and independently (Robinson, 1978, p. 74).

Can You Find the Hidden Outline?

READING AID 199

To reinforce the awareness that overviewing often reveals the author's plan of organization, the instructor might suggest: "We've discovered that the author's major chapter division headings and subheadings sometimes fall into an outline. Can you find the hidden outline in the chapter assigned for tomorrow?"

How Much Can You Learn In Just ______ Minutes?

READING AID 200

As students become adept in using overview techniques, a time limit can be imposed to jolt some of them out of unnecessarily sluggish habits. "How much can you learn about the contents of this chapter in just ______ minutes? Use your new overview techniques to hit the high spots of organized prose. List some of the important things you expect to learn from reading this chapter."

What Questions Will this Chapter Answer?

READING AID 201

The Baldridge Reading Strategy Program advises students: "Questions will occur during and after reading, but start them early, during Survey Reading." (*Seven Reading Strategies,* 1970, p. 5) What are some important questions you expect to find answered in this chapter? Jot them below:

____

____

____

____

____

____

Do You Know the Chapter Title?

READING AID 202

The teacher might alert unobserving students to the fact that chapters *do have titles* in this way: "When students were asked on a test, 'What was the title of the chapter you've just studied?' only a few were able to answer! Can *you* give the title of the chapter you've just studied?"

Can You See the Logic?

READING AID 203

When the chapter lends itself, students can be encouraged to discern the sweep of the chapter—its logical progression: "In this chapter how do the authors proceed from their introduction to their conclusion? What are the stepping-stones along the way? Can you see their step-by-step thought processes—the logical sequence—as they move from the first topic to the last?" (*Seven Reading Strategies,* 1970, p. 5)

The Table of Contents, an Unexpected Aid

READING AID 204

Most students are not aware that the table of contents can be an aid in overviewing. This listing of contents often includes not only the chapter title but also a concise, sequential listing of the topics and subtopics covered in the chapter. Students might be asked: "Turn to the table of contents and find the listing of topics and subtopics for this chapter. Judging *only* from these topics and subtopics, make jottings of what you expect to learn from this chapter. Make this a one-minute assignment." The one-minute time limit makes this activity more fun. The students dig in and concentrate better!

Students Can Prove Their Mastery

READING AID 205

After students have been taught overviewing in a content area and have perfected the techniques, why not let them prove on a test that they have mastered this important skill?

Students will take skill development *much* more seriously if they are checked on it in a regular testing situation. They will realize how really important their teacher considers the skill.

As their test question, the students can be asked to turn in their textbooks to a chapter they have not yet read and to carry out these directions: ''Practice your new overviewing techniques on this chapter. Get a 'mental map' of the chapter by overviewing, then jot down the answers to these questions: What, in general, is the subject of the chapter? What important aspects of the subject will be discussed? You'll have ______ minutes.'' (The time will vary with the difficulty and the organization of the chapter.)

Strategy 2: Go in with a Question

READING AID 206

SEE MASTER COPY PAGES 28–30

Detailed guidesheets for students introducing them to the questioning strategy appear on Master Copy Pages 28 through 30. They offer students *why-do-its* and *how-to-do-its* for Strategy 2.

''Be a Human Question Mark!''

READING AID 207

Practice with Strategy 2 should be especially meaningful for students if, as a chapter is assigned, they go through the chapter with their teacher and practice turning some of the headings into questions, then experience the value of this strategy as they study the chapter on their own. The teacher might suggest:

> Be a human question mark! *Constantly ask questions of the book all the while you're reading!* As you read the chapter for tomorrow, continue to formulate questions and make a very light [erasable] check mark or dot beside the material related to your question. Read searchingly—to find and learn the answers to your questions. We'll discuss and compare your questions in class.

''Now You're the Teacher!''

READING AID 208

A social studies teacher observed that some of her students were reading just ''words, words, words'' and gaining no real grasp of the content. She invited the school's reading teacher to come to her classes and work with them on comprehension. The reading teacher (Hillman, 1971) reports real success with the following class activity:

> Pretend *you* are the teacher. Read section ______ of the chapter, asking yourself, ''What would I want *my* students to get out of this section? What question or questions would I ask them on this section?'' Your own teacher goes through this very process.
>
> After you've formulated your questions, you're no longer the teacher. You're *you*, the student. Now really learn the answers to your questions. Then close your book and write the answers. You're asked to close your book so that you'll really *learn* the material, not just copy the answers by rote.
>
> Now that's the way you should study—*formulating questions, then reading to learn the answers.*
>
> Studies show that students who ''put themselves behind their teacher's desk'' can predict questions on their tests and exams more accurately than students who ''just read.'' (Hill, 1970, p. 19)

''Try to Outwit Your Teacher!''

READING AID 209

In other classes, the students were challenged to ''try to outwit their teacher.'' They read a textbook section and wrote down questions which they thought were likely, later on, to become test questions. The teacher spent a few minutes hearing the questions. She then projected on a screen the questions *she* would ask if she were actually giving a test on the chapter. The students discovered that the teacher's questions were in many cases identical to their own questions. The teacher has this word for other teachers: ''Don't underestimate the value of this discovery in selling the questioning strategy to students!'' (Bragstad, 1979)

Turn Headings into Questions

READING AID 210

To make sure that students actually practice the question strategy, they might be asked to fill in a table like the one that follows (see Figure 5–1) during their reading of an assigned chapter:

> As you are reading the chapter assigned, record, in the column to the left, important section headings from the chapter. Turn each heading into a question to hold in mind as you approach your reading of the section. Write your question in the column on the right. [The table is filled in with headings and questions that a student might formulate from Chapter 2 of *Biological Science: Molecules To Man,* BSCS Blue Version, 3rd ed. (Boston: Houghton Mifflin Co., 1973.)]

Heading for Section in Your Textbook	Question with Which You Might Approach Your Reading of the Section
Populations compete for survival	What are some ways that populations compete for survival?
Humans interact with their environment	What are some ways that human beings interact with their environment?
Early classification systems	What were the early classification systems?
Some organisms are difficult to classify	Why are some organisms hard to classify?
Organisms need each other	Just how do organisms need each other?

FIGURE 5–1

Working with a chapter that has been assigned, students practice turning textbook headings into questions. (Table adapted from Ralph C. Preston and Morton Botel, *How to Study*. Chicago: Science Research Associates, 1974, p. 25.)

Find the "Hidden Question"

READING AID 211

Students can be further encouraged to read with a questioning mindset by finding the "hidden question" in topic sentences of paragraphs. They can practice finding the "hidden question" with their teacher in class or conference or possibly through an activity like the one in Figure 5–2. Through practices like this, the students not only master the content of the paragraph better because they are curious and questioning when they approach it, but they also become more familiar with the organizational pattern of a paragraph. They experience how the topic sentence announces the topic of the paragraph and is followed (or perhaps preceded) by supportive information, and they learn to look as they read for that supportive information.

You'll sometimes discover "hidden questions" in the topic sentences of paragraphs. You can find one quickly in each of the following topic sentences from Chapter 2. Turn each topic sentence into a question, and then write your question in the column to the right. To start you, the first question has already been formulated. [The topic sentences are taken from *Biological Science: Molecules To Man,* BSCS Blue Version, 3rd ed. (Boston: Houghton Mifflin Co., 1973).]

Topic Sentences of Paragraphs	Question to Hold in Mind As You Read This Paragraph
"It is often difficult to place a given organism into one of the established categories.	Why is it often difficult to categorize organisms?
"In spite of this variety, members of each [monera and protista] have certain characteristics in common.	
"Any system for classifying living things brings up problems."	
"Many types of interactions exist within a great variety of living things."	

FIGURE 5–2. *Students practice finding the "hidden question" in topic sentences from a textbook.*

Strategy 3: Do "Stop-and Go" Reading

READING AID 212

SEE MASTER COPY PAGE 31

The guidesheet that appears on Master Copy Page 31 explains "stop-and-go" reading—and the *why* of it—to students.

Demonstrate "Stop-and-Go" Reading

READING AID 213

Teachers might demonstrate for students how they themselves do "stop-and-go" reading when personally studying difficult new material, stopping to master an "official" term . . . zeroing in on a graphic aid . . . saying to themselves "I didn't get that—I'll go over it again" . . . stopping to reflect and occasionally to argue with the author . . . looking away from the book and self-reciting.

Making a Sketch Helps You Really "See"

READING AID 214

Students may not be consciously aware of the existence, and the importance, of the skill of visualizing. Many will need encouragement, when visualizing is called for, to stop and "see" what they have just read. At the blackboard the teacher might quickly demonstrate for students how making their own sketch of the parts of a cell, for example, will speed and firm their learning.

Strategy 4: Remove the Roadblocks of "Official" Terms

READING AID 215

The guidelines that appear on Master Copy Page 32 alert students to typographical signals to help them recognize "official" terms and suggest ways to master important terms. The V.A.K. technique suggested in Strategy 8 will be a further help in mastering technical vocabulary.

SEE MASTER COPY PAGE 32

Can You Spot "Official" Terms?

READING AID 216

Teachers can raise the consciousness level of students for "official" terms through this one-minute assignment:

> Whenever you come to an important new "official" term, the authors flash a signal. What is the signal in your particular textbook? [The students note that it is boldface type—or it might be italic type or color.] Yes, terms printed in boldface are crucially important "official" terms.
>
> Make it a one-minute assignment to turn through the chapter and list as many "official" terms as you can. (Muelder, 1976)

Strategy 5: Use a "Back-and-Forth" Strategy

READING AID 217

The guidesheet for students on Master Copy Page 33 explains the *how* and *why* of "back-and-forth" reading between a printed column and a graphic aid.

SEE MASTER COPY PAGE 33

"This Is Clearing Up Something!"

READING AID 218

Many students regard graphic aids as blank spaces on the page where they can "rest their eyes." Early in the year, teachers can focus on graphic aids as timesavers:

> Each pictorial or graphic aid in the chapter is saying to you, "This is clearing up something important!" Students who skip graphic aids are skipping timesavers!
>
> List the titles of three pictorial [or graphic] aids in the pages assigned you:
>
> 1. ______________________________
> 2. ______________________________
> 3. ______________________________
>
> What important idea in the chapter is clarified or explained by each of these aids? (Preston and Botel, 1974, p. 15)
>
> 1. ______________________________
> 2. ______________________________
> 3. ______________________________

READING AID 219

Make a Quiz Question on Graphic Aids

To emphasize the importance of graphic aids, include a "graphic aid" question on quizzes. Ask the students for interesting information that has been offered in the graphic aid—and nowhere else. Students will take skill development *much* more seriously if they are checked in a regular testing situation. They will realize how important their teachers consider the skill.

READING AID 220

Strategy 6: Make Important Points Flag You

SEE MASTER COPY PAGES 34–37

The guidesheets that appear on Master Copy Pages 34 through 37 offer students a variety of methods for taking notes on important points or marking them. (Of course, a student may be at a loss to decide *which points in the passage are important.* Reading Aids 167 through 193 will help students with the selection process.

READING AID 221

Students Can Practice Selecting Important Points

If individuals or groups need this type of practice, the teacher might select an appropriate passage from reading assigned, then guide the students as they practice selecting and flagging the important points:

> Working with this section, select the important points. Then make notes or mark them in the way or combination of ways, you like best—marginal lines, underlining—your choice. As you know, your marks or notes should reveal levels of subordination.

Moving around the room, the teacher observes and offers guidance. A little later the students compare and discuss the points they have selected.

READING AID 222

Strategy 7: Adjust Your Speed to the Task at Hand

SEE MASTER COPY PAGE 38

The guidelines for students on Master Copy Page 38 are to alert students to the factors that should control their speed of reading. Reading Aids 236 through 260 in Chapter 6 offer suggestions for helping students to acquire a full range of reading rates and to use these in appropriate situations.

READING AID 223

Strategy 8: Use "the Most Powerful Study Technique"

SEE MASTER COPY PAGES 39–40

The guidelines for students on Master Copy Pages 39 and 40 offer students *why's* and *how-to's* of self-recitation.

READING AID 224

Self-Recite—with V.A.K.

Individuals and groups may not realize the *active* learning that is necessary to fix material firmly in their memories. And they may not realize the dividends they can gain from self-reciting unless someone walks them through the process. Using a passage in which the students have marked the important points or made notes (as suggested in Reading Aid 221), the students can be asked to look away from the book and "play back" these points to themselves, using triple-strength V.A.K. (visual, auditory, and kinesthetic) learning.

Then they can be given a quick quiz question covering this material. They will almost surely be sold on self-reciting if a control group in the class does not have the "playback" privilege!

Self-reciting will have high pay-off value when students are learning important "official" terms. Students might work on such terms under guidance, using the three sensory learning channels involved in V.A.K. The results will almost surely be convincing.

Use Mini-Notes to Trigger Recall

READING AID 225

Using marginal mini-notes as cues to recall is so effective that teachers may wish to spotlight this technique through a separate practice:

> Section ____ lends itself well to one of the most effective note-making devices—marginal mini-notes.
>
> Jot in the margin of your book, at the far left, key words or phrases that call to mind the main points of this section. Indented a little below these, jot down key words that suggest important subpoints.
>
> Now using your key words as "cue" words, review the important content. Cover the printed column and use your mini-notes as cues to trigger recall. Look at the print, whenever you need to, to check your accuracy.

Strategy 9: Zero in on the Self-Checks

READING AID 226

SEE MASTER COPY PAGE 41

READING AID 227

The guidesheet that appears on Master Copy Page 41 alerts students to the value of the self-check questions that are provided by the authors of textbooks.

If a student has become lost reading a difficult passage, the teacher might suggest in a conference:

> This passage is hard, and you're feeling overwhelmed. Let's turn to the author's questions at the end of the chapter. We'll find the ones related to this particular passage. . . . Now go back and reread the passage, holding these questions in mind. . . . Now can you "overwhelm" the passage?

Strategy 10: Review To Firm Up Learning

READING AID 228

The guidelines for students on Master Copy Pages 42 and 43 suggest how-to-do-its for deftly reviewing a chapter, and they disclose three memory secrets.

Take Advantage of a Memory Secret

SEE MASTER COPY PAGES 42–43

READING AID 229

In order to make overlearning more than just a word, the teacher might select a passage that calls for thorough mastery, then guide the students in actually overlearning the material: (Preston and Botel, 1974, p. 43)

> Time yourself from the moment you begin to study until you can say, "I have learned this material." Make a note of the time required.
>
> Now spend about one-fourth of that time in additional learning [overlearning] of the same material. This *overlearning* is a memory secret. This is what's involved in learning for the future.

Review Need Not Be Wearisome

READING AID 230

Students may be inclined to overlook the review step, thinking, "All that for an assignment!" Walking them through a deft review of the chapter should impress them with the fact that a skillful review—provided the initial steps have been properly carried out—is not wearisome restudy but a relatively quick *overlearning* step that clinches retention. The students might be guided through these steps:

> First, turn through the chapter to call back the broad chapter plan.
>
> Next, covering with your cover-card (or your hand) or just looking away from the book, check yourself once more—section by section—on the important content. Triple the strength of your learning with V.A.K. again.
>
> Finally, space out more reviews to freshen up your memory. Now everything you want from the chapter should be *yours—to stay*.

The Table of Contents, an Unexpected Aid

READING AID 231

It has never occurred to most students that the table of contents, provided it lists subtopics, can be a review device:

> Turn to the table of contents for an instant "guided review" of the chapter. There you'll find a capsule outline—a sequential listing of the major chapter divisions and, in slots between these, the subtopics. Turn each of these items into a question, then call to mind the important content of the chapter.
>
> As you do this, you'll not only review the big chapter points—you'll also call back to mind the broad sweep of the chapter.

A Conclusion to the Ten Strategies

READING AID 232

SEE MASTER COPY PAGE 44

We have mentioned that if Master Copy Pages 25 through 46 were reproduced consecutively, they would form a how-to-study booklet or a how-to-study section to be kept permanently in students' looseleaf notebooks. In that case, the caution, "Beware of Technique-itis," and the concluding comment, "What Do We Have in the Ten Strategies," would form an appropriate conclusion.

If the master copies are to form a booklet or a notebook section, it is probably best not to give them out all at once but part by part just before the teacher instructs the students on that section. Otherwise the material may lose its freshness. (Graves, 1979)

A Postscript—The OK5R Approach to College Reading

As we noted in the introduction to this chapter, students sometimes resist a study system like OK5R perhaps because, introduced all at once, it seems overwhelming. As a possible alternative, we have suggested offering ten study strategies in a take-your-choice approach, ideally at the point early in the course when each particular strategy is called for, then *later* inviting the students to combine the ten strategies into a smoothly operating system.

READING AID 233

The student guidesheets on Master Copy Pages 45 and 46 are an invitation to combine the ten strategies into "the OK5R approach to college reading."

The reader will notice references to college study in the introduction to the student guidesheets. These, as we have noted, are deliberate. In the writer's experience, high school students respond well to the suggestion that they streamline their study for college. They react, "Busy college students use these tips. Maybe I should try them!"

SEE MASTER COPY PAGES 45–46

Pointers for Instructing Students on OK5R

READING AID 234

One authority (Graves, 1979) offers the following suggestions about teaching OK5R:

> . . . It is going to be critical that you *sell* the method. Really go *all out* in suggesting its value to students. Cite studies testifying to the need for the technique, cite studies showing its results, argue that you use it yourself, and work out some sort of demonstration in which the students compare the results *before* using and *after* using the method. . . .
>
> Begin instruction with each phase of OK5R with your taking the students through the particular step. For example, preview a chapter or shorter unit aloud while the students follow along in their books. . . .
>
> Begin with short, relatively simple materials that lend themselves particularly to OK5R. Materials well suited will be informational materials that have clear introductions, plenty of boldface headings, clearly divided thought units, important terms italicized or in boldface, and clear summaries. Later, of course, the students will work with materials less ideally suited. . . .
>
> Provide students with opportunities to practice the method in class. Give them plenty of time, and insure that they are actively involved with the method. . . .
>
> Structure class discussions and quizzes so that students experience continual demonstrated success with the method. . . .

Teachers Can Share Their Own "Success Secrets"

READING AID 235

A college professor who taught the writer when she was a college freshman once demonstrated for the class how he himself studied an important textbook chapter. She can still see him sitting there behind his desk—overviewing the chapter, approaching with questions, focusing on "official" terms, going into action with his pencil, staring at the ceiling while he self-recited. Impressed that these study strategies had helped to give this teacher his impressive command of his subject, the writer was eager to try them herself!

Any teacher can give such a demonstration, sharing with students his or her own "success secrets." Example may prove to be one of the best teachers!

Bibliography

Baldridge Reading Instruction Staff. *Seven Reading Strategies*. Greenwich, Conn.: Baldridge Reading Instruction Materials (BRIM), Inc., 1970.

Biological Science: Molecules to Man, BSCS Blue Version, 3rd ed. Boston: Houghton Mifflin Co., 1973.

Norman, Maxwell H., and Enid S. Norman. *How to Read and Study for Success in College*. New York: Holt, Rinehart and Winston, 1977.

Pauk, Walter. *How to Study in College*, 2nd ed. Boston: Houghton Mifflin Co., 1974.

Preston, Ralph C., and Morton Botel. *How to Study*. Chicago: Science Research Associates, 1974.

Robinson, Francis P. *Effective Study*, 4th ed. New York: Harper and Row, 1970.

Staton, Thomas B. *How to Study*, 6th ed. Montgomery, Ala.: Box 6133, 1977.

Thomas, Ellen Lamar, and H. Alan Robinson. *Improving Reading in Every Class*, 2nd ed. Boston: Allyn and Bacon, 1977.

References

Baldridge Reading Instruction Staff. *Seven Reading Strategies*. Greenwich, Conn.: Baldridge Reading Instruction Materials (BRIM), Inc., 1970.

Bragstad, Berenice, reading consultant of La Follette Senior High School, Madison, Wisconsin, in remarks to the writer. January 1979.

Graves, Michael F., Department of Curriculum and Instruction, University of Minnesota, in conversation with the writer, April 1979.

Hill, Walter. *POINT: A Reading-Study System*. Belmont, Calif.: Wadsworth Publishing Co., 1970.

Hillman, Margaret, former director of St. Petersburg High School's Reading Clinic in Florida, in remarks to the writer, April 1971.

Hozinsky, Murray, University of Chicago Laboratory School science teacher, in remarks to his biology class, October 1976.

Muelder, Richard, University of Chicago Laboratory School mathematics teacher, in remarks to the writer, January 1976.

Preston, Ralph C., and Morton Botel. *How to Study*. Chicago: Science Research Associates, 1974.

Robinson, H. Alan. *Teaching Reading and Study Strategies: The Content Areas*. Boston: Allyn and Bacon, 1978.

Helping Students Adjust Their Reading Rate to the Task at Hand

Many students are unaware of the need to adjust their rate of reading. How can we gain insights about our students' attainments and needs in rate adjustment? How can we drive home the concept of flexibility in rate? How can we help students acquire a complete "collection" of reading approaches, then use these in the right places?

Janice covers the pages pell-mell, whatever the assignment, and gains little. Danny, no matter how light and easy the material, reads it as ploddingly as he would a difficult and crucial chapter.

Ideal "graduates" of reading programs adjust their rate to the task before them at the moment. They have at their command reading rates along a continuum from slow and careful to very rapid reading, they have developed techniques of scanning and skimming, and they have learned to identify the situation for which each approach is appropriate.

Flexibility in rate of reading deserves careful attention in the intermediate grades, a time when the students must read, for the first time, a variety of materials in such subject areas as English, social studies, and science. Since most students move slowly in the direction of rate adjustment, and since many students in high school and college have yet to meet the concept, teachers on advanced levels, too, will want to work with rate adjustment. Those who do so are helping students acquire strategies that will contribute to their success in high school and college, their efficiency in reading for information all through adulthood, and their lifelong enjoyment of personal reading.

Learning Students' Attainments and Needs in Rate Adjustment

How can we learn the answers to these important questions: Are our students aware of the need for rate adjustment? Which of the approaches that make up a complete "collection" have they already acquired? Can they scan for specific information? Skim for the general drift? Shift to slow rates when this is demanded by the type of study material? Speed up for *easy* informational reading? Attain high speeds on easy, fast-moving fiction?

Standardized tests, teacher-made tests, day-to-day classroom observation, and student self-appraisals—all these can be sources of helpful information. For detailed information on all four sources, the reader is referred to the companion volume (Thomas and Robinson, *Improving Reading in Every Class,* unabridged 2nd ed., 1977), pp. 198–208.

Standardized Tests Can Supply Some Information

READING AID 236

A great many schools have available the results of recently administered standardized reading tests. Many of these have rate-of-reading sections. Let us consider the insights that can be gained from one such test.

> *Cooperative Reading Test;* Cooperative Test Division, Educational Testing Service; Lower Level intended for grades 9–12; Upper Level intended for superior students in grades 11 and 12 and for college freshmen and sophomores; two forms. *The Cooperative Reading Test offers sub-scores in vocabulary, level (power) of comprehension, and speed of comprehension. The score on level of comprehension is based on the number of answers correct. The score on speed of comprehension is a function of both the number correct and the number completed. The content of this test is primarily fairly difficult study material. The speed score gives you some indication of the speed with which the student can handle reading matter of this type.*

A low speed score combined with a high comprehension score on the test above suggests that the student already comprehends well and should now learn to comprehend faster. A high speed score combined with a low comprehension score suggests that the student needs to adjust speed downward for closer, more reflective reading. A low speed score combined with a low comprehension score suggests that the student needs to upgrade both speed and comprehension. For reasons to be considered later, it is appropriate with this student to upgrade comprehension before focusing on speed.

Teachers who consult standardized test scores hoping to gain insights about their students' rates of reading should inform themselves concerning the number of minutes the students spent on the timed reading. If the rate scores are based on fewer than five minutes of timed reading, they are likely to fall far short in reliability. (Graves, 1979)

Standardized survey tests usually yield a single rate score based on the student's performance with only the type of material represented by the test items. While this information is somewhat helpful, we are obviously left in the dark as to the students' attainments and needs in rate *adjustment.*

The following diagnostic test, however, explores whether the student can adjust his or her rate of reading in the light of four different purposes:

> *Reading Versatility Test;* Educational Developmental Laboratories; three levels, 5–8, 8–12, 12–16; four forms: *In each of four sections the student is instructed to perform a different reading task—reading easy fiction, careful reading of study-type material, skimming, and scanning. The test is designed to indicate whether the student has these four essential approaches in his or her repertory.*

Students who performed these four diverse tasks at much the same rate clearly have a need for learning to adjust their reading rate. While experts who have reviewed the Reading Versatility Test alert us to some shortcomings, teachers may find it a useful source of ideas for making simple "homemade" tests to explore whether the student has acquired the reading approaches that will be called for in their courses.

Teacher-Made Tests Are Probably Most Helpful

READING AID 237

How different is the artificial sample students are asked to read on the speed section of most standardized tests from their actual reading assignments in their textbooks and other course materials! Because of this difference, teachers can probably get at the real needs of their students better through their own "homemade" tests.

A study task that students are often called upon to perform is to read study-type material and master its contents thoroughly. To explore the rates of students on this type of reading, select a passage representative of the material they will be expected to read and comprehend thoroughly, a passage not less than 1,000 words in length. Prepare short-answer questions, perhaps ten of these.

Have the students take your "homemade" test in class, following these directions: "When I give the starting signal, please read this passage carefully. Be sure you understand and remember the information. You will be asked to answer questions after you finish reading. Use the method of reading that will enable you to achieve maximum comprehension. As soon as you finish, look up at the board to learn the time that has elapsed. Divide [the number of words in the passage] by the figure you see on the board to learn the number of words you read per minute."

As the students are reading, write on the board, at quarter of a minute intervals, the elapsed time in minutes. To make the division easier for the students, write the elapsed time in decimals instead of fractions—"3 minutes," "3.25 minutes" "3.5 minutes," "3.75 minutes," and so on. After a student has finished reading and has recorded his or her rate in words per minute, hand the student the comprehension questions. As you examine the results of this test, your students' words per minute and their degree of comprehension on a typical passage, you should find that you now have deeper insights into how rapidly they can handle their day-to-day assignments that call for thorough study.

Procedures for making informal tests of scanning, skimming, and rapid reading, as well as thorough reading, are suggested in the companion volume (Thomas and Robinson, *Improving Reading in Every Class,* unabridged 2nd ed., 1977), pp. 200–208. Teachers can keep their insights current by testing informally as needed during the year.

Teachers Can Observe Needs from Day to Day

READING AID 238

READING AID 239

We have mentioned day-to-day observation as one way to identify students who have needs in rate adjustment, including the need to read more rapidly when this is appropriate. Students send us messages that they need to increase their speed when day after day they finish in-class reading tasks among the last in the group and when they shy away from recreational books, saying, "It takes too long to finish!"

Early in the school year, one English teacher (Rhinestine, 1978) gives her students a self-made reading inventory that yields a "speed score." They are asked to read a three-page short story and, after they have finished, to answer ten comprehension questions. She instructs the class: "Raise your hand as soon as you finish and I'll bring you the questions." As the students raise their hands, she jots down their names, inconspicuously, in the order in which they finish. In this way she obtains a list that suggests which students in the class may be the rapid readers, the average readers, and the slowest readers. The answers to the ten questions provide her with a check on comprehension.

Introducing the Concept of Rate Adjustment

*"Read Smarter, Not Just Faster!"**

READING AID 240

Teachers in every classroom can guide their students to "read *smarter,* not just faster." When teachers share with students understandings like those that follow, the students will

*This good counsel is slightly adapted from an interview with Alan Lakein, "How to Use Your Time Wisely" in *U.S. News and World Report,* 81, no. 3 (1976), p. 47.

quickly realize that indiscriminate speed does not characterize the "smart," sophisticated reader:

> You'll want to "read *smarter*, not just faster!" If someone asks you, "What is your rate of reading?" you'll know that person doesn't know much about reading.
>
> You should develop not a single rate of reading but *different rates*. Reading everything fast is a sign of a poor reader. The good reader develops *flexibility* instead of constant speed.
>
> What three considerations should control your speed?
>
> First, your *purpose*. Why are you reading this material? To get just the gist of an easy selection? To retain every detail? To find a single bit of information? To entertain yourself with light, easy reading?
>
> Second, the *difficulty of the material for you*. Is the selection easy for you? Or is it rough going?
>
> Third, your *personal familiarity with the subject matter*. Do you already have background on the topic? Or is it new to you?
>
> When you "read *smarter*," you'll shift from one approach to another within a single chapter or within an article—even within a single paragraph! Reading everything fast is about as smart as running everywhere you go! (Anderson, 1968, p. 1)

Suppose a teacher prefers to have the students themselves arrive at these insights. The teacher might ask: "Suppose someone should advise you, 'Read *smarter*, not faster!' What could that possibly mean?" Then, after the students have decided that "smart reading" does not mean covering everything rapidly, the teacher might ask: "When you 'read smarter,' what considerations should control your speed?"

READING AID 241

SEE MASTER COPY PAGES 47–48

Further guidelines for students about different reading approaches and the situations in which each is appropriate will be found on Master Copy Pages 47 and 48. The rates in words per minute suggested on the master copies are suggested as "target" rates for high school upperclassmen. Rates for high school underclassmen and for junior high school students should be adjusted downward.

English and reading classes, because of the variety of reading materials used, will be an especially appropriate place for students to examine, develop, and refine their concepts of rate adjustment. All teachers, however, will be concerned that students acquire the approaches essential in their particular courses.

Helping Students Acquire a Full Range of Reading Rates

After introducing students to the concept of rate adjustment, teachers will want them to practice sizing up real-life reading situations and making a deliberate choice of reading approach. Teachers will also want to help students acquire a full complement of approaches. The rest of this chapter will suggest possible ways to achieve these goals in rate adjustment. Much additional information is offered in the companion volume (Thomas and Robinson, *Improving Reading in Every Class,* 2nd ed. 1977), pp. 208–233.

"Assignment Time" Offers an Opportunity

Classroom teachers of every subject in which reading is carried on in class or assigned outside will want to help students develop the approaches that will be constantly called for in their courses. Assignment time will often be right for focusing attention on the particular approach (or approaches) appropriate for the coming reading. As teachers do this, they will be raising their students' consciousness-level about the need for rate adjustment. And they can suggest—or elicit from students—how-to-do-its for the approach (or approaches) called for.

Teachers will want to introduce—*repeatedly*—different selections to be read in different ways—some to be read rapidly, some to be skimmed for the drift, some to be scanned for some bit of information, some to be thoroughly studied. People need to read in all these different ways in daily life! Only with *much* reinforcement will students acquire a full repertory of reading approaches—to be used in lifelong reading.

A Quick Send-Off on Rapid Reading

The ability to read fairly rapidly for background information is called for in many school subjects (and all through adulthood, when much professional and personal reading can and should be covered rapidly). Students who attack all their reading with a slow, intensive approach will find themselves spending impossible amounts of time. Since many college courses require a great deal of reading, these students, unless they are "rescued," will find themsleves at a great disadvantage. Broad coverage is especially important in the social studies, for in this field depth of understanding demands extensive reading. Students will probably need guidance not only on *when to* but also on *how to* do rapid, broad coverage reading.

READING AID 242

Suppose the student's purpose is to get a general picture of what everyday life was like in Pompeii before Mount Vesuvius erupted and buried the ancient city. The teacher might suggest, "Read this easy selection rapidly to gain a general impression of what it was like to live in Pompeii before the great volcano erupted—just to catch the feel of living there during the 'last days,' not to remember all the details."

Then the instructor might ask, "How do you think you should do this type of reading?" With guidance, the students might suggest that they should move right along—picking up main thoughts, learning all they can from the pictures, not slowing down to learn details, looking up unknown words only if they block their getting the gist—pressing on to learn the general drift.

Students who have been "one-pace plodders" are learning, at last, that different approaches to reading exist—that they should not always read as if every detail were of supreme importance.

Once students have been introduced to rapid reading techniques, a word or two at the time the assignment is made will be a useful reminder to them to shift gears into this type of reading:

> Here's an easy, popular science article, "Fascinating Careers in Oceanography"—it doesn't call for close study. Read it as rapidly as you can for general impressions. You'll learn why more and more young scientists want to be "where the action is"—deep on the floor of the ocean! (Idea from Smith, 1971, p. 134)
>
> In this fast-action short story, your purpose is enjoyment. Fairly fast reading is suitable for "Dive Right In." Look for a double surprise near the end of the story!
>
> Read this account of a southern plantation owner about the "happy, carefree" life of the black slaves on his plantation. Then read *Up from Slavery* to see how a slave himself looked at those years. Read fairly rapidly—just to get the gist of these contrasting viewpoints.

Somewhere along the way some students have gained the impression that all their studying demands concentration on details—that it is almost a sin to cover anything rapidly. In send-offs like those just presented, students are being encouraged to cover the pages rapidly *when this is appropriate*. Other ways of helping students who need to develop more rapid rates will be considered later in this chapter.

A Send-Off on Slow and Careful Reading

Close, intensive reading is frequently demanded of students in their school courses. Here again the students will probably need *how-to* guidance followed by *when-to* reminders.

READING AID 243

Tips for close, intensive reading can sometimes be elicited from students, then combined with the expertise of the instructor to evolve guidelines. The instructor might ask the class, "Suppose you want to master the content of this difficult passage thoroughly without a word of help or explanation from your teacher. How would you go about reading it?" With their attention focused on how they would read a difficult passage ideally, the students themselves often come up with some highly practical pointers.

READING AID 244

Maturing student readers who have already been introduced to the OK5R approach to a textbook chapter, can be encouraged, at the time a chapter is assigned for thorough mastery, to practice this approach. (A detailed explanation of OK5R will be found on Master Copy Pages 45 and 46.) A physics teacher (Kimmel, 1975) gave his class this send-off on a difficult chapter:

> We've already talked about the contents of the coming chapter. So what you'll read tonight will not be completely new to you. Even at that, you may find yourself stopping and wondering, "What have I just read?" This is a good time to use the OK5R approach we learned a while ago. Let's go over it quickly to be sure you remember how it goes. [The class reviews the steps in OK5R.] Your work tonight will be a preview of what it's like in college—when you're reading a very difficult chapter.

Chapter 5 of this book offers much how-to-do-it guidance for students whose task is thorough reading. All ten study strategies offered in that chapter should be helpful when the student's purpose is thorough mastery of the content of a difficult chapter.

READING AID 245

GO SLOW reminders like the following can be *part* of a teacher's introduction of a difficult assignment:

> This chapter of twenty pages in science may be the equivalent—in study time—of a short novel to read for English! Read it to explore the mystery of how life originated on our earth aeons ago.
>
> Do tomorrow's reading slowly and thoroughly—to learn the disagreements that almost wrecked the Constitutional Convention and how each one of these was finally settled.
>
> As you read the essay "Friendship," you'll want to add *thought time* to reading time. What characteristics does Emerson value most in a friend? Be deciding: Are the characteristics *you* value most in a friend the same as Emerson's?

A One-Minute Send-Off on Internal Rate Adjustment

READING AID 246

Teachers can raise students' awareness about the need for *internal rate adjustment,* adjustment within a single chapter or within an article, as part of their prereading instruction. In the following paragraph, a social studies teacher sharpens this awareness when assigning a chapter, "Crises of the New Nation":

> Most of this chapter tells of crises facing the new nation. Read thoughtfully about each crisis and how it was met. But within this chapter you'll find an interesting "vignette" of how the British in the War of 1812 marched on Washington and set ablaze the Capitol and White House. While swarms of people fled the city, Dolly Madison refused to budge until the very last minute. Then—without panic—she stayed to rip the

precious portrait of George Washington from its frame and send it to safety. Speed up your reading when you come to this easier, story-type content!

A One-Minute Send-Off on Scanning

Some students plod doggedly down the page, line by line, when all they actually want is a brief passage related to their problem. Clearly, these students need to add rapid scanning to their repertory of reading approaches.

READING AID 247

After students have been introduced to techniques for scanning, just a word from the instructor will remind them to practice their new techniques. Here is the send-off a social studies teacher might give when assigning the question: ''What were the provisions and the date of President Kennedy's Alliance for Progress program to aid our have-not neighbor nations in Latin America?''

> Do fast scanning for your answer! ''Crack'' the page for what you want!
>
> Sweep your eyes down the page looking for clues that you've located your answer. What clues are likely to be signals? [Students will probably suggest: ''the words 'Alliance for Progress,''' ''the capital letters in these words,'' and ''the numerals in the date.'']
>
> Those are your targets! Good scanners concentrate, their attention unwavering! Take the attitude of expecting those signals to stand out from the rest. When you *think* you've found your information, *slow way down* to make sure. If you find that you have really found it, settle down to read carefully.

People scan *constantly* in adult life. Students should perfect this essential approach —to use in lifelong reading.

Detailed suggestions for developing scanning techniques are offered in the companion volume (Thomas and Robinson, *Improving Reading in Every Class,* unabridged 2nd ed., 1977), pp. 216–220.

A Quick Send-Off on Skimming

A skill extremely useful in study and personal reading is skimming for the gist of a passage. Often all the student wants and needs from a selection is a general impression. In daily life, adults cover *much* of their reading material by skimming. Why not teach young people to use this approach better and faster?

READING AID 248

To reinforce techniques of skimming, which had already been introduced, an English teacher searched for an interesting article that lent itself to skimming practice. She found one in the article, ''Marmosets: The World's Smallest Monkeys'' in Nila Banton Smith, *Be a Better Reader,* Basic Skills Edition, Level G (Englewood Cliffs, N.J.: Prentice-Hall, 1978), p. 29.

The teacher gave the skimming practice this introduction: ''You've already learned techniques for getting the gist of a passage quickly. How many of these can you remember?''

The students recalled the following techniques. Jottings of these went onto the chalkboard:

1. Examine the title and any blurb about the content.
2. Read the introductory paragraph(s), often the author's ''announcement'' of what is to come.

3. "Hit the headings" within the selection. These may announce the content of each section.
4. Zero in on the first and perhaps the last sentences of paragraphs. Main ideas of paragraphs are often found here.
5. Glance at the diagrams and pictures.
6. Read the concluding paragraph or two, often the author's wrap-up of what the selection contains.

After this send-off, the students skimmed the article, then took a preview test consisting of ten short-answer questions, all readily answerable if the students had zeroed in on the strategic spots. Good scores "sold" the new technique. Since speed rather than perfectionistic attention to detail was being encouraged, and since in skimming the reader intentionally accepts a lower degree of comprehension, 70 percent was considered a commendable score. The teacher deliberately planned a success experience. The students were surprised and pleased at how much they had gleaned from just a preview.

Detailed suggestions for instructing students in techniques of skimming will be found in the companion volume (Thomas and Robinson, *Improving Reading in Every Class,* unabridged 2nd ed., 1977), pp. 220–224.

READING AID 249

The classroom teacher who encourages students to skim a textbook chapter as the prelude to thorough study is developing a speed technique. Students who preview tend to comprehend both better and faster. A detailed discussion of skimming as the first step in studying a textbook chapter will be found in Reading Aids 195 through 205.

Detailed explanations for students and an abundance of practice material suitable for skimming (and also scanning) will be found in Edward B. Fry's *Skimming and Scanning* (Providence, R.I.: Jamestown Publishers, 1978).

Steps Toward Independence

READING AID 250

"Use this technique here . . . this one here . . . this one here" can be suggested to gradually maturing readers from day to day. Of course, students should be led more and more to select for themselves the appropriate approach. Their life need is to be able to set their own purposes, then read in the appropriate manner to accomplish these purposes. A question like this is a step in the direction of independence:

> We have talked about the purpose of this assignment. How do you think you should read to accomplish this purpose?

Then on, even closer to independence:

> What do you think it's important to learn from this reading? What will be the best method of reading in order to find this out?

*"Do the Flip!"**

READING AID 251

Students will need many experiences, under guidance, in setting their purposes and selecting their approach. Later, of course, they should move on to making these decisions alone. As they do so, they can "do the flip!"

*Paul D. Leedy uses this catch-phrase in *A Key to Better Reading* (New York: McGraw-Hill Book Co., 1968), p. 79.

A step toward efficient reading is to "do the flip!" Ask yourself, "What do I want to get out of this reading?" Flip through the passage asking, "How difficult does it look? To accomplish my purpose, should I read rapidly? Slowly and carefully? Scan? Skim? Use a combination?" Don't start to read *anything* unless you "do the flip!"

Helping Students Read More Rapidly When this Is Appropriate

On Parents Day, Danny's parents reported to the reading teacher: "He studies late at night—and most of the weekends, too. His grades are *A's*. He's conscientious and tries to read everything thoroughly. Can you help him read faster?"

Chris's parents reported: "Chris is 'into' science and math. He's read so much in these areas that now he reads the lightest novel slowly."

Ron told the reading teacher: "I read so slowly my mind wanders. I think about a soccer game or what I did last weekend."

Students who are over-conscientious, students who have done so much close reading that now they habitually read slowly, and dreamers whose wandering thoughts devastate their speed—these students may be promising candidates for training in more rapid reading.

Students are *not* candidates for training in rapid reading, however, if they are blocked by deficiencies in basic skills, as is the case with many who read slowly. A deficiency in word attack may be the interfering factor. Students can hardly profit from covering the page more rapidly if they do not know the meaning of the words on the page! Instruction in basic skills of comprehension may be essential before speed can be developed. Until students have the substructure upon which speed is built—word attack, vocabulary, and comprehension—pressuring them to read faster will be futile and *probably harmful*. The most competent teacher can't build a penthouse first! (Robinson, 1957)

When interfering factors are no longer present, direct attention to rapid reading is appropriate when students need it on or above the high school level. Below that level, school time is probably better spent developing essential skills and just learning to enjoy reading.

What Is the Plight of the Slow Reader?

A reading consultant (Grob, 1970, p. 285) in Ann Arbor, Michigan studied the range in reading rates among students who scored on standardized tests *on or above* their grade-levels. He calls that range "astonishing." He asks:

> How long would it take you to read *Great Expectations* at 150 words per minute? . . . While the average reader in the class will finish after five days of two-hour readings, the students falling below 100 words per minute will need to spend two hours a day for 21 days. . . . Assuming that these students would have other academic responsibilities, it seems fair to estimate that their pattern would have to be 42 days of one-hour readings, or 84 days of half-hour readings.

He calls attention to the academic crippling that may result from a low reading rate. And he urges us to make adjustments for the wide variations in study time required by students and help to prevent this crippling.

"Life-saving scissors" can sometimes save an assignment for slow readers. We can, as Grob suggests, sometimes make the assigned reading manageable by assigning them just

READING AID 252

parts of a selection. Omitting a few chapters from a novel, some scenes from a play, seems to him preferable to the alternative—having them give up and thus have no practice at all.

Of course, in addition to using "life-saving scissors" with slow readers, we will want to move on to *actively improve* their reading rates.

Teachers Can Improve Reading Rates in a Variety of Ways

Teachers can help students attain higher rates of reading in a variety of ways: 1) by providing practice with interesting material read for less exacting purposes, 2) by giving assignments that call for the general impression, 3) by providing timed practices on informational material, 4) by forcing more rapid reading through mechanical devices, among them the reading pacer, 5) by encouraging practice with easy, highly interesting material while doing some timing, and 6) by helping students have a definite purpose for reading day-to-day assignments. A discussion of all these methods is offered in the companion volume *Improving Reading in Every Class,* unabridged 2nd ed., (Thomas and Robinson, 1977), pp. 224–231 and pp. 109–124.

Commercial Practices Can Build Speed on Study-Type Material

READING AID 253

Students whose vocabulary and comprehension are already adequate can work directly on improving their speed of reading study-type material through timed practices. Groups or individuals read short selections under a time limit, then answer comprehension questions. Under time pressure, students often discard unnecessarily sluggish habits. Selections intended for rapid reading should, of course, include few unfamiliar words.

Reading and English teachers have found the following practice exercises helpful:

> *McCall-Crabbs Standard Test Lessons in Reading.* New York: Teachers College Press, Columbia University, 1979. *These booklets of short selections, long popular with teachers, are highly suitable for developing both speed and comprehension. Booklets are available for use on all levels up through grade 12. Reading time is three minutes. "Instant feedback" through a grade-level score (rough but an excellent motivator) helps to get the attention of students. Recently, the series has been completely revised.*

> *SRA Rate Builders,* a section of the SRA Reading Laboratories, 3B and 4A. Chicago, Illinois: Science Research Associates, Inc. *These short speed (and comprehension) practices offer the student high-interest content. Reading time is three minutes. The student is challenged to "climb" through the colors by completing more difficult and longer practices within the three-minute limit.*

Push Speed of Easy, Interesting Reading

Much practice with easy, highly interesting material, read for less exacting purposes, is a natural, effective means of increasing rates. The material should not present vocabulary or comprehension blocks. The students should be pulled along by intense interest.

Providing time for students to do free reading of such material while encouraging rapid reading should bring worthwhile gains. By graphing their rates on succeeding practices, the students should have convincing evidence of progress. This should spur their efforts.

The Reading Pacer—A Motivator for Students

READING AID 254

While reading pacers produced by different manufacturers vary, all pacers have a cover, a bar, or a beam of light that moves down the page, pressuring the student to read faster with each succeeding practice. A dial controls the speed of the descending occluder or light beam.

Pacer training is motivational for most students and profitable for many as long as vocabulary and comprehension are already adequate. If not, until such inhibiting factors are removed, forcing such training may be harmful. In one reading laboratory, a young man was in tears about his performance on the pacer. He was being forced to "read" faster and faster when he did not know the meaning of the words on the page.

The Controlled Reader—Another Motivator

READING AID 255

In addition to performing the functions of the pacer, controlled reading devices force specific left-to-right eye movements. Such techniques are used in connection with films or filmstrips. Probably the most popular of these techniques is the filmstrip approach used in the Controlled Reader (for four to fifteen students) or the Controlled Reader Jr. (for one to three students) produced by EDL-McGraw-Hill. Morris (1976, p. 13) cautions that students should be grouped for such training on the basis of reading achievement levels and rate of reading with comprehension.

The "Ten-Minute Speed Graph"

READING AID 256

Of course, expensive mechanical equipment like the reading pacer is not always available for all those who need rate training and is certainly not available for home practice. In that case, a number of simple devices can be used to push up reading rate.

In the following lesson, the students are encouraged to practice with the "Ten-Minute Speed Graph," which appears on Master Copy Page 49. The writer does not intend to be recommending this particular graph as the device for rate improvement. Some teachers report success with the "alarm clock graph." With this, the students set an alarm to ring at the end of an hour of practice, then they try to exceed the number of pages read on the preceding practice. Others prefer the "ten-page graph." With this, the students read ten pages, then try to reduce their time on the next ten pages. Others use a graph like the one on Master Copy Page 49 but extend the time to half an hour. As for the "Ten-Minute Graph," the writer has observed certain advantages. A senior girl mentioned one: "No matter how busy I am, I can always find ten minutes!" In the writer's experience, students who are in earnest about improving their speed will find time to work in extra practices. Whatever device is used for pushing up the student's rate, many of the insights in Reading Aids 256, 257, and 258 will be applicable.

SEE MASTER COPY PAGE 49

Let us observe a reading class where many of the students are working to increase their speed of reading. The students are asked to bring to class an easy, fast-moving fiction book or a fast narrative-style biography to read for pleasure: "Choose a book so exciting that it pulls you along fast." Or the students may select their book from among inviting books displayed in class. Each students is supplied with two paper clips and the "Ten-Minute Speed Graph."

The students read for a few minutes just to get into their book. After they have done this, the teacher explains:

> In a few minutes you'll be asked to read for ten minutes while being timed. A little later you'll be given tips on how to increase your speed. Then you'll read for another ten-minute period. You may be surprised at what happens!

Find the point where you are now reading in your book, and place one of your clips at that point. The longer loop of the clip should "point" to your starting point.

When I say "Start," please read at your usual speed. *Don't push yourself to go any faster—just read along at your comfortable rate.* We'll count the number of pages read, give you the speed tips, and then you'll try again. Are you ready? Start!

After ten minutes the teacher says:

Stop! Place your other paper clip in your book to mark the point you stopped. Please count the number of pages you read—to the nearest one-fourth or even one-eighth of a page. You may have read, for example, three and one-fourth pages. Then you will make a dot at that point on your speed graph. [The students record the number of pages they read on practice one.]

We'll practice again in a minute. This time you're out to "beat the clock." Here are four speed tips:

Tip 1: Your purpose is just to enjoy a good story. *Move right along!* Don't slow down for small details—you're not doing study-type reading. Six weeks from now it won't matter if you don't remember details.

Tip 2: *Push* yourself! Speed is largely a matter of habit. Push yourself a little faster than you want to go. This may be uncomfortable—at first. But later this faster speed should become your comfortable speed.

Tip 3: Set a goal to drive toward—*beyond* the number of pages you read in your first practice. If you read four pages the first time, you might set a new goal of four and one-fourth pages. Count ahead from where you stopped reading and place your paper clip in your book to mark this point, the long loop of the clip pointing to your target. Then read, intending to *reach* your clip and, if possible, to *read past* it.

Tip 4: Take a minute or two to "warm up" before you start each practice. Can you anticipate what's ahead in the story? Ask yourself, "What's likely to happen next?" . . . "What will that character do?" Anticipating will give you a mind-set—to find out *fast*. Please think over, right now, what may lie ahead in your story. [The students are given time for this.]

Now I'll time you on the second practice. You'll probably read faster. If you don't, there's probably a reason. You may have run into a more difficult passage—perhaps slow-moving description.

Remember: *Press right on! Push yourself! Drive toward your paper clip!* Are you ready? Start!

The teacher calls time in ten minutes. Again the students count the pages read, and make a dot on their graphs for practice two. Then they draw a line connecting their dots. Almost all the students are pleased with the results. Some exclaim about their increases. In the writer's experience, many students who read slowly need only to be convinced that they *can* read faster. The ascending lines on their graphs give positive proof of progress. Their success on this first try helps to keep them trying!

Students ask, "What about comprehension?" To make sure that they have comprehended, the teacher can have them write a brief summary. One expert reports: "I have my students do a brief recall after the first, then again after the second, faster reading. Then they compare the two. When their summaries tend to look about the same, the students feel confident." (Graves, 1979)

The students continue doing free reading when time is available and pushing speed upward with ten-minute practices.

Graphs of Former Students Lend Credibility

READING AID 257

The teacher has saved the ten-minute speed graphs for former students who markedly increased their speed and has placed these on display. The students perceive that many who practiced faithfully doubled—and some tripled—their rate of reading interesting fiction.

Students Can Increase Their Gains through Home Practice

READING AID 258

Some students respond to the suggestion of doing ten-minute speed practices at home. Those who practice faithfully usually make worthwhile gains. Friday may be the ideal time for reading for personal enjoyment and for an enthusiastic send-off on home practice. The weekend ahead offers less hurried hours for personal reading, and the book has a chance to "capture" the student in class.

Here is what a teacher might do and say in such a send-off. The students have already been introduced to the ten-minute speed graph and have practiced using it in class. Each student is given a copy of the "Tips for Using the Ten-Minute Speed Graph," which appears on Master Copy Page 50.

SEE MASTER COPY PAGE 50

> You can increase your gains in reading speed through home practice. Can you find ten minutes on Saturday and ten on Sunday to increase your speed? Try each day to top your record of the day before.
>
> You can read faster just by *trying*. Eyes—like people—get into habits. For years you may have moved your eyes across the page at a certain speed. But you aren't "locked into" that speed! Your ten-minute practices can break old sluggish habits!
>
> Select the right time and place for speed practice. When you have a choice, early in the day may be best. Try not to practice when you're worried, when there's a flow of troubles through your mind. A quiet place should help you send your speed upward. There's research evidence that high speeds are not attained in noisy, distracting surroundings.
>
> A kitchen timer is ideal for timing. Or you might have someone else time you. If an ordinary watch is used, bring both hands up to twelve. Stop reading in exactly ten minutes. Record on your graph the number of pages read.
>
> Will your speed *really increase?* Students who practiced faithfully have doubled and some have tripled their speed of reading fiction. Will the gains you make in reading fiction *help you study faster?* Your gains should filter down to certain types of study reading—to some of your materials in social studies, to some short stories and novels in English, to popular science books and articles—an article in *Science Digest,* for example. You probably won't be able to read a chemistry textbook faster. As you know, slow, careful reading is often appropriate in study.
>
> Will the line on your graph climb steadily? Probably not. Speed graphs do not climb in a well-behaved straight line—instead, they zigzag. You'll have good days and bad, depending on how tired you are—how preoccupied—even how warm or how humid it is! Your *average* speed, though, should definitely end higher than it began.
>
> Can you increase your speed indefinitely? No, eventually the line of your graph will level off. Then just continue on a high plateau. You'll need to do this in order to *hold* your gains and permanently change the habits of a lifetime.
>
> *You* are in the driver's seat. If, for any reason, a passage invites you to linger, call off the speed practice and slow down to savor the passage or to read more reflectively. You can always practice speed tomorrow.
>
> When you start a new book, make a note of this on your graph, or start a new graph. The opening pages of a book will—and *should*—go more slowly as you get acquainted with new characters, a new setting, an unfamiliar plot. Your speed will—and *should*—drop. The note on your graph will explain this drop.
>
> Sophisticated readers work on speed *indirectly*. Unknown words are hurdles in the way of speed. Each time you learn a new word, one of those hurdles tumbles! When you work on vocabulary, then, you're building speed indirectly.

Your teacher can only guide you—you can help yourself if you really want to.
For best results, practice daily. Little practice, little gain—much practice, much gain!
Work in extra timings if you can. They will help you *hold* your gains.

Some students respond by doing ten-minute practices at home two or three times each day. Students with urgent needs are encouraged to work in extra practices. They bring their graphs to class, and these go on display. Ten-minute timings continue from time to time in class.

Not all students will be motivated by the "Ten-Minute Speed Graphs." Practice with a reading pacer, the controlled reader, or with timed practices like the *SRA Rate Builders* or the *McCall-Crabbs Standard Test Lessons in Reading* offer possible alternatives.

The writer expresses special thanks to Leila M. Whitcombe, former reading consultant, East York Board of Education Office in Toronto, for sharing the idea of ten-minute timings in class and at home.

Use a "Push-Card" to Push Speed

READING AID 259

The teacher might offer students the "push-card" way to *remind* themselves to read faster:

> One of the hardest tasks is *remembering* to read faster. It's easy to lapse back into old habits. You might run your hand, or your index finger, down the page as a reminder to keep pushing *right on.*
>
> Some readers move a "push-card" down over the page. This can be an index card, an envelope, or a sheet of paper. You have a choice of two ways to use your "push-card":
>
> 1. Put your card *above* the lines you will be reading. Then move it down the page a little faster than you want to read, forcing yourself to keep ahead of the card.
> 2. Or put your card *below* the line to be read. Then move the card down the page, exposing one line after another. Try to keep up with your card. "Chase" it down the page.
>
> You can pick up extra gains in speed if you use your push-card with easy newspaper or magazine reading as well as light, fast-moving books.

Some students find the push-card distracting and respond negatively. Others quickly adjust to it and find it helpful.

"Jet" Down the Page!

READING AID 260

As students read fiction for personal enjoyment, they can time themselves, bringing both hands of their watch up to twelve as they start each full page. They read the first page at their usual, comfortable rate and record the time required. On subsequent pages, they "jet" down the page. A student might feel gratified by these successive timings: "3 minutes," "2 minutes, 50 seconds," "2 minutes, 40 seconds," "2 minutes, 45 seconds," "2 minutes, 35 seconds," and so on.

Students need to be convinced that they *can* read faster. And they need to overcome that arch foe of faster reading—mind-wandering.

Speed Is a Byproduct

Good teachers are constantly helping their students to build speed indirectly, and students should appreciate this. Every class hour that students spend on word study removes blocks that stand in the way of speed. Every class hour they spend on skills of comprehension removes roadblocks, too. Any work they do with paragraph patterns is a "speed device"—they can pull out main points faster. So is work with OK5R—they can master a chapter *faster*. Dr. Ruth Strang (1965) cited as one of the most important insights gained in her long and distinguished career: "Generally effective instruction in reading is a means of improving speed. A good reading program will have speed as a byproduct."

References

Anderson Albert William. *Speed Up Your Reading*. Perth: University of Western Australia 1968.

Graves, Michael F., Associate Professor, Department of English-Speech Education, University of Minnesota, in conversation with the writer, March 1979.

Grob, James A. "Reading Rate and Study-Time Demands on Secondary Students." *Journal of Reading*, 13, no. 4 (1970).

Leedy, Paul D. *A Key to Better Reading*. New York: McGraw-Hill Book Co., 1968.

Morris, Helen Frakenpohl. *EDL Controlled Reading Skill Development*, Teacher's Guide. Huntington, N.Y.: Educational Development Laboratories, 1976.

Rhinestine, Hope, English teacher at the University of Chicago Laboratory School, in remarks to the writer, March 1978.

Robinson, Helen M., in lecture to a class at the University of Chicago, Summer 1957.

Smith, Nila Banton. *Be a Better Reader*, Book 4. Englewood Cliffs, N.J.: Prentice-Hall, 1971.

Strang, Ruth, in a class lecture on the teaching of secondary school reading, University of Chicago, 1965.

Thomas, Ellen Lamar, and H. Alan Robinson. *Improving Reading in Every Class*, 2nd ed. Boston: Allyn and Bacon, 1977.

7

Turn Your Students into Readers—For Life

Teachers who turn their students into readers have given them a good gift—one that lasts for life. How can we find out how much personal reading our students do already? Get ''un-put down-able'' books into their hands? Have the classroom overflow with good reading? Make enthusiasms contagious? The chapter that follows suggests a host of possible ways to ''turn on'' lifetime readers.

We can dream of schools that graduate their students as lifetime readers who turn to reading for information and delight. They view a book as a close companion, always there for hours of rest and restoration, as a source of lifelong learning in areas of personal interest, as a counselor to turn to when they have personal problems. What a good gift we have given these students!

That is the dream—what is the reality? Many young people are leaving school unsure that what is between the covers of books has much to offer them. Yet never has there been a greater need for personal reading than there is today. Clashing viewpoints on controversial issues—social, political, ethical, moral—leave our graduates bewildered and in search of insights. The career education we give them may go out of date several times within their lifetimes. Automation will offer them more and more unfilled hours—some could well be filled with the joy of reading. An ''age of anxiety'' confronts them with personal problems, problems whose solutions could be explored through reading.

Can we bring reading close to these needs of students and to what they view as close to their own lives? They care about drug problems, contacts with the other sex, broken homes. They care about the generation gap, dropping out of school, ''stopping out'' of college. They care about their futures—lifestyle options, new marriage patterns, the jobs in their futures. They are ''into'' exciting hobbies—first cars, camping out, whitewater kayaking, mountain climbing, guitars, ''their'' music. Some care about the world they live in. They may wish to explore alienation, the environmental crisis, violence, poverty, public and private corruption, exploding populations, women today. What opportunities are offered to pull them into reading, to make them aware that reading offers insights and perhaps solutions!

What benefits will we give students when we motivate them to read widely? Students tend to improve in reading when they *practice*. While it is often true that "Johnny doesn't read because he can't," with other Johnnys, "Johnny *can't* read because he *doesn't*." (Witzling, 1956, p. 52) The following benefits in reading should go hand in hand with practice:

1. What students *bring to* the printed page in life experience and in vicarious experience is a powerful determinant of what they *take from* it. The more our students read, the broader their background for reading, and the easier, the better, and the *more* they read. By motivating reading, we set in motion this beneficial cycle.
2. The world of words has never been the world of troubled readers. But when they are guided to books that are right for them in difficulty and interest, they spend many hours in the world of printed words. As these students read, they are practicing basic skills of word attack, silently figuring out words they do not recognize at sight.
3. They are meeting new words repeatedly in similar and different settings, often with a little increment of meaning with each encounter, and gradually incorporating some of these words into their vocabularies. As a general rule, the broader students' reading interests, the richer their vocabularies. (McCallister, 1957)
4. The reading practice tends to strengthen their comprehension.
5. Easy, exciting readings "pull students along" and tend to increase their speed. Easy, exciting novels and fast-moving narrative style biographies can be effective speed builders.

While disabled readers will, of course, need planned remedial instruction, someone has observed with quite an element of truth, "The best reading school in the world is the library."

In addition to growth in reading power, wide reading offers young people important *personal* benefits:

1. It is in printed or written matter that ideas are most often presented in logical thought patterns. Here, more often than in speech, students meet *logical* presentations. Much of the oral language that surrounds them daily consists of "almost aimless meanderings." (Levine, 1972, p. 580) When students are exposed to the logical patterns in informational printed communications, they are more likely to assimilate and to use logical thought patterns.
2. Students who are surrounded in their classrooms with rich reading resources and who turn to these to solve in-class problems may form the habit of turning to reading to solve out-of-class personal problems.
3. Clashing values leave today's students adrift and uncertain. Not long ago, prescribed rules were passed on to the younger generation, who lived by these values without much question. Now change is so rapid it makes shock waves! The thoughts of contemporary and "classical" thinkers on social, political, ethical, and moral problems, thoughts accessible to young people through reading, can help provide them with a compass.

4. The career information we give students is growing rapidly—and growing out of date. Young people who have learned to search for solutions through reading should be better able to re-educate themselves for their careers during their working lifetimes—and for careers not yet in existence.
5. Trouble in the city streets may involve young people who have little to occupy their time. An athletic coach (Patlak, 1978) sees this opportunity: "Suppose a coach a boy looks up to pushes sports books. It might give a boy an interest—a habit, maybe. You might help keep him off the streets. It just might work."

Children come to us far from equal in their opportunity to become lifetime readers. With some, books were very much a part of a warm and happy childhood. As tots, they were read to—over and over again. *The Little Engine That Could* and a mother's or a father's warmth and closeness came to be associated. Birthdays and Christmases brought windfalls of books. These children recited their favorites by heart! Other children walk into the schoolroom from a bookless world. Some have never seen an adult reading a book in their homes, have never held a book in their hands.

As we consider developing committed readers, these questions may come to mind: "Won't books give way to other media?" "Why not let students learn from television, motion pictures, slide projectors, and recorders?" Surely these other media provide vivid learning experiences. Nevertheless, books have their own unique advantages. We can select a book that fits the mood, or the need, of the moment. We can pick up a book when we want to. We can take it wherever we want to and have it with us. We can turn to it again and again in the future. Images on the television screen flash by us and are gone forever. And the "relentless procession of ideas" on that screen can be a barrier to critical analysis. As someone observed, "Rereading is possible—relistening is often not."

In which subject can the classroom teacher best reach the unreached reader? Will it ordinarily be English? A student may loathe English and love another subject—auto shop, for example. The auto shop teacher may be able to reach that student when the English teacher could not possibly succeed! Under-par readers may have a built-in block to books offered them in English class—it is probably in English that they have experienced their worst failures.

What a world of books each subject teacher has to draw from! The shop teacher can convince a boy whose life is motorcycles that books can solve problems with *Two-Wheel Wonder: How Motorcycles Run and How to Keep Them Running*. The social studies teacher might captivate a young idealist with the dramatic *The Life and Death of Martin Luther King, Jr.* The science teacher might intrigue a "young scientist" with *Microbe Hunters*. The photography teacher might strike a spark with Eastman Kodak's profusely illustrated *How to Make Good Pictures;* the homemaking teacher with the thought-provoking anthology, *Family*. The music teacher might lure a music-minded student with *The Soul Brothers and Sister Lou* and give this student his or her first real pleasure from print. The track coach might win a "never-reader" with *How to Star in Track and Field.*

Classroom teachers who delight in their own personal reading—from English class to the playing field—will want to give their students the gift of lifetime reading. Principals may want to encourage a schoolwide effort. Many parents, if they are aware of ways to help, will want to contribute. Reading specialists and librarians will want to share with the school staff and with parents their insights about motivating reading. The pages that follow should be suggestive for all these groups as they seek their own effective ways of turning students into continuing readers.

As the writer rereads this chapter, its tone suggests that turning students into lifelong readers is a teacher's very first reason for being! Perhaps the reader who finds joy in personal reading will understand and forgive her enthusiasm. Surely time for encouraging love of reading should not run away with time for developing the skills of reading. Encouraging personal reading should have its appropriate place—and no more than its appropriate place—in a balanced reading program.

Finding Out About Their Personal Reading

What personal interests of students can you "plug into" as you work to turn them into readers? What are their attitudes toward reading? If they are already readers, what are their tastes? Do these tastes need broadening?

Quick Questions Can Give You Insights

READING AID 261

A few quick questions as classes start the school year can give you helpful insights about their personal reading. You will find a "sample" questionnaire on Master Copy Page 51. Students can write the answers in *just minutes*. Then their answers can help you guide them to the right books and zero in on those who tell you they are "never-readers."

SEE MASTER COPY PAGE 51

From this questionnaire you have some "starter" information. Questions 1 through 7 and question 10 probe for interests you can "plug into." Questions 8 and 9 reveal something about your students' tastes in reading if they are already readers. Question 11 suggests how much each student already reads. These insights as well as others that you gain can now be used in several ways: 1) in guiding individual students to the right books, 2) in selecting books for a classroom collection, 3) in choosing selections the class will read together, 4) in discovering interests of the group that you can "plug into" as you teach skills. You can zero in on students who report that they are "never-readers." It will be richly satisfying, later in the year, to see these "never-readers" lost in a book. This questionnaire can also help you become acquainted with your students quickly and develop rapport. One teacher comments: "If a student answers that he would spend his $500 on a motorcycle or a sailboat, I have an opportunity to talk to him about that motorcycle or that dream boat." (Bragstad, 1979)

SEE MASTER COPY PAGES 52–54

Question 3 offers a hint about each student's competence in reading. Students who list as favorite subjects English and social studies seem to be at home where there are heavy reading demands. Those who list as their favorites mathematics, industrial arts, photography, and the like, and as non-favorites the reading subjects may be more at home in areas that make fewer verbal demands. Their answers may be saying, "I need to improve my reading."

READING AID 262

You may prefer a more comprehensive questionnaire. In that case, the one on Master Copy Pages 52 through 54 should be suggestive.

Clues and Cues from Daily Contacts

READING AID 263

You can pick up clues to students' reading interests in informal contacts from day to day, then use these as cues to invite reading. What have their experiences been? What do they do in their spare time? What jobs have they held? What information do they want or need? What are their dreams? Listen to students as they talk informally—on the school steps, in the halls, on the stairs, at their lockers, walking into and out of class, in the lunch room, in the bleachers. What are they talking about? What are they caring about? Can you guide them to reading that is close to their lives?

Matching Book and Student

As teachers encourage reading, they will want to offer students books that match their reading reach. Give them books far beyond their reach, and we lose them! But how can a non-reading specialist assess each student's reading level? And how can a non-specialist assess each book's difficulty?

Standardized Reading Tests Offer Some Insights

READING AID 264

Most schools have standardized reading test scores on file for each student, scores that are yours for the asking. Jot these in your class record book the first few days of school, and you'll have a suggestion of the reading reach of every student. A reading specialist of your school or system may be available to help you interpret the scores. Of course, you'll supplement—and often supplant—these rough insights with all you learn from day-to-day observation.

How Can You Match a Book to a Student's Reading Level?

READING AID 265

Care is needed lest the difficulty of books exceed the student's *independent reading level.* Dr. Emmett Betts originated three descriptive terms for reading levels. The level that is so difficult for a child that even with help it is a source of frustration is referred to as the *frustration level.* The level appropriate for materials to be read with a teacher's direct assistance is the *instructional level.* The level of difficulty the student can handle without direct assistance is the *independent reading level.* This level, as Dr. Betts pointed out, is likely to be considerably lower than the instructional level. The student who checks out a book from the library or selects one from a reference list will probably be reading that book alone. The message of Dr. Betts' independent reading level is simple but often overlooked: in general, reading materials you intend for students to read on their own, books to which you guide them as you try to form patterns of lifetime reading, should be considerably easier than those they will read with your direct assistance. It should be noted, however, that a student's reading strength is not identical in all subject areas. A student consumed with interest in a certain subject (race cars, for example) may, by virtue of this interest, broad background information, and a strong technical vocabulary, *command surprising reading power* when reading on this subject.

Just how can we use a student's standardized score as an extremely rough but sometimes useful clue in matching a book for personal reading to the reading level of that student? It is important to note that the score the student makes on a standardized silent reading test usually indicates the *frustration* level for that student, the level that student can attain when *straining to the utmost* in a testing situation. As Burmeister (1978, p. 46) suggests, we must drop down a year or more to find the student's instructional level. And we must ordinarily drop down still farther to find the *independent level,* the level at which the student can comfortably read books alone.

Suppose Timmy, a ninth-grader, made a score of grade level eight on a standardized reading test. Dropping down about two grade levels, we might try guiding Timmy to a pleasure reading book on the sixth-grade reading level. Suppose the scores on a particular test were reported in terms of percentiles instead of grade levels, and Nick, a twelfth-grader, scored at the 50th percentile.* Since a 50th percentile rank is at the mid-point for the student's grade, Nick performed on that test on the level of the average twelfth-grader.

*A percentile score of 50 means that 50 percent of the students in the norming group scored lower than the student receiving that score. A percentile score of 30 means that 30 percent of the students in the norming group scored lower.

Dropping down those two grade levels again, as Burmeister suggests, we might try guiding Nick to a pleasure book on tenth-grade reading level. If Nick scored at the 85th national percentile, a ranking well into the college levels, we might try guiding him to a book on twelfth-grade reading level. If he scored only at the 25th percentile, a rank considerably below his grade level, we might try a book with mature content but on eighth-grade difficulty level.

Again, you will supplement—and often supplant—the rough insights gained from standardized test scores with your own day-to-day observations. As you will notice, students vary greatly in their ability and their desire to cope with easy and/or difficult materials (Burmeister, 1978, p. 59). Again, a student with a consuming interest in a subject may be able to read successfully *well beyond* his measured level. A school's reading specialist should be able to help a less experienced teacher with this important "operation matching." Some students, however, do not seem to need much guidance. When surrounded with inviting books and given freedom of choice, they select books suitable in difficulty.

How Can You Judge a Book's Difficulty?

What an opportunity we have in enrichment reading! A textbook that matches the average reader in a class may be years beyond or years below the reach of some of that student's classmates. But through supplementary materials, we have an opportunity to get the right book into the hands of the student. The poorest reader may be able to experience some measure of success, and the most gifted reader can have reading experiences that stimulate and challenge. (Muelder, 1970)

READING AID 266

How can a classroom teacher assess each book's reading difficulty? Your school librarian or the young people's librarian in your public library can guide you to book lists that suggest the level of reading difficulty and provide a helpful annotation about the contents. The books are classified by subjects; teachers can quickly turn to a list of books related to their subjects.

Several outstanding lists of books recommended for retarded and reluctant readers provide a maturity or interest level in addition to a reading difficulty level. The following book-length book lists can serve as helpful "book finders" for teachers.

Spache, George D. *Good Reading for Poor Readers.* 10th ed. Champaign, Ill.: Garrard Publishing Co., 1978. *This classic list annotates books, magazines, and newspapers likely to appeal to poor readers. Both an interest level and a reading level are suggested. A thought-provoking chapter, "Using Books To Help Solve Children's Problems," is included. The book also alerts teachers to the great variety of book lists that are available to strengthen their resources and provides an annotated list of these lists.*

Spache, George D. *Good Reading for the Disadvantaged Reader.* Champaign, Ill.: Garrard Publishing Co., 1975. *The author states as one purpose of his book building the self-concept: "It is our hope that this book will alert teachers to the need to help pupils find books with which they can identify—books in which they can find positive images of their race or ethnic type . . . We Must offer our minority children realistic stories—with central characters whom they can admire and imitate . . . We want the child to meet outstanding and respected members of his group, to learn more about their cultural and polictical contributions to America." Both an interest level and a reading level for each book are suggested.*

Palmer, Julia Reed. *Read for Your Life*. Metuchen, N.J.: The Scarecrow Press, 1974. *The books on this list are intended to appeal to young people who have had little or no experience with books. Choices are based on the cumulative experience of bookmobile operations and of school volunteers who spent thousands of hours working with children in deprived areas to lead them to enjoy reading. The books are generously annotated. A reading difficulty level as well as a maturity or interest level is suggested for each book.*

Strang, Ruth, Ethlyne Phelps, and Dorothy Withrow. *Gateways to Readable Books*. New York: H. W. Wilson Co., 1975. *This well-annotated graded list of books on a wide range of subjects is intended for use with below-grade readers in junior and senior high school. Books are selected for their appeal to troubled readers. A reading difficulty level is suggested for each book.*

Graves, Michael F., Judith A. Boettcher, and Randall J. Ryder. *Easy Reading: Book Series and Periodicals for Less Able Readers*. Newark, Del.: International Reading Association, 1979. *This new and different book list reviews materials written specifically to win secondary and upper elementary students who read considerably below grade level. Only book series, mostly fiction, and periodicals—no trade books—are reviewed. The various series include books on true adventure, race cars, mystery, sports, sea adventure, space adventure, westerns, monsters, problems of inner-city teenagers, and adapted classics. Some of the books are comics.*

The annotations are far more detailed than in the usual bibliography, and the evaluations should be extremely helpful. Each annotation includes a general description of the series, a more detailed description of a representative book, story, or article from the series, physical characteristics of the books, and prices. Of course, reading levels and interest levels are specified. Teachers in search of materials appealing to inner-city students, including black students, should find this list extremely useful.

You have available through your school or public library comprehensive annotated lists of thousands of books through the standard library catalogs. The teacher will find easy-to-read books on an infinite variety of subjects in *Subject Guide to Children's Books in Print,* 8th ed. (New York: R. R. Bowker Co., 1977). This volume classifies 39,000 books under more than 8,000 subject categories and suggests appropriate grade levels. The *Junior High School Library Catalog,* 3rd ed. (New York: H. W. Wilson Co., 1975, with yearly supplements) reveals by the very fact that a book was selected for this catalog something about its difficulty. The *Senior High School Library Catalog,* 11th ed. (New York: H. W. Wilson Co., 1977, with yearly supplements) includes books that vary widely in difficulty but sometimes suggests, through the annotation, the book's difficulty.

READING AID 267

The Fry Graph for Estimating Readability offers a quick, easy-to-use, helpful way to assess the reading difficulty level of a book, provided one realizes that the estimated grade level is rough. Readers who are interested in the rationale behind this handy graph and in evidence of its high correlation with more complicated readability formulas may wish to consult Edward Fry's article, "A Readability Formula That Saves Time," in the *Journal of Reading,* vol. 11, no. 7 (April, 1968), pp. 513–516 and 575–578. The graph itself and the directions for using it are reproduced on Master Copy Pages 55 and 56. Through the generous permission of the author and the editors of the *Journal of Reading,* anyone may reproduce this graph in any quantities. A sliding scale version in which the approximate grade level of the selection appears through a window, even handier to use, is available from Jamestown Publishers, Post Office Box 6743, Providence, Rhode Island 02940.

SEE MASTER COPY PAGES 55 AND 56

Of course, factors not measured in readability formulas influence how difficult it is for a student to read a given book. These factors are examined and the limitations of readability formulas are discussed in Anne Campbell's "How Readability Formulae Fall Short in

Matching Student to Text in Content Areas,'' *Journal of Reading,* vol. 22, no. 8 (May 1979): 683–689, and in Nancy Marshall, ''Readability and Comprehensibility,'' *Journal of Reading,* vol. 22. no. 6 (March 1979).

Over the years reading specialists develop a feel for the reading difficulty of books, as do school librarians. They will gladly share their insights. Through experience, classroom teachers also develop their own feel for the difficulty of books and for their appropriateness for individual students.

''Turning on'' Readers

On the pages that follow, you will find a variety of possible ways to motivate personal reading. Many are ''live'' reports from teachers—from English class to the gym. In view of the busy lives of students and the lure of television, guiding students to do more personal reading is not likely to be easy. The successes these teachers report, however, offer us encouragement. Nothing succeeds like the teacher's enthusiasm! Readers are invited, on the coming pages, to look for activities to their liking, adjust them in ways to their liking, and create their own effective ways exactly to their liking.

''Browse Box''

READING AID 268

A physics teacher who wanted to encourage personal reading (Kimmel, 1975) brought some attractive books into his classroom. When he lined these up on a traditional bookshelf so that only their spines were showing, almost no one reached for the books. Then he revised his strategy. He covered a carton with bright paper, printed a large sign, BROWSE BOX, and tossed the books into the carton. Next day he found his students crowding around the new ''browse box'' and reaching in. Now many of the books went home in his students' book bags or in the pockets of their jeans.

A Moment Can Sell a Book

READING AID 269

It takes just a moment of class time to advertise a book. A mathematics teacher might comment, ''Here's a fascinating book of mathematical games, puzzles, tricks, and problems,'' while holding up *Mathematical Carnival* for the class to see. A biology teacher whose class is studying genetics might hold up James D. Watson's *The Double Helix* and comment, ''Here's a fascinating, frankly revealing personal story of the co-discovery of the DNA molecule—a terrific book!'' A physics teacher might comment, ''Here's the inside personal story of Enrico Fermi and the first nuclear reaction. It's Mrs. Fermi's *Atoms in the Family.*'' A social studies teacher whose class is studying the tragedy of Hiroshima might hold up *The Great Decision* by Michael Amrine and comment, ''Here's a book about the atomic bomb and the agonizing decision to use it.'' A physical education teacher might show the class *The Complete Book of Cheerleading* with its lavish how-to-do-it pictures. After class, students are likely to come up to these teachers and ask, ''May I please have that book?''

A teacher of environmental studies (Lynch, 1978) sometimes wrote on the board or read aloud *one* intriguing sentence from a book. ''A book like *Our Vanishing Air,*'' she comments, ''would sell itself!''

''They Went Like Hot Cakes!''

READING AID 270

Bookstores entice us to browse and buy by surrounding us with a world of colorful, inviting books. Perhaps we can put students into just such a world. A teacher of basic English classes tells how she accomplished this in a school with a library especially well-stocked with books high in appeal to teenagers.

> I trundled colorful, eye-catching books from the school library into the classroom and stood them up in the chalk tray against the chalkboard. This was on Friday, a day when the students were more likely to have weekend hours ahead for reading. To make sure I had real book bait, I dropped by the library for several days in advance, walked around the bookshelves, selected popular books—books as enticing as Richards' stunning story of the world of motorcycles and their riders, *Into The Road*—and cached them away under the charging desk. Students who were wide readers helped me select the books. The school librarian, too, kept a sharp eye out for inviting books and saved them for me under the charging desk.
>
> When Friday arrived, I held up some of the books and caught interest with a sketch of the contents. Then the students went to the board, row by row, to select a book. Those books went like hot cakes! The students were so eager to have certain books that we had to work out rules as to which row could go first. One Friday the row by the window would have first chance at the books—the next week, some other row.
>
> The class period that followed was a "read-in." The students would dip into a book to see if they enjoyed it. If they did not, they would select another. Toward the close of the period we would go as a group to the library to check out the books the students wished to continue reading.
>
> At times, instead of trundling the books into the classroom, I would spread them out on tables in the school library. Each table would feature a different theme—adventure stories, mysteries, sports fiction and sports how-to-do-its, books about cars and other exciting hobbies, books about jobs and careers, teenage stories for girls, books about teenage problems, and so on. The students would crowd around the tables, examine books that looked appealing, and check out many. My biggest problem was keeping other students from raiding my tables before my own classes arrived!
>
> Students would sometimes comment, "That's the first book I've ever read all through." One remarked, "Thanks for the time to read in school!"

Read Aloud a Cutting

READING AID 271

How many of us learned to love reading when we were children by being read to at home? There's a homey saying:

> Richer than I you can never be—
> I had a mother who read to me!

Select a cutting from the book, the best passage to take the students captive. Lead into the passage with intriguing comments or exciting storytelling. Rehearse for an expressive, dramatic reading. Stop at a point where your students feel impelled to read on. Have several copies of the book on hand where students can check them out immediately or, if this is not possible, start a waiting list. If you can have multiple copies, several students will be reading the book at the same time and can share their enthusiasms. Reading aloud may prove to "tuned-out" readers that there's something to enjoy between book covers.

One writer (Karlin, 1977, p. 276) suggests reading aloud a few paragraphs, then "auctioning off" the book, i.e., offering it to the most interested student.

"Purposeful Projects" Create Friends of Books

READING AID 272

In classrooms that cross the curriculum, one of the most effective ways to create friends of books may be to involve students in "purposeful projects" that lead them to reading.

Harry W. Sartain's enthusiastic look at this technique is shared in Reading Aid 151. Students whose class projects are meaningful and "pull them into" reading may form the habit of turning to reading for personal reasons. The reader is urged to read and enjoy Dr. Sartain's enthusiastic comment.

One student became a "turned-on" reader while engaged in a "purposeful project" in a county park Nature Center! Her social studies teacher (Lynch, 1978) tells about it:

> My students had become concerned about preserving the environment and were considering what action a lone teenager could take. Each student selected a beyond-the-school-walls project. A senior girl chose to work at a county Nature Center, where a park naturalist trained her as a Nature Club leader for younger students. One of the buildings housed a small library of nature books, which the student soon discovered. One day she walked into class and exclaimed to her teacher, "Miss Lynch, they have the neatest books in that library! I never knew before that I liked to read!"

READING AID 273

"A Right On Read-In"

"Dim the house lights!" In the school's assembly a teacher and a librarian, both gifted in interpretive reading and in holding an audience, brought books to life through dramatic readings. (Davis, 1974, p. 9) They had prepared a cutting from each of ten books carefully selected to appeal to turned-off readers. They supplied each teacher with a shopping bag with multiple copies of the books. Their tour of ten schools was financed by a mini-grant from the Board of Education.

Here are some comments from teachers in the schools: "My nonreaders have been stimulated." . . . "Children feel that it is much more enjoyable to read a book they know something about." . . . "That was just marvelous—to have the books right away." . . . "An extra dividend was that *all* the children were reading the same books, which was supportive of the morale of the poor readers." . . . "The children said they were enthusiastic about these books because no one had ever introduced books that way to them before."

READING AID 274

School Libraries Can Offer Read-Along Tapes

We have mentioned the work of Laura Johnson (1973, p. 129), reading specialist at Evanston Township High School (Illinois), in preparing read-along cassettes for the opening pages of "fasten-your-seat-belt" fiction (see Reading Aid 145). Turned on by an exciting opening, the students sometimes read on to the last page by themselves. For those who cannot or do not, Mrs. Johnson sometimes records entire paperbacks—fast-paced ones—as read-along books.

English teachers in Laura Johnson's high school have asked her to tape full-length novels, among them *Native Son* and *The Incredible Journey*. Tapes of these books and others are made available in the school library. Students go up to the librarian and ask, "Is there a tape of Sammy Davis's *Yes, I Can?*" No stigma is attached to checking out a read-along tape—the motive might well be the heightened interest of hearing a dramatic reading. Once under way, some students finish the books alone. (Johnson, 1974)

Parents and students who wish to serve a school might assist teachers and librarians by tape-recording read-along collections. Future Teachers groups and National Honor Society might be a source of volunteers.

When reading centers and school libraries provide read-along tapes, some students for the first time in their lives experience an entire book, and this experience belongs in the Fun Department. Here, indeed, is strong motivation to learn to read!

Students who listen to read-along tapes should understand that dividends can be "theirs for the taking" in growth in reading. As they follow along, their eyes on the book, they may come to associate the *heard word* with the *printed symbol*. Gradually, some of the unknown words on the page may become theirs to use in future reading. It should be added, however, that the students should understand the *why* of keeping their eyes on the book and should be strongly urged to do this. Students who become engrossed in listening to an exciting story with their heads down on their desks are having the fun part of the read-along experience without collecting the dividends in growth in reading!

Students "Order" Books

READING AID 275

A teacher of small summer reading classes invited her students, many of them not-so-eager readers, to place "book orders." She asked, "What kind of book do you think you'd like best—what kind above all others? Just write me a note on this slip. The book you order will appear in class for you." Some of the orders read: "Bring me a story like *Star Wars*," "I'd like a book about race cars," "Good football story."

The next Friday, a day when the students were more likely to have time ahead for reading, they walked into class to find on their desks an inviting book, sometimes a choice of three or four books. The teacher, aided by the school librarian and by enthusiastic student readers who were well acquainted with teenage books, had filled the orders. Early in the course, standardized test scores were a help in selecting books appropriate for individual students. This filling of "book orders"—this careful matching of book and student—proved more successful early in the course than turning unenthusiastic readers loose in the library. Of course, students who preferred to select and bring their own books to class were encouraged to do so.

Tap Developmental Tasks and Other Needs and Problems

Robert J. Havighurst (1972, p. 43) has called to our attention the "developmental tasks," tasks which, as we develop through our lives, constitute the major business of living at different stages. The developmental tasks for the teen years, you may recall, include, among others, moving toward independence from parents, achieving more mature relations with age-mates of both sexes, looking ahead to marriage and family life, finding a life work, and acquiring values as a guide to living.

READING AID 276

Teachers in any subject area can be aware of the developmental tasks teenagers face and can invite their students to related reading. School libraries are often well-stocked with books related to the developmental tasks. The developmental task of *moving toward independence* might suggest to a science teacher a display of books on "Is There a Job in Your Future in Science?" The task of *preparing for marriage* might suggest to a homemaking teacher a book display on guidance in family living. An English teacher might prepare displays on "Problems of Teens—How to Cope!" These might include books on how to live with your parents, making and keeping friends, understanding dating relationships, increasing self-confidence, finding a part-time job, what to do after high school, what you should know about drugs, and exploring your values.

Now reading is brought close to students during the difficult growing up process. And they may come to view books as somewhere to turn when they have personal problems.

READING AID 277

Young people sometimes share a personal problem with a teacher with whom they feel a closeness. Often that teacher becomes, for the moment, the student's counselor. At times it may be appropriate for the teacher to offer a book. The book may lead the student to reflect, "I am not alone in this problem," and it may possibly suggest solutions. An athletic coach (Patlak, 1978) offers this comment:

> When a kid has a problem, sometimes I find a book about the same problem. I can talk up the book walking with the kid down the hall. Sometimes the student will read the book through and not apply it. But sometimes he thinks, "That sounds like my problem."
>
> When a kid has a setback and is feeling low, this book might be just right. It's *Fighting Back,* about Rocky Bleier, running back for the Pittsburgh Steelers. His foot was shattered by a grenade in Vietnam—he was told he would never play again. He fought his way back! Not so long ago he ran to victory in the Superbowl!

Of course guiding a student involves much more than bringing the book and the student together. Talking with a teacher about both book and problem—a teacher with a deep understanding of young people—may help the student come away with greater insight.

READING AID 278

Book lists that classify books according to their psychological, behavioral, and developmental themes, are available to help you identify books related to the student's need, concern, or problem of the moment.

> Dreyer, Sharon Spredeman. *The Bookfinder: A Guide to Children's Literature About the Needs and Problems of Youth.* Circle Pines, Minn.: American Guidance Service, 1977. *This superb, extremely comprehensive guide classifies more than 1,000 books—fiction, biographies, and some non-fiction—for children up to age fifteen. Examples of the many subjects included that are close to young people are divorce, fear, belonging, parents, siblings, boy-girl relationships, courage, responsibility, friendship, and death. An interest-level for each book is suggested.*
>
> Pilgrim, Geneva Hanna, and Mariana K. McAllister. *Books, Young People, and Reading Guidance,* 2nd ed. New York: Harper and Row Publishers, 1968. *This book list recommends books suitable through the teen years up to young adulthood. The chapter, "Books and the Needs of Youth," is not only informative but inspirational.*
>
> Baskin, Barbara H. and Karen H. Harris. *Notes from a Different Drummer: A Guide to Juvenile Fiction Portraying the Handicapped.* New York: R. R. Bowker Co., 1977. *This book analyzes more than 300 juvenile fiction books in which the handicapped—both physical and emotional—are depicted. Annotations are complete, and criticisms are sensitive and perceptive. A reading level for each book is suggested.*

Black children have a "developmental need" for a sense of identity, for an understanding of themselves, and for pride in their heritage.

> Rollock, Barbara, ed., *The Black Experience in Children's Books.* New York: The New York Public Library, 1974. *This list includes books suitable for children of all ages. The books listed are intended to give the black child "a sense of identity and a proper historical perspective of the struggles, hardships, and successes of his people." The books can also help sensitize the white child to the black experience. The books selected emphasize the similarities of people of different races and seek to develop an understanding of the human experience.*

Librarians Can "Catch" Readers

READING AID 279

School librarians can visit classrooms in every conceivable school subject and advertise books, including books newly received in the library. Holding up books with their bright covers, they can sketch the contents intriguingly. They can also bring along magazines and journals related to the work of the course. Students often respond to the novelty of the librarian's visit.

Teachers may not realize the variety of materials related to their subjects—books, magazines, and journals, especially new acquisitions—that are available in the library. Thus the librarian's visit can be informative to the teacher as well as the students.

There will be a *special plus* if librarians visit other classes as well as the traditional English class. A student who would never reach for a book voluntarily if it is offered in English class may soon be lost in Eve Curie's *Madame Curie* if it is suggested by a librarian who visits science class. Troubled readers gravitate to courses they consider "non-reading"—industrial arts, homemaking, business education, art, photography, music, physical education—driven there by fear of failure in reading subjects. Here the librarian has an opportunity to "catch" readers who are lagging in both ability and enthusiasm. A boy who has shied away from books may quickly check out an easy-to-read book that tells him how to build his own kayak if he is introduced to it in shop.

Visitors Can Touch Off Reading

READING AID280

In a previous chapter, we mentioned social studies teachers in LaFollette Senior High School in Madison, Wisconsin, who were teaching reading "holdouts." They invited a parole officer and some young ex-prisoners under his guidance to visit the class. The visitors talked about the influences that lead young people to crime, about whether the penal system discourages crime or fosters it, and about the need for change as they saw it. The visit touched off weeks of reading about young people and crime. (Bragstad, 1979)

Visitors to the classroom can start runs on books—a commercial or passenger airplane pilot or an instructor from a local flying school, a mountain climber, a sports writer for the local paper, a professional football star. On display nearby can be related books—where hands will reach for them. Sometimes the visitors themselves bring along and distribute inviting printed handouts.

Lifetime Reading—By Example

READING AID 281

When one school surveyed its students, only two percent could remember seeing a teacher practice the art of reading. (Petre, 1971, p. 194) Later this school scheduled half-hour "reading breaks" when the whole school—teachers, counselors, principal, athletic coaches, and the student body—read for recreation. Now reading was taught—and caught—by example and sharing.

In a junior English class, time was sometimes set aside for personal reading, and the teacher read, too:

> As Friday approached, the students were encouraged to find a book for weekend reading or to select one from attractive books displayed in class. Class time was available on Friday for dipping into the books. I brought a personal book to school that day, turned to my own book, and read it while the class was reading. Often we shared our excitement. Sometimes our sharing led to an exchange of books. My students brought me books to read, thus broadening my acquaintance with the literature that delights adolescents. I came to know Hermann Hesse when a student brought me her beloved *Siddhartha*.

Both class and teacher should feel free to share honest reactions. A student might exclaim, "*Lassie Come Home* is great!" The teacher might comment, "I'd like a dollar for every time I read it when I was your age!" With some other book, though, the teacher might remark, "I just can't get into that book!" In this way, the students will realize that they cannot expect to be enthralled by every book. (Haslam, 1978)

Parents, too, can be enlisted as models. Some young people have never seen their parents relax with a book and read for personal enjoyment or heard them talk about a book with enthusiasm. Parents who are concerned about their children's reading should realize that they themselves are teaching attitudes toward reading. A letter to parents to invite their cooperation will be found on Master Copy Pages 57 and 58.

READING AID 282

"These Are Our Favorites!"

One teacher asked each student to bring a favorite book to class, then made a display, "Our Favorite Books." Each book was labeled with the name of the student who had selected it as a favorite. Next she asked popular teachers, athletic coaches, counselors, and secretaries to bring in their favorites for a display, "Favorite Books of People You Know." Again, each book was labeled with the name of the person who had selected it as a favorite. The students gathered around this display, reached for, examined, and sometimes read the favorites. The favorite of a popular physics teacher, *The Effect of Gamma Rays on Man-in-the-Moon Marigolds,* quickly went home with a student.

READING AID 283

Vacation's Here! Here's a Book List!

Many teenagers *want* to read but do not find the time as long as school is in session. Summer vacation offers less hurried hours. Classroom teachers—of any subject—can use vacation book lists to encourage summer reading. A student might crumple and toss in the wastebasket a list of books supplied by an English teacher yet save and use all summer one that he or she is given in homemaking, science, music, or physical education. Of course, teachers will want the levels of the books on the list to span the reading levels within the class.

Many college-bound students respond to the suggestion that they strengthen their background for college through vacation reading. Instructors can obtain attractive annotated book lists for the college-bound in quantities at nominal cost from the American Library Association. These lists include "Outstanding Fiction for the College Bound," "Outstanding Biographies for the College Bound," "Outstanding Theater for the College Bound," and "Outstanding Books on the Current Scene for the College Bound."*

Teachers who have spent many patient hours helping below-grade readers achieve gains in reading will want to take care that these hard-won gains are not lost over the summer. They can list vacation books for these students, tapping their strong interests. A remedial teacher had patiently helped Dick, a high school sophomore, lift his reading level from the second to the sixth-grade level. Just before school was out, the teacher took Dick captive with a book about the Hardy boys, *Danger on Vampire Trail.* During the vacation that followed, Dick read a dozen or so of the Hardy Boys Series and had many hours of pleasant reading practice.

The class itself might compile a vacation book list of books widely read and liked. Students are responsive to book tips from other students.

READING AID 284

Passport to Reading—A Library Card

Adults in whose childhood a public library card was a passport to happy reading are well aware how much such a card can mean to a young person. Although procedures differ, a

*Write to the American Library Association, Young Adult Services Division, 50 East Huron Street, Chicago, Illinios, 60611.

library card can usually be secured easily and quickly. When a young teacher learned, to her surprise, that many in her classes had no library cards, she telephoned the public library and asked if she might send a student for the applications. That student brought the applications to class and supplied one to each classmate who had no card. The signature of a parent or other adult citizen of the community was required. Later a student returned the applications to the library, then a few days later picked up the cards for the class. The teacher placed a card in the hands of each student with an enthusiastic send-off.

As the students visit the library on their own and use their new cards, the teacher is no longer assigning or guiding their reading. They have taken a step toward independence as lifetime readers.

It's Vacation—Here's Your Library Card!

READING AID 285

"Sandy" Patlak, the physical education teacher who "sells" his students sports books, made sure that each student in his classes owned a library card. (Patlak, 1971) He did this in early June when vacation days ahead offered more time for reading. Just before school closed, the coach presented his boys with their library cards with enthusiastic comments about vacation reading.

Teachers who have helped handicapped readers upgrade their reading will not want them to slip back over the summer. Placing a library card in their hands just before school closes, and with it a list of vacation reading, will encourage pleasure and practice all summer.

Meet Your Public Library

READING AID 286

Some young people have never—no, not once—walked through the doors of their public library. That home of books, so much a part of the childhood of others, has played no part in their childhoods. Why not introduce these students to their local library?

A field trip to the library is most likely to be successful if the teacher plans carefully in advance, visiting the library to become acquainted with its resources and to talk with the librarian about the coming visit. The librarian may be available to take students on a guided tour—to introduce them to the reference section; to point out the helps it offers when they are working on assignments; to show them "the easiest encyclopedia" and "the hardest"; to introduce the reference librarian, a standby when they cannot locate what they want; to let them know that this librarian hopes that they will *never* leave the library discouraged and without what they came after.

The librarian–guide will want to show the students the location of books related to their subjects at school; to guide them to the young people's section and the fiction section; to show them the shelves of recent books, including best-sellers; to point out the biography section. The librarian can accent fascinating areas for personal reading—sports fiction and how-to-do-its, "how to" books on auto mechanics, career books, books on problems of growing up. The librarian can pull from the shelves "irresistibles"—books young people have heard mentioned, books they want to reach for.

The librarian will want to show students the stands with current newspapers and the colorful magazine racks and to let the students know how they may check out these periodicals. Some students will be surprised to learn that they may check out maps, pictures, and posters to illustrate talks they are preparing for school, and still more surprised to learn that they may check out favorite records, perhaps even paintings to hang on the walls of their homes!

The librarian can stress, as the students are walking past the bookshelves: "This is *your* property. These are *your* books. Your parents and others paid for them with their taxes. We hope you'll use what's *yours*."

During the visit, the students may learn for the first time of the library's program of activities for young people—the film offerings, the Junior Great Books program, the story hours for young readers. Browsing time, when each student can return to areas of special interest, will play an important part in a successful visit. The teacher will want to facilitate each student's having a library card, a passport to return to this world of books and enjoy it fully. Ideally, the students should receive their cards before their trip to the library.

The opening weeks of school is probably the ideal time for the library visit. At that time, students are hoping that the school year ahead will be successful and may welcome the facilities offered. To those whose homes are crowded and noisy, the library offers a possible haven for quiet study. Parents who are informed in parent meetings about this introduction to the public library can encourage their sons or daughters to make follow-up visits during the school year and to continue to use its resources during the summer.

"That Bookstore Was Neat!"

READING AID 287

Put together one bookstore owner who wants children to love reading—one teacher willing to do some advance planning—some parents who care and will provide transportation—and what do you have? A *great* experience for students—a visit to a bookstore's colorful world of books, perhaps for the first time!

Teachers throughout a Florida metropolitan area are aware that their classes are invited to take a guided tour of Haslam's Book Store in St. Petersburg, one of the South's largest book stores. After a date has been arranged, the teacher receives an advance letter from the owner suggesting how to prepare the children to gain the most from their visit. When the class arrives, the students are divided into two groups so that the tour will be "personal" and more students will ask questions.

The first stop on the tour is a new world for the children—the receiving and shipping room of a busy bookstore. The owner-guide explains: "Books are considered so important for people all over the world that they can be mailed anywhere for the same amount of postage. You can mail a copy of *Tom Sawyer* to a suburb of your town for 48¢; to San Francisco, for 48¢; to Singapore, for 48¢!"

The next stops on the tour are the rare book collection, the used book room, the new book room, the bargain book room, and the collector comics room. The last stop is the children's book room, where the guide demonstrates how a book is "born"—from the corrected galley proofs to the assembling of the page sections within the cover! Last comes what the children like best—time to browse among the children's books or to return to a favorite section of the bookstore.

After the visit, the children often write enthusiastic thank-yous: "That bookstore was neat!" "I would like to read all the books in your store!" "It was very fun!" "You're the nicest bookstore keeper I've known!" A teacher wrote: "It was one of our highlights for the sixth grade."

Reading Corners Invite Readers

READING AID 288

A schoolroom can be drab indeed when a teacher first walks into it in the fall. Such a room can be brightened by books with their colorful covers. These can advertise good reading to students—and advertise it every day.

Classrooms, especially in reading and English, can live and breathe reading. Books, many of them paperbacks, can be spread out on certain days, on shelves and tables where their covers beckon and where hands will reach for them. Window ledges with heavy-duty bookends can become inviting bookshelves. Students will be more involved if they help create their own equipment. Orange crates painted by students can become inexpensive but colorful bookshelves.

Displays might feature a specific interest for a short time—it might be "the job in your future"—then a display on another subject could take its place. You may wish to learn the interests of your students, then select books to match. Or you may wish to create displays to broaden their reading interests. A rack or windowsill of books can feature a certain theme, or books on a certain theme can stand up along the chalkboard. The "Book of the Week" might be spotlighted, with the cover or the book itself framed within a box cover. Students can have a part in selecting and displaying the books. Those who are wide readers of teenage books can suggest books likely to appeal.

Although newspapers offer content related to every conceivable school subject, how seldom do we see a copy in a classroom! Yet newspapers are available on an incredible range of reading levels—from *Know Your World* (Columbus, Ohio: Xerox Education Publications), with headline news at second to third-grade level, all the way to the *New York Times!*

Magazines, too, offer content related to every conceivable school subject. And often they talk to students about things they care about. For students who are "into" cameras, the photography teacher can have on hand *Popular Photography* and the *Photography How-To Guide*. For those who are "into" sports, the coach can have *Sports Illustrated.* For future homemakers, the homemaking teacher can have in the classroom *Coed.*

Student newspapers and magazines offer us the opportunity to attract older students who are reading *far* below their grade level with short, lively, interesting, "now" selections. Here is a highly selective list of such periodicals:

Student Newspapers

Know Your World. Columbus, Ohio: Xerox Education Publications. *Students can relate to the current news stories, special features, TV section, sports section, cartoons, and jokes in this appealing paper. Colored photographs and other illustrations give the paper strong visual appeal. Game-like skills exercises are provided. This paper is intended for students aged ten to sixteen. Those reading on only second- to third-grade levels should be able to read it successfully.*

You and Your World. Columbus, Ohio: Xerox Education Publications. *The content is much the same as that of* Know Your World *plus, since it is intended for older students, career information and consumer education presented appealingly. One typical issue included feature articles on cycle safety, skiing techniques, and new television shows. This paper is intended for students aged eight through twelve. Those reading at only third- to fifth-grade levels should be able to handle the reading successfully.*

News for You, Editions A and B. Syracuse, N.Y.: New Readers Press. *A strong plus value of this adult-looking weekly tabloid newspaper is that Editions A and B include the same content presented at different levels of difficulty. The paper can therefore accommodate students reading on different levels within a classroom, without obvious grouping. The paper is intended for students in grades 10 through 12 and for adult readers. Edition A is suitable for those reading on third- to fourth-grade level; Edition B, for those on fourth- to fifth-grade level.*

Student Magazines

Outstanding among the magazines designed especially for students are the lively and colorful Scholastic "family," including *Scholastic Sprint* (interest level, grades 4–8; reading level, grades 2–2.6); *Scholastic Action* (interest level, 7–12; reading level, 2–2.9); and *Scholastic Scope* (interest level, 7–12; reading level, 4–6).

You will find a well annotated list of magazines that cross the curriculum, magazines on all reading and maturity levels, in the chapter "Magazines and Newspapers," in

George D. Spache's *Good Reading for Poor Readers* (Champaign, Ill.: Garrard Publishing Co., 1978). Dr. Spache's book also annotates newspapers. Parents are often glad to donate recent magazines and have them put to good use at school.

In addition to providing time for the class to do personal-choice reading, teachers can encourage students to dip into the books and magazines in their classroom reading corner during any class period after they have completed their study tasks.

In some classrooms, simple procedures for checking out books, newspapers, and magazines encourage the students to practice out-of-class reading. They write in a notebook their name, the title, the author, and the date. The notation is crossed off when the item is returned. The loan period can be flexible, in keeping with the demand for the item by others. A reliable student librarian, on the alert, can insure that books are checked out officially and can help to prevent losses.

Television Instead of Reading?

Must television be something young people do *instead* of reading? Or can it *lead them into* reading? Librarians report that after a television program based on a book, their libraries are "borrowed out" of that book. Bookstores report that there was a run on the *Lord of the Rings* trilogy after the television presentation of *The Hobbit*. Both libraries and bookstores ran out of copies of *Star Trek* following the television series.

From day to day on television, young people can hear experts in many fields talk about their fields of specialization, they can view superb documentaries like *Microbes and Men,* they can watch screen versions of the classics, like *David Copperfield*. Afterwards these students can be encouraged to probe more deeply subjects that have caught their interest. Programs like these may touch off new interests and lead to completely new reading interests. (Arbuthnot, 1969,p.9)

A Tele-Guide to Books

READING AID 289

Teachers can alert their classes to coming events on television and suggest related reading. A corner of the chalkboard might be headed "Tele-Guide." Here the teacher (or a class committee) advertises for home viewing outstanding television offerings related to the course, announcing the channel, date, and time. Sometimes a related book is suggested. In science, the program might be "Jacques Cousteau." The related book might be Cousteau's own book, *The Silent World,* or Rachel Carson's *The Sea Around Us*. In social studies, a teacher might advertise *The Adams Chronicle*. The related book might be Lillian Bragdon's *Meet The Remarkable Adams Family*. In art class, the instructor might spotlight the Italian TV series, *Life of Leonardo da Vinci*. The book might be Dimitri Merejcovski's *Romance of Leonardo da Vinci*. The opportunities in English class are many. The program might be *Once Upon a Classic* or *Great Performances,* and the book, *Robin Hood* or *The Prince and the Pauper*. With exceptional programs guidelines for viewing can be suggested in advance, and discussion encouraged later.

READING AID 290

Educational television stations will provide teachers with guides to outstanding educational programs. The teacher's guide to *Nova,* a superb series exploring the frontiers of scientific research, offers background for the teacher, a synopsis of each coming program, possible discussion questions and class activities, and a list of books for students related to the program. The National Education Association recommends programs to teachers. The American Federation of Teachers offers *Teachers Guides to Television*. This bulletin alerts teachers to coming programs of outstanding educational value, provides guides for discussion, and comes complete with bibliographies from the American Library Association.

Parents, too, can use television to help young people "tune in" on books. They can share their children's viewing of dramatizations of books—one of these might be the sensitive movie classic, *The Yearling*. Soon afterward, a copy of *The Yearling* might "happen to be" lying within reach at home. Or parents might encourage a trip to the library to obtain a copy.

READING AID 291

English teachers and their students can view the television versions of masterpieces, see motion pictures, and attend live plays, then in class discuss these and compare them with the books. Now literature—and English—becomes part of the current scene.

READING AID 292

Tap "Rightful Rebellion"

READING AID 293

Young people—generation after generation—have wanted to "grasp this sorry scheme of things" and mold it more nearly to what is ideal. Some of them respond to books that talk to them about social injustice, about the lives of the poor and the powerless, and inspire them to want to finish the unfinished business of democracy. Not long ago, *Manchild in the Promised Land* and *Soul on Ice* were "big." Recently *Autobiography of Malcolm X,* Alex Haley's *Roots,* and Maya Angelou's *I Know Why the Caged Bird Sings* have been "big." Shirley Chisholm speaks of the younger generation "in rightful rebellion" and expresses bright hopes for their future. (Chisholm, 1970)

We can tap this "rightful rebellion" to send young people to books. Books brought from the library into the classroom—cuttings read aloud—visitors invited to class—lists of suggested books—units of study—can spotlight the literature of "rightful rebellion." A book like *I Know Why the Caged Bird Sings* can open eyes to social wrongs, lead students to consider these wrongs in relation to their own lives and values—and help to make them continuing readers. Books like these need not encourage cynical or iconoclastic attitudes. Instead, with a guiding hand present, they can generate thoughtful reaction, sometimes constructive action.

Now books are no longer seen as lifeless objects resting on cloistered shelves. Instead they become dynamic and vital things, capable of changing the direction of events! Iron-willed dictators standing resolute against change have burned books! (Downs, 1956, p. 7)

"It Isn't a Sin to Skip!"

READING AID 294

Reading may be a tedious chore for students because somewhere along the way they have picked up the notion, "It's a sin to skim or skip." Interested or uninterested, they plod through every page. Mature readers, on the contrary, do not read everything—they read selectively, concentrating on what is interesting or important *to them personally*.

Students may need these insights: "Good reading can be taking from a book three or four ideas that are important to you, not reading every page. Good reading can be reading chapters related to your purpose and skipping the others. Good reading can be following a certain thread through a book and skimming the rest." (Manolakes, 1976)

Help Them Find Time to Read

READING AID 295

Many teenagers really want to read but cannot find the time. Assignments for their classes, sports practice, club meetings, good times with friends, responsibilities at home crowd their days and nights. Some students report to their jobs after school, come home exhausted around bedtime, and fall into bed.

Students need time to browse among books, to dip into books, to select a book, then to read it in class until the book has made them captive. Friday, as we have noted, may be an opportune time to expose students to books. Time spent with books on Friday may be several times multiplied as the students read on over the weekend at home.

Up the Rungs of Reading Ladders

READING AID 296

As the school year passes, teachers will want their students to advance, when they are ready, up the ''ladder'' to more difficult books and to higher quality books. Teachers can have in mind sequences of gradually increasing difficulty and can advance a student through a sequence on some compelling interest.

Let's suppose that Joyce, a ''never reader,'' remarks to her teacher that she would like to read a teenage romance. Her teacher offers her Jeannette Eyerly's *The Phaedra Complex,* a light, easy, absorbing ''page-turner.'' When Joyce returns the book with ''It was terrific—is there another as good?'' her teacher recommends Maureen Daly's *Seventeenth Summer*. Considerably later, Joyce steps up several rungs of the ladder to *Portrait of Jennie*. Teachers have advanced students up ''ladders'' of sports books, mysteries, books about great black Americans, science fiction.

We have an opportune time to advance a student up a ladder when that student is consumed with interest in a certain subject. The days just before a vacation offer another opportunity to suggest a more difficult book. Unhurried vacation hours offer the student time to do more rigorous—and slower—reading. (Poole, 1978)

An outstanding list of books close to the interests of young people ranks books ''ladder fashion'' as a help to teachers:

> Reid, Virginia M. *Reading Ladders for Human Relations,* 5th ed. Washington, D.C.: American Council on Education, 1972. *Books, both fiction and non-fiction, are grouped according to four themes: creating a positive self-image, living with others, appreciating different cultures, and coping with change. Within each theme the books are grouped by gradually increasing maturity levels: primary, intermediate, junior, senior, and mature.*

Offer Students ''Bridge Books''

READING AID 297

Some young people become caught up with one type of reading to the exclusion of all others. Then their teachers look for opportunities to start them in new directions. One way is to offer them a ''bridge book,'' a book that may act as a bridge to a new type of reading. (Fenwick, 1964) Joyce, the ''never reader'' mentioned in Reading Aid 296, could easily become caught up with teenage romances and read these exclusively. A teacher might help her broaden her reading to include historical fiction by offering, as a ''bridge book,'' Irving Stone's *Love is Eternal* (the wedding band Abraham Lincoln placed on Mary Todd's finger bore this inscription). Later Helen E. White's *How Do I Love Thee?,* about Elizabeth Barrett Browning, might serve as Joyce's bridge to biographies. And the play, *The Barretts of Wimpole Street,* might become a ''bridge book'' to plays.

Parents Can Be on the Team

READING AID 298

Many parents, if they are aware how, will want to encourage young people to do more personal reading. They may wish to make attractive books available in the home and to encourage the use of the public library. PTA meetings and visits to the school offer an opportunity to talk with parents about ways to encourage reading. The school librarian or the reading specialist might display attractive books to an audience of parents and acquaint them with the rich variety of colorful, inviting, quality books available for young people. (Haslam, 1978)

Teachers might develop letters to parents, hoping to enlist their cooperation, and send these letters home where they would be signed by a parent and returned. Let us imagine that the ninth-grade English teachers of a school are planning a year-long effort to win their students to more extensive personal reading. Early in the year, these teachers might send home a letter something like the "sample" on Master Copy Pages 57 and 58.

SEE MASTER COPY PAGES 57–58

Sharing Reading Enthusiasms

When reading is a duty and reporting a chore, students have their own ways of reporting. They read the book's jacket, have a friend tell them the story, turn to the book digests of masterpieces of literature, the Monarch or Cliff notes, even to Classic Comics! One of the author's "creative" students returned to school years after his graduation and confessed that once, while giving an oral book report in her class, he made up the book as he went along—title, author, characters, and plot—and that this bit of fiction earned him a B+!

Ban Book Reports?

Formal written book reports have probably helped turn many students away from reading. While some find the task of writing pleasant, others find it mildly unpleasant, and some find it excruciating. It will be difficult for "reluctant writers" to enjoy reading if they must always report in writing. They will come to associate reading with a distasteful task. For these students, other ways of reporting are more likely to make them continuing readers.

Surely students should be encouraged to read books of their own choosing without having to report to their teachers. And when they do "report," perhaps they might have a choice of methods, for no one method will appeal to all. Some students enjoy sharing their books with their classmates—the variety of ways to share is limitless. Some prefer talking about their books alone with their teacher. Some take pride in keeping a log of their reading. Some enjoy writing about their books, especially when given the freedom to choose from a variety of interesting formats. If it seems desirable that all the students report in a uniform way, the class might vote on the form they prefer for their next book report.

Book Sharing Instead of Reporting?

Ideally, "book reports" would be a lively sharing of excitement and enthusiasm. The books would "catch on" with others, who would check out and enjoy their classmates' favorites. You will find on the pages that follow a collection of ideas for book sharing to help make enthusiasm contagious. Teachers, too, will want to share with students their own personal reading—and their own delight in reading.

Fill Up Your Pocket—with Books!

READING AID 299

Teachers in any subject classroom would like to see their students turning to books, then sharing their enthusiasms. Simple and easy to make, a poster with a "book pocket" for each student can be a stimulus for reading and for lively sharing. The heading of the poster might be "Books We Really Liked." On small book slips, the students record books they have just read—and liked, together with a brief evaluation, then insert these book slips into their pockets. The poster is colorful and eye-catching—likely to attract a crowd of students.

You might make the poster in school colors. Cut pockets from colored construction paper (2 by 4 inches is about the right size) and mount them on poster paper. Paste a white name label across the top of each pocket. You'll need a supply of book record slips. Cut these (3/4 by 4 inches) with a paper cutter by cutting 4-by-6-inch index cards crosswise. Student assistants can help prepare the book pockets, the name labels, and the book slips, and paste the pockets on the poster. One teacher used the school's colors of green and white, then trimmed the poster with the school's symbol, a jaunty green devil.

The poster forms an eye-catching bulletin board or wall display. The students are invited to go to the poster, write their name on one of the labels, and "move into" their pocket. Then they are to fill up their pockets—with books! As soon as they finish a book, they write on a book slip the title and author, and on the other side a few words of evaluation. Then they place the book slip in their pocket.

As the pockets begin to fill, students gather around the poster before class to examine each other's book slips. You will hear "book reports" like this: "I read it all night," "I'll lend it to you," "It's the best sports book I've read." On the slip, the student evaluates the book in just a word or two. Here are some appraisals: "Too good to miss!" "It helped me with a problem," "Clear instructions for kayak builders." Students sometimes meet "new" types of books through these exchanges.

Teenagers who live in a whirl of cars, sports, contacts with the other sex, broken homes, the environment in crisis, and drug problems respect a tip from another young person who has gained something from a book. A book suggested by a classmate often "hits the student where he lives." (Speigler, 1964, p. 91) Perhaps the very best book "ad," more convincing than any comment from a teacher, is "I just finished that book, and it was great!"

You can make a "big deal" of the pockets by going to the poster often to examine your students' book slips. Of course, you will want to have a pocket with your own name inscribed—one fairly bursting with book slips.

You can tap the influence of popular teachers and others—athletic coaches, counselors, secretaries, a well-liked principal—by inviting them to put their name on a pocket, make out slips for their favorite books, and "move in." Your students will examine the contents of these pockets with special interest.

In the writer's experience, book pockets appeal to students differing widely in ages. Sophisticated seniors in the University of Chicago Laboratory School have become excited about "filling up their pockets with books." Content area teachers might encourage reading related to their courses through book pockets.

What Book Is Your Favorite?

READING AID 300

A question like this can touch off an exchange of enthusiasms: "What is your favorite among all the books you've ever read? If you have difficulty selecting one favorite, what is *a* favorite? Or can you name two or three favorites?" Students who have been introduced to book pockets are asked to record their favorite book on a gold slip and place it in their pocket. (The slips can be cut from gold gift-wrap paper that has a reverse side suitable for writing.) The teacher, too, decides on a lifetime favorite and fills out a gold slip. Interest is high as the students examine each other's—and their teacher's—favorites.

Questions like these are catalysts for discussions: "*Why* is this book your favorite? Would you suggest it to others? To others with certain interests?" Teachers will leave these discussions "clued in" on the reading enthusiasms of teenagers. The writer of this book read and enjoyed Ann Fairbairn's *Five Smooth Stones* when a popular athlete named it as his favorite. Students check out and enjoy each other's favorites. Some favorites become epidemic.

Colorful "Covers" Can Represent Books

READING AID 301

Instead of a book slip, younger students may prefer to fold a slip of colored paper (perhaps 2¼ by 3½ inches) to simulate a book and to print on the cover the title and author of a book they have just completed. A brief reaction to the book can be written inside the folder. The names of the students might be printed on a poster, and the students' folded "books" taped after their names. Students feel pride as their record of reading grows.

"Load Your Airplane with Books!"

READING AID 302

Younger students may respond to something more exciting than book pockets or simulated book covers. Each child might have a cut-out airplane. (Harris, 1970, p. 470) These planes can be placed in rows on a wall chart headed "Load Your Plane With Books!" When a student finishes a book, the teacher [or the student] prints the name of the book on a colored slip of paper and places it "aboard" the child's airplane. Cut-outs of race cars, rockets, high-flying kites or balloons—whatever appeals most—can be used as pockets.

Fill Up Your Bookcase!

READING AID 303

SEE MASTER COPY PAGE 59

Here's a simple, inviting way for students to keep a record of their growing reading. (Harris and Sipay, 1975, p. 530) A bookcase with the outlines of books on the shelves is the student's record sheet. The students are to record each book as they finish it, printing on the spine of the book the title, the author, and the date they completed the book. Students experience satisfaction as they "fill up their bookcases with books." You will find such a bookcase on Master Copy Page 59. Coloring the books with a colored pencil makes the bookcase more attractive.

A "Bookworm" in the Schoolroom

READING AID 304

With young readers a "bookworm" is hung up along the wall or tacked on the bulletin board. The child cuts circles from colored construction paper and writes in the circle the title and author of each book he or she has read. The colored circles are overlapped to fill in the bookworm. As a variation, the teacher might create a very long segmented bookworm, with one segment for each child to fill in. (Spache, 1972, p. 227)

What Did You Read Over the Weekend?

READING AID 305

As class starts each Monday, the students share something they've read and enjoyed over the weekend—a bit from the sports page, a newspaper or magazine feature, a how-to-do-it item related to a hobby, a good book or a part of a book. The teacher, too, shares weekend reading. Enthusiasms are contagious. (Matthai, 1974)

Students Walk Out of the Pages

READING AID 306

Students "walk out of the pages" of biographies dressed as the famous person. They tell the class their life stories or a chapter from those life stories. Though the teacher suggests a pattern for the talks, the students are free to report in original ways. They read with heightened interest because they are going to bring their characters to life. On the day set, people like Mary Todd Lincoln, Martin Luther King, Jane Addams, Madame Curie, Johnny Bench, George Washington Carver, and Shirley Chisholm walk into the classroom and share their life stories. (Gregory, 1974)

Fill in a Bookmark

READING AID 307

A teacher or a student artist might design a colorful bookmark with spaces to write in the book's title, the author, the main characters (if fiction), a brief "recap," a brief personal reaction, or other appropriate information. Such a bookmark appears on Master Copy Page 60. One shop teacher made use of bookmarks in his graphic arts classes to stimulate his students to read books related to printing, offering credit for reading extra books. His students took pride in their collections. Librarians heard about the project and asked him to print two thousand bookmarks to be distributed schoolwide through the library. (Conroy, 1971, p. 60)

SEE MASTER COPY PAGE 60

A bookmark in school colors trimmed with the school pennant, mascot, or seal should appeal to students. Classes can be creative in designing their own bookmarks. Students who need more space for their comments on the book can use the reverse side. Bookmarks that have been filled in by a student can be displayed on the bulletin board where each one becomes a "book ad."

A Box of "Book Bait"

READING AID 308

Students put a three-by-five-inch index card, with their comments on books they have really liked, and only those they have liked, into a classroom card file. Dividers mark off sections: "Sports," "Sea Stories," "Adventure," "Teen Problems," "Mysteries," "Careers," "Life Stories," "Westerns," "Out of Doors," "Science Fiction," and so on. Students turn to the file for tips on good books. A tip from a classmate is often more persuasive than one from the teacher.

A Class Best-Seller List

READING AID 309

Toward the close of the year, a class may wish to compile a list of "best-sellers," books widely read and liked among the students. Students make their nominations and give their reasons. Then the class selects the "best-sellers." The "best-sellers" might be compiled into a vacation book list.

Keeping a Log of Personal Reading

READING AID 310

SEE MASTER COPY PAGES 61 – 62

What teacher is not gratified when students read widely in the teacher's subject? A personal reading log is one possible motivator. The students have an added incentive when the log becomes part of their record of progess in social studies, physics, homemaking, and so on, and "counts" in the course. Classroom teachers have used the "Personal Reading Logs" (on Master Copy Pages 61 and 62), asking their students to update them each week. The first form, on Master Copy Page 61, was designed for English and reading classes; the second, on Master Copy Page 62, for other subjects. As a check that the reading listed has actually been completed, teachers can ask students to evaluate what they have read and to staple their comments to their logs.

It should be richly satisfying to watch students' reading logs grow. An English teacher would be delighted to find on a student's log Marchette Chute's *Shakespeare of London;* a social studies teacher, *Profiles in Courage;* a science teacher, *Atoms in the Family;* a mathematics teacher, *Computers and You;* an art teacher, *Lust for Life;* a physical education teacher, *Your Career in Physical Education.*

Teachers of "non-reading" subjects, as we have already noted, have a special opportunity to reach the unreached reader. Students who lack interest in reading and who have lost hope about reading—gravitate to "non-reading" courses. A student who would never reach for a book in English class may check out, enjoy, and add to his or her personal log *Skin Diving and Snorkeling* if it is suggested by the swimming coach. A music student may list *Teach Yourself Guitar* or *Folk Song U.S.A.* if introduced to it in music class. An auto shop student may put to practical use, then list on the log *Fixing Cars: A People's Primer* if this is introduced in auto shop.

A busy senior boy remarked to his teacher: "Personal reading gets crowded out. Thanks a lot for making it part of our course!"

Freedom of Choice Is Appealing

READING AIDS 311–331

Freedom to take their choice appeals to young people. Teachers may wish to offer them a choice of activities related to books they have read instead of locking all the students into one book report assignment. The student's choice may include whether to carry out the activity orally or in writing.

One possible way to offer a choice is to prepare a Reading Activity Box. Inviting activities are typed on three-by-five-inch note cards, one on each card, and the cards are placed in a box. Students look through the cards until they find an activity to their liking, then later return the card to the box. Possible activities are suggested below.

- Choose a day or a few hours that were crucial in the life of a character. Give a brief "recap." Why was this period crucial?
- Are there any insights from the book that will help you in your own living? Help you understand yourself or others better? Help you in your relationships with others? If so, what are these insights?
- For a book about some moral, social, or ethical problem of today: Did some wrong or injustice trouble you as you read this book? Did the book stimulate you to think about a solution? To do something about it? Please explain.
- Was some incident in your book so good that you would like to live it? (Hunt, 1976)
- The author talked to you in this book. Now you can talk back to the author. Write a letter to the author about the book. Mail it, if you like, to a living author.
- Make an acrostic for your book. Arrange the letters of the title vertically. Then write a brief descriptive phrase or sentence about your book, starting with each letter of the title. (Shepherd, 1973, p. 183)

L
O
V
E

S
T
O
R
Y

- (The finished acrostics can be displayed. In this way each acrostic becomes a "book ad.")
- Pretend you are a book salesman. Make a two-minute sales talk in which you try to sell your book to your classmates. Advertise its strong points. Afterwards, we may ask which of the advertised books the class would like most to buy.
- What message do you think the author cared, most of all, to convey in this book? Did he convey it vividly or powerfully? If so, how?
- Like people in real life, some characters in books make us feel pride in our fellow human beings, and some make us feel shame. Select a character from your book and tell how he or she causes you to react in one of these ways.
- Is there a character in the book that you would like (or definitely would not like) to have been? If so, why?
- Suppose a friend asks you if he or she should read your book. How would you advise your friend?
- For a book you are enthusiastic about, write a short blurb for your book, three or four sentences that would catch interest if they were printed on the book pocket or on the cover of a paperback. Make the book cover, too, if you wish.
- Did any understandings you gained from the book cause a turnabout in your way of thinking, bring a change in some attitude or belief or conviction? What is the new understanding? And what is the change?
- What character in the story would you like (or not like) for a friend? Why?
- With what character in your book can you identify? Explain how and why you can compare yourself with the character. (Fraim, 1973, p. 122)
- What situation in the book makes you think of a situation you yourself have faced? Compare the situations. (Fraim, 1973, p. 122)
- Is there one idea from this book that you'll remember all your life? If so, what is it?
- Imagine that you are the main character in the biography (or novel) that you read. Select a moving or important episode, then write it in a diary or letter to someone as if it had happened to you.
- Would this book make *your* best-seller list? Explain why. (Hunt, 1976)
- Using well-known motion picture or television stars, cast the story for a motion picture or a television play. Give a brief reason for each selection of the star who will play a part.
- Imagine that your book is sealed up in a time capsule and that a man of the year 2500 finds it. Write or tell his reaction.

A Booklet of "Book Bait"

READING AID 332

As the students complete book activities, some of the results might be compiled into a class booklet—the "blurbs" for the paperback covers, the sales talks about books, the acrostics, the reactions to books on social wrongs. As this booklet circulates among the students, its pages will be advertisements.

How Are We Succeeding?

READING AID 333

How well are we succeeding in building reading into our students' enduring pattern of activities? We might ask ourselves questions like these:

1. How many of my students turn to reading voluntarily, when they are not required to do so by their school assignments? To what extent?
2. To what extent do they regard reading as a rewarding way to spend leisure hours?
3. To what extent do they see reading as "one of the best schools in the world," one to which they can go—always—for information important to them personally?
4. To what extent do they turn to reading to understand and solve their own personal problems?

READING AID 334

How can we be more certain about the answers to these questions? As the school year passes, we can sense answers as we hear enthusiastic comments about reading and see our students carrying paperbacks around with their schoolbooks. Teachers who want a more formal appraisal might use an end-of-the-year questionnaire. You will find one called "Please Help Next Year's Class" on Master Copy Pages 63 and 64. Some of the questions match questions on the "Information, Please" questionnaire (long form) suggested in Reading Aid 261 for use at the beginning of the year; thus they offer some suggestion about the students' growth in reading. The title "Please Help Next Year's Class" is deliberate. Had the focus been ostensibly on growth in reading, the students might have given "expected" answers. The appeal to "please help next year's class," in the writer's experience, helps to lift this pressure.

SEE MASTER COPY PAGES 63–64

When we observe our students turning to reading voluntarily for personal reasons and/or an end-of-the-year appraisal suggests that they are doing more personal reading, reading is likely to be built more solidly into their futures.

Bibliography

Arbuthnot, May Hill. *Children's Reading in the Home*. Glenview, Ill.: Scott, Foresman and Co., 1969.

Asimov, Isaac. "The Ancient and the Ultimate," *Journal of Reading*, 17, no. 4 (1974): 264–271.

Bell, Caroline R. "Library for All, All for Library." *Journal of Reading*, 17, no. 2 (1973): 119–121.

Graves, Michael F., Judith A. Boettcher, and Randall J. Ryder. *Easy Reading: Book Series and Periodicals for Less Able Readers*. Newark, Del.: International Reading Association, 1979.

Kolzow, Lee. "R & R—Read and Rap Program." *Journal of Reading*, 17, no. 1 (1973): 61.

Levine, Isidore. "Quantity Reading: An Introduction." *Journal of Reading*, 15, no. 8 (1972): 576–583.

McGuinness, Anne E. "Reading Guidance in the Junior High School." In *Teaching Reading for Human Values in High School*, edited by James Duggins. Columbus, Ohio: Charles E. Merrill Publishing Co., 1972.

Mueller, Doris L. "Teacher Attitudes Toward Reading." *Journal of Reading*, 17, no. 3 (1973): 202–205.

Robinson, H. Alan. *Teaching Reading and Study Strategies: the Content Areas*. Boston: Allyn and Bacon, 1975, pp. 239–246.

Russell, David H. and Caroline Shrodes. "Contributions of Research in Bibliotherapy to the Language-Arts Program, I." In *Teaching Reading for Human Values in High School,* edited by James Duggins. Columbus, Ohio: Charles E. Merrill Publishing Co., 1972.

Sartain, Harry W. "Content Reading—They'll Like It." *Journal of Reading,* 17, no. 1 (1973): 47–51.

References

Arbuthnot, May Hill. *Children's Reading in the Home.* Glenview, Ill.: Scott, Foresman and Co., 1969.

Bragstad, Bernice, reading consultant at LaFollette High School, Madison, Wisconsin, in remarks to the writer, January 1979.

Book jacket of *Shirley Chisholm Unbought and Unbossed* by Shirley Chisholm. Boston: Houghton Mifflin Co., 1970.

Conroy, Michael T. "Project Bookmark: Reading and Graphic Arts," *Journal of Reading,* 15 (October 1971): 60–61.

Davis, Mavis. "Right On Read-In," *Changing Education,* 5 (Summer 1974): 9–13.

Downs, Robert B. *Books That Changed the World.* Chicago: American Library Association, 1956.

Fenwick, Sarah, professor emeritus of the University of Chicago Library School, in a class lecture, November 1964.

Fraim, Emma Carville. "Book Reports—Tools for Thinking," *Journal of Reading,* 17 (November 1973): 122.

Gregory, Mary Sharon, former English teacher at the University of Chicago Laboratory School, in remarks to the writer, April 1974.

Harris, Albert, and Edward R. Sipay. *How To Increase Reading Ability,* 6th ed. New York: Longman, 1975.

Haslam, Elizabeth, bookstore owner, in remarks to the writer, January 1978.

Havighurst, Robert J. *Developmental Tasks and Education,* 3rd ed. New York: David McKay Co., 1972, pp. 43–82.

Hunt, Lyman Curtis, School of Education, University of Vermont, when a guest on the TV series, *Sunrise Semester,* April 28, 1976.

Johnson, Laura S. "Cool It, Teach! and Tape All of It!" *Journal of Reading,* 17 (November 1973): 129–131.

Johnson, Laura S., reading specialist, Evanston Illinois Township High School, in remarks to the writer, November 1974.

Karlin, Robert. *Teaching Reading in High School,* 3rd ed. Indianapolis: Bobbs-Merrill Educational Publishing, 1977.

Kimmel, Richard, former physics teacher at the University of Chicago Laboratory School, in remarks to the writer, May 1975.

Levine, Isidore. "Quantity Reading: An Introduction," *Journal of Reading,* 15 (May 1972): 580–83.

Lynch, Elizabeth K., former social studies teacher at Neshaminy Langhorne High School, Langhorne, Pennsylvania, in remarks to the writer January 1978.

Manolakes, George, professor of education at New York University, in his CBS television course on teaching reading, April 28, 1976.

Matthai, Ann, former English teacher, University of Chicago Laboratory School, in remarks to the writer, January 1974.

McCallister, James M., in remarks to the writer, July 1957.

Muelder, Richard H., University of Chicago Laboratory School mathematics teacher and former chairman of the Mathematics Department, in remarks to the writer, June 1970.

Patlak, Sanford, physical education teacher at the University of Chicago Laboratory School, in remarks to the writer, March 1971, May 1978.

Petre, Richard M. "Reading Breaks Make It in Maryland," *Journal of Reading,* 15 (December 1971): 191–194.

Poole, Winfred, University of Chicago Laboratory School librarian, in remarks to the writer, June 1978.

Shepherd, David L. *Comprehensive High School Reading Methods*. Columbus, Ohio: Charles E. Merrill Publishing Co., 1973.

Spache, Evelyn B. *Reading Activities for Child Involvement*. Boston: Allyn and Bacon, 1972.

Speigler, Charles G. "Give Him a Book That Hits Him Where He Lives" in *Improving English Skills of Culturally Different Youth*. Washington, D.C.: U. S. Office of Education Bulletin, 1964.

Witzling, Estelle H. "Johnny Can't Read Because He Doesn't," *High Points*, 38 (January 1956): 52–59.

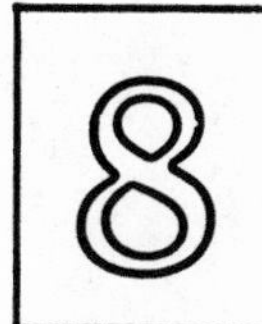

Helping Students Read with Critical Evaluation

CRITICAL READING BELONGS IN OUR STUDENTS'—AND IN PLANET EARTH'S—SURVIVAL KIT!

In an age when momentous problems face the world community, guidance for young people in critical reading belongs in Planet Earth's survival kit. And in their academic and personal lives, too, problems demand close and critical reading. This chapter stresses one important way to help students read with critical evaluation.

The young people we teach today belong to one of the most highly propagandized generations in the history of the world.

Words! Words! Words! From the television screen, from newspapers, from books, from billboards, from flaring advertising spreads, stimulus after stimulus makes its impression upon the minds of our students—shaping what they think and moulding what they do.

Clear, penetrating thinking was never more vital than in our times. Is it not ironical that in an age of bewildering and complex problems the forces that inform us should also confuse our thinking? Are we not strong in our conviction that training in critical reading and viewing is one of the most effective counter-forces, one of the compelling needs of the present, and one of the hopes of the future? (Thomas, 1960, p. 201.)

Yet observers in classrooms the nation over report that young people are usually asked questions that require only their faithfully repeating *what is literally stated on the page before them.* And these same classroom observers report finding with dismaying frequency a dearth of questions requiring the weighing of evidence in order to answer the question: *Is what is on this page before me true?* (Guszak, 1967, pp. 223–234.)

The Truth Will Not Be on the Page for Students, Theirs for the Taking

Is *What is true?* an easy question in the world our students live in? Powerful mass media survive in an intense struggle for existence by exciting interest. As journalists prepare a news report to print or broadcast a prime consideration is not always the question: How can I present a faithful picture of what happened? but what angle can I play up to excite interest? As political candidates contend for office, they surely do not always consider: How can I help constituents compare my qualifications—fully and fairly—with those of my opponent? but What image can I project so that voters will press my lever in the voting booth on election day? As ad writers prepare colorful advertising spreads and TV commercials, they may not consider: How can I inform consumers about just what they will obtain if they buy my product? but What appeals will reach into their billfolds and persuade them to buy?

National and global events and issues are daily interpreted to millions of readers by big-circulation newspapers and magazines and big-circulation television newscasters. Among these interpreters are many with a deep sense of responsibility, who offer their interpretations only after careful study and investigation. In contrast, there are others who write or speak from hidden motives, support their assertions with doubtful authority, draw hasty conclusions, offer distorted evidence, turn on persuasive and sometimes subtle and hurtful propaganda, stir readers and viewers with words loaded with emotion.

On the global scene, conflict among nations has, as Altick (1969, xix-xx) observes, become less military and more ideological. Most battles, he asserts, are fought at conference tables and through the various organs of propaganda and discussion that influence the minds of men. The ammunition, Altick points out, now includes such emotive, easily manipulated words and phrases as *neo-colonialism, aggression, provocation, mutual security, peace-loving, national interest, nuclear deterrent, balance of power, intervention.* . . . Multiply such instances of ambiguous word-use, he continues, in hundreds of speeches, pronouncements, broadcasts, editorials, and you see readily enough why the state of today's world more than ever demands close and critical reading. Language, he concludes, is the key to the ceaseless battle for men's minds. (Altick, 1969, pp. xix-xx)

In our students' lives from day to day, personal problems demand solutions. In an age when change is so rapid it makes shock waves, young people may be adrift and in search of values. Clashing viewpoints on controverisal issues—social, ethical, and moral—may leave them bewildered and in search of insights. Immediate problems—drugs, contacts with the other sex, broken homes, lifestyle options—may make this their "age of anxiety." Insights that will help them find solutions are often to be found through printed words.

The truth today's young people must learn to seek will often be elusive—not always plainly on the page before them, theirs for the taking. Yet influenced by what they read and hear, they will make important personal decisions and participate in crucial public decisions. Surely, training young people to respond to words with critical reflection is, again, one of the needs of the present and one of the hopes of the future.

At What Level Should Students First Receive Instruction in Critical Reading?

How early in their education should young people first be given guidance in sound reading-thinking procedures? Researchers Wolf, King, and Huck (1968, p. 438) urge us to begin this training early, and they explain their reasons:

> Research in child development indicates . . . that very young children . . . are capable of critical reasoning. If children are capable of such reasoning, it would seem important to begin instructing them in critical reading skills as soon as possible. Psychological research has shown that once habits are established, it is difficult to change them. The emphasis on word recognition skills and literal comprehension that characterizes reading instruction in the lower and intermediate grades may encourage naive acceptance of anything that appears in print. Through postponing instruction in critical reading, the habit of indiscriminate acceptance of printed material may become so well established that later instruction in these skills would be extremely difficult.

In a massive study at Ohio State University, elementary school children in experimental groups in grades one through six improved their skills of critical evaluation significantly. It should be noted that the time and attention devoted to critical reading did not crowd out work on basic reading skills nor interfere with the children's growth in other areas of reading. According to test results, in the experimental groups normal reading progress was maintained.

"Plenty of Truth Remains in the World"

Perhaps any discussion of critical reading should begin on a note of caution. Many young people accept as sacrosanct anything they see in print. A *claim in print*—black and white on paper—casts a magic spell of seeming truth. (Oliver and Shaver, 1966, p. 108) Then, as they begin to study critical reading, they suddenly experience a runaway reaction, refuting and rejecting too readily—delighting in rejecting—rather than seeking to determine what is true. Burmeister (1978, p. 257) expresses this caution:

> Critical reading should not be carried out in a predominantly negative way. Unfortunately, the word "critical" suggests fault-finding . . . . Persuasive language and techniques are, of course, not all bad. The word "critic" more nearly suggests the meaning intended when we talk about "critical" reading. Art critics, for example, are not fault-finders. They are *judges.* Part of their job is to *identify and describe the best.*
>
> What's wrong—and *what's right*—with this thinking should become the student's watchword. They should realize that persuasive writing is sometimes sly and hurtful and that it is sometimes noble and inspiring. Mankind would never have risen from barbarism, as Altick (1963, p. xii) observes, had there not been men—poets, orators, preachers—to stir it to action.

We profit little if we leave our students with questions substituted for convictions. The maturing student-reader should realize that "plenty of truth remains in the world—there is no dearth of things for him to believe in." (Altick, 1960, p. 121)

Believing nothing is as little to be desired as believing everything. Across more than 300 years, Francis Bacon's counsel is as timely today: "Read not to contradict and refute; nor to believe and take for granted . . .; but to weigh and consider."

What This Chapter Contains

Content area teachers in subjects that cross the curriculum—from the English classroom through physical education in the gym—may wish to build work with critical evaluation right into the regular course work, guiding students to respond critically in genuine reading situations. Teachers of English, reading, and social studies may wish to prepare, in addition, separate broad critical reading units. The questions that follow suggest some of the understandings that can—with important benefits for young people—be taught in either of these situations:

1. How can we make students aware of the force of their own biases as they interpret what they read? How can we help them to read with objective evaluation passages that reinforce or contradict those biases?
2. How can we help students become alert to the purposes of writers—and alert them to the possibility that writers sometimes say what they say from hidden motives?

3. How can students learn how to evaluate the authority of a writer or speaker to make pronouncements on a certain subject?
4. How can we help students understand how to proceed when the views of authorities differ?
5. How can students learn to differentiate between statements of fact and statements of opinion?
6. How can we help students weigh the evidence for a conclusion and evaluate the soundness of that conclusion?
7. How can we place students on their guard against common abuses of straight thinking?
8. How can we help students understand when emotion has been introduced into persuasive writing in place of evidence?
9. How can we help our students to recognize stereotyping of groups of people when they meet this in reading, listening, or viewing and to break stereotypes in their own thinking?
10. How can we alert students to the possibility that a certain passage they read or hear may possibly have been wrenched out of its context in order to hide or to distort the truth?
11. How can we help students detect propaganda, whether good or bad, note its proposed effect, and decide whether or not they care to be swayed by it?
12. How can students develop a critical response to the power of emotion-stirring words to turn off thought and turn on feeling?

Much has been written for teachers and students on the subject of critical reading. Since resources are easily available elsewhere, it does not seem essential to do repeating here. The writer will, for this reason, concentrate in this chapter on one aspect that has not been so thoroughly considered elsewhere. This aspect appears first on the list above: *How can we make students aware of the force of their own biases as they interpret what they read? How can we help them to read with objective evaluation passages that reinforce or contradict those biases?*

Teachers Will Want to Work with Additional Aspects of Critical Reading

As teachers work with critical reading, they will probably be interested in teaching other aspects in addition to counteracting the force of bias. The author would like to share with these teachers the following "finds" in the way of resources—books, transparencies, and dittomasters that she has found especially helpful:

Altick, Richard D. *Preface To Critical Reading*, 5th ed. New York: Holt, Rinehart and Winston, 1969. *Dr. Altick's classic on critical reading, intended as a textbook for students on the college level, offers the secondary teacher both ideas and inspiration. Readable and interesting, Dr. Altick's book can also serve the teacher as a source of background information. Secondary reading teachers and content area teachers will find Dr. Altick's explanations for students and his suggestions for practice work adaptable for students below the college level. The following sections are likely to be especially helpful: Chapter 1, "Denotation and Connotation" and Chapter 5, "Patterns of Clear Thinking" with subsections, "Inductive Reasoning," "Deductive Reasoning," "Other Steps Toward Clear Thinking," "Objectivity and Subjectivity," and "The Question of Authority."*

Hiatt, Donald A. *True, False, or In Between: An Elective Course in Logical Thinking* with *Teacher's Guide*. Lexington, Mass.: Ginn and Co., 1975. *Teachers can use this textbook as a source of teaching strategies and practice exercises to work into their own courses or as a textbook for a high school course in logical thinking that can be presented as a separate eighteen-week, twelve-week, or nine-week unit of instruction. The explanations of logical processes are clearly written. Practice work in which students analyze and evaluate "sample" assertions and arguments is abundant.*

Burmeister, Lou E. *Reading Strategies for Middle and Secondary School Teachers*, 2nd ed. Reading, Mass.: Addison-Wesley Publishing Co., 1978. *In Chapter 9, "Analyzing, Synthesizing, and Evaluating Ideas Through Reading," Dr. Burmeister discusses in some detail, with examples from various content areas, the following aspects of critical reading: judging the authenticity of sources of information and selecting appropriate sources, distinguishing between fact and opinion, propaganda techniques, and fallacies of reasoning. Dr. Burmeister's teaching strategies and examples are lively and close to students' interests. The fallacies of reasoning which Dr. Burmeister explains, again with motivating examples, include mistaken causal relationship, statistical fallacy, false analogy, oversimplification, stereotyping, ignoring the question, begging the question, and hasty generalization.*

Sherbourne, Julia Florence. *Toward Reading Comprehension*, 2nd ed. Lexington, Mass.: D. C. Heath and Co., 1977. *Dr. Sherbourne's book, intended to help students read successfully in college, includes material on critical reading that can be adapted for students below the college level. Chapter 5, "How To Evaluate What You Read," includes clear explanations of fallacies in reasoning and helps for avoiding them. Dr. Sherbourne's explanations are fortified by interesting examples and practice.*

Critical Thinking: Scholastic Social Studies Skills, Books A, B, and C. New York: Scholastic Book Services, 1978. *This series of three books, intended for students of average ability or better in the secondary grades, offers the teacher twelve especially attractive full-color transparencies, twenty-four spirit-masters for related student worksheets, plus a very helpful guide for the teacher. As the students work through the twelve lessons, they progress from analyzing the structure of a simple paragraph to evaluating and synthesizing a range of different viewpoints. Among other inviting contents are skills-practice lessons on evaluating information, including identifying valid inferences; distinguishing relevant from irrelevant facts, fact from opinion, primary from secondary sources; and drawing conclusions. Books A, B, and C gradually increase in difficulty. These sound and attractive materials are relatively inexpensive.*

Students Should Become Aware of Strong Forces within Themselves That May Affect Their Reading

Students' attitudes and biases may lock them into their present ways of thinking. How can we make them aware of these strong forces within themselves that may seal off the truth? And how can we help them to read with objective evaluation?

Are young people aware that their attitudes or mental sets can cause them to respond in a *pre*determined way to what they read or hear about an issue, a proposed course of action, an institution, or a person? Many young people undoubtedly are not fully aware of these powerful forces that exist within themselves to lock them into certain ways of thinking.

According to an investigation (McKillop, 1952, p. 8), we tend to remember longer those ideas we read that coincide with our opinions, and we tend to forget more readily material that contradicts those opinions. According to another investigation (McCaul, 1944, p. 456), we tend to interpret reading matter in a way that harmonizes with our own attitudes yet may not be supported by what is on the printed page. Furthermore, the more intensely and personally we feel about the content of the reading, the stronger the likelihood that our attitude will influence our interpretation. This researcher draws the following conclusion:

> Man reading does not differ from man listening, man speaking, man arguing, man living; he is not purged of emotion, prejudice, and attitudes just because he has a book in his hands. When he reads, he is as much a dupe of his attitudes as he is under any other circumstances.

Young people will advance toward maturity as readers when we make them aware that their own mind sets can seal off the truth, when we help them to understand the *force* of those mind sets, and when we guide them to read objectively and analytically selections that reinforce or contradict those mind sets. The explanations, activities, and other helps that follow may be suggestive to teachers as they develop their own effective ways to alert students to—and help them counteract—the force of bias.

What Is the Classroom Climate?

READING AID 335

The climate the teacher establishes in the classroom—from the middle school years and even earlier—is of real importance in developing in students habits of critical evaluation. Much "teaching" takes place through the teacher's personal example!

Questions like the following may be useful to new teachers as they consider the thinking climate of their classrooms:

1. What kind of thinking climate prevails in my classroom? Is the climate one of respect for independent thinking?
2. Do I sometimes unwittingly encourage in students only responses that echo my own beliefs and values? Or do I accept and welcome critical divergent responses?
3. Do my students give evidence from day to day that they feel free to make such divergent responses when these are well-supported?
4. Do I "come through" to my students as having mental sets that restrict my own thinking to certain habitual patterns? Or do I set a personal example of reading and thinking widely and examining all aspects of an issue?

"Are You Sensitive to Forces within Yourself?"

READING AID 336

Instructors may wish to develop—in discussions and during activities—background understandings about the force of bias. Here are some insights toward which they might lead students:

> Are you sensitive to powerful forces operating within yourself to lock you into your present ways of thinking?
>
> When a subject we are reading about is controversial, our own biases may strongly influence our reactions. We read not only with our eyes—but also with *our personal feelings!* It is as if our attitudes were lying in wait, *ready to pounce*—to attack by surprise, whenever they see an opportunity to shape our reactions to reading! (McKillop, 1952, p. 81)
>
> We actually comprehend better printed material that "agrees with us"! And we retain it better! We forget more easily ideas we read that we do not agree with—these

ideas just may not register! And we tend to twist what we read so that it harmonizes with our own attitudes! Thus our attitudes may *stand squarely in the way of our ability to think logically about important issues!*

Across more than 300 years, Francis Bacon's counsel in his *Novum Organum* is as timely today: "What a man had rather were true, he more readily believe . . . . In general, let every student take this as a rule—that *whatever his mind seizes and dwells upon with peculiar satisfaction is to be held in suspicion . . .*

"Check Out Your 'State of Mind'"

READING AID 337

In *The Art of Speaking,* Elson and Peck (1966, p. 101) suggest a number of questions students might use to check out their own open-mindedness. Slightly adapted to the reading situation, these questions are shared here:

> The best program on the air cannot reach you if your radio or TV is turned off. *Closed minds are like dead sets*! When you are determined to resist the plea of the speaker and when you already know what you are going to think regardless of what he says, your mind is closed. Neither accurate interpretation nor sound evaluation is possible. There are several questions you should ask yourself in your search for open-mindedness:
>
> 1. Do I immediately reject what has been said merely because it is *different* from what I believe?
> 2. Am I accepting or rejecting the idea(s) on the basis of a hasty reaction to the writer? Or after a careful evaluation of credentials?
> 3. Am I casting aside this proposal which affects group welfare because of my self-interests?
> 4. What is my own attitude? Do I *want* to believe this statement is true, or do I *want* to believe it is false?
> 5. Do I welcome the writer's ideas as I would want someone else to welcome *my* ideas?
> 6. Does personal, family, or group loyalty blind me to the truth?
> 7. When I see the truth, do I still cling to my loyalties?
> 8. Do I have such an exaggerated opinion of my own knowledge that I read with half attention, shutting my mind to the acceptance of what someone else says?
>
> You are indeed a superman if your honest answers to these questions verify yours as an open mind. You are fortunate if they do no more than indicate much room for improvement. Look upon reading as a kind of treasure hunt in which there are unlimited prizes if you'll just keep your mind open.*

"Are You Locked In?"

READING AID 338

The following activity in which students are led to focus on "problem areas" in their own thinking, areas where they may tend to have closed minds, might serve as a mind-opener for those students. Teachers might give this activity a send-off by sharing with the class their personal listing of their own "problem areas," areas where having an open mind requires special effort.

*Adapted from *The Art of Speaking, Third Revised Edition,* by E. F. Elson and Albert Peck, © Copyright, 1974, 1966, 1952, by Ginn and Co. (Xerox Corporation). Used with permission.

> Mature readers and TV viewers are not locked into their beliefs by influences from their past but are prepared to seek evidence, then still more evidence—to shift their point of view—often to disregard a preconceived viewpoint.
>
> Can you think of "problem areas" where you tend to have a closed mind? Are there public figures, groups, or institutions that you strongly oppose or favor? Are there local, national, or international issues about which you feel especially strongly? Please head one column STRONGLY FAVOR and another STRONGLY OPPOSE. Under these headings jot down topics on which you have strong leanings. After making your jottings, place a check mark before issues on which you have really made a thorough study.

The students' listings of "problem areas" can serve as springboards for discussion. The absence of check marks indicating thorough study can help the students appreciate that in many crucial areas they will need more information before forming a firm opinion.

Teachers might list for the class a number of possible "problem areas" as starters:

1. Nuclear power plants as energy sources
2. Reinstatement of the military draft
3. A unilateral moratorium by the U.S. on producing and testing nuclear weapons
4. Abolition of laws that make illegal possessing, using, or selling marijuana
5. Compulsory sex education in schools
6. Strict national control of handguns
7. Strict hair and dress codes at school
8. Spending billions on space shots instead of on improving the living conditions of those who live in poverty on earth
9. Euthanasia as a humanitarian solution for the terminally ill
10. Capital punishment as a deterrent for crime
11. The present welfare system
12. Easy-to-obtain legal abortions
13. Withdrawal of the U.S. from the United Nations
14. The Equal Rights Amendment
15. Genetic experimentation with human beings under controlled circumstances
16. President Jimmy Carter
17. Cesar Chavez
18. Ted Kennedy as a presidential candidate

What Forces Have Shaped Your Opinions?

READING AID 339

As a step in sensitizing students to forces within themselves that may predetermine their reactions to controversial reading (and viewing), we might guide them to ask: *Why do I hold the views I now have?* Teachers might give this activity a send-off by sharing with the class a personal analysis of influences that have helped to shape their own thinking on some highly controversial subject.

> Select some highly controversial subject—one on which you feel very strongly—a really explosive public figure or issue. [The teacher might suggest some of the explo-

sive subjects listed in Reading Aid 338.] Make an analysis of the forces that have predisposed you to respond in a certain way. Here are some possible influences you might consider: a parent or a relative, an influential teacher, a friend, a book, your viewing of television, a vivid personal experience. Your analysis may sharpen your awareness that you cannot always "call your thoughts your own"—that on certain subjects powerful influences tend to *pre*determine those thoughts.

Do you feel that on this particular issue you already have an *informed* opinion or that you should seek more information?

That Serious Mental Disorder—A "Closed Mind"

READING AID 340

Students—from the middle school years and even earlier—can share, discuss, read, or hear in comments from their teacher some of the following thoughts. These particular insights were shared with social studies classes in Thornton (Illinois) Township High School during their study of a unit, "Introduction To Clear Thinking."* The "telling" that follows occurred in the course of lively activities. Of course, "telling" by itself may not prove to be effective.

> Social studies students are often advised that like members of a jury they should not make decisions "until all the evidence is in." However, if this advice were followed strictly, no one could ever make any decision because *all* the evidence is never in. . . .
>
> We *must* make decisions based on as much evidence as we can get at the time. The important thing to remember is that *even the best* decision must be reviewed in the *light of new evidence,* and *there is almost always new evidence*. . . .
>
> All of this is important to remember because it will prevent you from developing that serious mental disorder known as a "closed mind." An individual who does have a closed mind denies the fact that more can be said on any subject. He is, to use a slang expression, "a know-it-all." Rarely do people close their minds to all subjects at the same time. The individual who is taking golf lessons or reading about sports cars with a mind open and eager for new facts and ideas may be close-minded about the Democratic or Republican Party, *Time* magazine, or our foreign policy.
>
> It would be interesting for you to try to decide why we close our minds to some types of information but not to others. Whatever the reason, the result may be *a careful preservation of ignorance*. . . .

Have You Changed Your Mind Lately?

READING AID 341

Students might examine their own past thinking to determine whether they have tended to look for and welcome other viewpoints or have been "fenced in" by their own biases. The teacher might give this activity a personal send-off by sharing with the class his or her own fairly recent mind changes.

> List three times during the past year or so when you have changed your mind about something related to world affairs, the national or local scene, or some well-known public figure. Explain what brought about the change. If you cannot think of any changes, why do you suppose there were none?†

Examine Closed Minds in Others

Students can become more aware of the minuses of having a closed mind and the pluses of having an open, receptive mind by focusing in on the closed minds of others:

**Introduction To Clear Thinking* (Harvey, Ill.: Thornton Township High School, Social Studies Department), pp. 13–14.

†*Introduction To Clear Thinking* (Harvey, Ill.: Thornton Township High School, Social Studies Department), p. 14.

READING AID 342

Find an example from the newspaper or from television [or from your own observation in conversation or elsewhere] of a person or group that, in your opinion, plainly shows a closed mind. Name the subject on which this person or group gives evidence of a tightly closed mind.

READING AID 343

List six or more "problem areas" where people tend to have closed minds. For each item, figure out, if you can, and jot down *why* people tend to have closed minds in this particular area.*

Another Mind-Opener for Students: "How Sure Can I Be?"

READING AID 344

A mind-opener for students—from the middle school years and earlier—can be to realize that they will weigh evidence, then draw conclusions, not often with finality but with *varying degrees of certainty*. Social studies teachers in Evanston (Illinois) Township High School suggested the following yardsticks to help students assess this degree of certainty: **

Even after carefully investigating, you will not always feel certain about the soundness of certain information or of a conclusion. One of the following statements will probably express your degree of certainty:

1. It is true—or false—*beyond reasonable doubt.* I have enough evidence, and no important evidence points to the contrary.
2. It is *probably* true—or false. There is more evidence on one side than on the other.
3. It is *impossible to judge* whether it is true—or false—because the evidence is not sufficient or is evenly balance on both sides.
4. I will *withhold judgment* until I can secure more information.

Students Read Clashing Viewpoints—Then Take Roles

READING AID 345

A high school science teacher (Hozinsky, 1979) comments: "Students walk into my classroom *hugging* their favorite biases. I soon make them aware that other viewpoints exist!"

Let's suppose the subject is genetic engineering. I introduce this fascinating subject and give the students a framework for their coming reading. I bring to life the controversies that have developed—between the safety of the community on one side and the promise of fantastic results—medical and genetic—for the future of humanity on the other. As starter reading I give the students two "clashing" reading selections—one stressing the advantages of genetic engineering; the other, the hazards. I ask the students to probe the question further through the *Reader's Guide*.

Before the students read, I point out that controversies like this one involve interest groups, that each interest group has a point of view in keeping with its own interest, and that each interest group tends to select—from all the available evidence—evidence to support its own views.

I bring to life the interest groups involved in the clash over genetic engineering—the citizens of a community where the research is going on, alarmed at the rumors of dangers that may result from such research—strange, new, uncontrollable diseases spreading in their community; the scientists in their laboratories poring

**Introduction To Clear Thinking* (Harvey, Ill.: Thornton Township High School, Social Studies Department), p. 14.

**Adapted from *Unit on Clear Thinking* (Evanston, Ill.: Evanston Township High School, Social Studies Department), p. 20.

over their research, inspired by faith in its promise for the future, irritated and alarmed by people in the community who, filled with vague fears, are trying to stop their life work!

The study ends with a free-for-all open discussion. My questions *cast the students in roles:* What if you were a scientist doing research in this area? How would you feel about the people who want to control—and even end—your research? What if you were a resident of the community, alarmed at possible perils? What if you were the mayor, responsible for the safety of the community? What if you were a legislator? What kind of bill would you support that would be fair to both groups?

During the discussion the students reveal the growth they have made in recognizing that any decision reached will involve a trade-off, that no one group will be entirely satisfied with the outcome, that the best that can be hoped for will be a reasonable working compromise. The students live with a growing awareness that crucial issues have more than one side.

As a finishing touch, the students sometimes write down what is *now* their own point of view about genetic engineering. Often their view is no longer a simple pro or con—no longer a biased viewpoint—but a trade-off!

Debates Help Middle-Schoolers "Hear" Other Opinions

READING AID 346

By the time students enter grade nine they are already confirmed in many of their social and political opinions. If we "catch them younger," we have a better chance of developing in students a much more thinking way of viewing issues. (Bernstein, 1979)

A middle-school social studies teacher (Kern, 1979) finds that informal debates in her classroom can be one means of developing this more thinking approach to issues:

> As school opens, I spend the first day giving a brief, hopefully an interesting, overview of the course. The students choose some area that catches their interest and select a long-term project. Among these projects are informal debates, in which four students participate.
>
> Let's say the subject is this one, an exciting one for my students: President Harry Truman should have used the atomic bomb in the war against Japan. The students have all term to prepare—up to the point in the course where their subject comes up. When "the day" arrives, the debate moves quickly. The team members on the affirmative share a five-minute opening statement, giving background and arguments; the negative team follows. The negative team then asks the affirmative team questions in a three-minute rebuttal; the affirmative team follows. Last, the affirmative team members present a two-minute summary, telling why they believe their arguments are stronger; the negative team follows.
>
> Just afterwards, the class fills out a debate evaluation, which includes a rating scale for different skills, *especially critical thinking skills,* and the points for each side are tabulated. Thus the class decides the winning team.
>
> Often my students emerge from these debates not with a biased viewpoint or even an informed pro or con viewpoint—but a middle-ground viewpoint.

"Consider the Arguments—Then Make Your Judgment"

READING AID 347

A high school social studies teacher (Bell, 1979) shares a way of helping students to consider the multiple factors that govern understanding a social problem and thus to replace a biased viewpoint:

> I want my students to look at *all* the evidence, so I confront them with crucial and controversial questions—high interest-getters—and ask them to make briefs in which they list arguments *on both sides.*

Let's suppose the subject is this: *Congress should prohibit the use of nuclear energy.* After the students have agreed on the definition of crucial terms, they construct a case based upon the three most crucial arguments for their side. The student starts the brief: "The three strongest arguments supported by the evidence are as follows." The student follows this with: "The three strongest arguments supported by the evidence on the opposing side are as follows." After stating the arguments, the student proves, in a summary paragraph(s), how the evidence does, in fact, support the conclusion. Last, the student presents his or her own conclusion(s), often a compromise position into which the student has integrated the best of the evidence from both—more often from *multiple*—sides.

I want my students to develop skill in drawing conclusions in an objective, analytical, and systematic way and, though progress never comes quickly, in a year I *do* see progress. The students develop a skeptical view of authorities (they so often find authorities to be in conflict!), develop a keen sense for the possible bias of their sources, and probe those biases. No longer do they react, "One book is the final word!" They develop a clear understanding of the partial nature of evidence. The quality of the evidence presented and of the writer's reasoning takes over. Now *this* determines what conclusion the students will "buy."

Making a brief can be followed by actual debate, or it can serve simply as an exercise in carefully examining all sides of a controversial question.

"Take a Look at Both Sides"

READING AID 348

The students of this same social studies teacher (Bell, 1979) examine both sides of a controversial question in yet another way:

To encourage my students to examine *all* the evidence, I ask them to write argumentative essays on crucial and controversial questions and to *argue both sides*. These questions, by the way, are one of my best interest-generators!

Suppose the question is this: *Is political détente with Russia in the national interest?* After the students have investigated the question, they write their essays—arguing first the affirmative and then the negative. On the closing pages they draw their own conclusion(s)—often a compromise position—into which they integrate the best of the evidence from multiple sides.

Most young people who walk into our classes are confirmed in their political viewpoints by the time they are thirteen or fourteen! My fond hope is to make students become more aware that on most social issues there is no simplistic "right" answer, that complex social issues do, indeed, have multiple sides, that conclusions are tentative, and that there is a strong possibility that they, the students, are sometimes wrong!

"Creative Interviews" Can Help Develop Sensitivity to Viewpoints

READING AID 349

Students imagine themselves transported into the long ago, interviewing an actual personage or an imaginary person who lived at that time. (Keller, 1979, p. 217) Transported to pre-Civil War days, for example, class members might interview a fiery abolitionist who urged the immediate end of slavery—violently if necessary, and/or a Southern slaveholder, committed heart and soul to the institution of slavery. The student prepares questions that probe the interviewee's reasons for becoming an abolitionist or a staunch defender of slavery, and, after "researching," writes out the answers. Later, the class—well-prepared now because they have written their interviews—discusses the clashing viewpoints.

In a variation of this activity, the students pair off and present their interviews orally, with a class committee awarding "Emmys" for the best portrayals. The teacher gives this activity a send-off by stepping into the role of someone who lived during the period and being interviewed by the class.

Simulations Help Students Experience Other Viewpoints

READING AID 350

A social studies teacher (Montag, 1979) speaks enthusiastically about simulations as a means of helping students "feel" the other person's viewpoint:

> Students "walk in another person's shoes" in simulations. In the simulation, "Radicals vs. Tories," * for example, some students step into the roles of Radicals, who favor breaking away from Great Britain; others into the roles of Tories, who favor close ties; others into the roles of Moderates. The players try to persuade the other factions to vote "their" way on a proposal to go to war against Great Britain. This simulation develops the understanding that the movement for American independence was *far* from unanimous—that there were convincing arguments both for breaking away and for reconciliation.
>
> Of course, simulations can help sensitize students to the viewpoints of others in present-day high explosive situations. Through a simulation, the students can ask themselves questions like this concerning, for example, the Arabs and Israelis: "What is it like to be in this situation? What does this person think and feel?"

Panel Discussions Can Create a "You-Are-There" Effect

READING AID 351

Panel discussions can lead students to ask: "What does the other person think and feel? What is it like to be in this situation?" Each panelist, Burmeister (1978, p. 284) suggests, can represent a real person. The student studies this person well, to learn the person's philosophy and patterns of reacting—examines the person's activities—analyzes the person's reasons for responding as he or she does. The student must also try to be able to predict how the person would react to a timely issue.

Students, Burmeister adds, might impersonate the following personages, among countless other possibilities:

1. Several senators, representatives, governors, the president, and/or the vice-president, discussing as timely issue.
2. A black person impersonated by a white student and a white person impersonated by a black student, conversing about civil rights, etc.

It's a Small World!

READING AID 352

In journalism class during the first few days of school, the instructor (Brasler, 1979) asks his classes to draw a map of "their" world—the actual physical world they live in from day to day. They draw their school, their home, the areas where they shop or have jobs, their transportation routes between home and these areas. Most of the students draw maps covering a few blocks or, at the most, a few miles. The teacher, too, makes a drawing of his world. It consists of two communities—his home community and his school community with an expressway—a ribbon—in between.

The teacher stresses: "Look how small our world—our own turf—is! Look how little we really see with our own eyes from day to day, how little we know about life

*Available from History Simulations, P.O. Box 2775, Santa Clara, Cal., 95051.

firsthand!'' The students react, ''I think I know so much, yet my world is so small!''

As Step 2, the students carry out the activity in Reading Aid 253.

''How Much Do You Really Know Firsthand?''

READING AID 353

The classes of the same journalism teacher (see Reading Aid 352) then list in one column on a sheet of paper how much they know about life *through their own eyes*—how much they actually know firsthand. In a second column, they list how much they know about life *through the media*—television, radio newspapers, magazines, and the like—and *through other people*. Of course, the items the students list in the second column as compared with the first come by the yard! The teacher comments: ''My students see that they know firsthand a very little corner of the world, that their personal viewpoint is extremely limited. I remind them of this all through the year to help counteract bias.''

Compare Clashing Editorials

READING AID 354

When an explosive issue is before the public, the teacher might suggest:

> Find an editorial in the newspaper on this highly controversial subject; then, in another paper search out one that expresses an opposing or a different view. You may find that your two editorials present the same person or event in a completely different light. Which editorial seems to you to offer more convincing evidence? Why? Should you withhold judgment until you have more information? Can you suggest possible ways that you could get more solid evidence, try to resolve these clashing viewpoints, and form at least a tentative conclusion?

READING AID 355

Students may not be aware that certain segments of the television newscasts they listen to from day to day are regularly devoted to editorials—that in these segments there is a sudden shift from straight news content to editorial content. When a controversial issue is before the public, students might listen for ''opposing'' editorials on different television channels, then, when they have found these editorials, carry out the activity suggested in Reading Aid 354.

Write Your Editor!

READING AID 356

When a ''dynamite'' issue is in the spotlight, students might write the editor of a local newspaper. This time, though, each student might be asked to write *two* letters to the editor—these would express opposing or differing viewpoints. The student might, for example, first write in the role of a citizen alarmed at pollution by a public utility company in the community. Next, the student would imagine that he or she was the public relations representative of that company, charged with polluting the community's land, air, and water. In the letter, the public relations representative would try to justify the company's stand and course of action. Or perhaps the student might write one letter to the editor proposing a middle-ground solution.

Dealing with Bias Will Call for the Teacher's Careful Attention

READING AID 357

Students with a strong bias, as we have noted, tend to ignore, forget, twist, or reject reading material that presents an opposing view. Our reaction to reading is, as Robinson (1977, pp. 125–126) expresses it, based on what is already stored in our minds and on our resulting readiness to accept or reject additional input. Without planned teaching, Robinson adds, it is unlikely that the student will attempt to alter an earlier opinion. Instead, the reaction will be rejection. In the following paragraph, an industrial arts teacher tells how he helped Tommy to overcome a strong bias, to practice reading, and to launch a dreamboat!

> My students come into woodshop, as they do their other classes, with their biases in tow. Tommy, for example, was having a love affair with one kind of wood—walnut. Now in woodshop he insisted on building a boat—of walnut! I guided Tommy to a chapter on types of wood and their functions. And I also did planned teaching on the physical properties and workability of types of wood. The upshot was a profitable reading experience *and* a seaworthy boat for Tommy—of mahogany instead of walnut—durable, more easily worked, and much easier on Tommy's allowance.

Bias Begins to Disappear as Students Read Multiple Sources

READING AID 358

Biases begin to disappear—in photography class! A photography teacher (Erickson, 1979) shares how he achieves this:

> You may not think of photography class as a place where the teacher must deal with bias. Take it from me, it *is!* Students in photography often see things in a very biased way. They may, for example, cling to this biased viewpoint—there is *only one way* to develop black and white film, and they may rush off to the darkroom to develop a roll in "their" way.
>
> Questions like these, posed by the teacher, can be mind openers: Should I develop this film in a tank or in a tray? In darkness or in daylight? Using an appropriate safelight or no safelight? Using standard film developer or non-standard? Should I develop for contrast or lack of contrast?
>
> The teacher guides the students to a variety of sources: the manufacturer's printed recommendations included with the film, the instructions on the containers of developers, books and magazines on photography, the opinions of experienced photographers. With guidance, the students match certain considerations against the printed guidelines—how the picture was taken (lighting, subject, exposure), type of film, size and shape of the end product, quality level they desire, and so on.
>
> As the students encounter in printed sources conflicting points of view, they must weigh a wide spectrum of viewpoints, then decide—again with guidance—the best process for the job at hand. Gradually bias begins to disappear. Being fully informed, the students are now less likely to be narrowly opinionated.

Consumers' Buying Guides Help Combat Bias

READING AID 359

Biases can begin to disappear—in driver's education class. A driver's education teacher (Patlak, 1979) shares one way he achieves this:

> Driver's ed class may not appear to be a place where a student would be boxed in by bias. But suppose a student has read about Car X, a "cool" compact, in ads and on billboards, and heard it acclaimed in TV commercials. To that student Car X is the greatest!
>
> I bring *Consumer Guide*, *Consumers' Research*, or *Consumer Reports* into driver's ed class, where perhaps this student holds one of these valuable buying guides in his hands for the first time. He learns that Car X has been put through rigid road tests by independent labs, through stresses and strains, through long-use tests, and he reads the results of those tests. He sees Car X ranked in the guide with other compacts in quality. He may revise his opinion of Car X!

If the students own their own cars and are caught up with an ad for a car accessory—a burglar alarm, for example—they learn to check the ad out with a consumers' guide. They may soon realize that price and advertising claims are no safe guides to the quality of a product and that consulting a consumers' guide, instead of "buying on bias," can help insure getting their money's worth.

Controversy Rages—in Homemaking, Too!

READING AID 360

We may not think of homemaking as an area where controversy rages. A homemaking teacher (Szymkowicz, 1979) offers this suggestion for dealing with a current controversy:

> Controversy sometimes rages—even in homemaking! What about microwave ovens? We can use the high interest this controversy generates to guide our students to practice reading, and at the same time, to guide them to fuller information.
>
> Suppose students have read and heard—and now believe—that the doors of a new microwave oven just installed in their homemaking room can leak dangerous radioactive waves. The teacher might seize this occasion to guide the students to the evidence offered in multiple sources—books, magazines, and the consumers' buying guides. Here is an opportunity to help the students realize that hearsay is seldom enough, and to guide them to weigh the evidence before drawing even a tentative conclusion.

Homemaking Teachers Run into Bias

READING AID 361

Here is how one homemaking teacher (Szymkowicz, 1979) copes with an unusual kind of bias she often observes in her classes—a bias in favor of foods that are old favorites:

> Students have a tendency to read and use, again and again, recipes that are old standbys, to prepare the foods they're accustomed to over and over again without variety. The colorful teenage magazines, *Seventeen* and *Coed,* are "standard" in my classroom. These and other magazines offer inviting items on preparing foods. The adjectives describing the foods are enticing; the full-color photos have eye-appeal. By guiding my students to these items, I encourage reading in my subject and entice them to new adventures in eating.

Business Education Teachers Can Deal with Bias

READING AID 362

A business education teacher has a special opportunity to combat bias—bias against labor unions or against management, bias against bosses! One business education teacher (Haehn, 1979) comments on how she combats among her students still another kind of bias. She does this largely through her own personal values:

> Students often walk into my classroom with a bias against blue-collar or against white-collar workers, as the case may be—a bias we don't need in a democracy! To some students, a plumber or a secretary is simply without status. I feel that in many cases the students are echoing what they have heard adults say in their homes. In class, we explore careers across a wide spectrum. We read—we discuss—we invite visitors to class to tell about their life work. One of my first purposes in career education is to develop an appreciation for the worthwhileness of different callings in the world of work—the vital contribution of each to our economy. I believe my own appreciation of contributions across the career spectrum—*my own personal valuing*—is by far the most effective force against bias.

Physical Education Teachers Can Help Combat Bias!

READING AID 363

One place to overcome bias is—of all places—in the school gym. A physical education teacher (Patlak, 1979) suggests a possible way to do this:

> Pete Rose, a third baseman for the Cincinnati Reds, had a great year not so long ago. His team traded him to the Philadelphia Phillies. His new four-year contract was fabulous—he pulled down more than three million dollars! It was all over the papers, and the kids read about it. Some of them asked: "Is that guy really worth all that money?" Others argued: "He draws the crowds in! He's dynamite! How can you say he's not worth it!" The pros and cons were all over the sports pages and sports magazines. A coach would grab this chance to get kids reading in all these sources—to ask, "Did you see this article in *Sports Illustrated?*"—to talk about the reading. Perhaps he could help his students see the problem as not quite so simple—he could encourage a more fully informed viewpoint.

Music Teachers Can Combat Bias, Too

READING AID 364

A music teacher, too, runs into bias. One music teacher (Abernathy, 1979) shares a possible way to deal with this—and, at the same time, to encourage reading in his music book collection.

> Suppose a student can see only rock music—reads about it, lives it, breathes it. One possible way to broaden his musical interests is to have him read about other styles of music. I have in class superb books on musical appreciation, like *Design for Understanding Music* by A. Verne Wilson and *Simplicity in Music Appreciation* by Anthony Apicella, Attilio Giampa, and Margarita Apicella. This latter book offers the students readings on a spectrum of musical styles—from the polyphonic music of 1100 to the popular music of today. I suggest that students who are really "into" rock music might like to look into its origins, see how it developed from other styles of music—then they should appreciate it even more! Sometimes as the student reads and as we discuss that reading, the student begins to develop an appreciation for a broader spectrum of musical styles.

A Checklist on Critical Evaluation

READING AID 365

The following checklist on critical evaluation, adapted by H. Alan Robinson from Thomas and Robinson (1977, p. 265) includes many of the considerations that are important in the critical evaluation of a piece of writing. In the chapter here on critical reading, we have dealt only with combatting bias. Some excellent resource books for giving students the following *additional* understandings are suggested near the beginning of this chapter.

1. Do students note the publication date and realize its importance in relation to events and attitudes of the writers?
2. Do they attempt to appraise the qualifications of the writers when feasible?
3. Do they ask, "What evidence supports this statement? Is it opinion? Are the writers trying to pass off opinion as fact?"
4. Do students ask, "Are the writer's implications reasonable in light of evidence presented? Are the writer's conclusions based on the information developed and supported within the piece of writing?"

5. Do students suspend judgment? Do they resist the impulse to accept the first plausible solution to a problem, holding on to that information, but waiting for other possible solutions?
6. Do they read widely and deeply, looking for and welcoming different points of view? Do they understand how to proceed when the viewpoints of authorities and/or researchers are in conflict?
7. Are students able to recognize writing designed to persuade—a conscious attempt on the part of a writer to get the reader to believe an idea, accept a fact, or buy a product?

In this chapter we have suggested a number of possible ways to alert students to, and help them combat, those strong inner forces—their own attitudes and biases. Students who have been so alerted will, as they are reading about an explosive subject, picture the pages as marked with little red flags that say DANGER—HANDLE THIS SELECTION WITH CARE! They will be aware that we human beings—quite humanly—tend to read not to alter but to reinforce our present viewpoints. They will be well aware that our biases can be "mind-forged manacles," chains forged by our own minds to imprison us within our present thinking.

We have considered in this section only *one* need of students in the area of critical reading—counteracting bias. In the opening section of this chapter, you will find listed other understandings that students should develop as they work in this area. These understandings, too, are vital for young people.

The activities reported in this chapter are not intended to be duplicated, just as they are, in other teacher's classrooms. Rather they are offered as catalysts to teachers to develop their own effective ways to handle bias.

References

Abernathy, Ralph, music teacher at the University of Chicago Laboratory School, in remarks to the writer, June 1979.

Altick, Richard D. *Preface to Critical Reading*. New York: Holt, Rinehart, and Winston, 1960, 1963, 1969.

Bell, Earl, social studies teacher at the University of Chicago laboratory School, in remarks to the writer, June 1979.

Bernstein, Edgar, social studies teacher at the University of Chicago Laboratory School, in remarks to the writer, June 1979.

Brasler, Wayne, journalism teacher at the University of Chicago Laboratory School in remarks to the writer, June 1979.

Burmeister, Lou E. *Reading Strategies for Middle and Secondary School Teachers,* 2nd ed. Reading, Mass.: Addison-Wesley Publishing Co., 1979.

Elson, E. F., and Alberta Peck. *The Art of Speaking,* 2nd ed. Boston: Ginn and Co., 1966.

Erickson, Robert, former art teacher at the University of Chicago Laboratory School, in remarks to the writer, June 1979.

Guszak, Frank J. "Teacher Questioning and Reading." *The Reading Teacher,* 21 (December 1967): 227–234.

Haehn, Faynelle, typewriting teacher at the University of Chicago Laboratory School, in remarks to the writer, June 1979.

Hozinsky, Murray, science teacher at the University of Chicago Laboratory School, in remarks to the writer, June 1979.

Introduction To Clear Thinking. Harvey, Ill.: Thornton Township High School, Social Studies Department.

Keller, Clair W. "Using Creative Interviews to Personalize Decision-Making in the American Revolution." *Social Education,* 43 (March 1979): 217–220.

Kern, Melissa, social studies teacher at the University of Chicago Laboratory School, in remarks to the writer, June 1979.

McCaul, Robert L. "The Effect of Attitudes Upon Reading Interpretation." *Journal of Educational Research,* 37 (February 1944): 451–457.

McKillop, Anne Selley. *The Relationship Between the Reader's Attitude and Certain Types of Reading Response.* New York: Bureau of Publications, Teachers College, Columbia University, 1952.

Montag, Philip, social studies teacher at the University of Chicago Laboratory School, in remarks to the writer, June 1979.

Oliver, Donald W., and James P. Shaver. *Teaching Public Issues in the High School.* Boston: Houghton Mifflin Co., 1966.

Patlak, Sanford, driver education teacher and athletic coach at the University of Chicago Laboratory School, in remarks to the writer, June 1979.

Pearson, Herbert, industrial arts teacher at the University of Chicago Laboratory School, in remarks to the writer, June 1979.

Robinson, H. Alan. *Teaching Reading and Study Strategies: The Content Areas,* 2nd ed. Boston: Allyn and Bacon, 1977.

Szymkowicz, Dorothy, home economics teacher at the University of Chicago Laboratory School, in remarks to the writer, June 1979.

Thomas, Ellen Lamar. "A Critical Reading Laboratory." *The Reading Teacher,* 13, (Feb. 1960): 201.

Thomas, Ellen Lamar, and H. Alan Robinson. *Improving Reading in Every Class,* 2nd ed. Boston: Allyn and Bacon, 1977.

Unit on Clear Thinking. Evanston, Ill.: Evanston Township High School Social Studies Department.

Wolf, Willavene, Martha L. King, and Charlotte S. Huck. "Teaching Critical Reading To Elementary School Children." *Reading Research Quarterly,* 3 (Summer 1968): 435–498.

"Please Help Me Learn to Study!"

Students' reading power may not come through because of helter-skelter study. Your guidance can help remove obstacles to learning that would have blocked students all through the year.

Through the years, students have asked the writer, "Please help me learn to study!" After working with them to improve their study habits, the writer has asked, "How many of you have ever had work like this before?" Almost invariably the students have answered, "No."

As we all observe, some students are lost souls in managing their time, some study under conditions that are chaotic, the notebooks of some are a disaster area. Working with groups or individuals to develop more efficient study habits can help to solve such problems. Yet seldom are students given this type of study guidance below the college level. Somehow this area of guiding students seems to be a "no man's land." Perhaps each individual who would care about giving this kind of guidance assumes that someone else has done it!

It is economy on the part of reading specialists, classroom teachers, and counselors to look to students' study habits. Students enrolled for remedial reading instruction usually need help with their study habits along with work on their actual reading. Some students improve their reading to a level that should enable them to succeed in school. Yet they continue to do failing or almost failing school work because of inefficient study. Many above-average, even superior readers need assistance, too. Because they do not know how to study effectively, their reading power does not come through as they work on their assignments. Time spent with these already able readers is especially well invested. It takes a tremendous expenditure of time and effort to *develop* reading power. It takes relatively little effort to *release* reading power that is already developed, when the students' block is inefficient study.

There's No One to Help!

All too often help with how to study is delayed until the college years when some guidance may be offered during orientation week or when the student may pick up one of the popular books on how to study in college. What a saving of time and energy for students—and for their teachers—if they were given guidance, on an appropriate level, in the grades *at the time they were given their first assignments that call for outside study,* again as the study load increases in the upper grades, again during the first year of high school (a crucial year for many), then again during the high school years as needed.

Students are likely to be receptive in the fall as each school year opens and they begin new courses. Many return to school with high resolve: "This year I'll really study." But often they do not know how, and often no one will help them.

The Job of Study—a Lifetime Job

A study expert at a top preparatory school (Armstrong, 1956, p. 3) urged students to look to their study habits: "Approximately one-third of your life will be spent in school, either accomplishing the hard job of study, or being exposed as a slave to it, lashed always by the lack of accomplishment. . . . When you finish college . . . you will have been studying about 22,000 hours." Then he asks a troubling question, "What percentage of this time is spent in developing efficient study habits?"

He continues: "When you finish college, is study over? No. You can only hope that you have had sufficient training for the studying which you, after college, commence in earnest. Beware of the commencement speaker who lauds you for the goal you have reached. You really have reached only the starting post. From this point on, your success will be measured largely by your ability to study."

Today's Living Conditions Make Study Guidance Crucial

Young people today need study guidance more urgently than young people did in the past. For many, television turned on at home is a distractor and a temptation. Often it makes concentration difficult; it invites the student to hurry through the study task. The homes of some students are crowded—it may be difficult to find a quiet place to complete home study assignments. Some young people report to part-time jobs daily right after school, return home exhausted at bedtime, and fall into bed. To students who are in earnest about securing an education in spite of these obstacles, the combined efforts of teachers and other concerned members of the school staff can be invaluable.

Whose Job Is Study Guidance?

Classroom teachers may wish to work with classes on how to study as the students begin a new course in September. These teachers should be rewarded as outside preparation improves—from September to June. Reading specialists will want to encourage productive study habits. They may decide to visit classes and hold how-to-study sessions. Conferences with individual students offer a special opportunity. Guidance counselors will want to help helter-skelter students "get themselves together." Administrators who are aware that some homes do not offer conditions favorable for study and that many students hold outside jobs may wish to schedule study time within the school day and to work to promote favorable surroundings in the school library or in study halls. They may also wish to encourage time for guided study within each classroom and thus reduce the need for outside study. Since the home is crucial in creating an atmosphere that favors learning, parents can play a part in a school's campaign for better study. Possible ways to enlist parents will be considered later.

"How Can I Find the Time?"

A question will come to the minds of teachers: "How can I find time for this?" Here is one teacher's comment (Hozinsky, 1979):

> Students' study can be extremely wasteful if unguided—and extremely unproductive. Instead of *taking* time, study guidance *stretches* time. It removes obstacles to learning that would have blocked students all through the year. We spend many hours trying to rescue our failures and near failures. We save time instead of losing time when we *prevent* failure.

Let's Face It!

Many study helps are likely to take best with academically oriented students. With others, we cannot hope for the "great impossible" but must rest content with the small possible. Teachers who get some students to study at all in any way deserve a halo! It may be a real accomplishment to persuade Sandy to clean out his chaotic notebook or Bobby to keep a record of his assignments. And it may be a *major* accomplishment to help Danny, who has his eye on a college athletic scholarship, to manage his time well enough to get *most* of his assignments done in spite of long practices every afternoon after school.

Rich Resources Are Available

The reader will find down-to-earth suggestions for improving the quality of study in the following sources. The writer has turned to these constantly in guiding students and has drawn ideas from them for this chapter.

Christ, Frank L. *Survey of Reading/Study Efficiency Resource Book* (Chicago: Science Research Associates, 1969)

Norman, Maxwell H. and Enid S. Norman. *How to Read and Study for Success in College,* 2nd ed. (New York: Holt, Rinehart and Winston, 1976)

Pauk, Walter. *How to Study in College,* 2nd ed. (Boston: Houghton Mifflin Co., 1974)

Preston, Ralph C. and Morton Botel. *How to Study* (Chicago: Science Research Associates, 1974)

Robinson, Francis P. *Effective Study,* 4th ed. (New York: Harper and Row, 1970)

Perhaps a distinction should be made here between the terms *study habits* and *study skills.* As they are used in this book, the term *study habits* refers to a student's accustomed ways with regard to management of time, physical setting, lighting conditions, equipment for study, certain factors that affect concentration, and the like. The term *study skills* refers to specific techniques and procedures for putting reading to work in study—locating information, making notes, making an outline, retaining what is read, summarizing, and so on. The present chapter is concerned with study habits. It is long and comprehensive because most books on teaching reading do not cover this area. Readers are of course aware that study habits should not run away with time and attention and that developing study skills is another area of very great importance. The reader will find possible procedures for developing study skills in Chapter 6, "How to Streamline Your Study." For one authority's coverage of a broad spectrum of study skills, the reader may wish to consult

Chapter 8, "Improving Reading Skills in Content Areas," in Robert Karlin, *Teaching Reading in High School: Improving Reading in Content Areas,* 3rd ed. (Indianapolis: Bobbs-Merrill Educational Publishing, 1977). The books on the preceding list should also prove rewarding.

The Study Helps that Follow

Most of the study helps that follow were prepared from time to time for students in the University of Chicago Laboratory School to meet needs that were observed there. Other helps shared in this chapter have been used with good results in public schools. Classroom teachers who plan study guidance for their classes may find these helps suggestive. Reading specialists and counselors may wish to refer to them as they share insights with teachers or work with students. Teachers and counselors may find them helpful as they work with a single troubled student. The writer of this book has found them especially useful in individual conferences where the help given can be closely tailored to the needs of the student. All who use the ideas will want to adapt them for younger or older students, for more or less academically inclined students, for a variety of situations.

The sections that follow are in "problem-solution" format—the statement of a problem likely to be faced in giving study guidance followed by possible solutions. First, we will consider some general problems that teachers often face. Then we will be concerned with the specific study problem of a group of students or of an individual student—Tom's problem, Jackie's problem, Mike's, Sandy's, Pam's, Judy's. While the names of the students are not their actual names, each problem is a straight-from-life problem and each student a flesh-and blood student.

Helping Students Want to Improve their Study Habits

Problem: *Some students resent being told how to study. They feel that it is their inalienable right to study as they please!*

READING AID 366

As a reading consultant and teacher, the writer was sometimes asked to give group presentations on how to study. She entitled the series "Take Your Choice of Study Tips." In her experience, students respond to a non-pressuring tone and to the suggestion that they consider the tips offered, then make their own personal choice of those that seem promising. They react well to comments like these: "We're all different—what works well for one may not work for another. Only you can decide which ideas are suitable for you—to meet your special needs in your courses this year." . . . "You may have ideas just as effective or more so. We hope you'll share them with us." They can be encouraged to find their own learning style through experience.

READING AID 367

In one high school the students themselves suggest the problems they want to investigate. They have selected such problems as "How can I control my time better?" "What can I do if my job crowds study out?" and "How can I learn to concentrate?" They search for solutions in books and articles on how to study, then share their findings with the class. During the next few weeks they try out the ideas, then decide by class vote which ones have proved the most effective. These they compile into a letter of tips on how to study effectively in high school, addressed to the members of next year's incoming Freshman Class. Here, indeed, is a reversal! The teacher is not telling the students what they should do; the students are telling others, including the teacher, what they *need* to do (Bragstad, 1979)

In the same school, teachers encourage students to share study pointers with the class by asking: "What helps *you* when you have trouble concentrating?" "How do *you* solve the time crunch?" Later the teachers compile the most helpful suggestions, in quotation form, into a handout for students. Attached to the quotations are names that carry weight—class officers, star athletes, honor students. Students are inclined to listen when fellow students testify, "This works!" (Bragstad, 1979)

READING AID 368

Prominent and popular seniors—students who have made outstanding contributions to the school while maintaining good scholastic averages—can be invited to visit how-to-study sessions of underclassmen and to talk on how they have solved their study problems, including the familiar one of "just too much to do."

READING AID 369

Dr. Ruth Strang (1965) suggested: "If you can't get interest and the cooperation of the students in upgrading study habits, change your strategy!" Students tend to react to study guidance partly according to their needs. If their reaction is not favorable, perhaps they do not really need the help being offered. Reading specialists and guidance counselors sometimes make attending how-to-study sessions voluntary. When this is the arrangement, many students who are already making good school records will volunteer. These students, it should be noted, are often well worth helping. Some of them achieve their *A's* and *B's* not because of their present study habits but in spite of them. Because of their strong motivation, these students may profit greatly.

READING AID 370

Problem: *Many students need to improve their study habits but do not seem to feel that need. How can a teacher make students aware of their need and encourage positive attitudes?*

Many students realize a need for "time control"; many, on the other hand, do not. To convince students of this need, Dr. Ruth Strang asked her students to keep a log for two or three days of how they spent their time. When they brought their logs to class, Dr. Strang asked: "What are some of the good features of your log?" and "How do you think it might be improved?" Some of the students exclaimed: "I spent as much time warming up as working!" "My study breaks had a way of filling the evening!" "If I dialed the phone once or twice, the evening was gone!" Now the students were more receptive to tips on how to manage time. (Strang, 1965)

READING AID 371

Dr. Strang saw a further use for the students' logs. She viewed them as an opportunity to learn more about her students—their friendships, their family life, their interests, their jobs—and to develop rapport and form a closer relationship.

SEE MASTER COPY PAGE 65

You will find on Master Copy Page 65 a "time log" by means of which students can evaluate the way they use their time and think through possible changes.

Some teachers find study habits inventories to be a source of motivation. Some give students complete questionnaires like the ones below; some select parts that suit their purpose at the moment. Others develop their own inventories.

READING AID 372

"Study Habits Checklist" in Ralph C. Preston and Morton Botel, *How to Study* (Chicago: Science Research Associates, 1974), pp. 3–8.

"Study Habits Questionnaire" in Francis P. Robinson, *Effective Study* (New York: Harper and Row, 1970), pp. 76–77.

"Wrenn Study Habits Inventory" (Palo Alto, Calif.: Consulting Psychologists Press, 1941).

College-bound high school students often react positively to references to the college years that lie ahead for them and to study helps they realize are drawn from college books on how to study. They react well to the comment, "These tips help busy college students

READING AID 373

streamline their study," and to references to books on college study which they see lying on a nearby desk or table in their classroom and are encouraged to examine. They respond well to the term "higher-level study skills."* Some say to themselves, "This is something new and promising—this is college stuff!"

READING AID 374

When students have long-term goals regarding college and their life work, they are more likely to appreciate the value of efficiency in learning. Students who have some idea of their life plans might profitably reflect on questions like these (idea from Lakein, 1976, p. 45):

1. What, so far as you know right now, are your lifetime goals?
2. Where would you like to be in achieving these life plans five years from now? Ten years from now?
3. How do the following areas of living play a part in your achieving your life goals: friends, family, recreational interests, school activities, school work?

Students who have thought seriously about their life goals may have a better perspective on where achieving at school fits into their life picture. Long-term goals may come to their minds as they set priorities!

READING AID 375

Students invited to or scheduled for how-to-study sessions can "put in their orders" for study guidance. They can be encouraged to take a look at their own personal needs and to make requests on or before the first session.

> What do you consider your three greatest strengths in studying? What three areas need strengthening most? What requests do you have about how we spend our how-to-study sessions? Your teacher will consider your requests carefully.

The teacher can now do advance planning so that the study guidance will be "on target." Students are inclined to take advantage of helps they themselves have "ordered."

READING AID 376

"Success stories" of actual students, drawn from the teacher's experience, lend credibility to study guidance. A visitor who had just observed a group how-to-study session held by the writer commented: "Those students *really listened* when you told stories of actual students!" After hearing this suggestion, the writer worked into her how-to-study presentations still more "success stories" of students. The stories she told of *A* students suggested that even honor students need and use the study helps offered. The stories of *D* and *F* students who had improved their grades gave discouraged students hope. A junior girl commented: "I really identified with those students!"

Helping Students Learn to Control Their Time

Problem: *In a high school where academic demands were heavy, students were concerned with the question, "How can I manage my time better?" They came to the reading consultant and asked for help. Classroom teachers, too, pointed out to the consultant this need of students for time control.*

*This term belongs to Francis P. Robinson, who used it in *Effective Study*, 4th ed. (New York: Harper and Row, 1970).

READING AID 377

In response to these requests, the reading consultant planned sessions on how to manage time, advertising these in advance. The students who attended were volunteers. Counselors and classroom teachers, however, encouraged students in whom they had observed a need, to volunteer.

In the writer's experience, high school upperclassmen are inclined to be more responsive to guidance on time control. This is understandable in view of the fact that their load of both activities and assignments is heavier than that of underclassmen. Of course, other students are likely to be responsive at times when they are really under pressure.

Some of the sessions were held for fairly large groups. Large placards, all with catchy headlines and some with Charlie Brown cartoons (enlarged on a photo-copier), were displayed on an easel before the group. Exposed one by one, these placards heightened interest, organized the presentation, and drove home main points. The "headlines" were written in script with broad felt-tipped pens in colors. While preparing these placards took time, they added the appeal of "show" to "tell." Once prepared, they became "instant" classroom resources, ready to use for the benefit of students year after year.

During the sessions, the reading consultant selected from among the following insights and activities, matching the helps to the needs of the particular group and offering them in manageable installments. Sometimes she shared her own insights; sometimes she elicited insights from the students. The students reacted to the ideas, discussed them, and contributed procedures they themselves had used and found effective. Let us imagine that you are attending some of these sessions.

A title placard, "TAKE YOUR CHOICE OF STUDY TIPS," is displayed on an easel before the class as the students walk in. On the poster is a cartoon of Charlie Brown holding an open book and looking like a winner. The teacher introduces the study helps in this way:

> Here are tips on how to study—offered on a take-your-choice basis. Many students have used them to make the school record they wanted to. Psychologists call them "higher-level study skills."* [The instructor reveals a placard with a drawing of Linus hugging his security blanket, with the headline, "HIGHER-LEVEL STUDY SKILLS —YOUR SECURITY BLANKET."] They can be your "security blanket" at school this year.
>
> Even Dan S——, a senior class president who went on to Harvard, needed—and used—tips like these. [The students in the group knew Dan and looked up to him—he was a senior last year.] In our school he had more *A's* than anything else, and as many activities as *A's*—president of the senior class, vice-president the year before, captain of varsity soccer, winner of fourteen track awards, sports editor of the yearbook, and a member of the Student Board!
>
> At the end of his junior year, Dan learned from his mother that he could return for his senior year only if he could earn almost everything he would need for his expenses. At first he was overwhelmed—and did nothing. Then realizing he must have a job quickly, he spent July selling magazines from door to door. Then he found a job as attendant and presser in a dry cleaning store. He worked seven days a week all summer and continued to work there after school and Saturdays all through his senior year.
>
> Princeton and Harvard both wanted this boy. Each kept upping the scholarship higher than the other until Dan went to Harvard with a full scholarship. How could he possibly do all this? His counselor commented, "His study habits were excellent, and he was an expert at managing time."
>
> You may be thinking, "But Dan's ability was inborn—achievement depends on that." Yet in your classes some of the students with the most ability achieve little.

*The term "higher-level study skills" belongs to Francis P. Robinson and is used in his *Effective Study*, 4th ed. (New York: Harper and Row, 1970).

Others with less ability achieve highly. What makes the difference? Often it's knowing how to study. After all, teachers don't grade a student's intellect but the quality of work he does. It's important to make the most of capabilities. Good study habits can help you do this. (Preston and Botel, 1974, pp. 2–3)

Terry, a junior, couldn't get himself together. He was always late—he couldn't meet deadlines. He collected one grade of *D* after another! But in basketball Terry was fantastic. The coach pointed out the possibility of an athletic scholarship if he could average *B* or better. A counselor helped Terry recycle his study habits. He learned to get his homework done even when there were long practices every afternoon, a heavy schedule of games, and on top of that, district, sectional, and state tournaments. Soon he raised his grades to *C's*. By the end of the year he was making solid *B's*. He won a college scholarship—to Indiana University. Recently Terry, a freshman doing good work in college—came back to school to see his buddies. (Roberts, 1977)

You may be thinking, "We're all different—what works for one may not work for another." And surely this is true. *Only you* can decide which ideas are suitable for you—to meet your special needs in your courses this year.

Here are the study tips. You may have ideas just as effective or more so. We hope you'll share them with us.

The teacher reveals a placard with the headline, "MAKE *YOUR* KIND OF TIME PLAN."

I wonder if anything will mean more to you this year than the way you manage time. You can use your time, as Dan and Terry did, for the achievement you want so much and a contribution to your school as well. Or your time can slip away, and you may never know what became of it, and things that mean a lot to you may slip away, too.

This year you'll have time on your hands—not just time at home but time within the school days, too. No one will tell you how to spend this time. Your teachers will assign readings, problems, papers. Then, without their nudging, it's up to you to complete them and hand them in on time. You may be absent for two or three days. Then it's up to you to catch up on whatever you missed and hand in those missing assignments. For some students the adjustment to time on their hands and the freedom to use it exactly as they wish is the biggest problem to be faced in high school.

How can you get more control over your time—and your life? College students are advised to solve this problem with a time plan. Of course, the same type of time plan will not suit every student. Some want and need a detailed schedule. Others are more comfortable with a minimum of planning and a very flexible schedule. (Preston and Botel, 1974, p. 147) Others operate best with just brief lists of things to do. Let's look at several different types of time plans. After examining these, you may want to make *your* kind of time plan.

Each student has been given blank forms for different time plans reproduced on ditto paper of different colors.

SEE MASTER COPY PAGES 66–67

You have a form headed "Your Personal Activity Plan for Study, Classes, and Recreation."* [On the easel before the class is an enlargement of this form, filled in with the time plan of a representative student. The instructor refers to this plan while explaining. See Figure 9–1. A blank form for "Your Personal Activity Plan" will be found on Master Copy Page 66 and tips for drawing up the plan on Master Copy Page 67.

Colleges advise their freshmen to make a general time plan. Here you set aside certain hours for study, then keep this schedule faithfully from day to day. These hours are saved for study. The rest are *freed* for other things you want to do. You'll find it a simple matter to work out such a plan. All it calls for is a *general* blocking out of time.

*The author is indebted to Ralph C. Preston and Morton Botel, *How to Study* for the title *personal activity plan* instead of the less inviting term *study schedule*.

YOUR PERSONAL ACTIVITY PLAN FOR STUDY, CLASSES, AND RECREATION

On this plan you block off certain hours for study. The rest are *freed*—for other things you want to do. Psychologists advise, ''Follow your plan each day. The *habit* of studying at regular times should develop. Then getting down to work and studying should be much easier!'' Here is the time plan of one senior boy.

A.M.	Monday	Tuesday	Wednesday	Thursday	Friday	Saturday	Sunday
7-7:45	→	→	Dress and breakfast	→	→		|
7:45-8	→	→	On way to school	→	→		|
8-9	Math	Math	Math	Math	Math		Free
9-10	Science	Science	Science	Science	Science	Study	|
10-11	Gym	Gym	Gym	Gym	Gym	Study	|
11-12	English	English	English	English	English	Study	Church
P.M.							
12-1	Lunch	Lunch	Lunch	Lunch	Lunch		|
1-2	Spanish	Spanish	Spanish	Spanish	Spanish	Guitar lesson	Free
2-3	Social studies	Social studies	Social studies	Social studies	Social studies		|
3-3:30	Free	Free	Free	Free	Free	|	|
3:30-5:15	Basketball	Basketball	Basketball	Basketball	Basketball	|	Study
5:15-5:30	→	→	On way home	→	→	Free	Study ? if this time is needed
5:30-6:15	→	→	Free (TV)	→	→	|	Study
6:15-7	→	→	Dinner	→	→	|	Supper
7-9:45	Study	Study	Study	Study	with friends	|	Study
9:45-10:30	→ TV –	gab fest –	personal reading	- listen to records	" "	|	Free

FIGURE 9–1.

Colleges advise their students to make a general time plan to fit their special needs.

Here is one senior's general time plan. [The instructor refers to the placard on the easel.] He prefers to do most of his studying evenings—each night except Friday from 7 o'clock to 9:45. Weekend study he plans for Saturday morning, Sunday evening, and part of Sunday afternoon—if he needs this extra Sunday afternoon time. The hours blocked off are, ordinarily, faithfully reserved for study.

But this is just a general plan, and it must be flexible. Open time should be available. This student has left free time everyday after school, Friday night, and part of Saturday and Sunday. There will be unexpected club, sports or family events, and good times with friends. With the time left unscheduled, he can adjust as special circumstances arise. Studying which has to be postponed or done ahead of time can be moved here.

Suppose tonight you want to work out a general plan to fit your needs this year. First, you would fill in your regualr activities, activities that are unchanging—your classes, lab periods, after-school sports, a part-time job, and regular weekly events like club meetings or music lessons. Then around these unchanging activities, work in your hours for study. You may prefer 6:30 to 9 o'clock, or 7 to 8:30, then a half hour's rest, then 9 to 10. A "cease study" time of 10 o'clock will be an incentive to drive hard to meet that deadline. (Pauk, 1974, p. 24)

Again, you are not locked into this plan—it has wide open spaces. Suppose on Wednesday you learn that a friend from out of town is coming Thursday evening. How can you finish a paper for English due Friday morning? By doing your paper ahead, during the free time you've left on your Wednesday's schedule, you can be with your friend and finish your paper, too. Or suppose there's a TV program you don't want to miss tonight at 8. Be flexible. Study in your free time before dinner, and listen to the program.

Again, this is a schedule for study—*and recreation, too.* You're planning an *activity schedule,* not just a study schedule. You're blocking off time for friends, physical activities, and rest, as well as study. Instead of denying yourself what you want, you're scheduling time for *what you want most.*

You may want to rough out your first trial schedule in pencil. You may soon find weak spots in your plan. Perhaps you've left too little free space. Or your evening's study may take another half hour. Then revise your schedule to meet your needs. (Preston and Botel, 1974, p. 149)

It's a good plan to place your schedule where you can see it often—in the front of your notebook or propped up on your desk or table. (Preston and Botel, 1974, p. 149) Psychologists advise, "Try to follow its pattern each day. The habit of studying at regular times should develop. Then getting down to work and concentrating should be much easier."

Now, with your time plan, you won't feel guilty about spending time in other ways than study. And, oddly enough, you may find that you now have more time for *non*-school activities. (Norman and Norman, 1976, p. 26)

This may be a good point for the students to react to the suggestions given thus far and to discuss them, to share their own ideas, and to draw up their own general time plan (though making a plan is not compulsory). The students understand that this first plan is tentative. They are encouraged to give it a trial run, then, after finding its weak spots, to make adjustments. During the days that follow, the teacher encourages the students to report on how their plans are working out and offers further guidance.

If the students need to make a weekly time plan and fit in the "far too many" things they have to do, the teacher may display a placard with the heading, "TRY A MUST-DO SCHEDULE TO SOLVE THE TIME CRUNCH." Here are the teacher's comments:

READING AID 378

We'll offer several different types of time plans for you to consider, adapt, combine, improve—in the way that suits you best. We have talked about a *general* time plan in which you block off certain hours for study. Along with a general plan, or instead of one, you may wish to make a weekly must-do schedule, one that gives a slot to each *specific* task you can foresee.*

You have a form headed "Make A Must-Do Schedule." [A must-do schedule filled in with the schedule of a representative student appears on the placard displayed before the class. See Figure 9–2. The reader will find a blank form for this schedule on Master Copy Page 68.]

SEE MASTER COPY PAGE 68

We all have rushed weeks when there are just too many things to do. Tasks like these are tugging at you: a test coming Friday in science . . . a book to finish and a paper to write for English . . . you promised you'd babysit . . . you're going on the bus to a game . . . you have three meetings coming up . . . you have to go buy a new notebook—yours is falling apart . . . your skis are broken and you're going skiing.

There's a way to help solve this problem—one that helps get each and every job done. It's to make a must-do list. First, take plenty of time to think out everything you have to do—the whole week long. Make a list of all the "must-do's" you can think of. You might "ABC" these items, separating what's more important from what is less important. Then place everything you really must do on your schedule. You might write in "Finish book for English" on Monday . . . "Write English paper—first draft" on Tuesday . . . "Finish paper" and "Start studying science" on Wednesday . . . and "Study science" and "Type paper" on Thursday . . . "Get those skis fixed" on Saturday . . . and so on.

Now the important things have their place, and you can see your way to finish. Now you won't be frantic and your concentration ruined by all those tasks tugging at you. Not all tranquilizers come in a bottle!

You'll want to revise your schedule and add to it as the week goes along and new "must-do's" come up. When you've attacked an item and finished it, check it off. This will give you solid satisfaction.

Ron, a junior, couldn't get a handle on all he had to do. His grades were failing. Then he met a man who interested him in engineering. Suddenly he saw a real reason for school! His counselor helped him to sit down each week, think through the week ahead, and make plans. He raised his grades to *A* in math and every other subject related to engineering. He felt satisfaction in being "in charge of himself."

This may be a good point for students to react and discuss the ideas, to share their own ideas, and perhaps, then and there, think out their "must-do's" and make a schedule. During the days that follow, the teacher encourages the students to report on how their "time control" is working out.

Students, it should be noted, are often given their assignments from day to day and cannot plan an entire week ahead. The weekly must-do schedule is for those who can—and should—look ahead.

If feeling overwhelmed and needing to set priorities is a special characteristic of the group, the instructor might display a placard headed "TOO MUCH TO DO? THEN 'ABC' YOUR TASKS!" Here is the teacher's explanation:

READING AID 379

Students exclaim, "I need a ten-day week!"

An expert on time management, who advises busy corporation executives, urges us to "work *smarter* rather than harder." He suggests that we list all the tasks we have to do, then assign to each task an *A*, a *B*, or a *C* priority. *A* means "This is an absolute must—I must do it soon"; *B* means "This is somewhat less important"; *C* means "I can postpone it, or perhaps I don't really need to do it." Be a do-it-soon person, he advises, with your high-value *A's!* "Make time" for yourself—by setting priorities! (Lakein, 1976, pp. 46–48)

*The idea for a must-do schedule is adapted from Maxwell H. Norman and Enid S. Norman, *How to Read and Study for Success in College,* 2nd ed. (New York: Holt, Rinehart, and Winston, 1976), pp. 233–234.

MAKE A MUST-DO SCHEDULE WHEN THINGS ARE RUSHED

We all have rushed weeks when there are just too many things to do. There's a way to help solve this problem—one that helps get each and every job done. Think out everything you have to do—the whole week long. Then give each item its place on your schedule. Now you have a handle on all the things you have to do. Now you can see your way to finish. Revise and make additions as the week goes along. When you've attended to an item, check it off. This will give you a feeling of real satisfaction.

A.M.	Monday	Tuesday	Wednesday	Thursday	Friday	Saturday	Sunday
						Get skis fixed	
		Classes					Free
						Dental appointment	Church
P.M.							
AFTER SCHOOL	Ski Club	Guitar lesson	Drama Club	Meet with college representative	Graduation Committee	Go skiing	Read—rest—rap
		Get notebook					
		at bookstore			Combo rehearsal		
		on way home					
7:00	Finish book for English	English paper—	English paper—	Study for	Go to game	Babysit	Do regular
to		first draft	final draft	science test			weekend
9:45	Other assignments	Other work	Start studying	Type English			assignments
			science	paper			

FIGURE 9–2

A must-do schedule on which students schedule specifically all the things they have to do may help them solve the "time crunch."

At this point, the students in the group list all the tasks that are overwhelming them at the moment, then label each one with an *A,* a *B,* or a *C*. Then they give the really important tasks a time slot on their schedules. In the process, they may discover that they've been spending time on their *C's* while their *A's* just haven't been done! (Bragstad, 1979)

Perhaps a simple daily, rather than a weekly, time plan seems more appropriate for the group. In that case, the teacher may reveal a placard with this heading: "USE A HANDY INDEX CARD FOR TODAY'S SCHEDULE." The teacher explains:

READING AID 380

> Some students operate best with just brief lists of things to do. Dr. Walter Pauk of the Cornell University Reading-Study Center helps college students streamline their study and raise their grade point averages. He suggests simply jotting your today's schedule on a handy index card (Pauk, 1974, p. 27):
>
>> A 3-by-5-inch card is just the right size. It will fit perfectly into your shirt pocket or handbag so that it will be on hand when you need it. Every evening before you leave your desk [or any other time you choose to do this] . . . determine your free hours and courses for the next day; then jot down on the card a plan for the next day: the subjects you plan to study, the errands, appointments, physical exercise, recreation, and any other activities you want to do, with their corresponding times.
>
> In just five minutes, Dr. Pauk comments, you'll unclutter your mind—you'll have a memo to refer to. And you will have mentally thought through your day, thus putting into action a psychological time clock. [See Figure 9–3.]

To Do— on Thursday
8:30-12 - Classes
12-1 - Lunch and bookstore for slide rule
1-3:15 - Classes
3:30-4 - Committee meeting
4-5:30 - Swimming practice
7-9:45 - Read Chap. 5 in science.
Find topic for Eng.
Do math.
Learn Spanish vocab.
9:45 - Rap on phone.

Some students operate best with brief lists of things to do.

FIGURE 9–3

READING AID 381

Making a time plan for the coming evening may seem appropriate for the students. If so, the teacher displays a placard with the heading: "MAKE AN EVENING'S STUDY BUDGET." Here are the teacher's comments:

> You may prefer doing most of your time planning after the close of school each day. At that time you have been given all your assignments for the next day and can estimate the time you'll need to spend on each task. A "study budget" slip may prove convenient.
>
> All you need is a small slip of paper. First, think out all the things you have to do during the evening. Then assign each task its place in your schedule. Estimate the time each task will take you. Now you have a handle on all the things you have to do.

STUDY BUDGET

Subject to Be Studied	Estimated Time to Be Spent
Do math problems.	7:00–7:50
Read science article.	8:00–8:30
Decide social studies topic.	8:30–8:50
Read story for English.	9:00–9:45
Copy over French.	9:45–10:00

FIGURE 9–4

The end of the school day may be a good time to make an evening's study budget, planning all the things to do and estimating the time to be spent on each task.

> Is there a special sequence for studying your subjects? [At this point the students will have their own ideas and will want to share them.] You may want to work on your hardest or least interesting subject first, so that you can study this when you're fresh instead of tired. Then you might study your next hardest subject, and so on, leaving the one that's easiest or most interesting until last. For example, there might be difficult thought problems in math, while for English you might need only to read an interesting short story. You might plan to do the math first. Later you could do the easier task of reading the short story.
>
> Or you may prefer to alternate different types of activities—an English assignment involving reading, then, for a change, drawing a map in social studies, then going back to reading again in science. You'll *actually remember longer,* psychologists claim, when you alternate activities. What you learn becomes "set" in your mind better if you alternate one type of learning with another. Often when you think you're tired, you're actually just "tired" of that particular activity or subject. Just switching from one activity to another may provide the "break" you need. (Pauk, 1974, p. 48)
>
> Or you may wish to use a "first-things-first" order, performing the evening's tasks in order of descending importance. (Pauk, 1974, p. 22) In this way you're likely to

> complete the tasks to which you gave an *A* priority. If some other task must be left undone because time runs out, it will not be your most important.
>
> The ten minutes unaccounted for on the budget are "breathers." An occasional break, psychologists assert, is absolutely necessary or your concentration will falter. You'll accomplish more if you stop for these brief rests. Walk around the house—raid the refrigerator—rest both your eyes and your mind. Work intensely while you work—then take your break. The break itself *actually helps you remember*. It allows one lesson to become "set" in your mind before you start a new one. The best time for the break, obviously, is between chapters or between assignments.
>
> How long should your "breather" last? You'll be most efficient, some psychologists suggest, if you plan in blocks of one hour—fifty minutes for study, then ten minutes for your break. (Pauk, 1974, p. 23) This, obviously, is a rough guide—you'll want to take your breaks at good stopping points.
>
> Your study budget should be completely flexible. It's often hard to judge how long an assignment will take. Or you may become so interested in a subject that you will want to work on. If you can't meet a deadline, just take a moment to revise your schedule. When you've attended to a task, check it off. Now you'll experience real satisfaction.
>
> Psychologists advise us to "get into the magnetic field" of an *immediate* goal. (Dudycha, 1957, p. 100) When we make an evening's study budget, planning to tackle one task after another, we are setting immediate goals. Now, like a magnet, each task "pulls us" to complete it before the deadline and reach that immediate goal!
>
> Students report that using a study budget helps their concentration. They focus their attention better because they're working against the clock. Students also claim that setting time limits helps them resist distractions. (Bragstad, 1979)

An evening's study budget may prove helpful with individual students whose after-school lives are chaotic. Don's time after school was slipping away and important assignments were being left undone. At his English teacher's suggestion, he came to the reading center for guidance. There the reading teacher sat down with him for a few minutes after school each day as he made his study budget for the coming evening at home. Next day he reported on how his plans had worked out. As the days passed, Don put time to work to better advantage.

Some students shy away from setting time limits for tasks. Those students may prefer to plan their sequence for the evening without setting deadlines.

READING AID 382

The teacher may display a placard with the heading, "DON'T WAIT FOR INSPIRATION TO STRIKE!" Comments like these may be appropriate:

> Some students lament, "The hardest part of studying is getting started!" One student kept a log for a few nights of how he used his time. He found he spent almost as much time warming up as he did working. If you are a slow-starter at some particularly uninviting or difficult task, you might list all the *pluses* you will have gained—your sense of satisfaction, your feeling of being "in control"—as soon as that task is done. And you might list all the *minuses* that will *cease* for you—having the task hang over you, your anxiety about it—the minute the task is done. (Idea from Lakein, 1973, p. 5)

This concludes the guidance on how to manage time, offered by a reading specialist, in manageable installments, to students who requested it. As we have noted, the guidance given was matched to the needs of the particular group. As we have also noted, the students discussed the pros and cons of the different time plans, suggested ways to adapt or improve them, and shared procedures they themselves had found effective.

In helping students with time control, emphasis on *flexibility* needs to be underscored. Dr. Ruth Strang (1965) cautioned: "There is danger of a great deal of frustration and anxiety if students set for themselves an overly rigid schedule, then cannot live up to it." She commented on the type of student most likely to be receptive to the idea of budgeting time: "Gifted students tend to like a time plan less—they like variety and surprises. Less gifted youngsters often appreciate having a certain amount of routine through a schedule." Dr. Strang would advise us to tailor our study guidance, whenever possible, to the individual student. She would also suggest emphasizing with students "making *your* kind of time plan" and keeping that time plan flexible.

"Time-Stretchers" for Students with Part-Time Jobs

Problem: *Tom needed a time-stretcher. He went to his part-time job right after school each day. Not having long uninterrupted hours for study, he needed—and wanted—to make the most of moments. A teacher helped him find ways to use scattered bits of time.*

READING AID 383

Here are some possible suggestions for students like Tom:

> Students with part-time jobs do not ordinarily have big blocks of uninterrupted time for study.* If you are in earnest about getting an education in spite of this obstacle, you can make some of your study materials portable so that you can study "on the run." You can paste or tack a metal clip near your mirror or on the wall at eye level and clamp in this clip note cards or pages of notes you want to study. Then, while you are shaving or combing your hair, you can read and recite the information. Formulas, definitions, or foreign language vocabulary can be written on note cards. With these, you can recite to yourself while driving to work or walking across a parking lot, then check your accuracy later.
>
> You'll want to use odd bits of time. At lunch, while munching a sandwich, you might work a problem or two in math. You can copy a short paper, type a page of a manuscript, or translate a paragraph of a foreign language in ten minutes. Learning vocabulary fits into odd moments. Dan, an honor student who worked long hours in a dry cleaning shop, would wait on a customer, then study until the next customer walked in. He even studied while pressing clothes!
>
> Early morning study may not be your "thing." Then again it just might be a busy person's "prime time"! Some students are their most productive when they're fresh and rested, with their minds uncluttered with thoughts of the day. There's research evidence that most of us can "put out" as much in one hour of daytime study as in an hour and a half at night. (Pauk, 1974, p. 22)

Some students like Tom have devised their own "time-stretchers," even recording class lectures on cassettes and listening to these while driving to work!

Spacing Out Long-Term Projects

Problem: *Jackie worked on important projects frantically the last night. When asked her greatest need in studying, she answered, "I leave important projects until the last minute."*

*Dr. Walter Pauk offers these suggestions to the job-holding student in his *How to Study in College* (Boston: Houghton Mifflin Co., 1974), pp. 30–31.

The following suggestions might appeal to Jackie:

READING AID 384

We've all left important projects until the last night—to our dismay! We meet one crisis, emerge staggering, recover from that crisis, then relax until the next crisis comes along! Yet major papers and projects are often assigned *far* ahead of the date due.

Why not make a calendar for long-term projects? With a calendar you space out your work in manageable stages—for example, doing the necessary reading, writing the first draft of a paper, revising, making the final copy.

SEE MASTER COPY PAGE 69

Let's suppose that on October 1 you're assigned a 2,000-word paper. Your calendar might look like this. [A blank calendar form appears on Master Copy Page 69.]

Part of the Project You'll Have Done	Date You'll Have It Done
Have reading completed.	Friday, October 11
Complete outline.	Tuesday, October 15
Complete first draft.	Monday, October 21
Complete revising and final typing.	Wednesday, October 23
Date Due	Friday, October 25

A student's calendar for a long-term project, spacing out the work in manageable stages.

FIGURE 9–5

When you're up nights until twelve or one banging out a paper, perhaps you've let weeks slip by before starting a big assignment. Your crash effort can lead to exhaustion—both physical and mental. Then your thinking becomes fuzzy, and you may lose time struggling over problems that should have been solved quickly. You may find yourself distracted by worry about that impending deadline. And you may be deeply disappointed in the final product—troubled because you didn't give yourself a chance to show that you can do good work!

When you "mark your calendar," you're ahead of the game—without last-minute panic. Not all tranquilizers come in a bottle!

Jackie planned with the teacher how to space out her work on a big project assigned for English, then reported at intervals how her work was progressing.

Is the Place Where Students Study "On Their Side"?

Problem: *When students in a reading class complained to their teacher that they couldn't concentrate, the teacher inquired about the surroundings in which they studied at home. Mike answered that he* *studied in the basement while his four brothers played pingpong nearby!*

READING AID 385

After asking the students about their usual study surroundings, the teacher might share some of the following ideas, encouraging the students to discuss them. (You will find more about the problem of concentration later in this chapter.)

Students ask, "How can I concentrate better?" The place you study can help you concentrate, or it can be a handicap impossible to surmount. Some students insist on studying in the living room on the floor in front of the television, sprawled on their stomachs or curled up like a pretzel. A younger brother may be nearby playing bomber pilot!

You'll probably concentrate better if you study in the same place each day. The same surroundings, psychologists tell us, exert a strong power of suggestion. It becomes habit to go there, clear your mind of other things, and study.

Most students study better in a quiet place. They may think that music doesn't distract them, but in one investigation reading comprehension was cut in half when students listened to popular music. And studies indicate that high reading speeds are not attained when distractions are present. Of course, we can perform purely mechanical study tasks in the presence of distractors, with little effect on our performance. [The students may want to talk over their personal reactions to different sounds.]

In one experiment, energy drain was measured under noisy and then again under quiet conditions. By pumping air from the room and analyzing it, it was possible to compare the energy expended. Individuals differed, but with most people noise drained away more energy and left them more tired. Again, many students don't realize that their efficiency is being reduced and their work impaired by distracting sounds. Most people fight against themselves when they try to read and listen to a TV program. A deep voice insisting on Nine Lives for finicky Morris distracts most people.

Since we live with other people, it's difficult to find complete quiet. We can become habituated to the lower levels of noise and block them out from our consciousness. (Christ, 1969, p. 22) We can also learn to block out background noises like the doorbell or the telephone ringing. Some large office supply stores offer a "Sound Barrier" or a "Study Buddy," a device that looks like earphones and helps shut out distracting sounds. Airplane mechanics wear devices like this while working on jet planes. Earplugs, which are inexpensive, can help, too.

Your homework may take two or three hours night after night. Why not create a study center in your home, complete with everything you'll need? You'll need a study desk or table with an adequate working surface. In college rooms, students place their desks so that they don't face their roommate or look out the window. College experts say you'll concentrate better if your desk faces a blank wall. Photographs of your friends on the desk, a paperback as exciting as *Jaws 2*, or a telephone nearby won't help much either.

If you can't concentrate, check the lighting of your study table. You can lose the concentration battle from poor lighting. Glare on the page or shadows on your work or light in your eyes can cause eyestrain, headaches, tiredness, and poor concentration. The old-style bare unshaded electric light bulb is as out of date as a candle. A study lamp scientifically designed by lighting engineers can ease your way in study. The entire working surface of your desk should be illuminated evenly. There should not be too much contrast between the lighting on your work and in the surrounding room. The rest of the room should be well lighted, without deep shadows. Be sure to check the ventilation. A stuffy atmosphere is conducive not to ticking off your tasks but to sound sleep!

You may be surprised to learn that the book you are reading should not lie flat on the desk before you. Instead, it should be propped up so that the top of the book is about thirty degrees above the desk surface and the light rays reflected from the page strike your eyes from that angle. You may have seen metal book rests for sale in bookstores. You can make a handy "book rest" for yourself by finding a box about two inches deep and cutting away the side toward you. Then place your book in a tilted position inside the box, supporting the top of the book on the side opposite the cut-out side. Of course, you should be looking down toward the book. If you read in bed with the book held over your head, the light is wrong, your eye muscles and nervous system are under a strain, and you'll tire easily.

You'll concentrate better if you collect everything you need before you begin to study. How can you concentrate if you must stop every few minutes to get something? Each "hunting expedition" breaks your continuity of thought. Your desk at home should have certain standard equipment right at hand and ready—paper, note cards, pen, sharp pencils, an eraser, a pencil sharpener, a ruler, paste, scissors, paper clips, graph paper and a compass, rubber bands, Scotch tape, a dictionary. Your desk should not be cluttered but free of things not needed.

Having the work of just one subject on the desk before you is good psychology. When you have the books and notebooks of four or five subjects piled high around you, you may feel swamped by it all. Put the other books aside and concentrate your efforts on the one task at hand. One assignment at a time done well adds up to five assignments all well done!

Last year Chris, a sophomore, was all helter-skelter. He would do anything to postpone studying—pick up a magazine, play a record, go get a snack, stay in the kitchen talking. By the time he got down to study, it was too late, and he was too tired. Or he would start to study, and if there was a newspaper anywhere near, he would be drawn to it, and he wouldn't have the slightest idea how he had gotten from his biology book over to that newspaper! He operated from day to day on a crisis basis. He constantly felt guilty about not getting his assignments done. Then he decided to revamp his study area. He moved everything that was distracting out of the area, so that he would have to move a long way to find any distractions. As time passed, he became more and more "in charge of" himself. Now he felt good about himself instead of guilty. He managed his time so much better that he raised his grades and took on a school activity, too—managing the track team. (Robb, 1977)

After a discussion of study surroundings, the students might focus in on the surroundings at home where they usually study. They might make a note of each distractor they can think of that disturbs their concentration and the steps they can take to reduce or eliminate that distractor. A chart that might be used for this purpose will be found on Master Copy Page 70. (Idea from Preston and Botel, 1974, p. 153)

READING AID 386

Using another chart, the students might examine the physical equipment they usually have for study, making a note of what's wrong or missing and of any changes they would like to make. A chart for this purpose appears on Master Copy Page 70. (Idea from Robinson, 1970, p. 93)

READING AID 387

SEE MASTER COPY PAGE 70

When Notebooks Are a "Disaster Area"

Problem: *The clutter in Sandy's notebook was incredible. He did not group the pages by subjects or keep his notes in chronological order. A Mixmaster must have mixed up those pages!*

The teacher might suggest:

READING AID 388

There's a positive correlation between the way students keep their notebooks and the grades they make. Will your notebook be a disaster area or a real help to you this year? Are its pages mixed up with a Mixmaster? Are they decorated with doodads, like hearts and arrows?

Notebook dividers with tabs for each subject will help you find what you're after faster. Your class notes should be dated in the upper corner, then kept in chronological order. Pages no longer used and just cluttering should be removed to make it easy to find what you want.

You may prefer, instead of one large notebook, colored folders with inside pockets, a separate folder for each of your subjects. You'll find these easier to carry around than a heavy notebook.

Your notebook is something you *live with—every school day!*

A little later Sandy cleaned out the clutter in his notebook in reading class. He carried out of the classroom a large wastebasket heaped high, pressed down, and running over with crumpled papers! Then he labeled a notebook section for each of his subjects and put the pages in chronological order. Now his notebook was "on his side" for more efficient learning.

Keeping a Record of Work Assigned

Problem: *Pam copied her assignments on any scrap of paper she could find. When the teacher gave special instructions, Pam did not always copy them. Sometimes she lost the scraps of paper.*

The teacher might suggest:

READING AID 389

SEE MASTER COPY PAGE 71

Top students make a careful record of work they have been assigned. You have a form headed "YOUR RECORD OF ASSIGNMENTS." You'll want to record what to do, the date due, and any special instructions. Now you'll be more likely to meet your deadlines—and to meet them well! Check off each assignment as you complete it, and you'll feel solid satisfaction. [A form for recording assignments appears on Master Copy Page 71.]

Encouraged by the teacher, students like Pam may want to set aside a special place to record assignments, perhaps a section of their looseleaf notebook, or to buy a small assignment notebook, and start to keep a careful record.

"How Can I Learn to Concentrate?

Problem: *Judy asked, "How can I learn to concentrate?" Many other students ask the same question. As Dr. Walter Pauk (1974, pp. 35–51) points out, the causes of poor concentration can be anything from poor diet to blue eyes!*

READING AID 390

Teachers will try to suggest those aids to concentration that seem appropriate for individual students. Some of the following insights might be shared with or elicited from the "right" students:

Students ask, "How can I learn to concentrate?" Your study schedule, psychologists observe, should help you concentrate. When you block off regular times for study, you become psychologically oriented to studying at those times. A quiet "study center" at home, equipped with everything you need, should also trigger concentration.

Sometimes a personal problem interferes with concentration. Our lives are seldom free from personal problems. When a problem is so serious that you cannot concentrate, talk it over with someone you trust, perhaps your counselor.

Can we hope to achieve unbroken concentration? Dr. Walter Pauk, widely known study expert, answers, "No." "Don't waste your energies," he advises, "trying to achieve continuous concentration. . . . Will-power alone can't make you concentrate. You will be breaking concentration whenever you say to yourself, 'I must use will-power to concentrate.' " Dr. Pauk suggests: "Rather . . . bring your attention back to the job in hand quickly every time your thoughts wander."*

Students report that setting time limits for certain study tasks definitely helps them concentrate and also resist distractions. The teacher might suggest for certain students:

READING AID 391

Suppose you have your English book open on the desk before you, and your thoughts are pulled to the game you're going to play in tomorrow or to a test you just "blew." You may be able to solve this problem with a "time box." [Blank "time box" forms appear on Master Copy Page 72.]

SEE MASTER COPY PAGE 72

TIME BOX

Your deadline for the task	60 minutes
Time you started	8:00 p.m.
Time you finished	8:45 p.m.
Actual time you spent	45 minutes

Students "beat the clock" with a time box.

FIGURE 9–6

You might set a deadline for finishing that English—perhaps sixty minutes. Then you concentrate all your powers to meet, or if it's humanly possible, to beat your deadline. With this pressure, you finish in forty-five minutes. You may have saved fifteen minutes of study time! Many people work best under pressure. As you try to "beat the clock," you're on the job every minute. With the clock ticking away toward the deadline, you don't dream your time away. But the deadline must be flexible. If you find you can't meet your first deadline, take a moment to set a new one.

The "time box" is for dreamers—to call back wandering thoughts. Use it with caution! If, in your haste, your work becomes careless, it can do more harm than good.

*This advice is offered students in Chapter 4, "The Ability to Concentrate," in Dr. Pauk's *How to Study in College*, 2nd ed. (Boston: Houghton Mifflin Co., 1974), pp. 43, 51. A number of other possible solutions to the problem of concentration are suggested in this chapter.

You may decide you want to spend *more* time on a task instead of less. And, obviously, the "time box" isn't suitable for certain types of assignments—it would be impossible, for example, to hurry difficult, controversial, and thought-provoking reading for social studies.

As we have noted, some students shy away from setting time limits. The "time box" is not for them. But others, those who are inclined to dream their time away, might, with their teacher's guidance, profitably use the "time box."

The reader is referred for many important insights on concentration to Chapter 4, "The Ability to Concentrate," in Walter Pauk, *How to Study in College,* 2nd ed. (Boston: Houghton Mifflin Co., 1974). Here Dr. Pauk discusses external distractors, among them noise, poor lighting, and lack of study equipment; internal distractors, among them disorganization, day-dreaming, and personal worries including anxiety about a school course; physical causes, among them inadequate diet, lack of sleep, and lack of exercise; and, last, so-called "mental fatigue," which Dr. Pauk believes is often caused by lack of interest. In this chapter Dr. Pauk suggests a diversity of possible solutions to the problem of concentration.

Students Need to Be Kept Going

Problem: *Students need all the encouragement they can get if they are to transform their study habits—the old habits are so persistent. Students need to be kept going!*

Students can be encouraged to get into the magnetic field of an immediate goal, then to enjoy the satisfaction of achievement. (Dudycha, 1957, pp. 100–101) Here a teacher suggests getting into the "field of force" of a promised reward.

READING AID 392

Psychologists suggest promising yourself a "high preference" reward when you achieve a goal you care about in study. You promise yourself a reward—something you prefer very highly—a rap session with a friend after an evening of solid study—a night off after you've finished a big paper. With long-term projects, you set stages and reward yourself whenever you complete an installment. When your energies are flagging, this reward helps keep you going. Your reward should not be distant and should be something really high among your preferences. (Robb, 1977)

Students in small how-to-study groups have sometimes set their goals together and decided on their "high-preference" rewards. The teacher sees that the rewards are not too distant. Rapport develops as the students talk about their goals and their hoped-for rewards—kayak trips, camping out, an evening developing photographs in the darkroom.

READING AID 393

Students should have realistic expectations—they should expect their progress to be gradual.

Many small steps can reach a goal! A sophomore last year was helter-skelter—he almost never got down to study. Then one day he decided to study in small "boxes" of time, trying at first to stick it out for just thirty minutes. He didn't try to go from *no* study to four hours of non-stop study. But gradually he concentrated longer and longer, and, in small steps, he studied his way to a good record.

If you're a human being, you will do some backsliding. Just go on from there with another step ahead. Many small steps make a giant step!

As we have mentioned, "success stories" of actual students help make study guidance ring true. Here are a teacher's remarks at the conclusion of how-to-study sessions held in September:

> Right now the school year is ahead for all of us. Good work this year can pay you well—in helping you make the record you want in high school, in helping you enter the college you want, perhaps in college scholarships.
>
> Keith didn't have a genius I.Q. He had always wanted to be a doctor. When I first knew him, he was a freshman with his high school years ahead—he could do what he liked with them. Toward the end of his senior year, he received a letter inviting him to the college he wanted—Yale. After that he went on to the medical school he wanted, Columbia. He plugged his way through eight years of college and earned his M.D. degree. Now he's ready to make the contribution he's dreamed of in medicine.
>
> Goals like that are within the reach of many of you here. Good study habits can make the difference!

Follow-Up, a "Big Deal"

READING AID 394

On the preceding pages we have mentioned drawing up activity schedules, cleaning out chaotic notebooks, making calendars for long-term projects, planning "high-preference" rewards, all in the presence of the teacher. Simply telling students how to study, teachers report, is likely to have little lasting effect. Guiding students as they *practice* promising procedures is more likely to bring a permanent change in habits. Teachers are likely to be disappointed with the results of a single how-to-study session or even two or three. But they can turn efficient study into a "big deal" through follow-up. Encouraging students to report on their progress helps to keep them going.

READING AID 395

At the close of several how-to-study sessions, a student asked, "Do you have a summary of all the study tips? I'd like one to take home." So the item, "A Summing Up," was prepared. You will find this item on Master Copy Page 73.

SEE MASTER COPY PAGE 73

Early in this chapter, we drew a distinction between *study habits* and *study skills* and explained that the present chapter is concerned with study habits. Perhaps it bears repeating that helping students develop *study skills* is another area of very great importance. For down-to-earth suggestions for developing study skills, the reader may wish to consult the references suggested in the introduction to this chapter.

Enlisting Parents in Encouraging Effective Study

Problem: *Many young people today need study guidance more urgently than young people did in the past. The homes of some do not favor quiet study. Can parents be enlisted in encouraging more effective study?*

READING AID 396

What do parents do when they feel concern about their son's or daughter's study? All that occurs to many is to ask the student, "Do you have homework? . . . Why don't you do it?" Many parents would like to do more than this. In one high school, the science and the foreign language departments wrote letters to parents explaining their expectations for outside study and sent these letters home, where they were signed by a parent, then returned to the school. (Bragstad, 1979) Individual teachers might prepare letters explaining their expectations and suggesting possible ways to help. When parents understand the

SEE MASTER COPY PAGES 74–75

school's expectations, some will do their best, even in a crowded home, to arrange a place of study apart and to encourage quiet. A "sample" letter to parents, one that might be sent home as school opens in the fall, requesting cooperation and suggesting possible ways to help, will be found on Master Copy Pages 74 and 75.

READING AID 397

Parent meetings to discuss the school's expectations for home study can be productive, especially as the school year opens. Guidance counselors and reading consultants might share with parents insights about motivating and facilitating study. Parents, in turn, might share with teachers, counselors, and with each other, ways they themselves have found successful. Closer ties should result when school and home thus communicate. Parents are often called in *after* students are in academic trouble. Perhaps meetings with parents can help *prevent* academic trouble!

Bibliography

Norman, Maxwell H., and Enid S. Norman. *How to Read and Study for Success in College.* New York: Holt, Rinehart and Winston, 1976.

Pauk, Walter. *How to Study in College.* Boston: Houghton Mifflin Co., 1974.

Preston, Ralph C., and Morton Botel. *How to Study.* Chicago: Science Research Associates, 1974.

Robinson, Francis P. *Effective Study,* 4th ed. New York: Harper and Row, 1970.

References

Armstrong, William H. *Study Is Hard Work.* New York: Harper and Brothers, 1956.

Bragstad, Berenice, reading consultant, La Follette Senior High School, in remarks to the writer, January 1979.

Dudycha, George J. *Learn More With Less Effort.* New York: Harper and Brothers, 1957.

Hozinsky, Murray, University of Chicago Laboratory School biology teacher, in remarks to the writer, January 1979.

Lakein, Alan, in an interview by John Poppy, "How to Find Time for What You Really Want to Do." *McCall's,* 99, no. 11 (1972).

Lakein, Alan. *How to Get Control of Your Time and Your Life.* Bergenfield, N.J.: New American Library, 1973.

Lakein, Alan, in an interview, "How to Use Your Time Wisely." *U. S. News and World Report,* 81, no. 3 (1976).

Norman, Maxwell H., and Enid S. Norman. *How to Read and Study for Success in College.* New York: Holt, Rinehart and Winston, 1976.

Pauk, Walter. *How to Study in College,* 2nd ed. Boston: Houghton Mifflin Co., 1974.

Preston, Ralph C., and Morton Botel. *How to Study.* Chicago: Science Research Associates, 1974.

Robb, Karen, Chairman of the Guidance Department, University of Chicago Laboratory School, in remarks to the writer, January 1977.

Roberts, Ursula, guidance counselor, University of Chicago Laboratory School, in remarks to the writer, May 1977.

Robinson, Francis P. *Effective Study,* 4th ed. New York: Harper and Row, 1970.

Strang, Ruth. Lecture to class in teaching secondary school reading, University of Chicago, Summer of 1965.

APPENDIX

Some Productive Greek and Latin Prefixes and Roots

In Chapters 2 and 3 we discussed our students' need to learn a strategy for breaking down words as an aid in arriving at their identities or meanings. A working knowledge of prefixes, roots, and suffixes is essential for students if they are to practice this strategy. A familiarity with frequently recurring word parts enables them to mentally separate the prefixes and suffixes and uncover the roots of words, then put the pieces back together as an aid in working out identities or meanings. Examples of this process will be found in Reading Aids 10, 12, 89, and 90.

The table that follows provides a list of some Greek and Latin prefixes and roots likely to be useful in reasoning out identities and meanings. For the convenience of the teacher they have been roughly assigned to five levels, increasing with respect to the difficulty both of the parts themselves and also of the derived words. Of course, a teacher should draw freely from anywhere on the list when the moment is right for teaching a certain word part.

A list of frequently recurring suffixes will be found just after this table.

Level I		
Latin Prefixes		
Prefix	Meaning	Derivatives
ad	toward, to	adjoining, adhere
ante	before	ante meridiem, antechamber
circum	around	circumnavigate, circumference
dis	opposite of, away	dissatisfied, disarm, dismiss, disperse
in	in, into, not	insert, ineligible
inter	between, among	interscholastic, intervene
mis	wrong(ly), incorrect(ly)	misspell, miscalculate
non	not	nonresident, nonpartisan, nondescript
post	after	postdate, postscript
pre	before	premeditated, preface
pro	in favor of, forward, in place of	pro-British, protrude, pronoun
re	again, back	recur, regress
sub	under	subcellar, subordinate
trans	across	transatlantic, transcontinental
Latin Roots		
aqua	water	aquaplane, aquarium
port	carry	portfolio, transport, portage
scrib, script	write	inscribe, scribble
spec(t)	look	inspect, spectator
vid, vis	see	video, vista, visible, vision
voc	call	vocal, vocation, convocation
Greek Prefixes and Roots		
anti	against	antitoxin, antiwar, anti-inflation
graph, gram	writing, record	telegram, autograph
micro	small	microscope, microbe
phone	sound	telephone, dictaphone
scope	sight	telescope, microscope
tele	far	television, telegram

Level II

*Number Prefixes**

Latin	Greek	Meaning	Derivatives
uni	mono	one	unicellular, monologue, monopoly
du(o)	bi	two	duplicate, bilingual, biped
tri	tri	three	triplicate, triumvirate
quad(ri)	tetra	four	quadruplets, tetrameter, tetrachloride
quin(que)	pent(a)	five	quintet, pentagon
sex	hex(a)	six	sextet, hexagon
sept	hept(a)	seven	septet, heptagon
octo	octa	eight	octave, octagon
non(a)		nine	nonagon
dec(im)	dec(a)	ten	decimal, decade
cent(i)	hect(o) hect(a)	one hundred	centipede, centennial, hectograph
mill(e) mill(i)	kilo	one thousand	millennium, kilometer
semi	hemi demi	half	semicircle, hemisphere demigod

Prefix Pairs

circum	peri	around	circumnavigate, perimeter
con, com, co	syn, sym	together, with	convention, cooperation, synchronize
lux, luc	photo	light	lucid, elucidate, photoelectric
magn(i)	mega	(very) large or great	magnate, megaphone
multi	poly	many	multimillionaire, polysyllabic, polygon
nov	neo	new	novice, neophyte
omni	pan	all	omniscient, Pan-American
prim	proto	first	primitive, prototype
super, ultra	hyper	over, above, beyond, excessive-(ly)	superfluous, ultrastylish, hypercritical

Latin Roots

Root	Meaning	Derivatives
aud, audit	hear, listen to	auditorium, audience, audition
cap	take, hold	captive, captivate
dic(t)	tell, speak	dictation, edict, dictator
fac	make, do	factory, manufacture, factotum
fid	faith, trust	fidelity, infidel
fract	break	fracture, infraction
mit(t), miss	send, sent	emit, remit, transmit, missive
ped, pod	foot	pedestrian, podium, tripod
rupt	break	interrupt, disrupt, eruption, rupture
spec, spic	look	spectator, conspicuous
ven, vent	come, coming	convention, intervene

*The lists of number prefixes and "prefix pairs" appear on pages 265 and 270 of Ward S. Miller, *Word Wealth Junior* (New York: Holt, Rinehart and Winston, 1962).

Greek Roots

auto	self	autobiography, automatic
bio	life	biology, biochemistry
geo	earth	geography, geology
hydr	water	hydroplane, dehydrate
meter, metr	measure	thermometer, symmetry
ology	study of	biology, psychology

Level III

Latin Prefixes

Prefix	Meaning	Derivatives
a, ab	away, from, away from	aversion, abnormal, abduct, abdicate
bene	well, good	beneficiary, benefactor
contra, counter	against, opposed to	contradict, counterspy
de	down from, away from, reverse the action	descend, deplane, decapitate, depopulate
ex	out, out of, away from, formerly	exclude, expel, ex-president

Latin Roots

Root	Meaning	Derivatives
acer, acr	sharp, bitter	acrid, acrimonious
amor	love	amorous, amour
carn	flesh	carnivorous, reincarnation, carnal
cogn	know	incognito, cognizance
cred	believe	credo, credulous, credible
crux, curc	cross	crux, cruciform, excruciating
duc, duct	lead	induce, conducive, abduction
fort	strong	fortress, fortitude, forte
frater, fratri	brother	fraternity, fratricide
gen	race, birth, kind	Genesis, congenital, genocide
man, manu	hand	manicure, manual
mute	change	transmute, immutable
nihil	nothing	annihilate, nihilist
pac	peace	pacifist, pacifier
pli, plic	fold	implicate, pliable, complicity
sequ, secut	follow	sequence, consecutive, consequence
sol	alone	solo, solitary
son	sound	unison, resonant, sonorous
viv	live	revive, vivacious

Greek Roots

cardi	heart	cardiac, pericardium
derm	skin	epidermis, dermatology
path	feeling, disease	antipathy, apathy, pathology
phil	love	Anglophile, philanthropist
phob	fear	claustrophobia
pseudo	false	pseudoscience, pseudonym
psych	mind	psychology, psychosomatic
theo	god	theology, theist, antheist
zo	animal	zoo, zoology

Level IV

Latin Prefixes

Prefix	Meaning	Derivatives
inter	between, among	interscholastic, interpose
intra	within	intrascholastic, introspection
mal	bad	malady, malignant
per	through	perforate, permeate, perceptive

Latin Roots

Root	Meaning	Derivatives
alter	other	alternate, alter ego, altruistic
ambul	walk	ambulatory, somnambulist
annu, enni	year	annals, millenium, perennial
corp, corpor	body	corporal, corpulent
culpa	blame	culprit, culpable
deus	god	deity, deify
equ	equal	equanimity, equable, equivocate
laud	praise	laud, laudable, laudatory
magn	great	magnify, magnate, magnitude
mort	death	mortal, post-mortem, mortuary
oner, onus	burden	onerous, onus
pater, patr	father	paternal, patrimony, patricide
plac, placa	please, appease	placate, implacable
string, strict	tighten	constrict, stringent, stricture
ten	hold	tenacious, tenets, tenable
tort	twist	distort, contort, extortion, tortuous
tract	draw, drag	tractor, tractable, extract
scien	know, knowledge	omniscient, science, prescient
terra	earth	terrain, terra firma, terrestrial
vert, vers	turn	divert, versatile, vertigo

Greek Roots

aster	star	astrology, asterisk
bibl	book	bibliography, bibliomania
caust, caut	burn	cauterize, caustic, holocaust
chrom	color	chromophotography, monochromatic
chron	time	chronological, synchronize
crat, cracy	power, rule	autocrat, democracy
dem	people	democracy, demagogue
gam	marriage	polygamy, bigamy, monogamy
miso, mis	hatred	misanthrope, misogamist, misogynist
nym	name	pseudonym, anonymous, acronym
ortho	straight, right, correct	orthodontist, orthodox, orthography
soph	wise	sophisticated, theosophy
tom	cut	appendectomy, epitome, microtome

Level V

Prefixes—Mostly Greek

Prefix	Meaning	Derivatives
a, an	not, without	asymmetrical, asocial, anarchy
ambi (Latin), amphi	both	ambidextrous, ambivalent, amphibious
dia	through	diagonal, diameter, diaphanous
dys	ill, bad	dysfunction, dyspepsia
epi	upon, above	epidermis, epitaph
eu	well, good	eulogy, euphonious, eugenics
hypo	under	hypodermic, hypoacidity
retro	backward	retrogress, retrorocket
se	away, apart	seclude, segregate, secede

Latin Roots

Root	Meaning	Derivatives
caput	head	captain, per capita, decapitate
flagr	flame, fire	conflagration, flagrant
flu, flux	flowing	influx, superfluous, confluence
greg	flock, herd	congregate, gregarious
gress	go	progress, egress, digress
jac, jec	throw	projectile, eject
junct	join	junction, conjunction, adjunct
locu, loqu	speak	circumlocution, solilquy, colloquial, loquacious, colloquy
nasc, nat	birth	nativity, renascence
pecc	fault	impeccable, peccadilloes
pend, pens	hang	dependent, pendant, impending
plen, plet	fill	replenish, plenary, deplete
preci	price	depreciate, deprecate
prim	first, early	primitive, primogeniture
pung, punct	point, prick	punctilious, pungent
quasi	as if, seemingly but not actually	quasi-official, quasi-intellectual
sanct	holy, sacred	sanctimonious, sacrosanct
sen	old	senior, senile
somn	sleep	somnolent, somniferous
tang, tact	touch	contact, tactile, tangible
verbum	word	verbal, verbose, verbiage

Greek Roots

Root	Meaning	Derivatives
anthropo	man	anthropology, anthropoid
arch	chief, ruler	patriarch, archenemy
crypt	secret, hidden	cryptic, cryptogram, cryptography
dox	belief	orthodox, heterodox
gyn	woman	gynecology, gynarchy
hetero	different	heterogeneous, heteronym
homo	same	homogeneous, homonym
lith	stone	monolith, neolithic
mega	great	megaphone, megalomania
morph	form	amorphous, anthropomorphic
peter, petri	rock	petrify, petrology
pyr	fire	pyre, pyromania
thana	death	"Thanatopsis," euthanasia

Some Frequently Recurring Suffixes

READING AID 399

A working knowledge of suffixes, too, is essential if students are to learn a strategy for breaking down words as an aid in arriving at their identities or meanings. Examples of this process will be found in Reading Aids 10, 11, and 89.

Dr. David L. Shepherd selected the following suffixes as especially useful to high school students. The list is reprinted from his *Comprehensive High School Reading Methods* (Columbus, Ohio: Charles E. Merrill Publishing Co., 1978, pp. 70–72), with the generous permission of the publisher.

Noun Suffixes	*Meanings*	*Example*
-ion	result of	fus*ion*
-sion	the act, quality, condition of result of	explo*sion*
-ation	the act of	form*ation*
-ity -ty	state or condition	dens*ity* plen*ty*
-ance	quality or state of being	disturb*ance*
-ence	quality or state of being	pres*ence*
-ment	result of or a means, agency, or instrument	govern*ment*
-ness	condition, state of being	good*ness*
-hood	condition, state of being	neighbor*hood*
-ship	condition, state of being or ability as in penmanship, friendship; or rank as in lordship	partner*ship*
-dom	rank of, position of, state of being one who has to do with; one of a size, capacity, value, date; resident of; agent	free*dom*
-or	state, quality, agent, doer	elect*or*
-ant	person or thing acting as agent	attend*ant*
-less	lacking or without	worth*less*
-most	the most	fore*most*
-able	able to, able to be	formid*able*

	Meanings	*Example*
-like	similar	life*like*
-ward	in the direction of	for*ward*
-itis	inflammation	appendic*itis*
-ize	to subject to, to render; to impregnate, treat, or combine with (chem); practice or carry on	minim*ize*
-fy	to make, to form into	solidi*fy*
-ate	combine, impregate, treat with (chem.)	agit*ate*

Adjective Suffixes

-able(-ible)	implication of capacity, fitness, worthiness to be acted upon; tending to, given to, favoring, causing, able to, liable to	service*able*
-ive	having the nature or quality of, given or tending to	excess*ive*

-al or -ial	belonging to, pertaining to, indicating the presence of the aldehyde group (-al, chem.)	natur*al* remed*ial*
-ful	full of, abounding in, characterized by; able to or tending to	master*ful*
-ish	of the nature of, belonging to;	mann*ish*
-less	without, destitute of, not having, free from; beyond the range of; unable or without power	self*less*
-ary	pertaining to, connected with; a person or thing belonging to or connected with; a place for	residu*ary*
-ous (-ious)	full of, abounding in, having, possessing the qualities of, like; denotes valence lower than that denoted by -ic (chem.); used to form adjectives corresponding to nouns of classification (biol.)	grac*ious*

Tips for Dividing Words into Syllables

As we noted in Chapter 2, many authorities question the value of spending long hours teaching rules for syllabication. As they see it, students can develop a working knowledge of syllable division in less formal ways. A few simple rules, however, if not overstressed, should be of value. Since some of the rules have numbers of exceptions and since students respond to the idea of being given helpful "tips," let us call them "tips" instead of rules.

As teachers help students break into parts words that come up in reading, the teachers will find it useful to have among their own resources a command of the rules for syllable division. Six of the most useful follow:

READING AID 400

Tip 1: Divide a compound word between the two words that make it up (and of course between any syllables within those words):

Examples: skate/board speed/boat wind/shield basket/ball

Tip 2: Prefixes and suffixes usually form separate syllables. These word parts are, in a way, units by themselves. They form separate syllables regardless of any other tips.

Examples: mis/spell dis/obey in/put im/pass/able

Tip 3: When two consonants stand together between two sounded vowels, you usually divide between the two consonants. For example, in the word *picnic,* the consonants *c* and *n* stand between the two sounded vowels *i* and *i,* so you divide between the *c* and the *n.* We can express it like this:

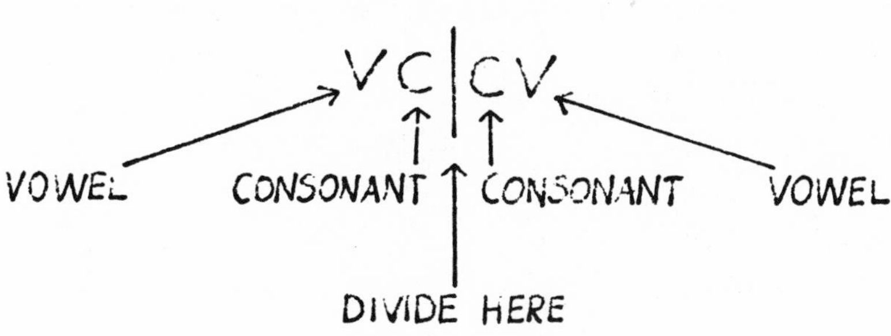

Examples: ten/nis kid/nap col/lide ad/ven/ture

Tip 4A: When only one consonant stands between two sounded vowels, you usually divide the word *before* the consonant. We can express it like this:

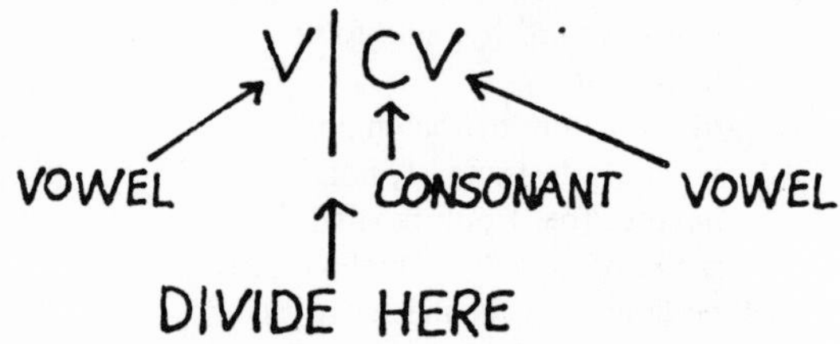

Examples: mo/tor pi/lot mu/sic va/ca/tion

Tip 4B: But there are some words in which one consonant stands between two sounded vowels that you will divide differently. If the word has three or more syllables or if the first syllable is accented, the consonant usually goes with the first syllable.

Examples: plan/et mag/ic pan/ic val/en/tine

Tip 5: Certain letter combinations are so close you can't separate them. *''Never separate the inseparables!''* Never split consonants or vowels that blend into just one sound when you pronounce them. Treat the ''inseparables'' as if they were a single letter.

Here are some examples of ''inseparables'':

1. *Consonant ''inseparables''* (blends) include *tr, pl, cl, st, gr, str, scr, thr,* and many others. The consonants in the word *trills* (*t, r, l,* and *s*) help to create blends. In order to spot blends, watch for these four consonants!

   Examples: de/**str**oy be/**tr**ay ex/**cl**aim

2. Vowel ''inseparables'' include *oi, oy, ou, ow, au, aw, eu,* and others.

   Examples: **poi**/son an/**nou**nce

   Exception: But two vowels may be divided if they are pronounced separately.

   Examples: gi/ant flu/ent

3. *Other ''inseparables''* include *ph, sh, ch, th, wh.*

   Examples: tro/**ph**y mis/**ch**ief a**th**/lete

Tip 6: When a word ends in a consonant and *-le,* the consonant usually goes with the final syllable.

Examples: pad/dle ri/fle bi/cy/cyle pin/ci/ple

An exception to this rule is the ''pickle words''—words that, like *pickle,* end in *ckle.* Here the letter *k* goes with the first syllable.

Examples: pick/le tick/le tack/le knuck/le

Master Copy Pages

TIC-TAC-TOE

Two students play tic-tac-toe, taking turns. Your teacher will give you several markers, either *Xs* or *Os*. You may place your marker on a space if you can do correctly the task written on the space. The first person to place three markers in a row—up, down, or across—is the winner!

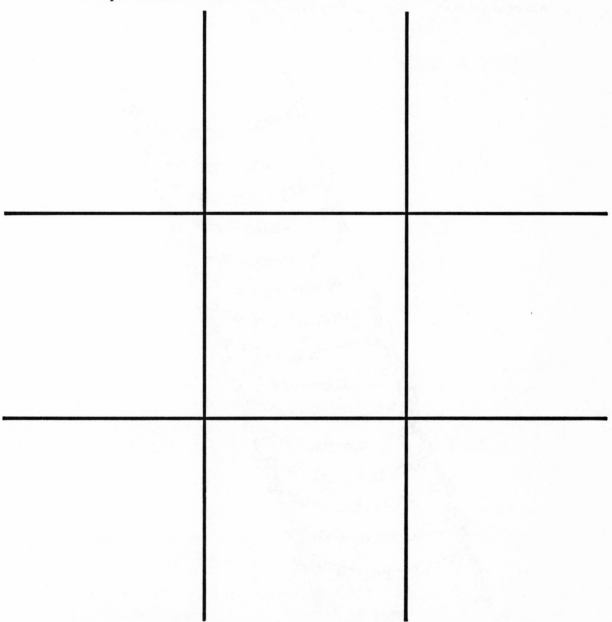

Note to the Teacher: Tasks appropriate for the students should be printed on the spaces of the grille, or the page can be placed in a plastic envelope and the tasks written on the plastic surface.

CLIMB THE WORD-LADDER!

Students climb rope "ladders" quickly in the school gym. Why not climb up word-ladders? You may climb to the next rung if you can do the task that's written on the space.

As you begin your climb, you will find the tasks fairly easy. They will grow harder as you climb to higher and higher rungs.

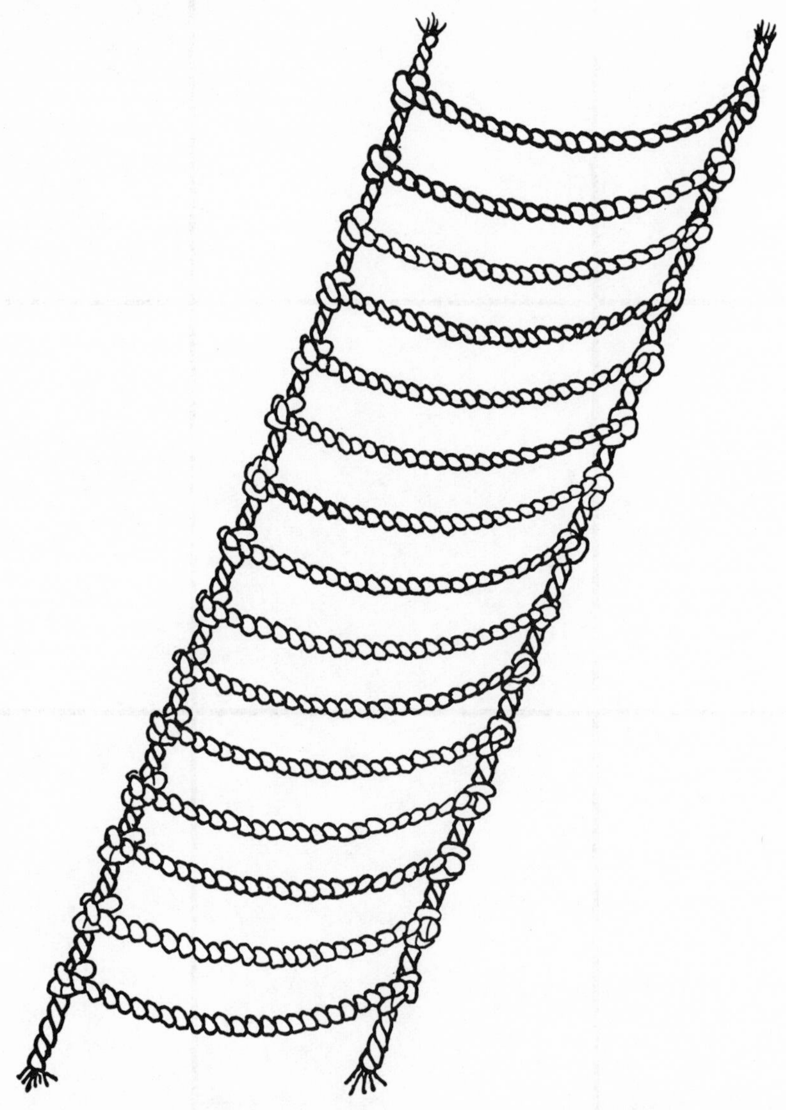

Note to the Teacher: Tasks appropriate for the student should be printed on the rungs of the ladder, or the page can be placed in a plastic envelope and the tasks written on the plastic surface.

NAME ______________________________ DATE ______________

serendipity paragon vociferous camaraderie respite perpetrate devotee poignant accolade

YOUR VOCABULARY SCORES *BEFORE* AND *AFTER*

This before-and-after vocabulary graph can give you solid evidence of progress. Obtain your score on the pretest by taking a try at writing the meanings of a few sample words from the coming vocabulary lesson. Of course, you are not expected to know the words on the pretest.

Then after you've studied the lesson, send your score *skyrocketing* on the final test! A row of good scores across the page will give you solid satisfaction!

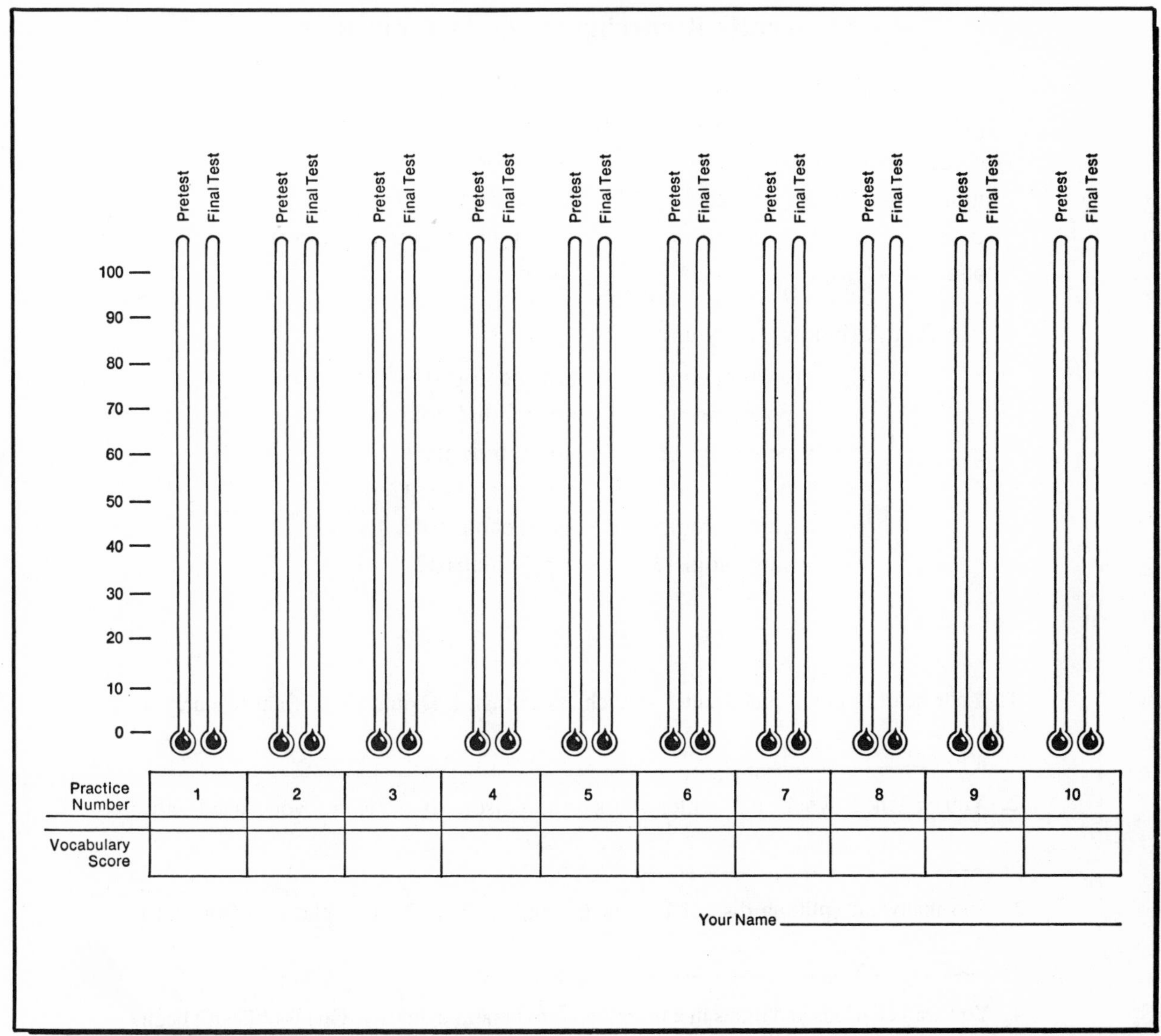

NAME ______________________________ DATE ____________

"DOCTOR UP" YOUR VOCABULARY!

Why not "doctor up" your vocabulary? You can do exactly that through this lesson.

The names of medical specialists are derived from Greek and Latin. Within their names, you'll find Greek and Latin word parts that appear in numbers of other English words. Learn the names of these specialists and, what's more important, the Greek and Latin roots, and you can unlock many other English derivatives. Now you have quick growth in vocabulary!

Do you need a doctor? Which one would you consult if you have the symptom, or special need, described in the exercise below? You'll find below a list of the useful Greek and Latin roots and also a list of the medical specialists:

Frequently Recurring Greek or Latin Root

derm	— skin	opt	— sight
path	— disease	pod (or ped)	— foot
cardi	— heart	tox	— poison
gyn	— woman	geras	— old age
psych	— mind	ortho	— right (meaning correct); straight
aud	— hear	neur	— nerve

In Part A (below), do you need:

an orthopedist?	a toxicologist?
a podiatrist?	an ophthalmologist?
a neurologist?	an audiologist?
a pathologist?	a dermatologist?
a gerontologist?	a gynecologist?
a cardiologist?	a psychiatrist?

Part A:

1. Your heart is going pitter-patter—much faster than it should! You want to hurry to a(n) ______________________.
2. You pitched your tent after dark—in poison ivy! Now you need a(n) ______________________.
3. Too many ear-splitting discos! Is your hearing impaired? Get a checkup from a(n) ______________________.
4. You walked miles and miles in a marathon—to benefit a charity. One foot hasn't been the same since! Better see a good ______________________.

5. You broke your leg while skiing—a compound break. You hope the bones will be aligned just "right." You want a highly skilled ______________________ to set it.
6. You're writing a major paper on the poisonous effects of pollutants poured into a river from a local chemical plant. You want to interview a(n) ______________________.
7. You hope to go to med school and specialize in the care of women. You want to talk this over with someone already in the field—a(n) ______________________.
8. You're looking for a specialist for a friend you care about—your friend is elderly. You want to find the right ______________________.
9. You studied your eyes out exam week. Now they've rebelled! You want a checkup from a(n) ______________________.
10. A friend has developed a facial twitch—you think it's caused by nerves. You suggest your friend's consulting a (n) ______________________.
11. You're studying disease prevention in your community. You plan to invite a(n) ______________________ from the Health Department to visit class.
12. A close friend of yours can't pull himself out of a deep depression. You know and recommend a capable and understanding ______________________.

Part B:

"Make a match!" Match the doctors and their medical specialties by drawing connecting lines between the two:

1. diseases	1. podiatrist
2. poisons	2. orthopedist
3. eyes	3. dermatologist
4. ears	4. neurologist
5. skin	5. gerontologist
6. women	6. pathologist
7. mind	7. cardiologist
8. heart	8. ophthalmologist
9. aging	9. toxicologist
10. nerves	10. audiologist
11. bones	11. psychiatrist
12. feet	12. gynecologist

Part C:

Now let's *prove* that you've "doctored up" your vocabulary. Using clues in the context together with your knowledge of the Greek and Latin parts, fill the blanks below.

1. Pam is in the grip of an extreme fear—*pathophobia*. What is she afraid of? ____________
2. The doctor moved toward the *audiometer*. What was he about to measure? ____________
3. A *neural* path is the path of one of your ____________.
4. He's a master physician! He attends to his patients' physical needs and to their *psyches*, too. What does *psyche* mean? ____________
5. Gloria Steinem has been described as *gynecocentric*. Around what do her interests center? ____________
6. Keep that liquid out of the hands of children! Remember its *toxicity!* What does *toxicity* mean? ____________
7. A person whose religious beliefs are *orthodox* holds beliefs officially approved in his or her church—beliefs regarded as ____________. (CLUE: What does *ortho* mean?)
8. The victim of *cardiac arrest* was rushed to the emergency ward. What had happened? ____________
9. A *monopode is a creature with* ____________.
   An *octopod* is a creature with ____________.
10. You are suddenly afflicted with *dermal* lesions. What is diseased or injured? ____________
11. The symphony conductor stepped up onto the *podium* [a small platform located under his ____________].
12. His paralysis was *psychogenic*. Where did it originate? ____________
13. Who's in command in a social organization that is a *gerontocracy?* ____________
14. Would an extreme advocate of women's lib like to live in a *gynarchy?* ____________

DID YOU NOTICE QUICK VOCABULARY GROWTH THROUGH THE GREEK AND LATIN PARTS IN THIS LESSON? YOU'LL FIND THAT YOU CAN USE YOUR NEW GREEK AND LATIN ROOTS TO UNLOCK OTHER UNKNOWN WORDS *BY THE HUNDREDS*.

THE "DIVIDED PAGE"

How can you speed up your learning? Use *the most powerful study technique known to psychologists*—the technique of self-recitation. In the question column to the left, record an important key term you want to master. Record the meaning in the column to the right. The dividing-line makes it possible to fold your answers underneath or cover them completely as you *recite to yourself and clinch your understandings*.

Important Term to Learn	Meaning of a New Term
	Test your understanding by covering this side or folding it underneath. Check and recheck until you have full mastery.

VOCABULARY SLIP

New Word ______________________

Pronunciation ______________________

Sentence in Which You Found It Used

____

____

Derivation (if helpful) ______________________

Meaning ______________________

Your Example of Its Use ______________________

____

VOCABULARY SLIP

New Word ______________________

Pronunciation ______________________

Sentence in Which You Found It Used

____

____

Derivation (if helpful) ______________________

Meaning ______________________

Your Example of Its Use ______________________

____

VOCABULARY SLIP

New Word ______________________

Pronunciation ______________________

Sentence in Which You Found It Used

____

____

Derivation (if helpful) ______________________

Meaning ______________________

Your Example of Its Use ______________________

____

VOCABULARY SLIP

New Word ______________________

Pronunciation ______________________

Sentence in Which You Found It Used

____

____

Derivation (if helpful) ______________________

Meaning ______________________

Your Example of Its Use ______________________

____

"COLLECT" WORDS
WITH THIS BOOKMARK!

Wide reading—and "collecting" new words—is one of the most effective ways to build your vocabulary. But you may not want to break your flow of thought when reading for enjoyment.

Just jot your new word below, together with its page location. Then work on the word later—whenever you want to.

IMPORTANT NEW WORD	PAGE LOCATION
1 ______________	____
2 ______________	____
3 ______________	____
4 ______________	____
5 ______________	____
6 ______________	____
7 ______________	____
8 ______________	____
9 ______________	____
10 ______________	____

"COLLECT" WORDS
WITH THIS BOOKMARK!

Wide reading—and "collecting' new words—is one of the most effective ways to build your vocabulary. But you may not want to break your flow of thought when reading for enjoyment.

Just jot your new word below, together with its page location. Then work on the word later—whenever you want to.

IMPORTANT NEW WORD	PAGE LOCATION
1 ______________	____
2 ______________	____
3 ______________	____
4 ______________	____
5 ______________	____
6 ______________	____
7 ______________	____
8 ______________	____
9 ______________	____
10 ______________	____

"COLLECT" WORDS
WITH THIS BOOKMARK!

Wide reading—and "collecting" new words—is one of the most effective ways to build your vocabulary. But you may not want to break your flow of thought when reading for enjoyment.

Just jot your new word below, together with its page location. Then work on the word later—whenever you want to.

IMPORTANT NEW WORD	PAGE LOCATION
1 ______________	____
2 ______________	____
3 ______________	____
4 ______________	____
5 ______________	____
6 ______________	____
7 ______________	____
8 ______________	____
9 ______________	____
10 ______________	____

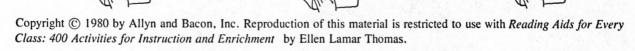

PARAGRAPH PATTERN 1—MAIN IDEA PLACED FIRST

To find the main idea, look for the *point the paragraph makes*—the message the writer wants most of all to drive home or leave with you. It is often a "Summing-up" idea, one that wraps up the content of the paragraph.

Take a good look at this paragraph pattern! You'll meet it—often! As you see, the main idea comes first. According to one authority's estimate, from 60 percent to 90 percent of the paragraphs you'll meet in informational writing are built like this!

The Main Idea is the point the paragraph makes →

(More general than the details that support it)

Your brain, your personal "super-computer," is an amazing organ. This extraordinary organ has more than ten billion nerve cells that serve you ceaselessly—whether you are awake or asleep. From your eyes, ears, nose, and skin, your brain receives a steady stream of messages that tell you what is going on in the world around you. Your brain is your "control center," sending out messages that control your life processes—including the beating of your heart. It stores the information of a lifetime—that is why you can learn, remember, and think. The total cost of duplicating all the brain's cells and connections—even at the ridiculously low cost of five cents per cell and one cent per connection—would come to more than a quintillion or a billion billion dollars! It is your billion billion dollar organ!*

Supporting Details:

- Ten billion cells serve you
- Your brain tells you about world
- It is your "Control Center"
- It stores information
- It is your billion billion dollar organ

*Most of the facts in the paragraph above are from the *World Book Encyclopedia* (Chicago: Field Enterprises Educational Corporation, 1978), p. 459. The estimate of the cost of duplicating the brain's cells and connections is from Gilbert Burck, *The Computer Age* (New York: Harper and Row, 1965), p. 127.

PARAGRAPH PATTERN 2—MAIN IDEA SENTENCE PLACED LAST

Here's the second most frequent paragraph pattern—main idea placed last. In this pattern, the last sentence sometimes expresses a general conclusion toward which a series of details has led. That makes sense! You have a line of argument or a chain of reasoning—then the point the writer hopes he or she has proved or driven home.

Details leading to and supporting the conclusion

You can use a razor to shave yourself or to slit a man's throat. Carbolic acid can sterilize—or kill. Under control, fire cooks for us and keeps us warm in winter; out of control, it burns our homes, sometimes our forests. Our cars take us places, but careless driving kills thousands each year. Atomic research has opened the way to the wiping out of cities, perhaps even of nations. It has also opened the way to medical research which may save the lives of millions otherwise doomed by such diseases as cancer. Newspapers, books, television, magazines, movies, radio—all these can inspire us to be good and noble, or they can give us false standards of living and even lead us into crime. *And so we see that there is no tool which cannot be used for either good or evil.**

Conclusion --------→

*Reprinted by permission of the publisher from Julia Florence Sherbourne: *Toward Reading Comprehension* (Lexington, Mass: D.C. Heath and Co., 1958), p. 91.

PARAGRAPH PATTERN 3—MAIN IDEA SENTENCE ANYWHERE IN BETWEEN

You'll find the main idea first in the paragraph, last in the paragraph, or *anywhere in between*. Any sentence that expresses the point or "message" of the paragraph, no matter where it's found, contains the main idea.

The main idea may be anywhere ----->

School dances, and especially that long-awaited night of nights, the Spring Prom, provide opportunity for relaxation and entertainment. Campaigns for positions of leadership in Student Government and for class offices can be diverting and a source of intense interest to students. *Surely the schools of today offer pleasure and interest as well as serious study and hard work.* What can be more exciting than a football game with an old rival on a crisp fall day? Even a lively class discussion on a favorite topic can enliven the atmosphere of a school day.*

*Joseph C. Gainsburg, *Advanced Skills in Reading*, Book 2 (New York: *The Macmillan Co. 1962), p. 33. Paragraph adapted.*

PARAGRAPH PATTERN 4—A "SPLIT" MAIN IDEA

Here the main idea is "split" between two sentences—part expressed in one sentence and part in another. To convey the main idea accurately, we must combine the two parts.

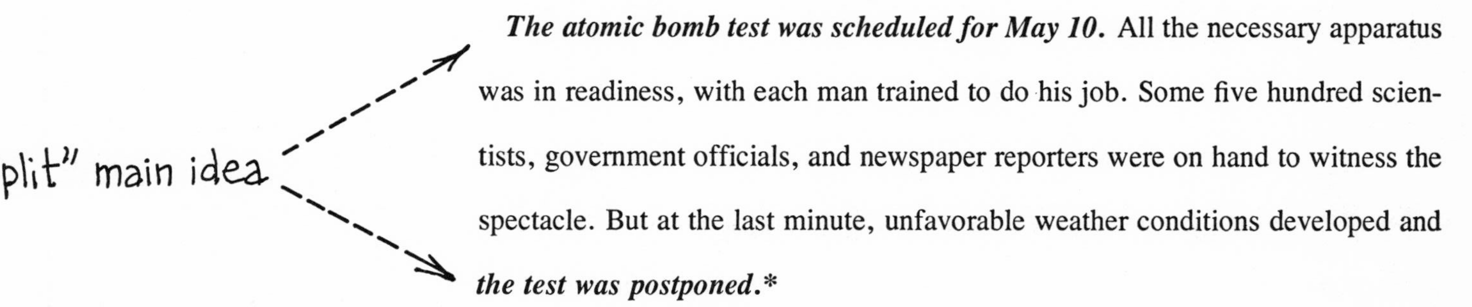

The atomic bomb test was scheduled for May 10. All the necessary apparatus was in readiness, with each man trained to do his job. Some five hundred scientists, government officials, and newspaper reporters were on hand to witness the spectacle. But at the last minute, unfavorable weather conditions developed and ***the test was postponed.****

At first glance, we might mistake the first sentence for the main idea sentence. But though the second sentence and the third support that idea, the last sentence definitely does not. That scheduled atomic bomb test didn't happen!

To convey the thought of the paragraph accurately, we must combine the first sentence and the last: "The atomic bomb test was scheduled for May 10, but it was postponed."

At times, then, we must combine sentences, or parts of sentences, to formulate the main idea of a paragraph.

* Doris Wilcox Gilbert, *Power and Speed in Reading,* © 1956, p. 35. Reprinted by permission of Prentice-Hall, Inc., Englewood Cliffs, New Jersey.

PARAGRAPH PATTERN 5—MAIN IDEA NOT STATED

Sometimes writers do not actually state the main idea in a paragraph. Then in order to find the main idea, you must reason it out for yourself.

Here every sentence supports a certain "unwritten" thought

But no one sentence stands out as the main idea sentence

The soil in this coastal area is not favorable to orange culture. It is largely glacial rubble with insufficient nutriment to support even the sturdiest seedlings. Fog and rain are with us at all seasons of the year, and there is little good, warm sunshine to ripen the fruit. Migrant workers are numerous, but they are used to digging for beets and know nothing of the care of citrus groves.*

Every sentence in the paragraph above is a detail—poor soil, unfavorable climate, untrained workers. All these details support an "unwritten" thought, which can be expressed something like this: "This coastal area, for several reasons, is not favorable for growing oranges."

* Doris Wilcox Gilbert, *Power and Speed in Reading,* © 1956, p. 35. Reprinted by permission of Prentice-Hall, Inc., Englewood Cliffs, New Jersey.

PARAGRAPH PATTERN 6—IS THE MAIN IDEA ALWAYS THE BROADEST IDEA?

A paragraph like the one below can be a real "fooler." Which sentence conveys the main idea of the paragraph—the first or the second? Take care!

Sentence one expresses the general idea that candidates use several methods of winning voters →

A candidate relying on the standard technique used by such office-seekers for influencing voters uses several methods. First, ***the candidate uses repeated affirmations to win votes.*** He says the same thing many times. He may make such a statement as "I shall serve you honestly and efficiently." But he does not explain how he will serve efficiently and he offers no evidence of his ability. He only repeats what he has said. He may, of course, use somewhat different words as he continues to make the same old affirmation. But all he really does is to say the same thing over and over again. . . .*

But the paragraph discusses only one of those methods →

Often it helps to ask: Which idea is *expanded* in the paragraph? Which has the *most said* about it? Which idea is developed by giving it the *most space?*

In the paragraph above, the first idea is stated, but it is not developed. It is the *second* idea—about the candidate's repeated use of affirmations—that is supported in the paragraph. (Note: In a paragraph like the one above, the first sentence may be introducing a longer selection in which a series of paragraphs will deal with several methods of influencing voters.)

* Reprinted by permission of the publisher from Julia Florence Sherbourne: *Toward Reading Comprehension* (Lexington, Mass.: D. C. Heath and Co., 1958), p. 108. Slightly adapted.

PARAGRAPH PATTERN 7—A SEEMING CONTRADICTION

Sometimes ideas expressed in a paragraph may seem to be contradictory. In that case we will need to ask: Which idea is the writer *really advocating?*

The reader loses out completely if he or she does not realize which idea is the "message" of the paragraph.

It is essential, for example, in the paragraph below to realize which the author is doing—belittling the super-importance of money, or calling its importance to our attention.

First, the writer expresses an idea which may seem contradictory to the rest →

But the idea she expands is this one →

All the details support the idea that money is important

Certainly money should not be your chief aim in life. ***But you ought not to despise it, for it can help you and your family obtain many of the good things of life.*** It can buy an adequate diet, one of the bases of good health. When necessary, it can provide medicine and medical care. It can be the means for a comfortable house, for travel, for good books, and for hobbies and recreation. It can make it easier for your children to secure an education. Finally, it can offer a great opportunity for you to help others.*

so this is the main idea

* Reprinted by permission of the publisher from Julia Florence Sherbourne: *Toward Reading Comprehension* (Lexington, Mass.: D. C. Heath and Co., 1958), p. 77.

PARAGRAPH PATTERN 8—MAIN IDEA CLARIFIED BY AN ANECDOTE

One method of developing a paragraph is by telling an anecdote or little story. The story is told solely for the purpose of clarifying the main idea.

In the following paragraph, the author tells the story of the "trial" of a prisoner in India. The story is interesting and catches our attention. But the story is included only to make clear the main idea, that *fear stops the flow of the digestive juices*. The idea about the effect of fear on our digestive processes, not the story of the prisoner, is the "message" of the paragraph.

The reader who understands how such a paragraph is built grasps its meaning more quickly. Once that reader has grasped the main idea, he or she can increase speed of reading on the anecdote.

Here is the main idea sentence ——————→ ***Fear, like anger, stops the flow of the digestive juices.*** In India a test was once used to tell whether or not a prisoner was guilty of a crime. The man was given a handful of dry rice to put in his mouth. He was told to keep the rice in his mouth a few minutes. If the prisoner had committed a crime and was very much frightened, his saliva would stop flowing and the rice would remain dry. If he was not guilty and had no fear of being punished, his saliva would flow as usual, and the rice would be wet.*

The anecdote is just to clarify the main idea

* Ruth Strang, *Study Type of Reading Exercises* (New York: Bureau of Publications, Teachers College, Columbia University, 1951), p. 39. Adapted from W. W. Charters, Dean F. Smiley, and Ruth M. Strang, *Health Problems* (New York: Macmillan Publishing Co.), pp. 22–23. Copyright 1935, renewed 1963 by Jessie Aileen House, Ruth M. Strang, and Dean Franklin Smiley.

MASTER COPY PAGE 18

PARAGRAPH PATTERN 9—MAIN IDEA SUPPORTED BY AN EXAMPLE

Sometimes the author makes the main idea clear by illustrating it with one or more examples. Then there's a DANGER! We can easily confuse the example with the main point! This may happen because the example is more interest-catching than the main point and therefore attracts our attention.

In the paragraph below, the canoe example is ''spectacular'' and catches attention, but it is *not* the main idea. It is intended only to illustrate the point that in a small Ohio town years ago the people made many of the things they wanted.

Skillful readers are careful to differentiate between the author's main points and the supporting examples.

This main idea, of course, is the important thing --->

Back in my old hometown, London, Ohio, at least part of our culture was homemade. If you wanted a thing, you did not always save up your money to buy it. Sometimes you made it. Our canoe, for example. Chubby Burnham, Dewey Culp, and I wanted a canoe to navigate the shallow waters of Deer Creek, three miles east of town. None of us had ever seen a canoe. We didn't even have a handbook. But build one we did—a strange craft of oak and barrel-hoops and painted canvas. But she floated. Indeed, for more than twenty years she was hauled out of one barn or another to serve the seagoing impulses of small boys who came after us.*

The canoe story is just a supporting example

* From *Who Owns America* by Herbert Agar and Alan Tate. Copyright © renewed 1964 by Herbert Agar and Isabella Gardner Tate. Used by permission of Houghton Mifflin Company.

PARAGRAPH PATTERN 10—MAIN IDEA IN JUST PART OF A SENTENCE

Often the main idea is expressed in just *part* of a sentence. In the paragraph below, the first sentence contains two ideas. But *only one* of these ideas is supported by the details in the paragraph. Which *part* of the first sentence, then, do you select as containing the main idea?

Earthquakes are sometimes so mild that one may hardly be aware of them, but some earthquakes create terrible disasters. The violent heaving of the ground may shatter thousands of homes into crumbling ruins. A river may be jolted out of its course, and its rushing waters flood the land. An entire city may be destroyed and all its inhabitants killed. One earthquake in Chile caused enormous waves that raced all the way across the Pacific Ocean and drowned thousands of people in several coastal towns of Japan.

As you noticed, the first sentence contains these two ideas: 1) that some earthquakes are mild; and 2) that other earthquakes are terrible disasters. The rest of the paragraph presents examples of catastrophes. The main idea of the paragraph, then, appears in the *second part* of the first sentence.*

* Joseph C. Gainsburg, *Advanced Skills in Reading,* Book 2 (New York: The Macmillan Co., 1962), p. 22. The writer expresses appreciation for permission to print this paragraph as well as for ideas in the explanation.

CAN YOU SPOT THE MAIN IDEA IN PARAGRAPHS?

Some textbook chapters contain more than 400 facts and ideas! Struggling to retain all these would be hopeless! The first step in retention is to be able to *select what's important* to remember.

The dozen tips below should help you pull out the main ideas of paragraphs:

1. The main idea is the most important idea—the central thought—that the paragraph expresses.
2. All the other sentences support or explain this central thought.
3. The main idea is always *more general, broader,* and *covers more* than the details that support it.
4. It is usually (but not always) the broadest idea in the paragraph.
5. It is often a ''summing-up'' idea, one that wraps up the content of the paragraph.
6. Often it is *the point the paragraph makes*—the message the writer wants most of all to drive home and leave with you.
7. It is sometimes the *point proved* by the details or the examples in the paragraph.
8. It is sometimes a conclusion toward which the line of thought or argument in the paragraph has led. In this case, it is often found in the last sentence.
9. Do not mistake for the main idea an idea that is too narrow—that does not really cover the content of the paragraph.
10. *Where* is the main idea? Most often it is in the first sentence of the paragraph—second most often, in the last sentence.
11. But it may be *anywhere* in the paragraph—in any sentence, in two sentences combined, in just part of a sentence, or in parts of two sentences. Or it may not be stated at all.
12. When the main idea is not stated, what can you do to find it? You can examine the details and infer, or reason out, the main idea for yourself.

SIGNAL WORDS OFTEN SIGNAL IMPORTANT DETAILS

Writers often use signal words in paragraphs. If you are alert to these, they will often help you spot important details.

"Full Signals"

"Full signals" in paragraphs flag you! You can hardly miss them! They announce, "Here comes the next detail!"

These "full signals" are quite obvious:

(1)
(2)
(3)
(a)
(b)
(c)

These "full signals" stand out, too:

"First"
"Second"
"Third"
"In the first place"
"In the second place"
"In the third place"
"Finally"
"The last step"

"Half Signals"

"Half signals" in paragraphs are less obvious. They stand out perhaps half as well. They often announce, "Here comes another subpoint." Here are some very common "half-signals":

"In addition"
"Another"
"Then"

"Next"
"Too"
"Furthermore"
"Moreover"
"Besides"

"Half signals" also include:

"One"
"Another"
"Still another"

These "half signals" announce, "Here comes an example":

"For instance"
"For example"

If a paragraph gives events in a time sequence (as is often the case in your social studies textbooks), these may be "half signals":

"Immediately after that"
"Soon"
"Next"
"After a short while"
"Later"
"After that"
"Then"
"At last"

Different degrees of the adjective may be "half signals":

"A common cause of war"
"A more common cause of war"
"The most common cause of war"
"A good ____"
"A better ____"
"The best ____"

"A bad ____"
"A worse ____"
"The worst ____"

HOW TO STREAMLINE YOUR STUDY

TAKE YOUR CHOICE OF TEN STRATEGIES

At the nation's top universities, college students learn to streamline their study. Their grade point averages go up when they use strategies like these.

Are there study strategies to help you complete difficult textbook assignments smoothly and efficiently? To enable you to remember what you learn more easily and longer? To eliminate some of your concern over tests and exams? To help you do assignments well—in less time?

Psychologists Have Discovered "Power Tools"

For many years psychologists have been experimenting to find out how students learn most easily. They have discovered powerful techniques for study and have found ways to fix material firmly into the memory.

What about intelligence? You may be thinking, "Intelligence is inborn—school achievement depends on that." High achievement depends a good deal upon intelligence. But in your classes some students with extraordinary ability achieve little. Others with less ability achieve highly. What makes the difference? Often it's knowing how to study. After all, teachers don't grade a student's intellect but the quality of work that student does. It's important to make the most of capabilities.* The psychologists' findings can help you do this.

The Most Powerful Study Techniques Known

You will find on the coming pages ten strategies for studying a textbook chapter—the most powerful techniques known for learning and retention. They should prove especially useful to you when you go on to college. There the assignment you get most frequently will probably be to read a textbook chapter and to master its contents thoroughly. Although the strategies are tailored here to science and social studies, their usefulness extends *far* beyond these courses. You can put them to work in reading any informational material—textbooks in other courses, documents in social studies, newspapers and magazines, non-fiction books—with *more learned and more remembered.*

What the Ten Strategies Can Do for You

Just reading about how to study probably won't be very productive. But if you put the procedures into practice, these results may follow:

*Ralph C. Preston and Morton Botel, *How to Study*, 3rd ed. (Chicago: Science Research Associates, 1974), pp. 2–3.

1. You'll know how to get the *greatest possible amount of learning and retention* from whatever amount of time you spend in study.*
2. If you practice and perfect the strategies, your hardest courses, those that demand thorough mastery of reading content, should be easier—now and in the future.
3. As studying becomes a smoother operation, you should find that it involves less strain and less frustration even when you are faced with difficult assignments.
4. What about grades? Grades depend on many factors, some of which you cannot control. But more efficient study usually results in more active participation in class and better performance on tests and examinations. Higher grades usually follow.†

"Is There Just One Correct Way?"

"Are you bothered by the mention of techniques for study?" a study expert asks. "Do you think you should be left to study in your own way? To be sure, there are individual styles of studying, just as there are individual styles of swimming, writing letters, and almost everything else. We encourage you to *develop your own style.* Research shows, however, that successful students agree about the importance of certain basic skills."** It is these that this booklet shares.

Choose the Strategies That Meet Your Needs

Of course, you will not need every one of these strategies with every assignment. Just "pull one out" whenever you need it. When you face a rigorous chapter, use as many as you choose in order to grapple with and grasp its content. Use them flexibly, vary them, adjust them to your needs and preferences. You may already have strategies of your own that are highly effective. We hope you'll share these with your classmates.

> *Suppose it's seven-thirty tonight. You've watched the news, had dinner, and now you've opened your textbook—you have a chapter to study for tomorrow. How can you pin down that chapter and make what's important yours—to stay? Turn now to the first strategy.*

*Thomas F. Staton, *How to Study,* 6th ed. (Montgomery, Ala: 1968), p. 13.

†Preston and Botel, *How to Study,* p. 2.

**Slightly adapted from Preston and Botel, *How to Study,* p. 2.

STRATEGY 1: OVERVIEW—TO SAVE TIME

You can get the gist of an informational chapter or article in just minutes.

President Kennedy's Speed Secret

President Kennedy sometimes read three books a day while carrying out his presidential duties! He explained that at these speeds he was doing overview skimming—hitting the high spots. He knew *where the strategic spots of informational writing were located,* those that would yield the general content, and he turned this knowledge into speed. President Kennedy followed his rapid survey with a more careful reading when this was appropriate.

Once you've learned, as he did, to get the gist very quickly, you'll want to *overview* almost everything you read—chapters assigned in textbooks, newspaper and magazine articles—everything but fiction. Of course, with textbook chapters, you'll *follow your overview with a careful reading*. Now let's turn to that chapter you're assigned for tomorrow.

Why Not Just Plunge In?

If you had to cross a stretch of rugged and unexplored territory you would never plunge in blindly if you could have in advance an accurate map of the region. When you plunge into a difficult chapter and "just read," you're trying to work your way through rugged territory without a map!

Learn where you're going—first! *Overview the chapter before you read it thoroughly*. Turn through the pages to find out what the chapter's all about and where it's going. Now you have your "mental map" of the chapter.

How To Make a "Smart Start"

Hit the high spots, as President Kennedy did, of well-organized informational writing. Make this your "smart start" in studying a chapter.

- *Examine the chapter title*. It offers an instant clue to the chapter's contents. Speculate as you read it about just what the chapter will offer.
- Now *zero in on the introductory paragraph(s)* to see if you can get the gist of the chapter. Here the authors usually "announce" what the chapter will contain, sometimes raise exciting questions to be explored, conveniently brief you on what lies ahead. (See Figure 1.)

The Immigrant Experience

CHAPTER 1

It has often been said that the only native American is the Indian. Certainly it is true that the Indian has been native to America for a longer period of time than any other people. But even the Indian was an immigrant.

Some time in the far off past the people whom we have called Indians came from Asia across the Bering Strait to what is now America. In those dim and far-off days, ice sheets and land joined the continents of Asia and America. Those early people must have suffered great hardships as they searched for food to eat and a place to live. By 8000 B.C. Indians were living in many places of what is now called North and South America. Today, almost 10,000 years later, people are still coming to live in America. Why do they come? What do they find when they get here? How have they shaped the history of America?

FIGURE 1. ***Chapter introductions "clue you in" on what lies ahead. (Text material from Gerald Leinwand,* The Pageant of American History. *Boston: Allyn and Bacon, 1975, p. 2.)***

- *"Hit the headings!"* These announce or suggest the content of each section of the chapter. You'll find within each chapter perhaps from two to five *super*-headings—often in large print and set off by white space. These signal the *major thought divisions* of the chapter. Within these sections you'll probably find a number of *smaller* headings. These signal *subtopics* within the big chapter divisions. As you examine the headings, ask yourself, "What aspects of the general subject will this chapter zero in on?" (See Figure 2.)

variety of living things

2–7
classifying living things

Biologists estimate that there are about two million kinds of organisms alive today on planet earth. And new kinds are constantly being discovered.

Living things include monerans, protists, plants, and animals ranging from tiny invisible organisms to redwood trees and giant whales.

2–8
early classification systems

The Greek philosopher and biologist Aristotle, who lived about 350 B.C., knew of only a few hundred kinds of animals and plants. Yet

FIGURE 2. ***"Hit the headings." These announce the content of each coming section. (Text material from* Biological Science: Molecules to Man, The Biological Science Curriculum Study (BSCS) *Blue Version, 3rd ed. Copyright © 1973 by Houghton Mifflin Co. Reprinted by permission.***

You may find that you've neatly discovered the authors' hidden outline—that the *big chapter division* headings and the *subheadings*, dropping into slots under these, *fall right into an outline*. Of course, finding the hidden outline makes the chapter easier to grasp. Now you have your "map" of the conspicuous features of the territory.

- You may want to *skim some of the columns and paragraphs*. Where within a paragraph will you look for key ideas? Examine the *first* and, less frequently, the *last* sentences. Beginnings and endings are strategic spots in informational writing. As you know, topic sentences are often (but not always) located in these "high spots."
- *"Official" terms will flag you*—they're usually printed in a dark type called *boldface* or in slanting *italics*. A glance at these terms will give you more clues to important content.
- *Look over the graphic aids*—photos, diagrams, graphs, and charts. Each one is saying, "This is clearing up something important!"
- *Read the chapter summary*. What do you think authors do in their conclusions? It's their last chance with you, their reader! So they often wrap up important content—review the major concepts and principles explored—drive home what they want most of all to leave with the reader! By reading the summary *first*, you'll learn important content to look for when you do your thorough reading. (See Figure 3.)

SUMMARY

The war was won by the Americans but the revolutionary principles for which it was fought still had to be put into practice. This was the great unfinished business of 1783. It remains the great unfinished business to this day. Much of the rest of the book is a review of how the nation tried to put into practice the ideals for which it fought.

FIGURE 3. *The chapter summary wraps up important content. (Text material from Gerald Leinwand,* **The Pageant of American History.** *Boston: Allyn and Bacon, 1975, p. 71.)*

- The authors often "giftwrap" something for you. It's a *package of chapter-end questions*. Here you have a giveaway of content the authors themselves consider crucial. Examine these questions, if you like, for clues to what to look for when you go back and really read the chapter.

- *You'll find exceptions.* We've talked about hitting the high spots of well-organized writing. Unfortunately, writing is not always well-organized. Introductions may fail to announce the content clearly, and conclusions may fail to wrap it all up. And in well-organized writing, topic sentences aren't always first or last—or even present at all—in paragraphs. So you'll often need to overview *flexibly,* running your eyes over the pages, following one promising lead after another.
- *As you overview, ask yourself, "What do I already know about this?"* Summon up your background information, your own ideas and experiences on the subject. You'll grasp new learnings better if they click with something you already know. Ask yourself, "How does this chapter link up with what I've been studying?"
- *Jot down questions.* Ask yourself as you overview, "Just what can I expect from this chapter?" "What should I look for when I go back and read it more carefully?" Jot down questions you'll want to answer when you read the chapter thoroughly. You might use slips from a memo pad and place them between the related pages or, if you own the book, jot your questions in the margin.

You'll Have a Speed Technique

Busy corporation executives enrolled in speed-reading courses learn to overview, to work through the load of reading matter on their desks. They're advised: "*Overview everything you read* before you read it thoroughly. Overview reports, correspondence, articles, news items, your weekly news magazine, chapters in informational books. Often, all you want from the item can be gleaned from this preview. And when thorough reading is called for, you'll do it *better and faster* because you've previewed."

When you overview a chapter, you're *looking where you're going!* You're walking down the street *looking ahead* versus walking head down, with your eyes glued on the sidewalk below. Which way do you think you'll reach your destination?

It Takes Longer to Tell About It than to Do It!

Let's quickly sum up how to do it:

1. Focus on the title.
2. Zero in on the introduction.
3. "Hit the headings."
4. Skim the columns, if you like.
5. Glance at the graphic aids.
6. Read the chapter summary.
7. Look through the authors' questions.
8. Ask, "What do I already know?"
9. Ask, "How does this chapter fit in?"
10. Make jottings of questions.

You'll perfect this strategy through practice. Give it a dozen or so trials! Later it should become a fast and smooth operation.

Why Overview?

- *You've taken the chill off the reading.* You've grasped the authors' organization. And you've already caught the drift of the chapter.
- *Main points should stand out better.* If with no advance survey you just plunge in and plod on through, you may find yourself lost among details—you may have missed out on main points completely.
- *Details should now fall into place in relation to the whole.* You'll retain them *more easily and longer*.
- *Now you should concentrate better.* You'll be more alert since you'll know what to look for.
- *You'll build up momentum, then read the chapter faster.* Remember those corporation executives whose time was so important? They overviewed to *save* time!

STRATEGY 2: GO IN WITH A QUESTION!

After you have your "mental map" of the chapter through your overview, how would you master the chapter? We've mentioned the subsections of a textbook chapter. Each subsection, marked off with a boldface or italic sideheading, should be a "bite" the right size for you to digest. Work through the chapter, then, one headed subsection after another.

Questions Will Help You "Overwhelm" the Most Difficult Chapter

What, perhaps more than anything else, will help you grasp difficult reading? Approaching that reading with questions in mind!

More than one thousand college students took part in an experiment. Those who approached their reading with questions showed *decided* gains in comprehension.* In another experiment, students who approached their reading with questions showed better *immediate retention* on tests taken just after reading—and better *long-term retention* on tests taken later.†

Turn Headings into Questions

In the boldface or italic headings that start each section, the authors are shouting, "We're giving you these headings as clues to key ideas. Shift them into questions, and you'll be guided to the key ideas!"

Suppose a section in science has the heading, *Early Classification Systems.* Quickly shift it into the question, "*What were* the early systems of classifying living things?" You might jot down your question as the student did in Figure 4. The margin is a convenient place if you own the book, or you might use a sheet from a memo pad and place it between the related pages.

What were the early classification systems?

2–8
early classification systems

The Greek philosopher and biologist Aristotle, who lived about 350 B.C., knew of only a few hundred kinds of animals and plants. Yet he faced the same problems of classification that biologists do today—whether to emphasize the common characteristics of a group or to

FIGURE 4. ***Approaching your reading with questions in mind should help you "crack" the most difficult chapter. (Text material from* Biological Science: Molecules to Man, *The Biological Science Curriculum Study (BSCS) Blue Version, 3rd ed. Copyright © 1973 by Houghton Mifflin Co. Reprinted by permission.***

*John N. Washburne, "The Use of Questions in Social Science Material," *Journal of Educational Psychology*, 20 (May 1929): 321–359.

†Eleanor Holmes, "Reading Guided by Questions Versus Careful Reading and Rereading Without Questions," *School Review*, 39 (May 1931): 361–371.

Suppose you find this heading in science, *Some Organisms Are Difficult to Classify*. Recast it quickly: "*Why* are some organisms difficult to classify?"

What If Headings Are Too General?

Some headings are so general they leave you guessing about the content—this one, for example: *The Growth of Giant Corporations*. You might formulate this question: "What important points are made here about the growth of giant corporations?" Or you might skim the passage while asking yourself: "If I were the teacher making out test questions on this passage, what would I ask the class?" You might decide on these test questions: "What caused the giant corporations to grow?" and "What opposition developed?"

Discover "Hidden Questions"

You'll sometimes discover hidden questions in the topic sentences of paragraphs. You'll find one quickly here: "Few wars have been more unpopular than the war in Vietnam." Rephrase it quickly: "*Why* was the war in Vietnam so immensely unpopular?"

Be a Human Question Mark!

As you're reading, you'll want to add questions and adjust your questions. Above all, you'll want to ask your own *below-the-surface,* deeply *thoughtful* questions. As you read about starvation in the world, for example, this question might come to your mind: "*Why,* in spite of the amazing increase in technology and the Green Revolution, are half the world's people still undernourished or hungry?"

Won't I Miss Something Important?

You may be thinking, "If I read just to answer questions, won't I overlook important content?" Take care not to skim for bits and pieces of information and bypass the rest. Read to find the answers to your questions *and other important content.*

Mark Your Book or Make Jottings

Mark key ideas and any important subpoints. Or make brief notes, perhaps in the margin your textbook provides. Again, if the book is not yours to mark, you might use slips from a memo pad and insert these between the related pages.

When Will Questions Help You Most?

The question strategy should prove extremely helpful when you're confronted with passages that do not interest you and passages that are especially difficult. You may find yourself reading effectively *without* this conscious questioning. In that case, *just pick out the key ideas from the supporting material.*

Why Approach Reading with Questions?

- *Try it when the going's rough.* A passage that would have been a "stopper" for you may be easy to grasp when approached with a question.
- *Try it if you can't sort out what's important.* Since the authors announce their big thought divisions in their italic or boldface headings, questions formulated from these should help you *cut through* what's less important *to main points.*
- *Try it if you want to retain the content.* Remember that experiment in which college students approached this reading with questions? They retained more on tests taken right away and later.
- *A crystal ball?* As you perfect the questioning strategy, you'll find yourself predicting some of the questions your instructors will ask on tests and exams.
- *Try it if you want a powerful tool for independent learning.* As you develop skill in formulating your own questions, you'll become less dependent on teacher-given questions and gain a lifetime tool for independent learning.

Gradually your use of the question strategy should become almost automatic. You'll sharpen this strategy with practice.

STRATEGY 3: DO "STOP-AND-GO" READING

In recent years, claims for speed reading courses have been in the national spotlight. In demonstrations advertising these courses, graduates give the impression that it's possible to read an informational book straight through without stopping, then give a brilliant recital of its contents. Top scholars would disagree, maintaining, "Certainly not true in my subject!"

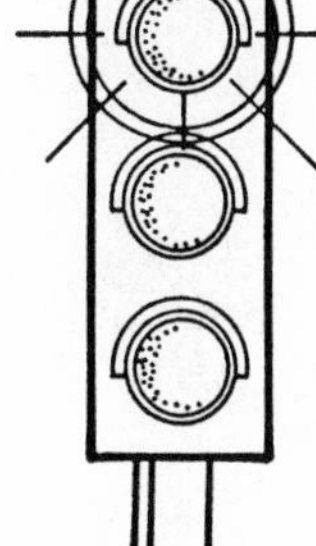

When the passage is easy and retention of details is not your purpose, a reading-straight-through pattern may be appropriate. Not often so in textbooks! There highly skilled readers do "stop-and-go" reading. Part of the time they read standing still! *Thought time* is added to reading time!

"I'll Go Over It Again"

Stop to "play back" what you've just read—that is, *self-recite* and test your learning. Successful students say, "I didn't get that—I'll go over it again." A passage that blocked you at first may come completely clear with rereadings.

Throw Pictures on a Screen in Your Mind

Textbooks, especially in science, call for stops to form an "eye picture" of what you are reading. As you read about the parts of a cell, for example, look away and *see* in your mind's eye that thin outer membrane, the grainy cytoplasm, the tiny nucleus, the clear vacuole. You might make a quick sketch of that cell and label those parts. Making your own sketch helps you really *see*—brings hazy relationships into sharp focus.

Stop to Reflect!

Do you ask as you're reading, "What is the basic *why* of this?" "What can I conclude in view of this?" "How can I apply this?" Do you sometimes ask, "How do the authors have a right to say this?" Perhaps they have no right! All of us fall short—authors are no exception. Bring your arguments with the authors to class. Some authors, in their preface, invite the suggestions of students—even supply an address to write to. If you have a good suggestion, by all means write the authors. *Applaud* the authors, too. Authors of reputable textbooks usually support what they write with the best evidence the present stage in the development of knowledge through the centuries provides.

Do you relate what you're reading to what you've read before? to experiments in class? to the world outside your classroom? Do you make imaginative leaps, speculate, and wonder? Is reflective thinking *built right into* the way you operate in reading?

STRATEGY 4: REMOVE THE ROADBLOCKS OF "OFFICIAL" TERMS

New technical terms say, "STOP! LOOK! AND LEARN!" A single key term left unknown (the meaning of *genus,* for instance, in science) will devastate your understanding of not just one passage but many passages throughout the book. The term will be used *time after time* all through the course.

How can you recognize "official terms," terms critically important to your understanding? Boldface or italic type is likely to flash the signal.

Key Terms Can Be "Collector's Items"

A technique many students find useful is recording the meanings of important "official" terms on flash cards (or small slips of paper). Record the term by itself on one side of the card and the meaning on the reverse side. Take a minute or two—that's all you'll need—to make each entry. (See Figure 5.)

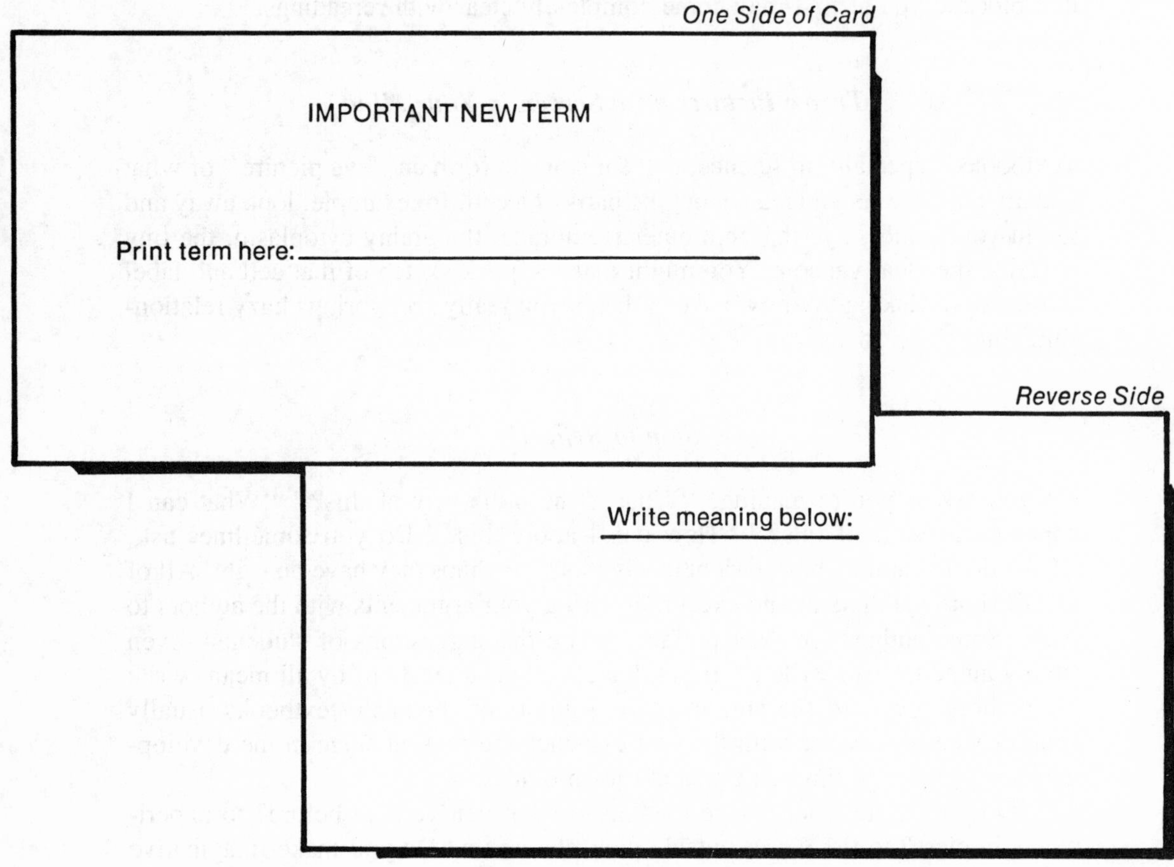

Figure 5. ***Take a minute or two to record "official" terms on flash cards. Then check yourself until the terms are yours—to stay.***

To check yourself, look at the term, then ask yourself the meaning. Or check yourself the other way—look at the meaning and ask yourself the new term. As you study, you can separate your cards with rubber bands into an ''I do know'' pile and an ''I don't know'' pile. Then work on your ''I don't know'' terms until you know them perfectly.

You might prefer making a dividing line down a page in your notebook, then writing the term on one side of the dividing line and the meaning on the other. The dividing line makes it easy to cover the meaning while you recite to yourself and clinch your understanding.

By the way, if you were to do nothing more than write down the terms and their meanings and then lost your flash cards forever, you would still be ahead. The very muscular act of writing, in and of itself, would have already *strengthened your learning*.

STRATEGY 5: USE A "BACK-AND-FORTH" STRATEGY

Tired students sometimes come to a photograph or diagram and think, "Good! Here's a part I can skip!" Often they're skipping a *time saver!* A single photograph may be quick, vivid, and easy-to-grasp—it may make the printed explanation instantly clear!

Focus on the Graphic Aids

Focus on photos, diagrams, charts, graphs. Each one is saying, "This is clearing up something important!" It has always cost book publishers several times as much to print a graphic aid as it does to use ordinary print. Now the costs have skyrocketed still higher with inflation. A graphic aid is supplied, you may be sure, only to drive home something of special importance.

What should be your strategy when you encounter graphic aids? *Shift into "back-and-forth" reading!* Words like the following are flashing a signal: "See in Figure 2–1," "Notice in Figure 2–5." They're signaling: "Read back and forth between the printed column and the graphic aid!"

When a figure is present, read the textual explanation with special care. At the point where you're referred to the figure, *shift your eyes and thoughts to the figure*. Zero in on the caption. Those few words may be *packed* with essential information. Or they may ask a searching question. When the caption refers you to specific features of the diagram or photograph or graph, locate these precisely in the figure.

In Figure 6, you'll want to shift your eyes back and forth *at least three times* between the printed column and the pictorial aid. How quickly you can now understand the movement of your forearm!

In moving the forearm, for example, the upper armbone, or *humerus*, is held rigid. The biceps muscle contracts (Fig. 15-25, A to B), pulls on a bone of the forearm, and the forearm moves up. You can feel the contracting muscle grow tense and hard.

To move the forearm back, the biceps relaxes. An opposing muscle on the other side, the triceps (C), contracts and pulls the arm down. Most body movements in animals involve such opposing muscular contractions.

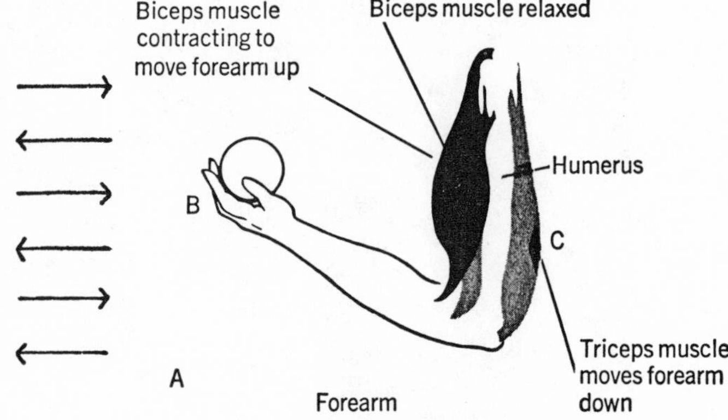

Opposing muscles control movement of limbs.

FIGURE 6. *Graphic aids are time savers! Do "back-and-forth" reading between the printed explanation and the graphic aid. (Text material from Stanley L. Weinberg,* **Biology: An Inquiry Into the Nature of Life,** *4th ed. (Boston: Allyn and Bacon, 1977). Reprinted by permission.*

STRATEGY 6: MAKE IMPORTANT POINTS "FLAG" YOU

Students exclaim, "I've read that chapter twice, but I still can't remember it! How can I *retain* what I study?"

"Select out" What You Want to Remember

You will often find *as many as 400* different bits of information and concepts crowded into one of your textbook chapters. You simply can't remember all of these! The first step toward retention, then, is "selecting out" what's important to remember. Having decided on what's important, your next step is to mark it in the book or make notes.

Delay Making Notes or Marking until the End of a Section

Some students plunge into a chapter and make notes or mark the book immediately. They copy or mark whatever their eyes first glimpse on the page. It's probably best to delay making notes or marking until you've read to the end of a headed subsection. Why wait? Only when you have encountered *all* the ideas in the section can you see their relationships, and only then can you judge their relative importance.

The Change of Pace as You Make Notes or Mark the Book Is a Definite Plus in Study

How will making notes or marking bring you a bonus benefit? The rapid succession with which ideas come crowding in one after another during reading tends to block your learning because of *retroactive interference.** The new ideas you meet tend to muddle the ones you've just met. But the *break* you take as you mark or make notes interrupts this rapid rush of ideas and provides "fixating" time—time for the ideas to make an impression.

Take Your Choice of Notemaking or Marking Methods

Make the key ideas stand out in some way so that they will flag you later. Techniques like those that follow—any one or a combination—will enable you to spot the high points of a chapter instantly when you want to review them later on. Now you won't have to reread, page by page, the entire chapter. And you'll collect another fringe benefit: pencil work has a "no-doze" effect.

Neatness in notemaking or marking requires only a little effort, not much added time. Later your orderly notes or markings will tend to encourage you. And they will *save you time* since you will quickly and clearly perceive the high points of the chapter.†

*H. F. Spitzer, "Studies in Retention," *Journal of Educational Psychology*, 30 (December 1939): 641–656.

†Walter Pauk, *How to Study in College*, 2nd ed. (Boston: Houghton Mifflin Co., 1974), p. 154. Many of the ideas about marking a book were suggested in Dr. Pauk's outstanding book on how to study, pp. 153–159.

If the book is not yours to mark, the following notemaking methods are appropriate:

1. *Make quick, labor-saving notes (or an outline).* A shorthand of your own will save you time. You can soon develop a personal "notehand" something like this:

about	=	abt	development	=	dev
be	=	b	observation	=	obsrv
before	=	b f	environment	=	env
no	=	n	hypothesis	=	hypth
are	=	r	evolution	=	evol

   Notetaking sometimes amounts to an absentminded copying of the book. Don't take notes—*make* notes. Use your own words when possible. This forces you to *really think over* what you have read.

   How complete should your notes be? That varies with the person and the purpose. Enough for *you* to recall as much of the content as you need.

2. *Memo slips can be useful.* Your large looseleaf notebook offers plenty of space for uncrowded notes. Or you might prefer to jot your notes on slips from a memo pad (a little smaller than the page size of the book) and insert the slips between the related pages. When you've finished studying a chapter, remove the slips from your book. Otherwise your book will bulge with these inserts. Just clip them in order, label an envelope with the title of the book or chapter, and place the envelopes in order as "pockets" in your notebook.

3. *The "divided page" is sometimes handy.* Make a dividing line down a page in your notebook. In the "QUESTION" column to the left, record an important question. In the "ANSWER" column to the right, jot quick notes that call to mind the answer. (See Figure 7.)

   The "divided page," you'll find, is handy when review time comes. The dividing line makes it easy to fold your answers underneath (or cover them) as you recite to yourself and clinch your understandings.

   The "divided page" is convenient for recording important new terms and their meanings. Mark the end of a unit, perhaps with a double line. Now when you want to go back and check on the words you've studied in a certain unit, you'll know exactly where to find them.

4. *The divided notebook offers all the space you need.* You may prefer the divided notebook to the divided page. Open your looseleaf notebook so it lies flat on the desk before you. On the left-hand page, record an important question. Just across, in a corresponding position on the right-hand page, jot notes that call to mind the answer. Check your memory later by folding the right-hand half of the notebook underneath so that the questions are exposed and the answers out of sight.

   You may wish to leave extra space between your questions for making class notes on related discussions and lectures.

The "Divided Page"

Important Question (Or "Official" Term)	**Answer (Or Meaning of Term)**
	Test your understanding by covering this side or folding it underneath.

FIGURE 7. *Cover your answers while you self-recite and clinch your mastery.*

5. *What about your own brainstorming?* What about your own reflections, your own interpretations, your own evaluations, your own ''great ideas''? If it's a case of inserting your own ideas right into notes you are making from other sources, you should enclose ideas of your own inside of brackets. Or you might jot your own reflections on slips from a memo pad, mark them with the word ME or with your initials, and again, place them between the related pages.

If the book is yours to mark, the following marking methods—your preference—are likely to be useful:

1. *Use quick marginal lines.* This is a high-speed marking method. Much quicker than underlining, it's the quickest marking method of all. Draw a *solid vertical line* down the margin (just to the left of the column of print) next to a *major point* that you wish to stand out. Carefully mark the exact extent of the part you've selected as important. Since your markings should show relative importance, use a *broken line* to mark an important *subpoint.* Using light pencil makes it possible for you to reconsider and perhaps revise your markings later. (See Figure 8.)

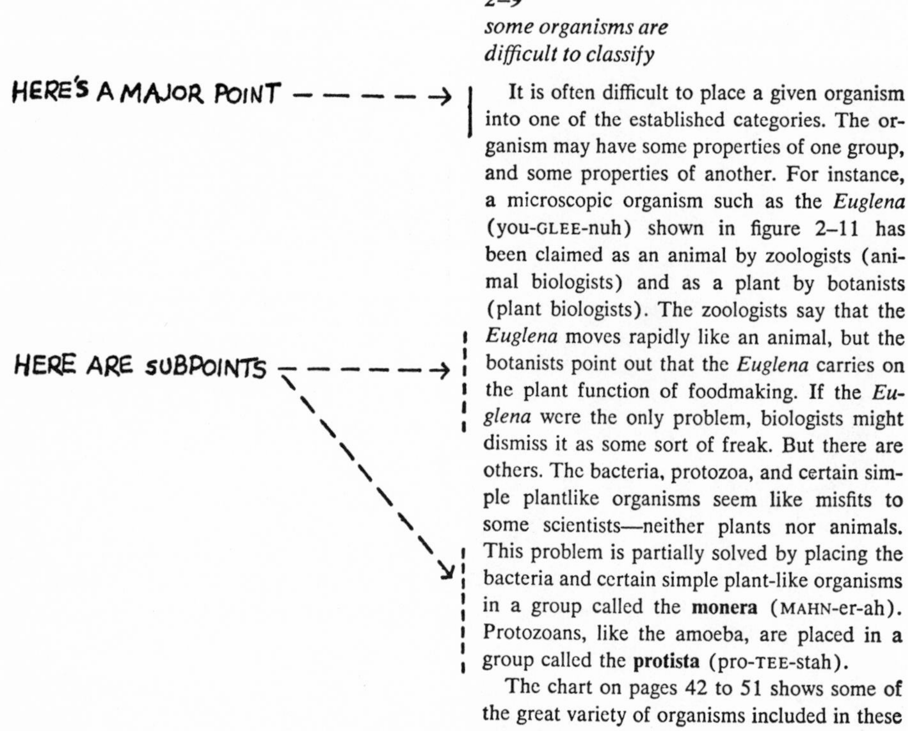

HERE'S A MAJOR POINT
HERE ARE SUBPOINTS
2–9
some organisms are
difficult to classify
It is often difficult to place a given organism into one of the established categories. The organism may have some properties of one group, and some properties of another. For instance, a microscopic organism such as the Euglena (you-GLEE-nuh) shown in figure 2–11 has been claimed as an animal by zoologists (animal biologists) and as a plant by botanists (plant biologists). The zoologists say that the Euglena moves rapidly like an animal, but the botanists point out that the Euglena carries on the plant function of foodmaking. If the Euglena were the only problem, biologists might dismiss it as some sort of freak. But there are others. The bacteria, protozoa, and certain simple plantlike organisms seem like misfits to some scientists—neither plants nor animals. This problem is partially solved by placing the bacteria and certain simple plant-like organisms in a group called the monera (MAHN-er-ah). Protozoans, like the amoeba, are placed in a group called the protista (pro-TEE-stah).
The chart on pages 42 to 51 shows some of the great variety of organisms included in these groups.

FIGURE 8. *Marginal lines will make high points stand out when you want to review them later. (Text material from* **Biological Science: Molecules to Man,** *The Biological Science Curriculum Study (BSCS) Blue Version, 3rd ed. Copyright © 1973 by Houghton Mifflin Co. Reprinted by permission.*

2. *Underline to show relative importance.* You might underline *main ideas* with a *solid* line and *important details* with a *broken* line.

    __________________ = main idea
    _ _ _ _ _ _ _ _ _ = important detail

    Be selective. As a general rule, underline no more than 15 to 20 percent of the page. When you *over*-underline, none of the ideas flag you as outstanding, and the task of learning such a mass of detail looks overwhelming.

    If you find you need to underline several successive lines, just enclose those lines in brackets as a time saver.

3. *Use see-through color accents.* Use color if you like, but use it sparingly. Because of the ease with which color-accents can be applied, there's a tendency to become color-happy and "paint the pages in pastel colors."* Some students accent main points with one color, subpoints with another.

4. *Make marginal mini-notes, brief jottings of key words or "cue" phrases.* Here's a device college experts recommend highly. Key words or phrases that call to mind main points are jotted at the *far* edge of the *left margin* of your book. Key words that suggest subpoints can be jotted below these, indented a little. (See Figure 9.)

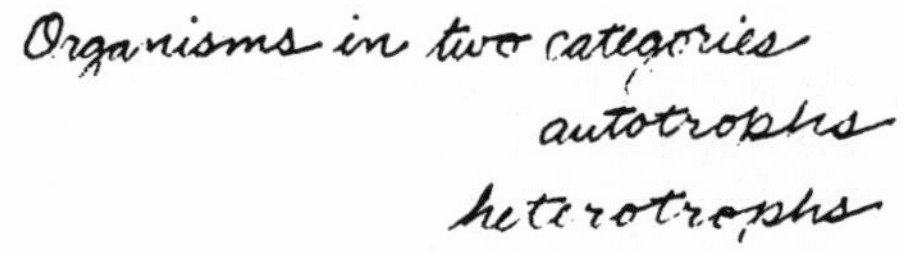

Organisms in two categories
autotrophs
heterotrophs

The new system places all organisms in two categories: producers and consumers. The producers, or **autotrophs** (auto-trohfs), are able to make and store food. The consumers, or **heterotrophs** (HET-er-oh-trohfs) are unable to make food. Heterotrophs must therefore depend on the autotrophs for their food, directly or indirectly.

FIGURE 9. ***Use marginal "mini-notes" as cues for review. (Text material from* Biological Science: Molecules to Man, *The Biological Science Curriculum Study (BSCS) Blue Version, 3rd ed. Copyright © 1973 by Houghton Mifflin Co. Reprinted by permission.***

Later when test time comes along and you need to review, your key words out in the margin become "cue" words. Cover the column of print and use the "cue" words to trigger your recall of important content. You can look at the print for a quick checkup on your answer.

*Walter Hill, *POINT: A Reading-Study System* (Belmont, Calif.: Wadsworth Publishing Co., 1970), p. 30.

5. *Use marginal numerals.* You can place numerals in the margin beside a series of steps or points to be remembered. Notice in Figure 10 how the numerals make the three basic parts of a cell flag you.

> You might notice, for example, that each organism contains a material called **cytoplasm** (SYT-uh-plaz-um). The cytoplasm is surrounded by a thin covering called a **cell membrane.** You might also notice that inside each cell is a small body called a **nucleus** (NEW-klee-us). The cytoplasm, membrane, and the nuclear area are the three basic parts of a cell. A **cell** is considered the basic unit of living things.
>
> ← 1 (beside "cytoplasm")
> ← 2 (beside "cell membrane")
> ← 3 (beside "nucleus")

FIGURE 10. *Note how the numerals out in the margin make the three parts of a cell flag you. (Text material from* Biological Science: Molecules to Man, *The Biological Science Curriculum Study (BSCS) Blue Version, 3rd ed. Copyright © 1973 by Houghton Mifflin Co. Reprinted by permission.*

You can use *a's* and *b's,* indented under your numerals, as in Figure 11, to indicate important subpoints.

> 1. The new system places all organisms in two categories: producers and consumers. The pro-
> a. ducers, or **autotrophs** (auto-trohfs), are able to make and store food. The consumers, or
> b. **heterotrophs** (HET-er-oh-trohfs) are unable to make food. Heterotrophs must therefore depend on the autotrophs for their food, directly or indirectly.

FIGURE 11. *Here the numeral* 1 *and the* a *and* b *mark the major point and the important subpoints. (Text material from* Biological Science: Molecules to Man, *the Biological Science Curriculum Study (BSCS) Blue Version, 3rd ed. Copyright © 1973 by Houghton Mifflin Co. Reprinted by permisssion.*

6. *"Capsulate" important content.* Your capsule summary of a concept, principle, or other crucial content can be jotted in the book itself (if you own it) in the upper, lower, or side margin. Or you can use a small slip of memo paper and slip it between the corresponding pages.
7. *Make marginal question marks.* A question mark out in the margin can indicate a statement you question or with which you disagree. Or it can indicate something you don't understand and want to check with your instructor in class.

8. *Make asterisks.* An asterisk (*) can guide your eye to an idea of supreme importance, the major idea of a chapter, for example, or an underlying concept or principle.

Why make jottings? Now you've involved motor memory—in many students one of the strongest learning channels of all. If you were to do nothing more than record your notes and then lost them forever, you would still be ahead. The muscular act of writing, in and of itself, would have already strengthened your learning.

STRATEGY 7: ADJUST YOUR SPEED TO THE TASK AT HAND

In television "spectaculars," students of commercial speed reading courses give the impression of racing through nonfiction at fantastic speeds, then brilliantly reciting the contents. You may have heard claims like these: "The greater the speed, the greater the comprehension," even "Read a page at a glance—with total recall!"

How Well Do Graduates of these Speed Courses Really Read?

When Dr. George Spache, renowned reading authority, gathered together graduates of highly advertised speed reading courses and tested their comprehension at these phenomenal speeds, they performed poorly, averaging only 50 percent. The carefully selected demonstrators, in Dr. Spache's opinion, already had, in many cases, an excellent background of information in the field covered in the book they read during their demonstrations. And his photographs of the eye movements of these "readers" proved that they were not really reading but skimming and skipping—not a very useful skill in thorough study!* Other investigators report that the demonstrators are often brilliant, extremely well-informed people who can already talk glibly about the subjects on which they are "reading." Even then, when the books are actually examined, they are sometimes in error in what they report about the content.

What Factors Should Control Your Speed?

If someone asks you, "What is your speed of reading?" you may be sure this person does not know much about reading. Of course, you should have not a single speed but *different* speeds. Reading everything rapidly is a sign of a poor reader. The mature reader develops *flexibility* instead of constant speed. What three considerations should control your reading speed? First, *your purpose at the moment;* second, *the difficulty of the material for you;* and third, *your familiarity with the subject matter.*

*George D. Spache, "Is This a Breakthrough in Reading?" *The Reading Teacher,* 5 (January 1962): 258–263.

You may want to shift from one speed to another within a single chapter (even within a single paragraph). Let's suppose you're assigned a fact-packed chapter in a science textbook. Ordinarily, read slowly! But suppose within this chapter you come upon an easy ''short short'' item about a great moment in science—it might be Newton's pondering the fall of that apple in his garden and discovering the law of gravitation. Speed up for this easier content!

Where Speed Reading Has Little Status

How fast should you read difficult new material? Here speed reading has little status. Even your instructors with their broad background and long experience in reading in their fields find that they must read difficult new material slowly.

Put the brakes on a runaway speed as you read the opening chapters of new textbooks. Spend time to *save* time! Get the basics firmly through precision reading—then build on these for a successful year.

STRATEGY 8: USE "THE MOST POWERFUL STUDY TECHNIQUE" OF ALL

Students exclaim, "I've read that chapter twice, but I still can't remember it!" Solve this problem by using the most powerful study technique known to psychologists. This is the technique of *self-recitation.**

"Play It Back!"

The most powerful study technique is a "playback"!† As you complete a paragraph or section, ask yourself, "Just what have I read here?" Look away from the print and see if you can "play back," or recite to yourself, important points.

Put the ideas into actual words—preferably your own words. Trying to express an idea in different words rivets your attention on the meaning. If you can't do this, that's your cue to reread appropriate parts.

At Cornell University's Reading-Study Center, students are advised, "Keep the print out of sight at least 50 percent of the time you're studying!" When these students, in repeated experiments, spent just one minute looking away from a passage and "playing back" its contents, they nearly doubled their retention.‡

Try a Cover-Card

Use a cover-card—or just your hand—to conceal parts of your textbook (or notes) while you "play back" important content. A cover-card is an index card of a convenient size—perhaps 5 by 8 inches.

Expose just the section heading and/or the first sentence or two of a paragraph. Can you really recite the important points? Lift your card and check. Expose an "official" term and cover the explanation. Can you explain the meaning? Look at the page and check. Cover an important diagram. Have you grasped its message and perhaps its parts and labels?

Turn on Triple-Strength Learning

Turn on triple-strength learning. If you learn with your eyes alone, you're using just one-third of your sensory learning channels for mastering the printed page. Why not use all-out, V.A.K. learning—*visual* plus *auditory* plus *kinesthetic* (muscular) learning?

*Pauk, *How to Study in College,* 1st ed., p. 25.

†H. Chandler Elliott, "The Study Unit" in *SR/SE Resource Book,* edited by Frank L. Christ (Chicago: Science Research Associates, 1969), p. 13.

‡Pauk, *How to Study in College,* 1st ed., p. 76.

Use your eyes in study, then add your ears and muscles.

See it!
Say it!
Hear it!
Draw it or write it!*

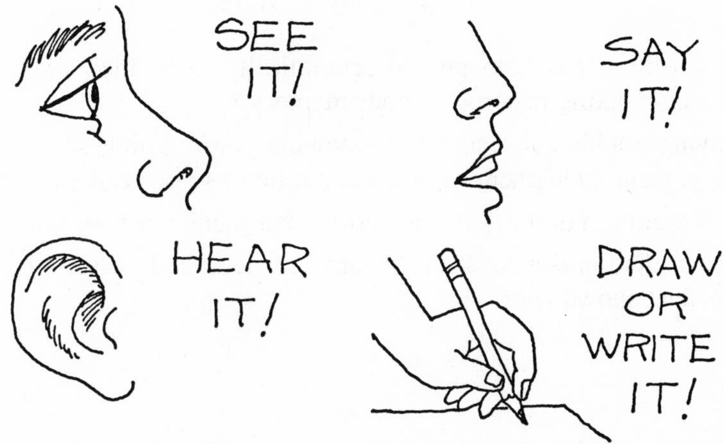

FIGURE 12. *For triple-strength learning, turn on V.A.K.—your visual, auditory, and kinesthetic learning channels. (Adapted illustration from p. 97* **Learn More With Less Effort** *by George J. Dudycha. Copyright © 1957 by Harper and Row Publishers, Inc. By permission of the publishers.)*

Use your eyes as you *see* the printed words. Now you've brought your visual memory into play.

Say what you're learning—aloud or in a whisper. Now you've added kinesthetic (muscular) learning as you involve the muscles of your throat, lips, and tongue.

Strengthen learning with your *ears* as you hear yourself say it. Now you've brought your auditory memory to bear.

Add *kinesthetic learning* again as you make jottings (exceedingly brief) of cue words and phrases to *prove* that you've learned the main points. Now you've involved *motor memory,* which, in many students, is the strongest learning channel of all.

"See it! Say it! Hear it! Draw it or Write it!" is *four-way reinforcement*. The variety itself helps you retain the material. The change of pace—eyes, voice, ears, pencil—keeps you alert and increases your "intake."

*George J. Dudycha, *Learn More with Less Effort*. (New York: Harper and Row, 1957), p. 96.

You Are Not Being Urged to Memorize—in Fact, You Are Being Urged Not to Memorize

Your textbook is the condensation of a broad field of knowledge—the distillation of many lifetimes of experiences of scholars—and deserves your thoughtful study.

Why "Play It Back"?†

1. Self-reciting has been proved scientifically to be the *most powerful of all means* of fixing material in your memory.
2. Having trouble concentrating? Knowing you're going to try to "playback" the content strengthens your concentration as you read each section.
3. Self-reciting faithfully reveals errors and blanks in your knowledge.
4. Self-recitation is a constant rehearsal for tests and exams—of great value in the final showdown.

*The writer expresses appreciation for these ideas to H. Chandler Elliott, "The Study Unit" in *SR/SE Resource Book*, edited by Frank L. Christ (Chicago: Science Research Associates, 1969), p. 13.

STRATEGY 9: ZERO IN ON THE SELF-CHECKS

Authors of textbooks often "giftwrap" something for you—it's a package of chapter-end questions. Here you have a giveaway of content the authors themselves consider important. In some books you'll find self-check questions placed at strategic points throughout the chapter.

In many books you'll also find "in gift wraps" at the end of each chapter a list of the most important terms and concepts, as in Figure 13.

Reviewing the Essentials

Man the Newcomer

1. How long has the earth been in existence? How long has man been on earth?
2. Name important Hominids and describe their accomplishments.

Races of Mankind

3. Name the major races of mankind. On a map locate those parts of the world where each race predominates.
4. Define the term race. Is language a characteristic of race? Religion? Nation?
5. What traits are used by anthropologists as a basis for placing men in racial categories?

Evolution of Man

6. What contribution to scientific thought did Charles Darwin make in his *On the Origin of Species?*
7. What is meant by (a) mutation, (b) natural selection, (c) isolation, and (d) adaptation as they relate to the evolution of man?

Explain or Identify

Caucasoid	Cro-Magnon man
Mongoloid	Neolithic man
Negroid	*Homo habilis*
Homo sapiens	*Zinjanthropus*
Java man	evolution

FIGURE 13. ***Check yourself with questions that the authors themselves consider important to your understanding. (Text material from Leften S. Stavrianos et al.*** **A Global History of Man.** ***Boston: Allyn and Baocn, 1974, p. 51.)***

Are you having trouble selecting what's important from among the *hundreds* of details in the chapter? Through their questions, the authors are standing right beside you as you study, saying, "This is what we consider most important."

Are there some passages you "just can't get"? Questions, you recall, can help you "crack the most difficult passage. Try going back and rereading the passage, holding in mind the self-check questions that relate to that particular passage. Now you may get a breakthrough.

Your "gifts" from the authors, then, can help you *check on* and *firm up* your learning.

STRATEGY 10: REVIEW TO FIRM UP LEARNING

Unless you learn *for the future,* a lot of hard work goes by the board. How can you "break the memory barrier"?*

Regain the Broad View

Suppose you've just completed your close, intensive reading of the chapter. You've been concentrating on sections—even on bits and pieces, like the meaning of a single key term. As you've focused on each part, you may have lost the broad chapter plan.

Add a last quick runthrough. Can you recall the broad plan of the chapter? Try to recite its *broad organization* and to recall its *big thought divisions*. You've attended to the tiny pieces of the jigsaw—now look once more at the *total picture*.

Then Check on Important Subpoints

Run through the chapter again, section by section, checking yourself once more on main points and important subpoints. Use your cover-card, or cover the print with your hand again. Reread parts that have slipped away.

Use Triple-Strength Learning Again–Eyes, Ears, Muscles

Turn on V. A. K. power again—visual and auditory and kinesthetic. Use your *eyes* as you reread selectively. *Say* things aloud and *hear* yourself. *Write* jottings of key words in points you want to remember.

Take Advantage of a Memory Secret

Learning for the future requires overlearning. A football player learns to take his man out for a run around left end. Then he goes over and over the play until he overlearns it. He does this so there will be no forgetting or confusion. An actor memorizes his lines well enough to deliver them without error. Then he continues to go over them until they are automatic.†

Psychologists say, "Minimal learning is not enough. When you can say, 'I have learned this material,' you will need to spend perhaps one-fourth the original time overlearning it." In one study, students who overlearned a vocabulary lesson remembered *four times* as much after four weeks had passed.

*James D. Weinland, "Memory Improvement: General Principles" in *SR/SE Resource Book*, edited by Frank L. Christ (Chicago: Science Research Associates, 1969), p. 139.

†Richard Kalish, *Making the Most of College* (Belmont, Calif.: Wadsworth Publishing Co., 1959), p. 119.

Another Memory Secret

You can remember longer *simply by the way you place your reviews*. Suppose you read an assignment today. When will forgetting take its greatest toll? The greatest loss will be *within one day*. Notice the flight of knowledge in Figure 14! Arrange your first review to check this flight. Place it from twelve to twenty-four hours after you first study. Reinforce at this point, and you will remember much longer.

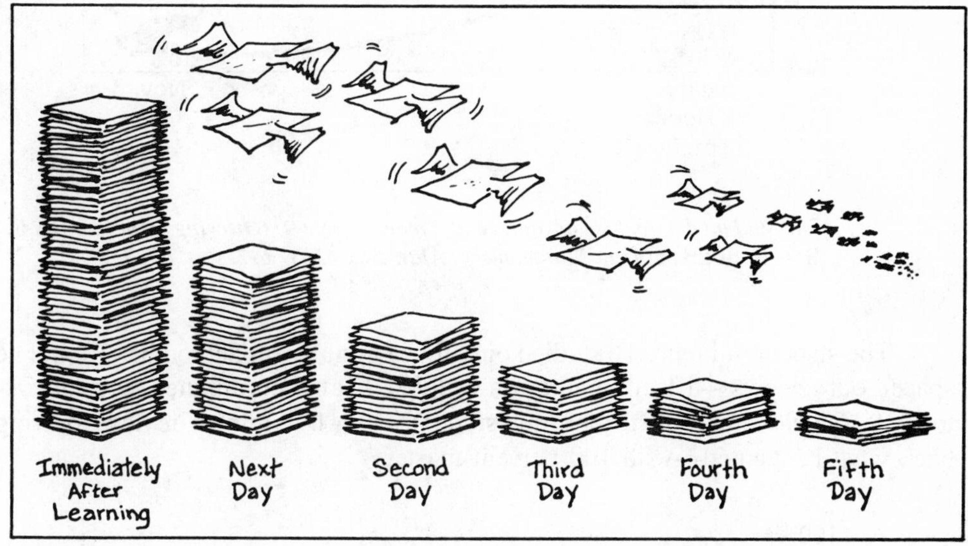

FIGURE 14. ***The greatest memory loss takes place within one day. You can check this loss! (Adapted illustrations from p. 74 in*** **Learn More With Less Effort** ***by George J. Dudycha. Copyright © 1957 by Haper and Row Publishers, Inc. By permission of the publishers.)***

A study expert points out to college students the curve of forgetting.* The student in Figure 15 studied one hour on September 30, then six weeks later retained very little.

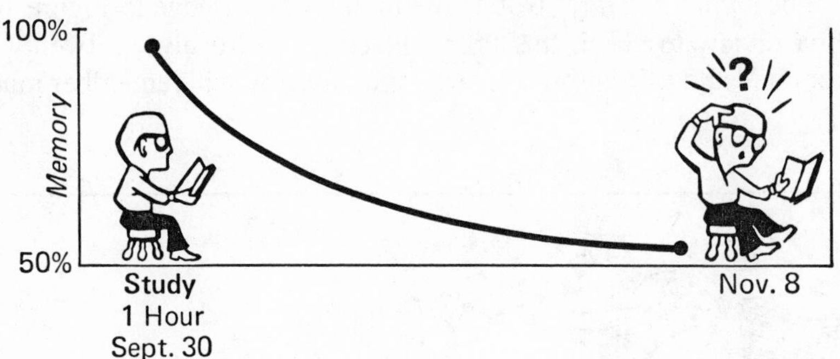

FIGURE 15. *This student did not take advantage of a memory secret. (Drawing from Thomas F. Staton,* **How to Study,** *6th ed. Montgomery, Ala.: Box 6133, 1977), p. 47.*

The student in Figure 16 studied only thirty minutes on September 30, but he spaced out reviews—fifteen minutes on October 1, and ten minutes more on October 8. On November 8, it took this student just a five-minute review to bring back what he wanted—with 100 percent mastery.

FIGURE 16. *This student knew the memory secret of spaced review. (Drawing from Thomas F. Staton,* **How to Study,** *6th ed. Montgomery, Ala.: Box 6133, 1977), p. 47.*

Both students studied just one hour, but the one who spaced out his reviews had *far* better retention. For best results, then, space out your own reviews, as he did, one within twenty-four hours, one perhaps a week later, another perhaps six weeks later—or whenever a test comes along.

*Staton, Thomas F., *How to Study*, 6th ed. (Montgomery, Ala.: Box 6133, 1977), p. 47.

Beware of "Technique-itis"

You've been introduced to a number of study techniques. Now a word of caution. Try not to become so conscious of techniques that you lose the meaning of the passage! You may get excellent results when, with your interest caught up, you become absorbed in your reading and forget all about techniques. And we do not recommend that you try too many new techniques at once or use those that are not your "own thing."

"Beware of an overload," one psychologist suggests. "Don't be like the overburdened knight in armor. At first the armor of a knight consisted of a shield, then a helmet to protect the head. Next came the coat of mail to protect the heart and chest. After that there were concocted all sorts of special armor. By the time the knight was fully armored, he was as protected and heavy as a hippopotamus, and as slow as a snail. Worst of all, he couldn't do the job (fighting) that he was originally supposed to do. Don't let the weight of the technique keep you from doing your main job, studying."*

What Do We Have in the Ten Strategies?

The ten strategies are research-designed procedures to help you *comprehend better and faster, concentrate better, and remember longer,* useful not just with textbooks but with any informational reading.

Are they cumbersome? Actually, they are based on a study method designed during a wartime crisis when young men had to be rushed through training courses at Maxwell Air Base and other military locations.

Will there be difficulties applying the strategies? Poorly organized material will present difficulties. But poorly written material makes procedures that facilitate reading even more essential.

They form a package of techniques and skills. If you use much of the package, in your own individual way, you'll have a powerful approach for mastering a textbook chapter.

Use as many of the ten strategies as you choose to, adapt them to your needs and preferences, and add effective ways of your own.

*Abridged from Walter Pauk, *How to Study in College*, 2nd ed. (Boston: Houghton Mifflin Co., 1974), p. 149.

THE OK5R APPROACH TO COLLEGE READING*

You can combine your study strategies into a smoothly operating system. At Cornell University's Reading-Study Center such a system is called OK5R. This approach incorporates *the most powerful study procedures yet known* for mastering a textbook chapter.

At Cornell students' grade point averages go up when they build OK5R into their permanent habits. A similar system is recommended in almost every book on how to study in college.

The steps in OK5R are as follows:

1. *O*verview
2. Pick out *K*ey Ideas
3. *R*ead
4. *R*ecord
5. *R*ecite
6. *R*eview
7. *R*eflect

There will be much overlapping of steps 2–7.

O OVERVIEW

Sample the chapter to discover what it's all about.

Examine the title. Read the chapter introduction. "Hit the headings." Glance at the pictures, charts, and diagrams. Read the chapter summaries. Look over the self-check questions. Jot down questions of your own.

Overviewing will build up momentum for your study of the chapter.

K KEY IDEAS

One of your main jobs will be to "select out" the key ideas from the supporting material.

R_1 READ

Work through the chapter, one headed section at a time.

You may find that some of these sections are quite easy. Then just "pick out" the key ideas from the supporting material. Try to go into each section with a question. Turn headings (and sometimes topic sentences) into questions. These should guide you to key ideas.

Read and reread parts as often as necessary. Remove the roadblocks of "official" terms. Shift to a "back-and-forth" reading strategy for graphic aids. Adjust your reading speed as needed within the passage.

*Dr. Walter Pauk, former Director of the Cornell University Study-Reading Center, originated the name OK5R. He sums up the approach in *How to Study in College*, 2nd ed. (Boston: Houghton Mifflin Co., 1974), p. 151.

R2 RECORD

Make notes on the key ideas, or mark them. Make the key ideas stand out. Now you won't have to reread the entire chapter when you return to review it later.

R3 RECITE

"To counteract forgetting, recite!"*

As you complete a section or a paragraph, ask yourself, "Just what have I read here?" Cover the passage with your hand or with a card, or just look away from the book. Can you recite the important points to yourself? Now look back at the column of print and check your accuracy. Reread whenever you need to.

One expert on how to study calls self-recitation a "playback." Immediate "playback," he asserts, has been proved scientifically to be *the most powerful of all methods of fixing material into the memory.*†

R4 REVIEW

Add a last quick run-through of the chapter.

First, turn through the chapter to call back to mind the broad chapter plan. Next, run through the chapter section by section, checking yourself once more on the main points and the important subpoints.

Space out quick reviews later.

R5 REFLECT

Build reflective thinking into every step—*into the way you operate in reading.*

Are you locked into a rigid system in OK5R? That is not intended. You'll want to vary any study system from one purpose to another, one textbook to another, one passage to another.

Is OK5R slow and labored? A similar approach was used to rush officer candidates and other young men through their training courses during a wartime crisis.

You may want to try OK5R as it is offered here—you may want to modify it—or you may find it suggestive as you create your own study system to suit your own personal learning style.

*Pauk, *How to Study in College,* p. 151.

†H. Chandler Elliot, "The Study Unit" in *SR/SE Resource Book,* edited by Frank L. Christ (Chicago: Science Research Associates, 1969), p. 13.

CAN YOU ADJUST YOUR READING RATE TO THE TASK AT HAND

If someone asks you, "What is your speed in reading?" you'll know that this person does NOT know much about reading.

You should have not a single rate but *several different rates*. Reading everything fast is a sign of a poor reader. The good reader develops *flexibility* instead of constant speed.

1. Shift from one rate and method to another in view of these considerations:
   a. Your purpose
      Why are you reading this material?
      to get just the gist of an easy selection?
      to learn, point by point, a specific process or a detailed sequence?
      to find one particular point in a selection you've already read?
      to entertain yourself with light, easy reading?
   b. What is the *difficulty* of the material for you?
      is it easy?
      or is it rough going?
   c. How *familiar* are you with the subject matter?
      do you already have background on the topic?
      or is it new to you?
2. You should have in your "collection" of rates the following approaches. The rates in words per minute suggested below are intended as "target" rates for high school upperclassmen.

Approach	How Fast	When to Use
Scanning, not a true reading rate—just glancing until you find what you want	*Maybe* 1500 or more words per minute (rate is an individual matter)	when glancing down pages to find a single piece of information
Skimming (previewing or overviewing), not a true reading rate—just getting the gist of the article, hitting the high points.	*Maybe* 800–1000 words per minute	to get the general content of an article, "what it's all about"
Actual Reading Rates		
1. *Very rapid*	*Maybe* 500 words per minute	for light, easy, fast-moving fiction (entertainment reading)

Approach	How Fast	When to Use
2. *Rapid*	*Maybe* 350 words per minute	for fairly easy materials when you want only the more important facts, ideas
3. *Average*	*Perhaps* 250 words per minute	for magazine articles such as *Science Digest;* some chapters in social studies; some travel books; some novels like *My Antonia* or *Cry the Beloved Country*
4. *Slow and careful*	From 250 words per minute—all the way down to a *slow* 50 words per minute or even *slower*	for difficult concepts and vocabulary for thorough reading of technical material for retaining every detail for weighing the truth of difficult reading (Here *"thought time"* is needed in addition to reading time.)

Internal Rate Adjustment

You may need to *shift* from one rate (and approach) to another *within* a *single chapter* of a textbook or within an article—even within a single paragraph. This shifting of speed within a selection is called *internal rate adjustment.* Let's suppose, for example, you're reading a chapter in science, "Fish and Fishlike Vertebrates." The introduction is a narrative—the story of how deadly eel-like sea lampreys invaded the Great Lakes. Read this fairly fast! The body of the chapter is closely packed with information. Reduce speed! Later you find some easy paragraphs on sports fishing as a hobby. Speed up again!

So, do not work for *indiscriminate speed* in reading; rather, work for *flexibility* of *rate. Adjust your approach to the demands of different types of reading tasks!*

NAME ______________________________ DATE ____________

TEN-MINUTE SPEED GRAPH

The reading material best suited for speed practice is easy, fast-moving fiction or a fast narrative style biography read for enjoyment. Set aside ten minutes each day—more if you can—for speed practice at home. Time yourself while you read for ten minutes. Count the number of pages read, to the nearest one-fourth or even one-eighth of a page. Then chart the results below. Try each day to outdo your record of the day before. You may be surprised at what happens!

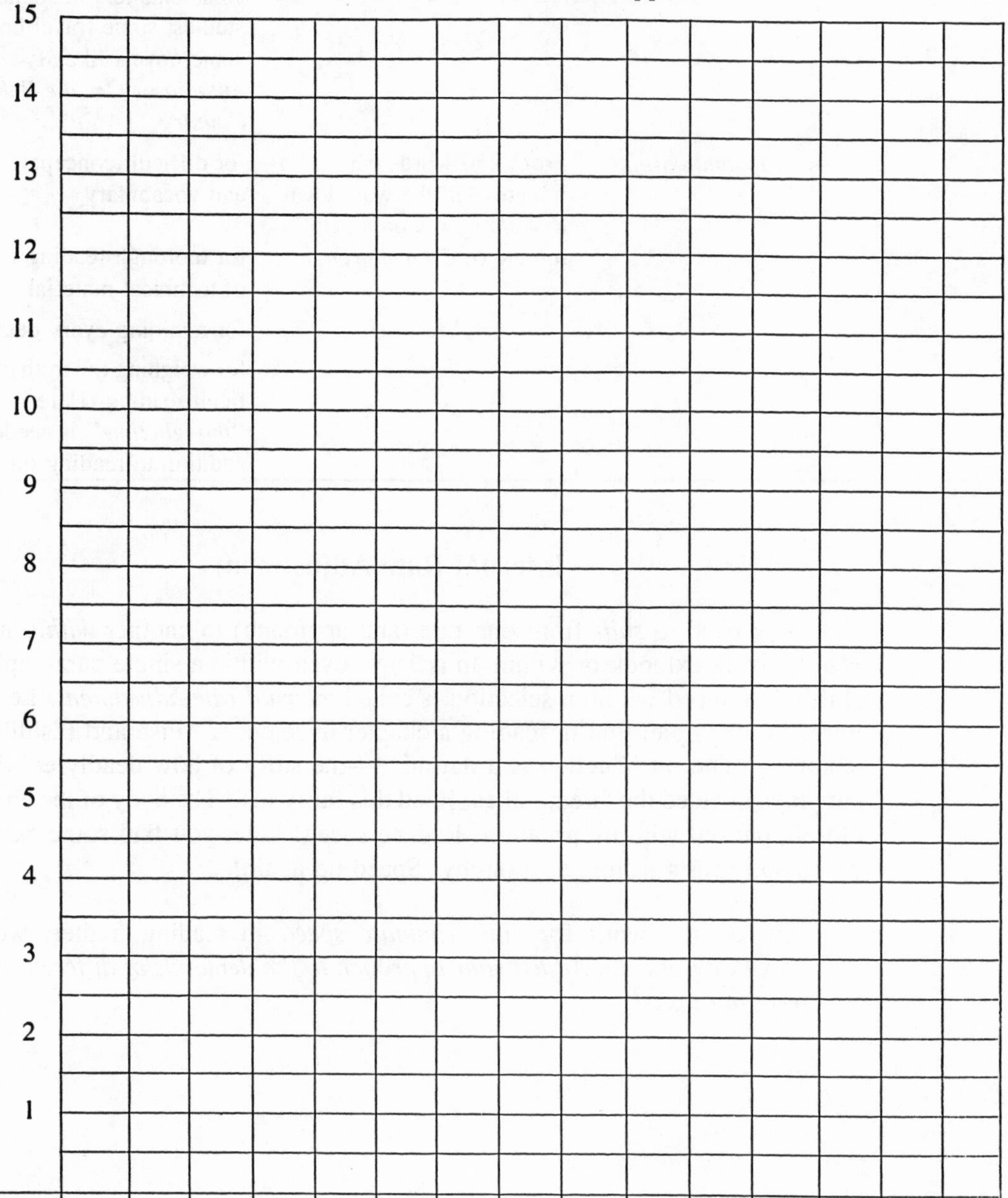

15
14
13
12
11
10
9
8
7
6
5
4
3
2
1

PRACTICE NUMBER	1	2	3	4	5	6	7	8	9	10	11	12	13	14	15
NUMBER OF PAGES READ															

TIPS FOR USING THE TEN-MINUTE GRAPH

These Tips Should Help You Increase Your Speed:

1. During your first practice, read at your comfortable rate. Don't push yourself to read any faster. Record the number of pages read. This is your starting speed.
2. Then, using the tips below, set out to improve your speed.
   - Tip 1: Remember your purpose—enjoyment! Press right on! Don't slow down for small details.
   - Tip 2: Set a goal to drive toward—*beyond* the number of pages you covered during your last practice.
   - Tip 3: Anticipate what's ahead in the story.
   - Tip 4: Push yourself *beyond* your comfortable rate.

How To Use this Graph:

1. Each time you practice, place a clip to mark your starting point in the book. The longer loop of the clip should ''point'' to your starting point.
2. Set a goal for this ten-minute practice—*beyond* the number of pages you completed in your last practice (five-and-a-half pages, for example, instead of five).
3. An oven timer set for ten minutes is ideal. Or you might have someone time you. If you're using an ordinary watch, bring both hands up to twelve.
4. Record, by making a conspicuous dot on your graph, the number of pages you've read—to the nearest one-fourth or even one-eighth of a page. As you complete more practices, draw a line to connect your dots.
5. Practice again, *pushing* to outdo yourself.
6. Whenever you start a new book, make a note of this on your graph, or start a new graph. The opening pages of a book will—and *should*—go more slowly as you become acquainted with new characters, a new setting, an unfamiliar plot. Your speed will—and *should*—drop. The note on your graph will explain this drop.
7. Your teacher can only guide you—you can help yourself if you really want to. FOR BEST RESULTS, PRACTICE DAILY AND WORK IN EXTRA TIMINGS. These will push your speed upward and help you *hold* your gains.

YOU'RE IN COMMAND! If, for any reason, a passage invites you to linger, call off the speed practice and slow down to savor the passage or to read more reflectively. You can always practice speed again tomorrow.

NAME ______________________________ DATE ______________

INFORMATION, PLEASE

Your reading is a very personal thing. Some young people like the sports page, some like magazines, some like books about a strong interest—like whitewater kayaking or space flight. Your teacher will use your answers to the questions below to guide you to reading you will enjoy all through the year.

1. What are your favorite pastimes, hobbies, and interests? (What sports do you take part in? Do you collect things? What pets do you have? What other interests?) ______________________________

   ____

2. Have you decided on your life work? (If you are considering two or three possibilities, please name them.) ______________________________

3. What are your favorite subjects at school? ______________________________

   What are your least favorite subjects? ______________________________

4. Is there any kind of information you feel a need for right now? If so, what kind? ______________________________

   ____

5. Suppose you could have one wish come true now or in the future. What would it be? ______________________________

6. If you had $500 and *had* to spend it, how would you spend it? ________

____

7. If you had one whole day to spend exactly as you please, how would you spend that time? ____

8. Have you read some books that you really liked? ____ If so, please name one or two. ____

9. Do you have some favorite types of books? ____________________

   Other types of reading? ____

10. What three TV programs do you like best? ____________________

11. Would you describe yourself as a *frequent* reader for pleasure? One who *sometimes* reads for pleasure? One who *never* reads for pleasure? ______

____

12. What could your teacher do so that you might enjoy reading more? _____

____

____

NAME ____________________ DATE __________

INFORMATION, PLEASE

Your reading is a very personal thing. Some young people like the sports page, some like magazines, some like books about a strong interest—like whitewater kayaking or space flight. Your teacher will use your answers to the questions below to guide you to reading you will enjoy all through the year.

1. What are your favorite pastimes, hobbies, and interests? (What sports do you take part in? Do you collect things? What pets do you have? What other interests?) ____________________

   ____

2. Have you decided on your life work? (If you are considering two or three possibilities, please name them.) ____________________
3. What are your favorite subjects at school? ____________________

   What are your least favorite subjects? ____________________
4. Is there a kind of information you feel a need for right now? If so, what kind? ____________________
5. Suppose you could have one wish come true now or in the future. What would it be? ____________________

6. If you had $500 and *had* to spend it, how would you spend it? ________

____

7. If you had one whole day to spend exactly as you please, how would you spend that time? ____

8. If you could be anyone in the world, who would you be? ____________

9. What was the happiest day of your life? ____________________

____

10. Have you read some books that you really liked? ____ If so, please name one or two. ____

11. What is the best book you've ever read? ____________________

12. Do you have some favorite types of books? ____________________

13. If you could wish for a book right now and have it appear on your desk, what kind would it be? ____

14. Did you read any books for your own pleasure or information during the past summer? ____ About how many? ____ Please name one or two: ______

____

15. Do you have some books of your own? ____ If you do, how many? ____

16. Do you read a newspaper or part of one? ____ If you do, which one(s)?

____

________ Which part(s)? ____

17. Do you read a magazine? ______ If you do, which one(s)? __________

____

18. Do you read comic books? ______ If you do, which one(s)? __________

__________________________ Please underline your favorites.

19. What three TV programs do you enjoy most? ________________

____

20. Do you have a part-time job? ______ What do you usually do on a school day from after school to bedtime? ______________________

____

____

21. Would you describe yourself as a *frequent* reader for pleasure, a person who *sometimes* reads for pleasure, or a person who *never* reads for pleasure?

____

22. Do you have a public library card? Yes ______ No ______ Do you use the public library often? ______ Sometimes? ______ Never? ______

23. What could your teacher do so that you might enjoy reading more? _____

____

____

24. Please check below some subjects that interest you that you think you might like to read about:

Adventure _______
  Any special kind? _______
Exploring _______
The sea _______
Mystery and thrills _______
Detectives _______
Sports _______
  Any special kind? _______
Outdoor life _______
Science fiction _______
Westerns _______
Pioneers _______
Historical fiction _______
Faraway lands and people _______
Travel _______
War _______
Love and romance _______
Fanciful tales _______
Flying _______
Animal stories _______
Interesting people _______
  Any special kind? _______
Conquering handicaps _______
Family life _______
Animal life _______
Information about pets _______
Humor _______
Music _______

Religion _______
Today's world _______
Politics _______
Man's yesterdays _______
  Any special period? _______
Theater _______
Television _______
Radio _______
Science facts _______
Space flight _______
The arts _______
  Any special area? _______
Drawing or painting _______
Photography _______
The world of mechanics _______
Self-improvement _______
Looking ahead to a job _______
  Any special field? _______
What to do after high school _______
Making money _______
School problems _______
Home problems _______
Being in a minority _______
Making and keeping friends _______
Understanding the other sex _______
Looking ahead to marriage _______
Drugs, alcohol, and/or smoking _______
Understanding the law _______

24. Can you think of something else that you might like to read about?

GRAPH FOR ESTIMATING READABILITY

by Edward Fry, Rutgers University Reading Center

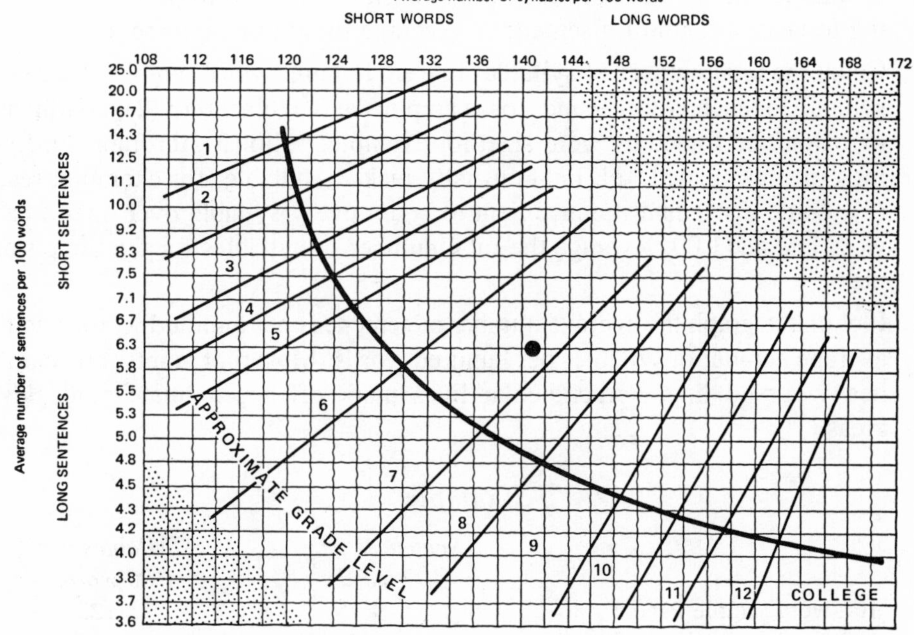

DIRECTIONS: Randomly select three one-hundred passages from a book or article. Plot average number of syllables and average number of sentences per 100 words on the graph to determine the grade level of the material. Choose more passages per book if variability is observed and conclude that the book has uneven readability. Few books will fall in the dotted area but when they do, grade level scores are invalid.

EXAMPLE:	**SYLLABLES**	**SENTENCES**
1st Hundred Words	124	6.6
2nd Hundred Words	141	5.5
3rd Hundred Words	158	6.8
AVERAGE	141	6.3

READABILITY 7th GRADE (see dot plotted on graph)

From Edward Fry, *Reading Instruction for Classroom and Clinic* (New York: McGraw-Hill, 1972), p. 232. Reproduced with the permission of the publisher.

Directions for Using the Readability Graph

1. Select three one-hundred-word passages from near the beginning, middle, and end of the book. Skip all proper nouns.
2. Count the total number of sentences in each hundred-word passage (estimating to nearest tenth of a sentence). Average these three numbers.
3. Count the total number of syllables in each hundred-word sample. There is a syllable for each vowel sound; for example: cat (1), blackbird (2), continental (4). Don't be fooled by word size; for example: polio (3), through (1). Endings such as -y, -ed, -el, or -le usually make a syllable, for example: ready (2), bottle (2). I find it convenient to count every syllable over one in each word and add1 00. Average the total number of syllables for the three samples.
4. Plot on the graph the average number of sentences per hundred words and the average number of syllables per hundred words. Most plot points fall near the heavy curved line. Perpendicular lines mark off approximate grade level areas.

Example

	Sentences per 100 words	*Syllables per 100 words*
100-word sample Page 5	9.1	122
100-word sample Page 89	8.5	140
100-word sample Page 160	7.0	129
	3)24.6	3)391
Average	8.2	130

Plotting these averages on the graph we find they fall in the 5th grade area; hence the book is about 5th grade difficulty level. If great variability is encountered either in sentence length or in the syllable count for the three selections, then randomly select several more passages and average them in before plotting.

These directions are from "A Readability Formula That Saves Time," by Edward Fry, April, 1968 *Journal of Reading*. Reprinted with permission of the International Reading Association.

Dear Parent,

We are writing to share with you our plans for "Operation Reading" at school this year. We are aware that you, as a parent, care deeply about your son's or daughter's reading. We, too, want your son or daughter to have the reading power needed to secure a quality education, to advance in the lifework he or she chooses, to do lifelong reading for information and enjoyment.

We plan a special effort at school this year to encourage growth in reading. We will do this in two ways. First, we will be working from day to day to extend the skills of study-type reading. And, second, we will encourage growth in reading in a very pleasant way--through personal reading.

What benefits should go hand in hand with personal reading? Among other benefits, it should help develop more efficient readers. Wide reading is one of the most effective vocabulary builders. As children read, they meet new words again and again and gradually incorporate some of these into their vocabularies. As a general rule, the broader students' reading interests, the richer their vocabularies. The hours that students spend in reading practice tend to strengthen their reading comprehension. Highly interesting fiction and fast-moving, story-type biographies "pull them along" and tend to increase their speed.

We feel that young people today need guidance in personal reading far more than they did in the past. Assignments for their classes--sports practice--club meetings--good times with friends--home and job responsibilities crowd their days and nights. And television is often an ever-present distractor!

Many parents, already encouraging reading, ask, "How can we do more?" One possible way is by arranging a place at home, if the student does not already have one, that is quiet for reading. Encouraging the student to visit that home of books, the public library, and to have--and use--that passport to reading, a library card, may stimulate reading. A subscription to a colorful magazine close to the interests of young people may lead to pleasant hours of reading. Inviting the young person to share newspapers and magazines that are available in the home should encourage reading. Sharing what you yourself are reading--exchanging enthusiasms--may be best of all. Example may be one of the best of teachers!

Must television be something young people do instead of reading? Perhaps it can lead them into reading. Television programs can touch off new interests and lead to completely new reading interests.

*Arbuthnot, May Hill, *Children's Reading in the Home* (Glenview, Illinois: Scott, Foresman and Company, 1969), p. 9.

Librarians report that after a television program based on a book, their libraries are "borrowed out" of that book! When a subject has caught a child's interest on television, we can encourage the child to probe that subject more deeply through a related book--even provide the book. Surely programs like <u>Once Upon a Classic</u> invite us to do this!

How often young people have "growing-up" problems! At times it may be appropriate to offer them a book. The book may lead the young person to reflect, "I am not alone in that problem" and it may possibly suggest solutions. School and public libraries offer rich resources to choose from--books on making and keeping friends, understanding dating relationships, increasing self-confidence, finding a part-time job, what you should know about drugs, exploring your values, how to live with your parents! Now reading is brought close to young people during the difficult growing-up process.

Young people feel pride and pleasure in owning personal books. Owning a few books can stimulate interest in owning--and reading--<u>more</u>! A special place at home to keep books that are their own-- a personal bookshelf or a brightly painted box or a carton covered with colorful self-stick paper can give young readers still greater pride and pleasure.

Where can a parent learn more about books and other reading-matter high in appeal to young readers? Your school librarian is well acquainted with the rich variety of colorful, inviting, quality books available to interest, guide, and inspire students. He or she will gladly answer questions about young people's reading and will guide you to books to attract both eager and less eager readers.

We will welcome your comments about "Operation Reading" at school this year, and we invite your help at home. We will welcome your suggestions about what we can do to increase your child's delight in reading. We ask you to share with us ways you yourself have found successful. To your son or daughter, this is our wish: "Happy reading--and a happy and successful school year!"

Sincerely,

NAME ______________________________ DATE ______________

FILL UP YOUR BOOKCASE!*

Fill up your bookcase with books! When you finish a book, print the title and author on one of the books below. Turn the bookcase sideways to fit your printing in. You'll feel real satisfaction as your record of reading grows.

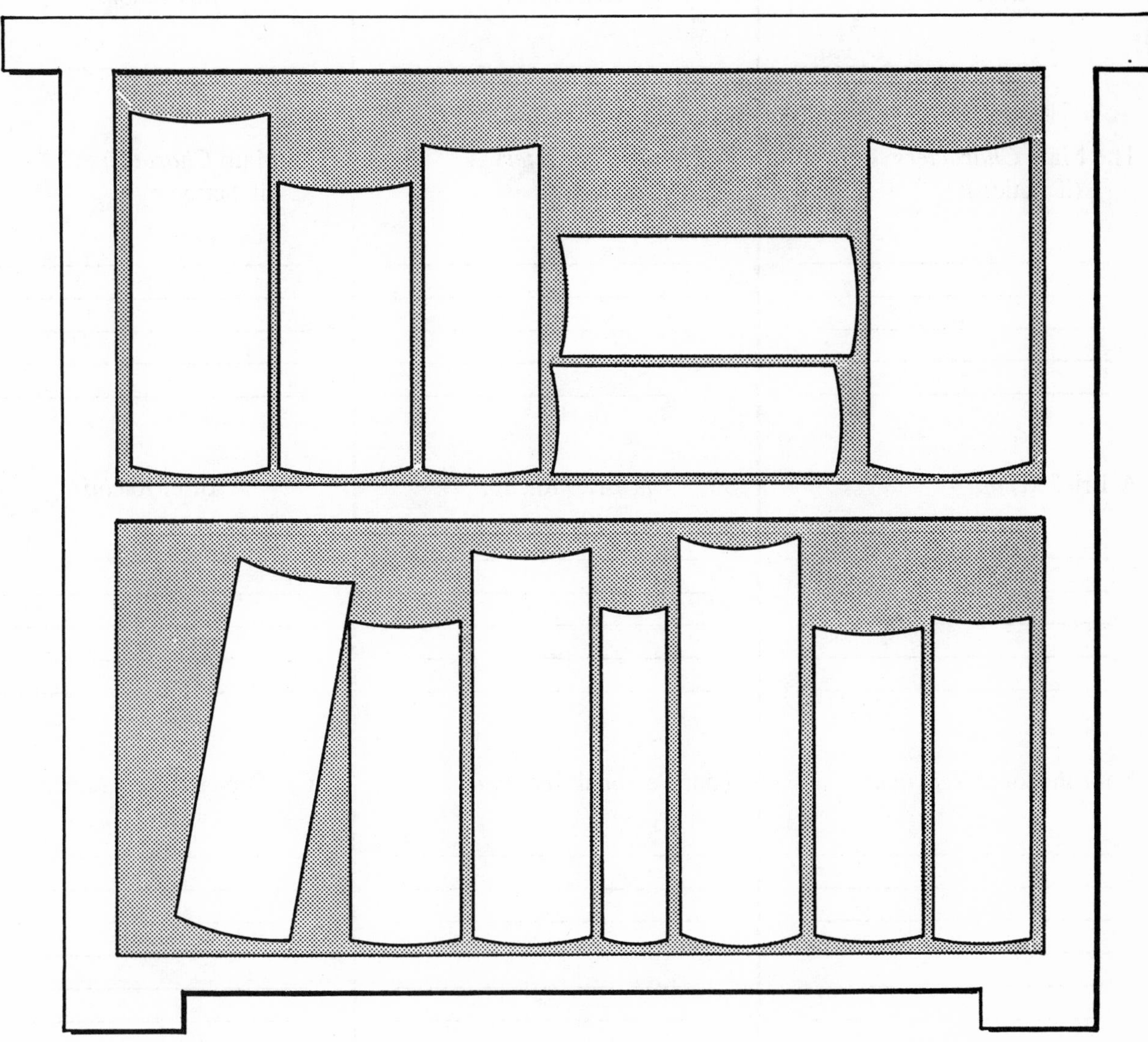

*From How *How To Increase Reading Ability*, 6th ed. by Albert J. Harris and Edward R. Sipay. Copyright © 1975 by Longman, Inc. Reprinted by permission.

The *Title* of Your Book:

____

Its *Author:*

____

The Main *Characters* (if fiction):

____
____
____
____
____

A Brief *Recap:*

____
____
____
____
____

Your Personal *Reaction:*

____
____
____
____
____
____

Your *Name:*

____

(more space on other side)

The *Title* of Your Book:

____

Its *Author:*

____

The Main *Characters* (if fiction):

____
____
____
____
____

A Brief *Recap:*

____
____
____
____
____

Your Personal *Reaction:*

____
____
____
____
____
____

Your *Name:*

____

(more space on other side)

The *Title* of Your Book:

____

Its *Author:*

____

The Main *Characters* (if fiction):

____
____
____
____
____

A Brief *Recap:*

____
____
____
____
____

Your Personal *Reaction:*

____
____
____
____
____
____

Your *Name:*

____

(more space on other side)

NAME ______________________________ DATE __________

YOUR PERSONAL READING LOG

You can educate yourself to the last day of our course—and beyond—through your own personal reading. As someone observed with quite a bit of truth, "The best school in the world is the library."

Wide reading can bring you information and delight. And it can make you a more efficient reader! Do you want a superior vocabulary? Wide reading is one of the most effective vocabulary builders. As you read, you meet new words again and again and gradually incorporate some of these into your vocabulary. Do you want to read more rapidly? Highly interesting fiction and fast-moving narrative-style biographies tend to "pull you along" and thus to increase your speed.

Keep this record up to date each week. The personal reading you do in our course will become part of your record of progress. You may want to make a voluntary commitment to yourself—to decide on the approximate number of pages you plan to read each week.

During the week of *I read*

______ to ______ ______ pages in ______________________ by ______________________.
(date) (date) (title) (author)

______ to ______ ______ pages in ______________________ by ______________________.

______ to ______ ______ pages in ______________________ by ______________________.

______ to ______ ______ pages in ______________________ by ______________________.

______ to ______ ______ pages in ______________________ by ______________________.

______ to ______ ______ pages in ______________________ by ______________________.

______ to ______ ______ pages in ______________________ by ______________________.

______ to ______ ______ pages in ______________________ by ______________________.

______ to ______ ______ pages in ______________________ by ______________________.

______ to ______ ______ pages in ______________________ by ______________________.

______ to ______ ______ pages in ______________________ by ______________________.

NAME ______________________________ DATE ____________

YOUR PERSONAL READING LOG

You can educate yourself to the last day of our course—and beyond—through your own personal reading.

Keep this record up to date each week. Your personal reading that is related to our course will become part of your record of progress.

During the week of *I read*

______ to ______ ______ pages in ______________________ by ______________________.
(date) (date) (title) (author)

______ to ______ ______ pages in ______________________ by ______________________.
______ to ______ ______ pages in ______________________ by ______________________.
______ to ______ ______ pages in ______________________ by ______________________.
______ to ______ ______ pages in ______________________ by ______________________.
______ to ______ ______ pages in ______________________ by ______________________.
______ to ______ ______ pages in ______________________ by ______________________.
______ to ______ ______ pages in ______________________ by ______________________.
______ to ______ ______ pages in ______________________ by ______________________.
______ to ______ ______ pages in ______________________ by ______________________.
______ to ______ ______ pages in ______________________ by ______________________.
______ to ______ ______ pages in ______________________ by ______________________.
______ to ______ ______ pages in ______________________ by ______________________.
______ to ______ ______ pages in ______________________ by ______________________.
______ to ______ ______ pages in ______________________ by ______________________.
______ to ______ ______ pages in ______________________ by ______________________.

NAME ______________________________ DATE __________

PLEASE HELP NEXT YEAR'S CLASS

You can help next year's class by answering the following questions. Your teacher will consider your comments thoughtfully in planning for next year's class.

Teachers need to know what teenagers really like to read and how to guide them to reading they will enjoy. There isn't any grade on this!

1. Have you read some books for your own pleasure or information during that past school year—books you were not required to read for your school assignments? ______ About how many? ______ Please name one or two:

   ____

   ____

2. If you read some books for personal pleasure this year, what were your favorites?

   ____

   ____

3. Has your personal reading included any new *types* of books during this past school year? ______ If your answer is yes, what type(s)? __________

   ____

4. Do you think you have done about the same amount of personal reading that you did during the school year before this? ______ Less personal reading than before? ______ More personal reading? ______

5. Do you have some books of your own? ______ If you do, about how many? ______ Did you add some books during this school year? ______
6. Do you read one or more magazines? ______ If you do, which one(s)?

____

7. Do you read a newspaper or part of one? ______ If you do, which one(s)?

____

8. Have you used the school library for your own personal reading about as much as you did during the school year before this? ______ Less than last year? ______ More than last year? ______
9 Do you own a public card? Yes ______ No ______ . Did you take out your library card during this school year? ______
10. Have you used the public library for your own personal reading about as much as you did during the school year before this? ______ Less than last year? ______ More than last year? ______
11. Would you describe yourself as a *frequent* reader for pleasure, a person who *sometimes* reads for pleasure, or a person who *never* reads for pleasure? ______
12. What could your teacher have done during this school year so that you might

have enjoyed reading more? ______________________________

____

____

NAME ______________________ DATE __________

HOW DO YOU SPEND YOUR "TIME INCOME"?*

We all have an "income" of 168 hours each week. How are you spending your "income"? Keep a log for two or three days of how you spend your time. Be specific—"15 minutes phoning," "10 minutes playing a record." The purpose is not for someone else to tell you how to spend your time but to help *you* see where your time is now going. Ask your teacher for extra "log" sheets like this to keep a record of the extra days, or keep your record on notebook paper.

Are you spending your "income" in the way you really want to? Make jottings of the good features of your present schedule and of any changes you would like to make.

Your Time Log for __________ (date):

7:00 ______________
7:30 ______________
8:00 ______________
8:30 ______________
9:00 ______________
9:30 ______________
10:00 ______________
10:30 ______________
11:00 ______________
11:30 ______________
12:00 ______________
12:30 ______________
1:00 ______________
1:30 ______________
2:00 ______________
2:30 ______________
3:00 ______________
3:30 ______________
4:00 ______________
4:30 ______________
5:00 ______________
5:30 ______________
6:00 ______________
6:30 ______________
7:00 ______________
7:30 ______________
8:00 ______________
8:30 ______________
9:00 ______________
9:30 ______________
10:00 ______________
10:30 ______________

Good Features of Your Present Use of Your "Time Income":

____
____
____
____
____
____
____

Changes that Would Help You Make Better Use of Your Income

____
____
____
____
____
____

*Alan Lakein speaks of "spending your time income" in his book, *How to Get Control of Your Time and Your Life* (Bergenfield, N.J.: New American Library, 1973). Mr. Lakein has made a career of helping people make better use of their time.

YOUR PERSONAL ACTIVITY PLAN FOR STUDY, CLASSES, AND RECREATION

On this plan you block off certain hours for study. Thr rest are *freed*—for other things you want to do. Psychologists advise, "Follow your plan each day. The *habit* of studying at regular times should develop. Then getting down to work and concentrating should be much easier!"

A.M.	**Monday**	**Tuesday**	**Wednesday**	**Thursday**	**Friday**	**Saturday**	**Sunday**
P.M.							

TIPS FOR DRAWING UP YOUR PERSONAL ACTIVITY PLAN

Do you want to get more control *over your time—and your life?* A personal activity plan should help you solve this problem. On your plan you block off certain hours for study. The rest are *freed*—for other things you want to do.

Below are tips to help you draw up your personal activity plan:

1. Rough out your first trial schedule in pencil.
2. First, fill in your regular activities—activities that are unchanging—your classes, lab periods, after-school sports, hours on the job, and any regular weekly events like club meetings or music lessons.
3. Then, around these unchanging activities, plan the hours you'll spend in study, and block these off on your plan.
4. You are making a plan for study—*and recreation, too.* Be sure to block off some free time spaces to make time for friends, physical activities, and rest.
5. Your open spaces will give you flexibility. There will be unexpected club, sports or family events, or good times with friends. With the time left unscheduled, you can adjust as special circumstances arise. Just move your studying into one of your open spaces.
6. Place your schedule where you will see it often—in your notebook or on your desk or study table.
7. Give your plan a trial run. If you find weak spots, revise your schedule to meet your needs.
8. Try to follow your plan each day. Now, because you *really concentrate* during the hours you've set aside for study, you may find you have more time for non-school activities!

MAKE A MUST-DO SCHEDULE WHEN THINGS ARE RUSHED

We all have rushed weeks when there are just too many things to do. There's a way to help solve this problem—one that helps get each and every job done. Think out everything you have to do—the whole week long. Then give each item its place on your schedule. Now you have a handle on all the things you have to do. Now you can see your way to finish. Revise and make additions as the week goes along. When you've attended to an item, check it off. This will give you a feeling of real satisfaction.

A.M.	**Monday**	**Tuesday**	**Wednesday**	**Thursday**	**Friday**	**Saturday**	**Sunday**
P.M.							

CALENDAR FOR A LONG-TERM PROJECT

We've all left important projects until the last night—much to our dismay. Why not try this calendar for long-term projects? Here you space out *parts* of your project in manageable stages—for instance, doing the reading for the paper, writing the first draft, revising, writing the final copy. Now you'll be *ahead* of the game without last-minute panic. Not all tranquilizers come in a bottle!

Part You'll Have Done	**Date You'll Have It Done**
____________________	____________________
____________________	____________________
____________________	____________________
____________________	____________________
____________________	____________________

CALENDAR FOR A LONG-TERM PROJECT

We've all left important projects until the last night—much to our dismay. Why not try this calendar for long-term projects? Here you space out *parts* of your project in manageable stages—for instance, doing the reading for the paper, writing the first draft, revising, writing the final copy. Now you'll be *ahead* of the game without last-minute panic. Not all tranquilizers come in a bottle!

Part You'll Have Done	**Date You'll Have It Done**
____________________	____________________
____________________	____________________
____________________	____________________
____________________	____________________
____________________	____________________

IS THE PLACE YOU STUDY "ON YOUR SIDE"?

Revamping the area where you study at home may bring a decided increase in your study efficiency—even raise your grades! Using the chart below, zero in on any "distractors" and decide what you can do to reduce or eliminate them.

"Distractor" that Hurts My Concentration	What I Can Do about It?

Using this chart, examine your usual conditions for study at home and note any changes you would like to make.

Condition to Examine	What's Wrong or Missing?	What I Can Do about It
Room where I study		
Working space on desk or table		
Lighting equipment		
Study tools (paper, note cards, pen, sharp pencils, eraser, pencil sharpener, ruler, paste, scissors, clips, rubber bands, dictionary, etc.)		

RECORD OF ASSIGNMENTS

Subject	What to Do	Special Instructions	Date Due	Check When Finished

TIME BOX

Your deadline for the task ________

Time you started ________

Time you finished ________

Actual time you spent ________

TIME BOX

Your deadline for the task ________

Time you started ________

Time you finished ________

Actual time you spent ________

TIME BOX

Your deadline for the task ________

Time you started ________

Time you finished ________

Actual time you spent ________

TIME BOX

Your deadline for the task ________

Time you started ________

Time you finished ________

Actual time you spent ________

TIME BOX

Your deadline for the task ________

Time you started ________

Time you finished ________

Actual time you spent ________

TIME BOX

Your deadline for the task ________

Time you started ________

Time you finished ________

Actual time you spent ________

TIME BOX

Your deadline for the task ________

Time you started ________

Time you finished ________

Actual time you spent ________

TIME BOX

Your deadline for the task ________

Time you started ________

Time you finished ________

Actual time you spent ________

TAKE YOUR CHOICE OF STUDY TIPS

Would you like to streamline your study and perhaps raise your grade average, too? Tips like those below have helped students *do exactly that!* Take your choice of the tips that suit your learning style.

1. Ask yourself, "What, so far as you know, are your *life goals?* Where does achievement at school fit in?"
2. *Take control* of your time. Now you're in charge of yourself.
   - Make a time plan, giving a place on it to all your "must-do's." Now you have a handle on everything you have to do. Not all tranquilizers come in a bottle!
   - Space out long-term projects—in manageable installments.
   - Do you need a "time-stretcher"? Use scattered bits of time!
3. Is the place you usually study "on your side"? The right surroundings can help you *turn on concentration!* What are your distractors? Can you reduce or eliminate them?
4. Do you have everything you need for study *right at hand and ready?* Each "hunting expedition" breaks your continuity of thought!
5. You *live with* your notebook—every school day. Will yours be a disaster area or a real help to you this year?
6. Keep a *record of your assignments,* including any special instructions.
7. With the books and papers of four or five subjects piled up high around you, you may feel swamped by it all. Having the work of *just one subject* on the desk before you is good psychology.
8. Having trouble concentrating? *Set a time limit* for certain tasks, then beat the clock! Now you won't dream your time away!
9. Promise yourself a *"high preference" reward* when you achieve a goal you really care about in study.
10. Expect your progress to be gradual. *Many small steps make a giant step!*

AND HAVE A HAPPY AND SUCCESSFUL SCHOOL YEAR!

Dear Parent,

We are writing to share with you our plans for "Operation Effective Study." We know that you, as a parent, care deeply about your son's or daughter's success at school this year.

We are planning a special effort this year to guide our students in effective study. Young people today need this guidance far more urgently than young people did in the past. Television may be an ever-present distractor. The responsibilities of an out-of-school job may make it difficult for students to meet responsibilities at school. Our guidance counselors comment that even our top students can, in many cases, benefit from guidance for still more effective study.

Parents ask, "How much time will my son or daughter be expected to spend on homework?" While expectations will vary with the course load and the efficiency of the student, and while assignments will be heavier certain days than others, your son or daughter should probably average at least __________ of study on school nights and over the weekend.

Many parents, already encouraging study at home, ask, "How can we do more?" One promising way is by arranging a place, if the student does not already have one, that really facilitates study. Students will probably concentrate better if they study in the same place every day. The same surroundings, learning experts tell us, exert a strong power of suggestion. It becomes habit to go there, clear the mind of other things, and study. Most students study better in a quiet place. Surely the study desk or table should be away from that distractor of distractors--television! A deep voice insisting on Nine Lives for finicky Morris distracts most people!

Students can be encouraged to design their own study center in the home, complete with everything that's needed for the job of study. This will include a study desk or table with an adequate working surface. Experts on college study suggest that students place their desk so that they face a blank wall instead of a friendly roommate. A telephone nearby isn't an aid to study, and a well-stocked refrigerator nearby probably won't help either!

You may wish to check the lighting of the student's study table. Students can lose the concentration battle from poor lighting. Glare on the page, shadows on their work, or light in their eyes can cause eyestrain, headaches, tiredness, and poor concentration. The old-style bare unsheded electric light bulb is as out of date as a candle. The entire working surface of the desk should be illuminated evenly. There should not be too much contrast between the lighting on their work and in the surrounding room. The rest of the room should be well lighted, without deep shadows.

Students will concentrate better if they have everything they need before they begin to study. Each "hunting expedition" breaks their continuity of thought. The desk at home should have certain standard equipment right at hand and ready--paper, note cards, pen, sharp pencils, an eraser, a pencil sharpener, a rule, paste, scissors, paper clips, graph paper and a compass, rubber bands, Scotch tape, and a dictionary.

Parents ask, "How can I help my son or daughter concentrate?" If noise is the distractor, that quiet place apart should be extremely helpful! Some large office supply stores offer a "Sound Barrier" or "Study Buddy," a device that looks like earphones and helps shut out distracting sounds. Airplane mechanics wear devices like this while working on jet planes! Earplugs, which are inexpensive, can serve the same purpose.

Parents may wish to encourage young people to take advantage of the school library before and after school and of the resources of their public library, including the expert assistance of the reference librarian.

Parents inquire, "What causes failure to concentrate?" One study expert replies, "Anything from poor diet to blue eyes!" He calls our attention to a variety of possible causes. These include "external distractors," among them noise, poor lighting, and lack of study equipment, and "internal distractors," among them disorganization, daydreaming, personal worries including anxiety about schoolwork, and physical causes, including poor diet, lack of sleep, and lack of exercise. If you suspect a serious concentration problem, we invite you to consult your son's or daughter's counselor.

We also invite you to talk with the counselor if you observe a need for study guidance but feel that the young person will "take" that guidance better from someone at school.

We invite your comments about "Operation Effective Study." We will welcome your suggestions about what we can do at school to promote effective study. We ask you to share with us ways you yourself have found successful.

To you and to your son or daughter, this is our wish--"Have a happy and successful school year!"

Sincerely,

*Pauk, Walter, *How to Study in College,* 2nd ed. (Boston: Houghton Mifflin Co., 1974), p. 36.

Index

Abstraction ladder, 54
Accent
  listening for, 25–26
  shifting, 26, 27
  using dictionary for, 85–86
  using textbooks for, 103
  in word attack, 8, 25–27
  in word meaning, 64
Additive learning, 75
Advance organizer, 104, 113
Allusions, understanding, 86
Alphabetical order, 82
Altick, Richard D., 216, 217, 218
American Heritage Word Frequency Book (Carroll, Davies, Richman), 57
Art, motivating personal reading, 202
Art of Speaking, The (Elson, Peck), 221
Assignments
  recording, 254
  using context clues in, 71–72
Audio-visual aids, 119, 123
Auditory discrimination, 29, 31, 32, 33, 49
Ausubel, David, 104

Bacon, Francis, 217, 221
Baldridge Reading Strategy Program, 157
Banks, James A., 116
Be a Better Reader (Smith), 10, 28, 175
Becker, Wesley C., 53
Betts, Emmett, 189
Bias
  awareness of, 217, 218, 219–232
  combatting, 228–231
  developing sensitivity to viewpoints, 226–227
  examining in others, 223–224
  making judgments, 225–226
Biology
  "fine-tuning" dictionary meanings, 85
  motivating personal reading, 192
  pre-teaching multi-meaning terms, 64
  reducing polysyllables in, 64
  using realia in, 61, 115
Black Experience in Children's Books, The (Rollock), 196
Bookfinder, The: A Guide to Children's Literature About the Needs and Problems of Youth (Dreyer), 196
Book lists, 190, 196, 198, 204
Book reports, 205
Books
  judging difficulty of, 190–192
  matching to students, 123, 189–192, 204
Books, Young People, and Reading Guidance (Pilgrim, McAllister), 196
Bookstores, 200
Burke, Carolyn L., 14
Burmeister, Lou, 10, 19, 34, 37, 43, 77, 189, 217, 227

Business education
critical reading in, 230-231
relating words to experience, 61-62

Campbell, Ann, 191-192
Chapter titles, 157
Comprehension, 99-126
collecting resources, 122-123
diagnosing problem areas, 100-102
difficulty of materials and, 124-215
helping with opening pages, 119-120
motivating students, 99-100, 102-103, 107-115
open book lessons in, 120
previewing materials, 104-107
projects and activities, 113-115
providing background experience, 118-119
questions for, 115-117, 158
rate-of-reading and, 170, 171, 177, 180
reading aloud to students, 120-121
reading with purpose, 115-117, 123, 172
removing roadblocks to, 86, 92, 103-104
rewriting materials for lower levels, 125-126
using study guides, 117-118
word meaning and, 53, 92
Comprehension skills, 128
application to course materials, 144-145
identifying details, 128, 138-145
main idea from paragraphs, 127-137
selecting materials for practice, 136
testing for mastery, 136, 145
Comprehensive High School Reading Methods (Shepherd), 266
Concentration, 238-239, 249, 251-256
Concepts, and word meaning, 65-66
Consonant sounds, 29
activities, 41, 43, 44
Consumer buying guides, 229
Context clues
for assignment words, 71-72
defined, 8
do's and don'ts for using, 71
for new words, 63
in phonic analysis, 31-32
soft and hard *c* and *g*, 37, 40, 45
syntactic and semantic, 67-70
testing for mastery in, 72
timely use of, 73
in word attack, 9, 14-16
in word meaning, 14-15, 67-74, 77, 92
in word recognition, 67
Cooperative Reading Test, 100, 170
Critical reading, 215-232
activities, 221-222, 226-228
checklist on, 231-232
and classroom climate, 220
counteracting bias, 218-232
importance of, 215-216
and reading level, 216-217
resources, 218-219
Critical Thinking: Scholastic Social Studies Skills, 219
Critics, 217

Dallman, Martha, 19
Davis, Frederick B., 53
Details
to be disregarded, 139-141
in paragraphs, 138-145
signal words in paragraphs, 138-139, 141-144
Diagnostic Reading Test (Vocabulary), 55
Diagnostic testing. *See also* Standardized testing
for rate-of-reading, 170
for vocabulary, 55
for word attack, 11
Dialect, 106
Dictionaries
simplified, 81-82, 83
unabridged, 86
Dictionary skills, 9
alphabetical order, 82
building speed in using, 82, 83
locating entries, 81, 83-84
for pronunciation, 8, 46, 81, 85
selecting correct definitions, 81, 84-85, 90
using guide words, 81, 83
for word attack, 46
for word meaning, 8, 71, 80-86, 92
for word origin, 80, 90
Digraphs
au, 37, 38-39, 40
aw, 37
Diphthongs, 43
oi, oy, 37, 40, 41
ou, 37, 40
ow, 37, 39, 40
Documents, 107
Dougherty, Mildred, 10, 19

Dramatic readings, 194
Driver education, combatting bias in, 229-230
Durkin, Dolores, 8, 9, 17, 27, 28, 50

e, silent final, 35-36, 40
Easy Reading: Book Series and Periodicals for Less Able Readers (Graves, Boettcher, Ryder), 191
Editorials, 228
Educational television, 202-203
Ekwall, Eldon E., 31, 87
Encyclopedias, 124
English
  building bridges to students' emotional experiences, 107-108
  critical reading in, 217, 227
  determining reading rates, 171
  "fine tuning" dictionary meanings, 85
  motivating personal reading, 112-113, 187, 192-193, 202
  pre-teaching multi-meaning terms, 64
  previewing difficult material, 105-107, 119-120
  providing background, 118
  reading for purpose, 115
  reading to students, 120-121
  taping stories for motivation, 111
  teaching "stopper" words, 63
  using supplementary materials, 125
Estes, Thomas H., 56, 109
Evaluating Reading and Study Skills in the Secondary Classroom (Viox), 102

Figurative expressions, 72-73
Fry, Edward B., 176, 191
Fry Graph for Estimating Readability, 191

Gates-MacGinitie Reading Test, 55, 100
Gateways to Readable Books (Strang, Phelps, Withrow), 191
Generative learning, 75
Geography, "fine tuning" dictionary meanings, 84
Geometry, pre-teaching multi-meaning terms, 64
Glossary, 67, 103
Goodman, Kenneth S., 13
Goodman, Yetta, 14
Good Reading for Poor Readers (Spache), 190, 202
Good Reading for the Disadvantaged Reader (Spache), 190
Graphic aids, 103, 161-162
Graves, Michael F., 165
Greek and Latin word parts, 62, 74
  limitations to using, 77
  prefixes, 261-265
  roots, 18-19, 79, 80, 261-265
  value of learning, 75-76, 78
Grob, James A., 177
Guide words, 81, 83
Guiding the Social Studies Reading of High School Students (Preston), 102

Havighurst, Robert J., 195
Heilman, Arthur W., 29
Hennefrund, E. R., 125
High-frequency words, 48
Hill, Walter R., 67
Hillocks, George, 73
Home economics
  critical reading in, 230
  "fine tuning" dictionary meanings, 85
  motivating readers, 187
  teaching "stopper" words, 63
"Homemade" tests, 101, 102, 170-171
How to Study in College (Pauk), 256
Huck, Charlotte S., 216
Hull, Marian A., 28, 36

i, consonantizing of, in final syllables, 37, 40, 43-44
Improving Reading in Every Class (Thomas, Robinson), 36-37
Index, 67, 103
Industrial arts
  critical reading in, 229
  terminology in, 54
Inflected forms, 8, 74
  in the dictionary, 81, 83
Informational articles, 138
Introduction, paragraphs of, 137

Johnson, Laura, 111, 194

Karlin, Robert, 31-32, 33, 54, 105, 238
Kind, Martha L., 216
Kinesthetic reinforcement, 49
Klare, George R., 125
Krug, Mark M., 107

Latin. *See* Greek and Latin word parts
Letter sounds, 8
Librarians, 123-124, 190, 196-197, 199
Libraries, 194-195, 198-200
Library card, 198-199
Living Word Vocabulary, The (Dale, O'Rourke), 57
Long-term projects, 250-251

McCabe, Bernard J., 73
McCall-Crabbs Standard Test Lessons in Reading, 178, 182
McCallister, James, 128
McCampbell, James F., 73
McCullough Word Analysis Tests, 11, 20
Magazine articles, 124
Magazines, 201, 202, 216
Main idea, 127-137
  defined, 130, 131-132
  importance to students, 129-130
  of longer selections, 145-151
  not stated, 133-134
  skimming for, 130
Marksheffel, Ned D., 16
Master copies, 131, 154, 271-325
Mathematics
  ensuring retention in, 64
  "fine tuning" dictionary meanings in, 85
  motivating personal reading, 192
  previewing assignments in, 109
  relating words to experience, 62
  teaching "stopper" words, 63
  terminology in, 54
Measurement of Readability, The (Klare), 125
Medical profession, roots in, 79
Memory, David, 10, 19
Miller, Ward S., 60
Miscue Analysis: Applications to Reading Instruction (Goodman), 13-14
Morris, Helen Frakenpohl, 179
Multi-meaning words, 64
Music
  combatting bias in, 231
  "fine tuning" dictionary meanings in, 85
  motivating readers, 187
  pointing out root words, 63-64
  relating to students' thoughts and concerns, 108-109
Myth or fact questions, 110

Newspapers, 201, 216
Niles, Olive Stafford, 10, 19, 35-36
Notebooks, neatness in, 253-254
Notes from a Different Drummer: A Guide to Juvenile Fiction Portraying the Handicapped (Baskin, Harris), 196
Note taking
  from paragraphs, 139
  skills, 140
  strategies with textbooks, 162
  to trigger recall, 163

"Official" terms, 161
OK5R approach, 154, 164-165, 174, 182-183
Open-book lessons, 120
Oral language abilities, 8
Oral reading
  miscues in, 13-14
  in word attack diagnosis, 11-14
Outline, overviewing to find, 156
Outlining paragraphs, 148
Overviewing, 155-158, 176
  proving mastery in, 157-158

Paragraph(s)
  identifying details in, 138-145, 160
  main idea from, 127-137, 160
  outlining, 148
  patterns, 128, 130-136, 137, 182
  signal words in, 137-139, 141-143
  from subject areas, 133
  topic sentence, 160
  types of, 137
Parents
  encouraging good study habits, 257-258
  encouraging personal reading, 204-205
Pauk, Walter, 154, 247, 255, 256
Periodicals, 201
Personal problems, 254
Personal reading, 185-211
  activities, 205-211
  areas for, 200-201
  benefits of, 186-187
  gaining insights into, 188-189
  matching books and readers, 123, 189-192
  motivating readers, 185, 187-188, 192-205, 211
  resources, 190-192, 196, 201
  sharing, 205-211
  time for, 197-198, 203-204
Phonic analysis
  activities, 37-46
  basic skills needed in, 28-29, 44

defined, 8, 27
resources, 27-28, 29, 31, 34, 37
teaching guidelines for, 36-37
in word attack, 9, 11, 27-46
Phonics for the Reading Teacher (Hull), 28, 36
Phonics in Proper Perspective (Heilman), 29
Photography, combatting bias in, 229
Physical education
combatting bias in, 231
motivating personal reading, 187, 192
Physics
motivating personal reading, 192
vocabulary development in, 90
Piercey, Dorothy, 80
Poetry, 115
Polysyllabic words
deciphering, 74, 79-80
reducing, 64
using context for, 73-74
using knowledge of word parts for, 74
Preface, 102
Preface to Critical Reading (Altick), 218
Prefixes, 74
defined, 17
Greek and Latin, 261-265
high-yield, 75-76, 78
meanings of, 8, 18-19
Pre-reading activities, 100
Preston, Ralph C., 102
Previewing, 104-107
Printed aids, for vocabulary, 66-67
Pronunciation
c and *g*, 45
dictionary use for, 8, 46, 81, 85
Pronunciation keys, 46, 67, 86, 103

qu, 32-35, 40
Questions
myth or fact, 110
overviewing with, 157
for reading with purpose, 115-117
for self-checking, 163
in textbook headings, 158-160

Readers
gifted, 100
low level, 121-122, 124, 125, 154, 190-191
matching books to, 123, 189-192
slow, 177-178
unreachable (*see* Personal reading)
Reading
for background information, 173
brainstorming before, 105
close-intensive, 174
critical (*see* Critical reading)
devices, 179
dramatic, 194
"hurdles," 58
importance of word meaning in, 53
increasing the difficulty in, 123, 124
ladders, 204
levels, 100, 121-122, 189-190, 216-217
oral (*see* Oral reading)
with purpose, 115-117, 123, 172
removing roadblocks before, 103-104
"stop and go," 160-161
to students, 120-121, 193
textbooks (*see* Textbook reading)
for vocabulary development, 48, 186
wide, 48, 186-187
Read for Your Life (Palmer), 191
Reading Miscue Inventory Manual: Procedure for Diagnosis and Evaluation (Goodman, Burke), 14
Reading Strategies for Middle and Secondary School Teachers (Burmeister), 219
Reading rates, 169-183
and academic success, 177-178
acquiring a full range of, 172-177
adjusting to task, 162, 169-183
building speed, 177-183
and comprehension, 170, 171, 177, 180
and concentration, 252
diagnosing attainment and need in, 169-171
flexibility in, 169
internal adjustment in, 174-175
in scanning, 175
in skimming, 130, 175-176
teaching concept of adjustment in, 171-172
techniques for improving, 173-174
testing for, 178-182
Reading Tactics (Niles, Dougherty, Memory), 10, 19
Reading Versatility Test, 170
Recall, using notes for, 163
Retention
of content, 138-139, 163-164
of vocabulary, 61-62, 64, 87-88, 91
Reviewing, 163-164
Richards, Norman, 149-151
Roberts, Clyde, 27-28
Robinson, Francis P., 153
Robinson, H. Alan, 36-37, 228-229, 231
Root words, 8, 74

Root words (*continued*)
defined, 17
for dictionary use, 81, 83-84
disguised, 75
finding familiar, 17-18, 74
Greek and Latin, 18-19, 79, 80, 261-265
high-yield, 75
limitations for using, 77
spotlighting in long words, 63-64
value of learning, 79
Rudd, Josephine, 82

Sartain, Harry W., 114, 194
Scanning, 175
Science
critical reading, 224-225
dealing with poor readers, 121-122, 124
major patterns of writing in, 137
motivating readers, 187
open-book lessons, 120
pointing out root words, 63
preparing for reading assignments, 105
pre-teaching multi-meaning terms, 64
providing background, 119
terminology in, 54
textbook study guidance, 154
using Greek and Latin word parts, 19, 74, 75
using live issues, 110
using realia in, 61, 114-115
using skills of librarian, 123-124
using supplementary materials, 124
Self-recitation technique, 162-163
Semantic clues, 67, 68-69
Shaw, Philip B., 92
Shepherd, David L., 30, 77, 83, 266-267
Sight words, 47-51
Singer, Harry, 60
Skimming, 130, 156, 175-176, 203
Skimming and Scanning (Fry), 176
Smith, Nila Banton, 10, 28, 175
Social studies
adjusting reading rate in, 174-175
advance organizing, 104-105
critical reading in, 217, 223, 224, 225, 226, 227
figurative expressions in, 72
having visitors to turn on interest, 111
major patterns of writing in, 137
motivating personal reading, 187, 192, 202, 203
pointing out root words, 63
pre-teaching multi-meaning terms, 64
previewing primary sources, 107, 119
providing background, 118
questioning, reading for purpose, 115, 116
reading for background information, 173
teaching "stopper" words, 63, 67
terminology in, 54
textbook strategies, 158
using live issues for motivation, 110, 114
using realia in, 61
using self-assignments, 112
words and concepts through pictures, 62
Spache, George D., 202
SQ3R approach, 153, 154
SRA Rate Builders, 178, 182
Standardized testing. *See also* Diagnostic testing
for comprehension, 100-102
to determine reading level, 189-190
for rate-of-reading, 170
for vocabulary, 55-56
Stauffer, Russell G., 14
"Stopper" words, 63
Strang, Ruth, 30, 89, 183, 239, 249
Strategies for Identifying Words (Durkin), 10, 17, 28
Stress. *See* Accent
Structural analysis
defined, 8, 17, 74
testing for skills in, 76-77
in word attack, 9, 11, 17-19
word meaning through, 74-80
Student assistants, 39-40
Study guides, 117-118, 125
Study habits, 238-258
concentration problems, 236, 238-239, 249, 251-256
defined, 237, 257
distractions, 236, 252, 253
in home environment, 236-237, 253
with long-term projects, 250-251
Must-Do Schedule, 245-246
notebooks, 253-254
parental encouragement in, 257-258
with part-time jobs, 241, 250

Personal Activity Plan, 242–244
place of study and, 251–253
recording assignments, 254
resources, 237–238
teaching, 238, 239–240, 257
time limits, 255, 256
time planning, 239, 240–250
time wasting, 237
transforming, 256–257
wanting to improve, 238–240
Study skills, 138–139, 235–238. *See also* Textbook reading
defined, 237, 257
Suffixes, 8, 18, 74
defined, 17
high-yield, 75, 78
lists of, 266–267
Summaries
chapter, 103
paragraph, 137
Summarizing skills, 138
Supplementary materials, collecting, 122–123, 124
Syllabication
activities, 21–25
"chunking," 21
rules for, 23–25, 267–268
in word attack, 8, 9, 17, 19–25
in word meaning, 64
Syllables, 22, 64
Synonyms
available concepts for, 65
as contextual clues, 69–70
Syntactic clues, 67–68

Table of contents, 102, 157, 164
Tachistoscope, 50–51
Tapes, read-along, 194–195
Teacher, as author, 125–126
Teacher Handbook of Diagnosis and Remediation in Reading, The (Ekwall), 31
Teachers Guides to Television, 202
Technical terms, 58
Television, 202–203, 216, 236
newscasts, 228
Textbook reading, 153–165
graphic aids in, 161–162
OK5R approach, 154, 164–165, 174, 182
overviewing, 155–158, 176
reviewing, 163–164
self-check questions for, 163
self-recitation in, 162–163
spotting "official" terms, 161
SQ3R approach, 153, 154
"stop-and-go" method, 160–161
taking notes, 162, 163
V.A.K. technique, 161, 162–163
Textbooks
guiding students in using, 102–103
selecting for vocabulary development, 67
Thomas, Ellen Lamar, 36–37, 231
Title, 146
chapter, 157
Topic, in longer selections, 146. *See also* Main idea
Topic sentence, 160
Toward Reading Comprehension (Sherbourne), 219
Transition, paragraphs of, 137
True, False, or In Between: An Elective Course in Logical Thinking (Hiatt), 219
Typeface, used as signals, 86, 102

"Using Paragraph Clues as Aids to Understanding" (McCallister), 128

V.A.K. (visual, auditory, kinesthetic) technique, 161, 162–163
Vaughn, Joseph L., Jr., 56, 109
Viox, Ruth J., 102
Visual discrimination, 29, 31, 32, 49
Visualizing, 161
Vocabulary
and academic success, 54
activities, 60, 92–95
figurative, 72–73
and job success, 54
and rate-of-reading, 177
retention of, 61–62, 64, 87–88, 91
sight, 47–51
technical, 58
Vocabulary development, 53–95
through context clues, 65–66, 86, 91, 92
diagnosing student ability in, 55–60, 74, 101
enriching background experiences for, 61–62

Vocabulary development (*continued*)
guidelines for teaching, 56-57, 63-67, 91-92
importance of, 53, 58
through living examples, 62, 64, 69
motivating students, 58-60, 88-89
through pictures, 62
through printed aids, 66-67
reading "hurdles," 58
through realia, 61
recording and reviewing words, 91-92
resources for, 57, 60, 81
"stopper" words, 63-67
through structural analysis, 74-80, 86, 91, 92
student techniques, 53, 57, 86-91
teaching concepts for, 65-66
testing for mastery, 72
textbooks for, 67
using dictionary for, 71, 80-86, 90, 91, 92
wide reading for, 48, 62-63, 186
through word origins, 80, 86, 91
Vowel sounds, 29, 31, 35-36

Williamson, Ann, 108
Wolf, Willavene, 216
Word Attack (Roberts), 28
Word attack, 7-51
accent and, 25-27, 46
activities for, 21-25, 37-46, 50-51
through context clues, 14-16, 46
defined, 7, 46
diagnosing student needs in, 10-14, 31, 36, 55-56
through dictionary use, 46
guidelines for teaching, 10, 31-32, 46-47
with older students, 9-10, 20, 25, 29-31
through phonic analysis, 27-46
and rate-of-reading, 177
resources, 10, 27-28, 37
strategies for, 46-50
through structural analysis, 17-19, 46, 74
through syllabication, 19-20, 46
and word recognition, 55
Word blending, in phonics, 31
Word frequency, 57
Word ladders, 42-43
Word meaning, 8. *See also* Vocabulary; Vocabulary development
through context clues, 14-16
through structural analysis, 18-19
Word origins
learning new words through, 80
using dictionary for, 80, 90
Word parts, 17-19. *See also* Greek and Latin word parts; Root words; Structural analysis
activities, 77-80
diagnosing student knowledge of, 74-75
enriching stock of, 75
limits to using, 77
lists of, 19, 77
teasers, 79
for word meaning, 92
Word recognition
using context for, 167
defined, 8
with flash cards, 49-50
word attack as aid in, 55-56
Word-use, ambiguity in, 216
Word Wealth (Miller), 60
Words–from Print to Meaning (Burmeister), 10, 34
"Writing for the Reluctant Reader" (Hennefrund), 125